SKEPTICISM, JUSTIFICATION, AND EXPLANATION

PHILOSOPHICAL STUDIES SERIES
IN PHILOSOPHY

VOLUME 18

JAMES W. CORNMAN

SKEPTICISM, JUSTIFICATION, AND EXPLANATION

with a Bibliographic Essay by
Walter N. Gregory

D. REIDEL PUBLISHING COMPANY

DORDRECHT : HOLLAND / BOSTON : U.S.A.
LONDON : ENGLAND

Library of Congress Cataloging in Publication Data

Cornman, James W
    Skepticism, justification, and explanation.

    (Philosophical studies series in philosophy; 18)
    Includes indexes.
    1. Skepticism. 2. Certainty. 3. Probabilities. 4. Justification
(Theory of Knowledge) 5. Hermeneutics. I. Title.
BD201. C6   121   80–37
ISBN 90–277–1041–4

Published by D. Reidel Publishing Company,
P.O. Box 17, 3300 AA Dordrecht, Holland.

Sold and distributed in the U.S.A. and Canada
by Kluwer Boston Inc., Lincoln Building,
160 Old Derby Street, Hingham, MA 02043, U.S.A.

In all other countries, sold and distributed
by Kluwer Academic Publishers Group,
P.O. Box 322, 3300 AH Dordrecht, Holland.

D. Reidel Publishing Company is a member of Kluwer Group.

TABLE OF CONTENTS

ACKNOWLEDGEMENTS

Material from Chapter 3 was previously published in the *Journal of Philosophy* and material from Chapter 6 was previously published in the *American Philosophical Quarterly*. Permission to reprint that material is gratefully acknowledged. Material from Chapter 2 was previously published in *Noûs*, and is reprinted with the permission of the editor from *Noûs* **12** (1978), 93–118.

JAMES W. CORNMAN

PREFACE

This book is a manuscript that was virtually complete when James W. Cornman died. Most of the chapters were in final form, and all but the last had been revised by the author. The last chapter was in handwritten form, and the concluding remarks were not finished. Swain took charge of the proofreading and John L. Thomas compiled the indices with the assistance of Lehrer. It is our opinion that this manuscript, like the other books Cornman published, is one of exceptional scholarly and philosophical importance. As do all of his philosophical publications, this work reflects Cornman's great love for philosophy and his commitment to the search for truth. Every serious student and author of epistemology will benefit from and admire the thorough scholarship and rigorous argumentation they will find herein. It has been our privilege to participate in the preparation of the manuscript for the philosophical public.

KEITH LEHRER
MARSHALL SWAIN

INTRODUCTION

Many philosophers try to refute skepticism, but few try to give a precise characterization of the thesis they attack. My first aim, consequently, is to characterize skepticism, or, more precisely, several species of skepticism. Then I shall choose those species I wish to consider and justify my choice. To begin, let me distinguish what I shall call "epistemological skepticism" from the thesis I shall call "ontological nihilism" and from what is believed by someone whom I shall call an "ontological skeptic".

ONTOLOGICAL NIHILISM AND ONTOLOGICAL SKEPTICS

As I shall interpret ontological nihilism, it is a thesis stating that some thing or things does not or do not exist, rather than one concerning the lack of human knowledge or justification of statements or beliefs about what there is. Theses of this second, epistemic type are versions of epistemological skepticism. Thus ontological nihilism about some entity, such as God, is a factual thesis that does not entail any epistemic statements, that is, statements that themselves entail that something has some epistemic status, such as being certain, indubitable, evident, acceptable, reasonable, unreasonable, justified, unjustified, confirmed, disconfirmed, verified, or falsified. We can, consequently, characterize the schema for ontological nihilism as follows:

> Ontological nihilism about x (ϕ's) $=_{df.}$ x neither exists nor occurs (there are no ϕ's).

Note that in this and subsequent definitions, 'x' takes singular referring terms as substituends, and 'ϕ' takes general terms.

One who believes the thesis of ontological nihilism about ϕ's is an ontological nihilist about ϕ's. But some have doubts about a thesis as well as its denial. All such persons are skeptics rather than nihilists, but whether they are ontological or rather epistemological skeptics depends on how this doubtfulness is interpreted. Where the doubt is merely psychological,

xi

and implies only that the person refrains from believing either the thesis or its denial, then the person is an ontological skeptic. That is:

> At time t, s is an ontological skeptic about x (ϕ's) $=_{df}$. At t, s refrains from believing that x exists (that there are ϕ's), and also refrains from believing that x does not exist (that there are no ϕ's).

There is, then, no thesis of ontological skepticism, to be believed, not believed or disbelieved, because being an ontological skeptic is to keep oneself from believing certain theses. If, however, a person ascribes doubtfulness to a thesis, and he means something like 'worthy of being doubted' rather than 'capable of being doubted', then he is an epistemological skeptic, because he assigns a doubtful epistemic status to the thesis. And the claim that the thesis is epistemically doubtful is one species of epistemological skepticism. Because, however, there are so many epistemic terms, there are many other species as well. I wish to consider here only those three which I find best exemplify the most plausible kinds among the broad spectrum of theories.

EPISTEMOLOGICAL SKEPTICISM

I shall list the three theses in ascending order of strength, that is, the strong version will entail the other two, and the moderate version will entail only the weak version which will entail neither of the other two. First, the 'weak' thesis:

> Weak epistemological skepticism about x (ϕ's) $=_{df}$. *It is never known* by any human being that x exists (that there are ϕ's).

Second, the 'moderate' thesis:

> Moderate epistemological skepticism about x (ϕ's) $=_{df}$. *It is never more reasonable* on purely epistemic grounds for any human being to believe that x exists (that there are ϕ's) than for him to believe its denial (that is, I shall say, it is never, epistemically, reasonable for any human being to believe that x exists, that there are ϕ's).

Third, the 'strong' thesis:

Strong epistemological skepticism about x (ϕ's) $=_{df}$. *It is always less reasonable* on purely epistemic grounds for a human being to believe that x exists (that there are ϕ's) than to believe its denial (that is, it is always unreasonable for a human being to believe that x exists, that there are ϕ's).

Note in each definition the phrase 'on purely epistemic grounds'. This is added to allow a skeptic to admit there are ways to justify someone's believing something when the relevant evidence disconfirms what is believed. For example, someone washed overboard at sea may be justified in believing he can swim to safety, when the epistemic evidence is clearly to the contrary, because only by believing does he have even the slightest chance of succeeding. From here on, I shall assume, but not mention, that we are considering only epistemic grounds for believing, that is, grounds that affect the reasonableness of hypotheses themselves. Note also that I have abbreviated 'it is not more reasonable to believe x than its denial' by 'it is not reasonable to believe x.' This also abbreviates 'it is at least as reasonable to believe not-x as x', and is equivalent to 'it is *not un*reasonable to believe the denial of x.' I have also abbreviated 'it is less reasonable to believe x than not-x' by 'it is unreasonable to believe x.' This also abbreviates 'it is more reasonable to believe not-x than x', and is equivalent to 'it is reasonable to believe not-x.' Finally note that the strong thesis, which is the hardest to establish, entails the moderate thesis, which entails the weak thesis. The latter is because s's knowing that p entails that p is fully justified, given s's total evidence, and this entails that it is reasonable for s to believe p. But if it is never reasonable for anyone to believe p, then it is not reasonable for s to believe p, and so he does not know p.

Second-Level Skepticism

Many epistemoloical skeptics believe one of the preceding three versions of epistemological skepticism. The philosophical interest in such a person is in refuting his skeptical claim. However, other skeptics often go farther and believe not only that their skeptical theses are true, but also that they are reasonable, or at least not unreasonable. And still others might go so far as to claim that they know their theses are true. However, what is crucial for a person's knowledge claim is whether his evidence justifies his thesis. And what is crucial for such justification is whether his evidence makes the thesis reasonable for him. Consequently, the reasonableness of the thesis is of central importance for such a skeptic who claims knowledge of his thesis. Of course, if his thesis should prove not to be reasonable, he could always retreat from claiming knowledge to the view that his thesis is not unreasonable. Refutation would then become the much more difficult task of showing that his thesis is unreasonable.

There would also seem to be skeptics who have beliefs about the epistemic status of a skeptical thesis, but are agnostic about its truth. Indeed, there may be some – perhaps Hume – who are unable to believe certain skeptical theses, but who, nevertheless, find them reasonable, or, at least, not unreasonable. Consequently, because we are to be interested in the epistemic status of skeptical theses, we should consider more than just the previous three species, which I shall call 'first-level' skeptical theses. We should also consider what I shall dub 'second-level' theses, because they concern the epistemic status of an epistemic statement. What is important for our purposes at the second level are claims that certain first-level skeptical theses are reasonable, and claims that they are not unreasonable. Because of this, I shall define two second-level theses for each of the trio of first-level theses previously defined. First:

> Moderate second-level (weak, moderate, strong) epistemological skepticism $=_{df}$. *It is always reasonable* for human beings to believe (weak, moderate, strong) first-level skepticism.

Second:

> Weak second-level (weak, moderate, strong) epistemological skepticism $=_{df}$. *It is never unreasonable* for any human being to believe (weak, moderate, strong) first-level skepticism.

The difference, then, between a first- and second-level skeptic is that the former believes that a certain first-level thesis is true, but he need have no beliefs about the reasonableness of the thesis. A second-level skeptic, however, is committed to some belief about the comparative reasonableness of a skeptical thesis, but he can remain agnostic about its truth.

There is also an important difference between moderate and weak second-level skeptics (hereafter, moderate$_2$ skeptics and weak$_2$ skeptics). The former face the task of showing their first-level thesis to be reasonable. Weak$_2$ skeptics, however, need only show that it is as reasonable to accept as to reject their first-level thesis, and they can do this by casting doubt on every attempt to make the denial of their thesis reasonable. This is a much easier task than producing a cogent argument for a thesis. Furthermore, it is likely that someone who is primarily interested in refuting arguments needs to use only a fraction of the resources required by someone who attempts to prove a thesis. For example, it may well be that a weak$_2$ skeptic would not need to use induction, and so from his secure position he can ask his opponents for reasons for using induction and try to show that none is cogent. But if a moderate$_2$ skeptic uses induction to justify his skeptical thesis, as he might well do, then he must allow his opponents to use it also, and his job is likely to become much more difficult.

I am sure that many people are convinced that I have multiplied distinctions well beyond necessity. In particular, someone might object that nothing more is needed for someone interested in refuting skepticism than the three first-level theses. It is true that these three are at the center of any debate about skepticism, but the crucial philosophical issue about them is not whether they are believed, and not whether, by unknown luck, they are true. It is whether they are at least as reasonable as, and perhaps even more reasonable than, their denials. That issue takes us to the second-level theses.

HUME AS AN EPISTEMOLOGICAL SKEPTIC

Another way to realize the value of the second-level set of distinctions is to see that it provides a helpfully accurate classification of the view of an historical figure. Consider Hume. If, as I believe, he is to be understood as some sort of skeptic, he was both a first- and second-level epistemological skeptic, but he was not an ontological nihilist or skeptic.[1] It is obvious that Hume at least accepted weak first-level skepticism (hereafter, weak$_1$ skepticism) about external physical objects, the past, the future, and other minds. I believe he also held the moderate, but not the strong positions (hereafter, moderate$_1$ skepticism, and strong$_1$ skepticism). For example, he argued that we have no reason to believe any 'external' matter of fact, that is, any claim about what is distinct from our own present experiences. At one point, he says:

The only existences, of which we are certain, are perceptions, which . . . are the first foundations of all our conclusions. The only conclusion we can draw from the existence of one thing to that of another, is by means of the relation of cause and effect, . . . But as no beings are ever present to the mind but perceptions; it follows that we may observe a conjunction or a relation of cause and effect between different perceptions, but can never observe it between perceptions and objects. 'Tis impossible, therefore, that from the existence or any of the qualities of the former, we can ever form any conclusion concerning the existence of the latter, or ever satisfy our reason in this particular.[2]

And since I believe that Hume would also agree it is not reasonable for us to deny the existence of things distinct from our own present experience, he would state that existence claims about such entities are neither more nor less reasonable for us than their denials. Thus, he would reject the strong$_1$ thesis, which requires such existence claims to be unreasonable, while accepting the moderate$_1$ view.

Hume, however, was not merely a moderate$_1$ skeptic. His skeptical beliefs were not more dogmas, because, as the preceding quotation indicates, he argued for them. This makes him also what I have called a second-level skeptic (hereafter, a skeptic$_2$). But which kind is he? Again, the preceding quotation indicates that he held at least weak second-level, moderate skepticism (hereafter, a weak$_2$-moderate$_1$ skepticism). That is, he held that it is not unreasonable for us to think that any claim asserting the existence of an external object is not reasonable. And, because it seems quite clear that he would also hold it is not reasonable for us to think such an existence claim is unreasonable, he would *not* accept moderate second-level, strong skepticism (hereafter, moderate$_2$-strong$_1$ skepticism). The most interesting remaining question, then, is whether he held moderate second-level, moderate skepticism (hereafter, moderate$_2$-moderate$_1$ skepticism), that is whether he believed it is reasonable to claim it is not reasonable to accept that there are things distinct from our own present experience.

Hume's Skepticism About Reason

Hume's "skepticism with regard to reason" in the *Treatise*[3] is some evidence that he is not a moderate$_2$-moderate$_1$ skeptic, which would seem to require reasoning to justify moderate$_1$ skepticism. Yet, as in the preceding quotation, and in his attack on induction, Hume does continually argue for his first-level skeptical claims. Also, it is not clear that Hume rejects all reasoning in the *Inquiry*, where he clearly opposes only reasoning that is neither "abstract reasoning concerning quantity or number", nor "experimental reasoning concerning matter of fact and existence".[4] Furthermore, Hume's statement of what he did in proving skepticism about reason, gives a Humean skeptic – if not Hume – a way to be skeptical about reasoning, yet use it to prove something. He says, "For I have shown, that the understanding, when it acts alone, and according to its most general principles, entirely subverts itself, and leaves not the lowest degree of evidence in any proposition, either in philosophy or common life".[5] In making this statement, Hume can be interpreted to claim that he has produced a *reductio ad absurdum* argument against the use of reasoning to justify claims of philosophy and common sense. That is, he is stating that if we assume the general principles needed to justify such claims, we can show by correct inferences that no attempt at such justification by means of reasoning succeeds. This, of course, requires that this Humean agree that certain *forms* of reasoning are justifiable, because he uses them to establish his conclusion. These forms would, of course, be deductive. But this is all he needs for such a *reductio* argument. Thus this Humean can consistently be a moderate$_2$ skeptic. That Hume actually is one is bolstered by what he *does* in the *Treatise*. Whether what he *says* there is consistent with these actions is debatable, however.

There is, nevertheless, a rather more subtle way to interpret Hume on reasoning that clearly absolves him of inconsistency in being a moderate$_2$ skeptic. This view derives from his statement: "In all demonstrative sciences the rules are certain and infallible; but when we apply them, our fallible and uncertain faculties are very apt to depart from them, and fall into error".[6] Because of this, although deductive forms of inference justify conclusions when correctly applied, none of us fallible beings is justified in claiming to establish a conclusion. This is because if we assume that the general principles of reasoning are correct and that some persons do correctly use them to infer conclusions correctly, then one conclusion established in this way is that for each person the probability that he has reasoned correctly is vanishingly small.[7] Thus if some person has reasoned correctly and thereby established a conclusion, then it is unlikely that he has established the conclusion. That is, either no one has ever established a conclusion, or each person is justified in thinking that he has not established any conclusion. Surely, this is a skeptical thesis about human reasoning, and it is one that is consistent with the claim that it is reasonable for us to believe that no existence claim is reasonable. That is, Hume would be consistent in believing this disjunctive claim and in believing moderate$_2$-moderate$_1$ skepticism. Of course, he could not consistently claim that it is reasonable that he has established this thesis.

Although much of the preceding reconstruction of Hume – or, at least a Humean – is debatable, I believe that it shows that the second-level distinctions I introduced are helpful in clearly classifying Hume as a skeptic where his position is clear, and clearly highlighting where he is unclear. Thus these distinctions have some value. Using them, it is plausible, although debatable, to classify Hume as a moderate$_2$-moderate$_1$ epistemological skeptic.

Hume Is Not an Ontological Nihilist or Skeptic

Hume is not an ontological nihilist or skeptic, contrary to the view that seem to be attributed to him by certain of his critics. For example, Thomas Reid says, "Mr. Hume, after annihilating body and mind, time and space, action and causation, and even his own mind, acknowledges the reality of the thoughts, sensations and passions of which he is conscious".[8] But Hume did not claim to have annihilated anything, nor did he believe there are no minds, bodies, causation, and the like. It is true that he argued that there is no mental substance and that men "are nothing but a bundle or collection of different perceptions, which succeed each other with inconceivable rapidity, and are in perpetual flux and movement." And, "they are the successive perceptions only that constitute the mind".[9] However, these identity claims imply that there are minds and men. Furthermore, I believe, these arguments, like all others in the sections of the *Treatise* on skepticism, are merely attempts to show the conclusions to which we are led when we rely on reasoning alone.

Consider that Hume "take[s] it for granted, whatever may be the reader's opinion at this present moment, that an hour hence he will be persuaded there is both an external and internal world".[10] He finds that he is like others: "absolutely determined to live, and talk, and act like other people in the common affairs of life". And, like the others, "my natural propensity, and the course of my animal spirits and passions reduce me to this indolent belief in the general maxims of the world"; indeed, "I must yield to the current of nature, in submitting to my senses and understanding".[11] That is, nature forces even him and his readers to believe in "an external and internal world".[12] What bothered Hume so much was that he could not establish by reason what he and most of the rest of us could not stop believing. He could only try to explain what causes us to have these beliefs, and agree we have no obligation to avoid having them. Thus he is not an ontological nihilist or skeptic. As he says about inductive inference, "As an agent, I am quite satisfied in the point; but as a philosopher, who has some share of curiosity, I will not say scepticism, I want to learn the foundation of this inference. No reading, no enquiry has yet been able to remove my difficulty, or give me satisfaction in a matter of such importance".[13]

I have interpreted Hume as a moderate$_2$-moderate$_1$ skeptic, but my interest here is not primarily historical. It is principally to evaluate skeptical theses about physical objects, the past, the future, and other minds.

Nevertheless, this discussion of this Humean skeptic is a helpful introduction, because this skeptical thesis is the first one that I propose to examine in detail. I have chosen to consider it first not primarily because it may be Hume's position, but because it and its less exposed kin, that is, weak$_2$-moderate$_1$ skepticism, are the most philosophically interesting and important skeptical theses that have some initial plausibility. It might be objected that second-level theses about weak$_1$ skepticism, which opposes knowledge, are not only interesting and historically important, but are also more plausible than their stronger relatives. But, as I have already indicated, the crucial issue for the thesis that something is not known by someone is not whether it is false or not believed by him, but whether it is not reasonable for him. Thus what is crucial for weak$_1$ skepticism is just what moderate$_1$ skepticism states. We should, then, concentrate on the latter thesis, and what is required, at minimum, to refute it.

ON REFUTING SKEPTICAL THESES

To refute a thesis is to provide reason or evidence that shows at least that it is reasonable to reject the thesis. I shall assume *for present purposes*, as would many skeptics, that it is reasonable for human beings to reject a thesis, T, if and only if there is a simple, valid deductive argument with clearly reasonable premises and a conclusion that, with certain exceptions, is the denial of T. Exceptions occur when T is of the form: 'It is reasonable to believe P'. In such cases, the conclusion itself can be the denial of P, because the argument makes it reasonable to believe the denial of P, and this claim, rather than P, clearly contradicts T. Consequently, three different conclusions of cogent simple, deductive arguments are sufficient to refute moderate$_2$-moderate$_1$ skepticism about ϕ's, because of its imbedded epistemic operators. These are:

(a)   There are ϕ's;
(b)   It is reasonable today for any human being to believe there are ϕ's;
(c)   It is not reasonable today for any human being to believe it is never reasonable for human beings to believe there are ϕ's.

Here (b) clearly contradicts moderate$_1$ skepticism, just as (c) contradicts moderate$_2$-moderate$_1$ skepticism. Conclusion (b), when it is justified by a simple, cogent, deductive argument, is itself reasonable for human beings to believe. But if it is reasonable for us to believe (b), then it is false that it is reasonable for us to believe the denial of (b). That is, (c) is implied and once again justified. And, where conclusion (a) is justified by an appropriate argument, then it is reasonable for us to believe (a), that is, (b) is true. But then there is an argument that justifies (b), namely, if the first argument suitably justifies (a), as it does, then it is reasonable for us to believe (a), that is, (b) is true. But this second argument is a simple, valid deductive argument, and so whenever its two premises are reasonable, it justifies (b), and (b) is reasonable for us to believe. Then, as previously, (c) can once again be justified, and the second-level skeptical thesis is refuted.

Surely, a refutation by means by an argument with (a) as its conclusion is most satisfying. It not only refutes moderate$_2$-moderate$_1$ skepticism, but also refutes weak$_2$-moderate$_1$ skepticism, and justifies that there are ϕ's. However, failing this, a simple, cogent deductive argument concluding with (b) would be satisfactory, because it would refute the same three skeptical theses, even though it would not justify that there are ϕ's. It would refute both second-level theories, because it would make it reasonable for us to believe (b), which entails it is unreasonable for us to believe it is not reasonable for us to believe there are ϕ's. It would refute moderate$_1$ skepticism, because its conclusion is the denial of that thesis. Unfortunately, when we instantiate 'ϕ' to entities distinct from our own present experiences, such as unperceived physical objects, the past, the future, and other minds, I find that no argument to justify (a) or (b) will succeed unless (c) is justified first. This is because, as will become clearer as we proceed, any argument directly for either (a) or (b) involves premises that clearly beg questions against skepticism. We shall, then, begin by considering how to establish (c) or, rather, some particular instantiations of (c).

An Epistemic Principle for Refuting Moderate$_2$-Moderate$_1$ Skepticism

Moderate$_2$-moderate$_1$ skepticism is a thesis to the effect that some statement is reasonable. Although there may well be statements that should be considered epistemically innocent until proven guilty, I would argue that this is not true of certain epistemic statements. Where a thesis entails that some statement, P, is epistemically preferable to another (for example, it is more reasonable than its denial), then, I claim, if P is not initially (non-inferentially) reasonable (acceptable), the burden of proof is on anyone who maintains the thesis. That is, such a thesis, P, is reasonable for someone, only if there is some means available to that person for justifying P. Because of this, we can adopt the following epistemic principle:

E.　　　　*If* a thesis, P, is not initially reasonable for entities of kind K (for K's), and it is reasonable, at a time t, for K's to believe that all attempts to justify P that are available to K's at t fail, *then* it is not reasonable at t for any K to believe P.

It should be noted that the consequent of E does not imply that P is unreasonable, but only that P is no more reasonable than its denial. We can also use the preceding discussion to characterize *refutation*:

　　　　Thesis P is refuted (for K's) at time $t =_{df}$. P is unreasonable relative to the evidence relevant to P that is available (to K's) at t.

Refutation of skepticism for everyone forever is an ideal at which to aim, but because, I believe, it is unattainable for human beings, I suggest that we rest content with achieving more modest goals. I propose that we begin by trying to produce a cogent argument whose conclusion is an instantiation of the consequent of E, namely, that moderate$_1$ skeptical theses about physical objects, the past, the future, and other minds are not reasonable for human beings today. While this would not refute moderate$_2$-moderate$_1$ skepticism for ever after, it would at least succeed for the present.

To use E to refute a second-level (skeptical$_2$) thesis in the present day seems to require that we establish the failure of all arguments for the appropriate skeptical$_2$ thesis which are available to human beings today. But this would seem to require an inductive argument from observed failures to the conclusion that all available arguments fail. This raises a problem. I do not want to beg any questions against skepticism about induction, and so I would like not to rely on induction to establish the antecedent of E until – or unless – we have refuted skepticism about induction. But because I also wish to use E to counter such skepticism, I want to find a method that avoids the use of any form of induction. Furthermore, because such a method would rely only on deduction, it will not be vulnerable to the objection that it fails because it uses induction which is an unjustified form of inference. But what about deduction? I shall say only two things about that. First, it is at least allowable when aiming to refute a moderate$_2$ skeptic, because he needs reasoning of some sort, and presumably this requires at least deduction. Second, as noted above, I believe it is quite reasonable for a person to use any deductive argument that is simple enough for him to grasp its validity easily and quickly. In this, I agree with Descartes when he says that "many things are known with certainty, though not by themselves evident, but only deduced from true and known principles by the continuous and uninterrupted action of a mind that has a clear vision of each step in the process".[14] And, I maintain, the arguments I shall use to attack second-level skeptical theses will be deductive arguments that are simple enough to meet this 'Cartesian requirement'.

A Deductive Argument for Refuting Moderate₂-Moderate₁ Skepticism

I wish to refute, for human beings today, a certain moderate$_2$-moderate$_1$ skeptical thesis, or, more precisely, all versions of such a thesis. I make this clarification, because, as we shall see as we proceed through the book, there are three different versions of moderate$_1$ skepticism about physical objects, the past, the future, or other minds, and I wish to refute all three of them. I shall call these theses M_1S_1 through M_1S_3, and when discussing them in general terms, I will use the variable expression, 'M_1S_i', where $1 \leqslant i \leqslant 3$. Given this stipulation, I suggest the following deductive argument as one that meets the Cartesian requirement of simplicity and justifies the rejection of all three M_1S_i's:

(1)   Principle E.

(2)   No skeptical thesis, M_1S_i, is initially reasonable for human beings.

Therefore

(3)   If it is reasonable at t for human beings to believe that all attempts to justify each M_1S_i that are available to human beings at t fail, then it is not reasonable at t for any human being to believe any M_1S_i.

(4)   It is reasonable today for human beings to believe that all attempts to justify each M_1S_i that are available to human beings today fail.

Therefore

(5)   It is not reasonable today for any human being to believe any skeptical thesis, M_1S_i.

The preceding sorites is simple enough for us to grasp its validity easily and quickly. So it is reasonable for us to assume its validity. And, if its premises are clearly reasonable, its conclusion is justified and it is reasonable to reject all three forms of $moderate_2$-$moderate_1$ skepticism about physical objects, the past, the future, and other minds. So, if successful, this argument refutes this brand of skepticism for us now. Yet obviously, many skeptics would protest my use of some of the premises in this argument. But which? I believe I have exhibited the plausibility of principle E, and, consequently, premise (1). And, surely, premise (2) is quite reasonable. Each skeptical thesis, M_1S_i, is a general thesis to the effect that four classes of existence claims are never reasonable for any human being. As Hume pointed out, such a thesis implies the implausibility of a huge number of claims we have an overwhelmingly strong inclination to believe. Surely, no general claim as controversial and counterintuitive as this is more reasonable for human beings than its denial, unless it has been justified for human beings by some sort of inference from other statements. But that is enough to show that no M_1S_i is initially or noninferentially reasonable for human beings. So premise (2) is clearly true. Of course, this reasoning does not apply to every $moderate_1$ skeptical thesis, such as one about the existence of four-sided triangles. For such an entity, what corresponds to premise (2) is false, but, of course, we are not interested here in skepticism about four-sided triangles.

On Justifying Premise (4): Failure of Best Attempts to Justify Skepticism. Some skeptics would surely attack premise (4) on the grounds that there is no way to justify that every argument for each M_1S_i that is available to us now has failed. Even if it is true that all these arguments fail, there is at present no way to confirm this without relying on induction from a sample of past failures. But I have forsworn induction for now, and no skeptic about past events would allow us to argue from past cases. There is, however, a way to approach (4) that relies neither on induction or on the past. Furthermore, it is the sort of approach that we find used by a $moderate_2$ skeptic such as Hume, who claims that some $moderate_1$ skeptical thesis is reasonable. For example, Hume's skepticism about our reasoning concerning matters of fact is based on his repeated attempts to find cogent chains of inference which support the conclusions we actually infer regarding matters of fact. His attempts fail; he can find no such chains. And he says, "This negative argument must certainly, in process of time, become altogether convincing, if many penetrating and able philosophers shall turn their enquiries this way and no one be ever able to discover any connecting proposition or intermediate step, which supports the understanding in this conclusion".[15] In other words, Hume seems to be saying, this argument from the repeated failure of able philosophers to find any justifying chain of reasoning, to the conclusion that there is none, is fully convincing. That is, I take it, such an argument justifies the claim that there is no form of inference that justifies the claims we make about matters of fact.

One way to construct an argument from what Hume says here is to use premises of the following forms:

(6)   If all of the many attempts by able philosophers, as of time t, to justify P have failed, then it is reasonable, at t for human beings to believe that all attempts as of t have failed.

(7)   All of the many attempts by able philosophers as of t to justify P have failed.

One Humean substituend for 'P' would be, of course, 'reasoning about matters of fact'. Our premise (4) would follow if 't' is replaced by 'today', and 'P' by 'any M_1S_i'. Unfortunately, neither of these premise forms seems to be helpful for a Humean skeptic. The problem with (6) is that it may be true that all the attempts have failed, but, nevertheless, the available evidence points to one succeeding. Then (6) would be false. We can correct this flaw, however, by requiring the antecedent of (6) to concern not what is true, but rather what it is reasonable at t for us to believe about these attempts. A Humean's concern about (7) would not be its truth, but, instead, how he is to justify it, because the obvious way is to rely on induction from past failures. Nevertheless, there is a way, which is suggested by what Hume says, for a person to justify (7) without using induction from past cases. He should consider at one time, t, all the strongest, most plausible attempts to justify P that he can find. He can do this by examining, at t, the relevant work of the most able philosophers he can find. Then he should modify each of these attempts to make it as strong as he can. If he can still show that each of these strengthened arguments fails, then he has evidence that justifies (7).

The preceding suggestions about how to amend (6) and how to justify (7) provide us with what we need to justify premise (4) in a way that does not rely on induction from the past. I propose that we use the following pair of premises which yield (4):

(8)   If it is reasonable, at t, for K's to believe that the most plausible attempts to justify P that are available to K's at t have failed,

then it is reasonable, at t, for K's to believe that all attempts
to justify P that are available to K's at t fail.

(9)   It is reasonable today for human beings to believe that the
most plausible attempts to justify each M_1S_i that are available
to human beings today fail.

I find that (8) is clearly acceptable, and I should think that it is agreeable
to a moderate$_2$ skeptic, especially one who attempts to argue the way
Hume does. Surely, if it is now reasonable for us to believe that the most
plausible attempts to justify something fail, then it is also reasonable for us
to believe that the other, less plausible attempts fail. But, of course, premise
(9) is not so easily justifiable, especially without using induction from past
cases. But I believe that I can justify it now by following the Humean procedure for (7): present and refute in one document, namely, this book, the
strongest arguments for each of the M_1S_i's that I can find or construct in
the present day. If I am successful in doing this, then the results stated in
this document will provide evidence that makes it reasonable for us now
that the most plausible, available arguments for the various M_1S_i's fail.
Thus premise (9) would be justified. I am sure that this procedure will not
satisfy all skeptics, but I believe that it is at least plausible enough to put
the burden of proof on those who reject it as a means of justification.

On Refuting Versus Convincing a Skeptic. I have argued that principle
E and premises (2) and (8) of the preceding argument are quite plausible,
and that there is a usable procedure for justifying premise (9) and, thereby,
(4). Indeed, we can replace (4) by (8) and (9), and restructure the preceding
argument to show what we have accomplished:

(10)   If premises (1), (2), (8) and (9) are true, then (5) is true.
(11)   Premises (1), (2), and (8) are true.

Therefore

(12)   If (9) is true, then (5) is true.

Premise (10) is clearly true and, I claim, the preceding discussion justifies
(11). So it is reasonable for us to accept (12), and one task remains before
us in our attempt to justify (5) and thereby refute, for now, moderate$_2$-
moderate$_1$ skepticism about physical objects, the past, the future, and other
minds. This last task is to establish (9), and that will occupy us throughout the rest of the book. Indeed, it will help provide the broad outline of

the path that we shall follow and that leads, at its end, to the rejection of skepticism and the acceptance of a particular theory of justification.

It might be objected at this point that I am doomed to failure before I begin, because no self-respecting skeptic would accept all I propose. Indeed, he might well maintain that I have failed miserably in attempting to justify my premises. Is my attempt frustrated because of this? It may well fail to convince even one skeptic, but that would make it no less a success. My aim in justifying principle E and premises (2), (8), and (9) is not to convince a skeptic. Indeed, my aim here, as in all my philosophical argumentation, is not to convince any actual person, let alone a committed opponent. My only aim is to present arguments that succeed in justifying their conclusions.

If, however, I were to state my aim in terms of convincing someone, I would say it is to convince anyone who would be a disinterested spectator of my attempts at argumentation, and who would be ideally rational in the sense of being capable and willing – both intellectually and emotionally – to evaluate arguments solely on the basis of their rational merit. Of course, he must beg no questions for or against any thesis whose plausibility is at issue. For example, he must avoid using or accepting inductive arguments when the justification of induction is in question. Thus in some cases he would be required to be behind a certain sort of "veil of ignorance" regarding certain relevant issues. Nevertheless, I would claim we could rely on his rational intuitions when he is rendered ignorant in the appropriate way. I suggest, furthermore, that any such individual would agree, first, that I have shown that the preceding argument refutes moderate$_2$-moderate$_1$ skepticism about physical objects, the past, the future, and other minds, if premise (9) is justified; and, second, that the procedure I described for justifying (9) is correct. I believe I neither can do, nor need to do, any more than that.

ON REFUTING WEAK$_2$-MODERATE$_1$ SKEPTICISM

I have proposed and argued for a way to refute moderate$_2$-moderate$_1$ skepticism. But, unfortunately, this procedure leaves weak$_2$-moderate$_1$ skepticism unaffected. To refute this less-exposed thesis, we must at least provide a cogent argument with a conclusion that entails that it is unreasonable to believe the thesis of moderate$_1$ skepticism. The problem for refuting this skeptical$_2$ thesis can be seen by realizing that modifying the previous argument so that it refutes this thesis has implausible results. The obvious move is to change the consequent of E so it becomes:

It is *un*reasonable, at t, for any K to believe P.

The resulting principle is implausible. The reasonableness of the failure of all attempts to justify a thesis which is, initially, no more reasonable than its denial, does not imply that the statement is less reasonable than its denial. This is especially easy to see in cases where it is reasonable that all attempts to justify the thesis and also all attempts to justify its denial have failed. This does not imply that it is both more and less reasonable to believe the thesis rather than its denial. This objection, however, can be avoided by replacing the first conjunct of the antecedent by:

P is initially unreasonable for K's.

But although this may salvage the new principle, it requires a change in the second premise that makes it implausible. It is true that moderate$_1$ skepticism is not initially reasonable, but I see no reason to think it is initially unreasonable. The most plausible view, I find, is that initially (that is, independently of any other evidential statements) moderate$_1$ skepticism and its denial are about equally reasonable for human beings.

Unfortunately, I know of no way to reconstruct the previous argument so it refutes weak$_2$-moderate$_1$ skepticism. Indeed, the only way I can find to refute this skeptical thesis requires that we first refute moderate$_2$ skepticism, and then use that result to help attack its less-exposed kin. This is how I propose to proceed.

How to Refute Weak$_2$ Skepticism by Refuting Moderate$_2$ Skepticism

As stated previously, there are three statements each of which would refute moderate$_2$-moderate$_1$ skepticism if it were the conclusion of a cogent simple, deductive argument. The argument previously discussed concludes with statement (5) which instantiates (c): 'It is not reasonable today for any human being to believe that it is never reasonable for human beings to believe there are ϕ's'. This alone does not provide reason to reject weak$_2$-moderate$_1$ skepticism. However, if either the corresponding instantiation of (a): 'There are ϕ's', or (b): 'It is reasonable today for human beings to believe there are ϕ's', should be established now, then, as noted above, not only would the moderate$_1$ thesis be refuted now, but so also would moderate$_1$ skepticism, and, consequently, weak-$_2$moderate$_1$ skepticism.

Unfortunately, I do not know of a non-question-begging way to argue for (a), even indirectly by way of justifying (c). But I shall propose such an argument for (b).

If, as I hope to show, the preceding argument for conclusion (5) is successful, then it justifies that it is *not unreasonable* today for human beings to reject the three versions of moderate$_1$ skepticism about ϕ's, where, as previously, the substituends for 'ϕ' concern physical objects, the past, the future, and other minds. What else is needed is something that, with this first conclusion, establishes that it is now *reasonable* for us to reject the three moderate$_1$ skeptical theses, M_1S_1 through M_1S_3. Then we would have shown that weak$_2$-moderate$_1$ skepticism about ϕ's is mistaken because it implies that it is not now reasonable for us to reject all three of these theses. My approach, in rough outline, will consist in three steps in addition to the previous one of refuting moderate$_2$-moderate$_1$ skepticism. The first is to show that it is reasonable for human beings to adopt a particular theory of the justification of empirical statements, if it is the most reasonable available to them for achieving a certain worthwhile and important goal, and it is not reasonable for them to accept moderate$_1$ skepticism. The next step is to argue that a particular theory of the justification of empirical statements provides, at present, the most reasonable means for reaching this goal. So, this theory is 'vindicated', and it is now reasonable for us to adopt it. The last step is to establish that this reasonable theory has consequences that contradict what is required by the three forms of moderate$_1$ skepticism, and that, consequently, it is reasonable now for human beings to reject all three of these skeptical theses, contrary to weak$_2$-moderate$_1$ skepticism. Furthermore, as an added bonus, we shall also be able to use the theory to help refute skepticism about induction.

The crucial tasks set for us by this extended argument, which I shall call the "master argument" of the book are: first, justifying premise (9) of the previous argument for (5); second, determining the conditions that are sufficient for its being reasonable for us to adopt some theory of justification; third, developing a precise theory that satisfies these conditions; and last, using this reasonable theory to derive consequences that contradict all three skeptical theses, and, in addition, skepticism about induction. I shall attempt the second task in the next chapter, where I shall lay out and discuss the "master argument" in detail, but the other three will be completed only after extended examinations of the relevant skeptical theses and arguments, and the various competing epistemic theories of empirical justification. These examinations will constitute the great bulk of this book.

JAMES W. CORNMAN

NOTES

[1] Not everyone considers Hume to be a skeptic. See for example T. Beauchamp and T. Mappes, 'Is Hume Really a Skeptic About Induction?', *American Philosophical Quarterly* **12** (1975), 119–130.

[2] D. Hume, *A Treatise of Human Nature*, L. A. Selby-Bigge (ed.), Oxford: Clarendon, 1888, p. 212.

[3] *Ibid.*, pp. 180–187.

[4] Hume, *An Inquiry Concerning Human Understanding*, C. W. Hendel (ed.), Indianapolis: Bobbs-Merrill, 1955, p. 173.

[5] Hume, *Treatise*, pp. 267–268.

[6] *Ibid.*, p. 180.

[7] *Cf.* Hume, *Treatise*, p. 182.

[8] *Philosophical Works*, W. Hamilton (ed.), Edinburgh: James Thin, 1895, p. 442.

[9] Hume, *Treatise*, pp. 252–253.

[10] *Ibid.*, p. 218.

[11] *Ibid.*, p. 269.

[12] For a similar view of Hume, see R. Popkin, 'David Hume: His Pyrrhonism and His Critique of Pyrrhonism', *Philosophical Quarterly* **1** (1950–1951). Reprinted in *Hume*, V. C. Chappell (ed.), New York: Doubleday, 1966, pp. 53–98.

[13] Hume, *Inquiry*, p. 52.

[14] R. Descartes, 'Rules for the Direction of the Mind', in E. Haldane and G. Ross (trans.), *The Philosophical Works of Descartes*, 2 vols., New York: Dover, 1955, vol. 1, p. 8.

[15] Hume, *Inquiry*, pp. 48–49.

CHAPTER 1

AN ARGUMENT FOR THE EXPLANATORY
FOUNDATIONAL THEORY AND AGAINST SKEPTICISM

In the introduction, I hinted at a four-step master argument that would have the conclusion that it is unreasonable now for human beings to believe any of the three versions of moderate$_1$ skepticism about physical objects, the past, the future, and other minds. As we shall see as I develop and explain the argument here, it has the beneficial side effect of also refuting skepticism about induction for us now.

FIRST STEP OF THE MASTER ARGUMENT: REFUTATION OF
MODERATE$_1$ SKEPTICISM

Happily, the first step of the argument has already been laid out in the introduction, so I need only restate it and briefly explain it here. It is the step that refutes the three relevant moderate$_2$-moderate$_1$ skeptical theses. Its premises – (12) and (9) from the introduction – constitute the first two premises of the master argument. Thus we begin with:

I. If it is reasonable today for human beings to believe that the most plausible attempts to justify each skeptical thesis, M_1S_1 through M_1S_3, that are available to human beings today fail, then it is not reasonable today for any human beings to believe any M_1S_i.

II. It is reasonable today for human beings to believe that the most plausible attempts to justify each skeptical thesis, M_1S_1 through M_1S_3, fail.

Therefore

III. It is not reasonable today for any human being to believe any M_1S_i (that is, any version of moderate$_1$ skepticism about physical objects, the past, the future, and other minds).

As previously argued for (12), premise I is quite reasonable, and, as mentioned about (5), the justification of II must await the end of an examination which will occupy the rest of the book. The only detail about the

1

first stage that might be helpful at this point is some elucidation of the
precise nature of M_1S_1 through M_1S_3. Since the second and third theses
are successive retrenchments which, as we shall see, are forced upon skeptics at later stages in the discussion, let me here merely state the thesis
which we shall first examine, namely:

> M_1S_1. It is not (epistemically) reasonable at any time, t, for any
> human being, s, to believe a statement *if* it entails either (a)
> the existence of some particular physical object at t, or (b)
> the occurrence of some particular event before t, or (c) the
> occurrence of some particular event after t, or (d) the existence
> of mental phenomena of a being other than s, at any time.

There are two points worth noting about thesis M_1S_1. The first concerns
how to understand the disjunctive antecedent of M_1S_1. The claim is that
any of these four entailments is, by itself, sufficient for a sentence's not
being reasonable. Thus we need only show that some statement with just
one of these entailments is reasonable in order to refute M_1S_1. This might
prompt the objection that we should replace M_1S_1 by a less easily refutable
thesis, namely, one that is true if at least one of these entailments excludes
reasonableness. Or, at least, we should consider, separately, each of these
four theses that M_1S_1 implies. My answer is twofold: the most plausible
arguments I can find for the three M_1S_i's also apply to all four of the theses
that they imply, and so the refutation produced by the master argument
will refute not only M_1S_1 through M_1S_3, but also each of the four theses
they imply. That is, the argument is designed to refute not only "conjunctive" moderate₁ skepticism about physical objects, the past, the future,
and other minds, but also "disjunctive" skepticism about physical objects,
the past the future, *or* other minds.

The second point is that the reason for the term 'particular' in all four
phrases in thesis M_1S_1 is to emphasize that the thesis would not be refuted
if it is now reasonable for me to believe a general statement, such as,
'There are now physical objects, there have been past events, there will be
future events, or someone other than me is in a mental state'. What is
needed are statements about specific physical objects, past events, future
events, or mental phenomena, such as my desk, my birth, tomorrow's
sunrise, or your present pain. Consequently, M_1S_1 is not as exposed to
attack as a skeptical thesis that is refutable by the very general claims.
Nevertheless, as previously noted, it will have to be revised to avoid some
clear objections to it, until finally we arrive at M_1S_3, which is the minimal

conjunctive thesis that someone can believe and still be a moderate$_1$ skeptic about physical objects, the past, the future, and other minds.

SECOND STEP: ON VINDICATING A THEORY OF EMPIRICAL JUSTIFICATION

The second step of the master argument is relatively simple logically, but I find it the most difficult to make plausible. This is because at this point in the argument, I shall be trying to find what, together with the conclusion of the first stage, is a sufficient condition for it to be reasonable now for us to adopt a theory of the justification of empirical statements. Once this is achieved, there remain the more complex and time-consuming tasks of showing that a particular theory meets this condition and also conflicts with a skepticism. The crucial problem for the second stage is that we want a sufficient condition for reasonableness that is plausible and whose instantiation by a particular theory can, in practice, be verified or falsified. Since we are allowing ourselves at each stage in the argument only simple deductive arguments, it is clear that we have available for justifying arguments only deductive forms of something like what Feigl calls "validation" and "vindication". Will either sort of argument help?

Feigl has not provided much detail about the characteristics of validation and vindication, but perhaps the following two quotations are of some help. First:

When we speak of 'justification' we may have reference to the legitimizing of a knowledge-claim; or else we may have in mind the justification of an action. The first case may be called '*justificatio cognitionis*' (validation) the second, '*justificatio actionis*' (vindication). The rules of deductive and inductive inference serve as the justifying principles in validation; purposes together with (inductively confirmed or at least confirmable) empirical knowledge concerning means-ends relations . . . serve as the bases of vindication (pragmatic justification).[1]

And also:

Validation terminates with the exhibition of the norms that govern the realm of argument concerned. If any further question can be raised at all, it must be the question concerning the pragmatic justification (vindication) of the (act of) adoption of the validating principles.[2]

Limiting our discussion to deductive arguments, which are the only arguments available to us here, how might we best explicate the differences between validation and vindication, based on what Feigl has merely indicated somewhat roughly? For one thing, the difference he emphasizes between justifying a knowledge claim and justifying an action seems irrelevant, especially if we construe validation as making it reasonable to believe something and allow the adoption of or belief in a principle to be (mental) actions. Then we would have, as I think we should, merely two different ways to justify adoption of or belief in principles. It is no more helpful to contrast the two in terms of validation using but not justifying certain principles of inference or canons of evidence, but vindication justifying but not using some of these principles or canons. This is doubly mistaken. There is no reason to forbid the validation of some principles of inference, and vindication is not restricted to the justification of such principles. I believe that the best way to view the difference is to see deductive vindication as one species of deductive argument in which a premise that is required for validity states a sufficient condition for some degree of reasonableness of a principle or statement that entails that the principle or statement is in some way suitable or required as a means to achieve some goal.[3] All other cogent deductive arguments validate their conclusions.

On Three Principles of Vindication

Consider one principle of vindication that might be used to justify a principle:

> VP1.   If the adoption of a principle of kind K by human beings is required for them to reach a goal G, and G is worthwhile and important for human beings, then it is reasonable for human beings to adopt principle, P, if P provides human beings a better means of achieving G than any other principle of kind K.

To justify a principle deductively using VP1, we must also establish that P is the best of its kind to achieve a certain goal, and that this is a worthwhile and important goal. This second task is often ignored and seldom discussed, presumably because the goals mentioned are assumed to be of the right sort. For example, in discussing the vindication of the scientific method, Sellars says, "In the case of scientific theory, the end is presumably the goal of providing scientific understanding, the ability to explain and predict phenomena falling under the scope of the theory".[4] I would guess that Sellars assumes it to be so evident that this goal is worthwhile and important that there is no need to debate it. I would agree with him about the worth of the goal, but think it deserves debate.

Some Problems for Vindicating Enumerative Induction. The task of showing that a certain principle is the best for achieving a certain goal, which the use of VP1 in vindication imposes on us, raised a serious problem which neither Feigl nor Sellars seem to notice. In many cases, it is known to be false that there is just one best principle. Consider, for example, the problems confronting Reichenbach's attempted vindication of enumerative induction. Reichenbach identifies the values of conditional probabilities with the limits of relative frequencies of infinite series, and then argues for what is called the "straight rule of induction", that is, the inductive rule stating that each limit of these infinite series equals, or closely approximates, the relative frequency of the initial observed segment of the series. At one point, he summarizes his pragmatic justification in this way:

If the series converges toward a final percentage, we must eventually arrive at values which are close to the final value. The inductive inference [the straight rule] is thus shown to be the best instrument of finding the final percentage, or the probability of an event, if there is such a limiting percentage at all, that is, if the series converges toward a limit. [And if the series does not converge, then, obviously, no method will find it.][5]

It follows from Reichenbach's claims that wherever there is a probability, the straight rule provides the best means of finding, or at least, reaching it. And since the goal of obtaining the values of conditional probabilities is important and worthwhile, we can infer, with principle VP1, that it is reasonable for us to adopt the straight rule.

The well-known, defeating objection to this deductive vindication of the straight rule is that there is no reason to think the straight rule is *the* best for finding limits of relative frequencies. So, even if, contrary to what I shall propose, probabilities are to be taken as limits of relative frequencies, Reichenbach's vindication fails. As he saw himself there are infinitely many "asymptotic rules" which will also reach every limit there is. So Reichenbach's argument fails to pick out one rule as uniquely best, as it must for VP1 to apply. The unsolved problem, then, for vindication via principle VP1, is to find other characteristics of the straight rule which uniquely identify it as the best. Reichenbach tried to use a notion of "descriptive simplicity" to isolate the straight rule,[6] but, as Salmon notes, that attempt fails.[7] Salmon tried to improve on what Reichenbach started by proposing three characteristics of the best rule which he thought belonged uniquely to the straight rule.[8] But later he admitted the three do not single out the straight rule, and said, "Additional conditions are needed, but I have no idea what they might look like, or even whether there are any acceptable ones".[9] And even though Hacking produced three conditions that conjointly pick out the straight rule, neither he nor Salmon found any reason to prefer a rule having them.[10]

The point of all this is that it is extremely difficult to justify what is, uniquely, *the* principle that is best suited to guide induction by enumeration, or, more broadly, the best principle of justification. This problem, then, seems clearly to vitiate any attempt to vindicate such principles using premise VP1. It also casts grave doubt on Sellars's hint about how the scientific method can be vindicated, because even if this method were to replace enumerative induction by what I shall discuss in Chapter 4 under the names 'hypothetical induction' and 'inference to *the* best hypothesis', the uniquely best would be no more easy to uncover.[11] However, deductive vindicating arguments are not limited to those using premise VP1. Even in the case of the straight rule with its infinitely many asymptotic competitors, I believe that we can argue that it is *not unreasonable* for us to adopt the straight rule, *if* we have no reason *of any sort* to prefer any other inductive rule, and no reason to think it would be unreasonable to adopt any rule of kind *K*. This is because we need to adopt some rule or other to achieve a worthwhile and important goal. Of course, this also allows it not to be unreasonable for us to adopt any other asymptotic rule instead, if there is no reason to prefer another rule to it. But, I find, this as it should be. We need to adopt some rule, and so we are epistemically permitted to adopt exactly one of those that are maximally reasonable. Consider, then, a second principle of vindication:

> VP2.   *If* (1) the adoption of a principle of kind *K* by human beings is required for them to achieve a goal *G*, (2) goal *G* is worthwhile and important for human beings, and (3) it is not reasonable, at *t*, for human beings to believe that it is unreasonable for them to adopt a principle of kind *K*, *then* it is *not unreasonable*, at *t*, for human beings to adopt exactly one principle, *P*, of kind *K*, if it is *at least as reasonable*, at *t*, for human beings to adopt *P* as to adopt any other principle of kind *K*.

It should be noted that VP2 is not trivial, as it may seem. Principle *P* being as reasonable as any principle of kind *K* does not guarantee that it is not unreasonable to adopt *P*. It might be unreasonable to adopt any rule of kind *K*. But the need to use some principle of kind *K* for a worthwhile and important goal, and there being no reason to believe it unreasonable to adopt some such principle, do guarantee that it is not unreasonable to adopt such a principle, according to VP2. It is this that makes VP2 a principle of vindication.

Given the present situation concerning induction, I believe we have no reason to prefer any inductive rule to the straight rule, provided we can find a formulation of the straight rule that avoids a certain problem for its usual formulation.[12] If this should be accomplished, and, contrary to what I believe, a frequency view of probability is the most reasonable one, then we could conclude, by VP2, that it is not unreasonable for us now to adopt exactly the straight rule, because some inductive rule is needed to achieve a worthwhile and important goal, no rule is more reasonable for us now than the straight rule, and it is not reasonable for us to think adoption of such a rule is unreasonable. What would then remain before us would be the difficult, unsolved problem of finding something, other than suitability for reaching limits, that makes it more reasonable for us to adopt the straight rule than any other that is otherwise as reasonable as the straight rule. If we should find this additional reason, we could fully vindicate the straight rule by using, instead of VP1 or VP2, the following principle of vindication which corresponds closely to VP2:

VP3.   *If* (1) the adoption of a principle of kind K by human beings is required for them to achieve a goal G, (2) goal G is worthwhile and important for human beings, and (3) it is not reasonable, at t, for human beings to believe that it is not reasonable for them to adopt a principle of kind K, *then* it is *reasonable*, at t, for human beings to adopt a principle, P, of kind K, if it is *more reasonable*, at t, for human beings to adopt P than any other principle of kind K.

I find VP3 acceptable, if, as I have argued, VP2 is. This is because the two principles differ only concerning levels of reasonableness. Principle VP2 states that if certain conditions are met and it is not reasonable to believe adoption is unreasonable, then P's being as reasonable as any other principle of kind K, makes P not unreasonable. Similarly, VP3 states that if the same conditions are met, and it is not reasonable to believe adoption is not reasonable, then P's being more reasonable than any other competitor ensures P's being reasonable. These two implications seem equally plausible. Note that there is no similar relationship between VP1 and VP3. Principle VP3, like VP2, concerns how the overall reasonableness of a principle compares with its competitors, but VP1 merely considers how they compare as means for reaching a goal. Reasonableness might well be affected by more than that.

The Relevance of Vindicating Induction to Vindicating Theories of Empirical Justification. There are two reasons why I have spent so much time discussing the vindication of induction by enumeration: it is where the most detailed attempts at vindication have occurred, and the goal that induction is used to achieve is obviously closely related to the more general goal for theories of the justification of empirical statements. My next task, then, is to transform the preceding first, hypothetical step in the vindication of the straight rule into the first step in vindicating some theory of justification, and that requires finding a worthwhile and important goal that such theories serve to achieve. It might be objected, however, that it would be premature for me to begin this task, because I have not yet shown that there is no hope for validating such a theory, and validation is preferable to vindication. I agree. We should stop and consider whether some sort of validation is avilable.

Interlude on Validating Theories of Empirical Justification

The usual view seems to be that vindication becomes appropriate when attempting to justify the ultimate or basic principles of some theory. As Sellars says, "Our rational warrant for accepting the first principles of the theory clearly cannot consist in the fact that they have been logically derived from other statements of the theory. If this were the case, it would simply mean that they were misdescribed as the *first* principles of the theory".[13] Sellars then says that vindication is available for first principles. However, it would be a mistake to assume validation is not available. For a theory, T_1, there may be another more general theory, T_2, from which the first principles of T_1 are deducible. Such validation does not imply that the justified principles are not first principles of T_1. This might lead someone to suggest that a theory of the justification of empirical statements is like T_1, because its 'first' principles might be derivable from a more general theory of justification. So, while it is clear that we would have to use vindication to justify a theory for justifying any sort of statement or principle whatsoever, validation would succeed for the derived theory that concerns only empirical statements.

I believe that there is a more general method of justification, which I call 'methodological naturalism' because its paradigmatic species is justification by 'the' scientific method. And I believe, as I shall argue at a future time, that this more general method has certain other distinct species. One, which concerns us in this book, is a theory for justifying empirical statements of all sorts. Two others concern the justification of metaphysical theories, and justifying standards of moral obligation.[14] But I also believe that the way to justify this general principle is, first, to justify one of its most common species, namely, the one concerning empirical statements, and, then, to show how, by suitable adaptations, it produces plausible results in other areas, including metaphysics and ethics. Thus, for me at least, the crucial theory to justify first is the one which shapes our current interest. So, although no theory of the justification of empirical statements is ultimate in one sense, because it is a species of a more general theory, it is ultimate in the sense that its justification is needed as part of what justifies other species of the general theory, and, indeed, the general theory itself.

I have just claimed that a theory of empirical justification is not to be validated by derivation from a vindicated more general theory. But, as I have construed validation, this does not show that no such theory is to be deductively validated, because any cogent deductive argument validates if it does not vindicate. Nevertheless, I know of no hint of a nonvindicating, cogent, deductive argument for any theory of this sort that does not involve derivation from a more general theory. Once again, the similar case of induction by enumeration is instructive. After many attempts, no argument of any sort has yet succeeded in justifying some inductive principle. And if validation has failed for enumerative induction, it is reasonable that it also fails for theories of empirical justification. Of course, this evidence also argues for the failure of vindication of some theory of empirical justification, but in that case, I intend, next, to provide new reasons to hope for success.

Theories of Empirical Justification and Human Goals

To what goal that is worthwhile and important for human beings are theories of empirical justification relevant? We have seen that Sellars enunciates a goal to be achieved by adopting the methods of science, namely, providing explanations and predictions. And Carnap has called probability "a guide of life", in the sense that "any man X has to base his decisions on expectations concerning events which are independent of his actions and also concerning events which might happen in consequence of certain acts which he might decide to carry out. For expectations of both kinds, X has no certainties but only probabilities. And if his decision is to be rational, it must be determined by these probabilities".[15] In other words, determining here and now the probabilities of events happening at other places or times is crucial for a person deciding what he should do now to guide his life on some particular path. More generally, it is clear and generally agreed that, in a wide variety of situations, human beings need some method for making explanations and predictions in order to arrive at decisions about what to do. And this need is clearly not limited to areas where scientific explanation and prediction hold sway. The need is much wider, because science is, so far, mute or of little help, when, for example, deciding whether to buy a new house or continue renting, or deciding whether a friend would be hurt by your doing a certain act.

For many of our mundane, everyday decisions, we neither need nor use any method to determine what it is reasonable for us to expect to happen either independently of but relevant to our actions, or as consequences of them. In these cases, everthing relevant is often quite simple and very clear. Decisions about whether to carry an umbrella today, or whether to have meat for dinner tonight are usually of this sort. But, obviously, all too many human decisions are not of this sort, and, for them, some method of prediction based on present and past information is essential. Furthermore, many of our decisions are to be based not merely on predictions about future events but also on those concerning the thoughts, feelings, and desires of others. Thus it is clear that our goal of making effective, efficient, and – I should emphasize – moral decisions to guide us through life, requires a method for making predictions, about unexperienced present events, future events, and the mental phenomena of others, that are based on reasonable claims about the present and the past. Clearly, then, in order to achieve this goal, we need some theory that provides the means to determine which statements about the present and past provide acceptable bases for prediction, and what these statements make it reasonable for us to expect about those other places, other times, and other persons that are relevant to our present decisions. Theories of the justification of empirical statements are what provide these means, and so some one of them is required to achieve the human goal of making effective, efficient, and moral decisions about what to do. Consequently, if this goal is worthwhile and important, then according to vindicating principle VP3, it is reasonable for us to adopt the most reasonable theory of empirical justification that provides these means, if it is not reasonable to think the adoption of such theories not to be reasonable.

We now have all we need to construct the second step of the master argument, if two claims can be established: first, the goal that requires some theory of empirical justification is worthwhile and important for human beings; second, it is not now reasonable for us to believe that it is not reasonable to adopt a theory of empirical justification. It is at this point that the previous refutation of moderate$_2$-moderate$_1$ skepticism becomes relevant to the second step of the master argument. I believe that the only reason we would have now for thinking that it is not now reasonable to adopt some such theory, would be that it is reasonable to accept some form of moderate$_1$ skepticism about physical objects, the past, the future, and other minds. The only other candidate I can find would be that it is not reasonable to believe there is any way to formulate any such theory in a problem-free way. But there is always the method of drawing straws to determine what to do, and that method is easy to state. Of course, it may be that all those that can be formulated without problem are not reasonable because of other defects, but this mere possibility does not count as a reason. I believe, then, that we can take the refutation of moderate$_2$-moderate$_1$ skepticism as sufficient for it not being reasonable for us to think that the adoption of some theory of empirical justification is not reasonable.

We can also see that the goal toward which theories of empirical justification contribute is both worthwhile and important for human beings. It is clear that to act morally, and to do so in an effective and efficient way, is a worthwhile and important goal for human beings. In any situation, to do what we ought to do, or at least what is morally permitted, and to achieve the intended results effectively and efficiently is an important ideal well worth our efforts. It is also clear that in many complicated situations it is very difficult for human beings to act either morally or effectively and efficiently, unless they act on the basis of some decision about what should be done in the situation, and what is the most effective and efficient way for them to achieve it. There are many examples of cases where it is vitally important for a person to act in one very precise way, but it is very unlikely that he would act that way without basing it on a carefully reasoned decision. Consider a doctor who is faced with a wide variety of things he might do to save a seriously ill patient. Often, one precise course of action may be required to save the life, and it is unlikely he would take that course without a decision about how to proceed in the most effective and efficient way. We can conclude, then, that because the goal of acting morally in effective and efficient ways is worthwhile and important for human beings, and because, in many situations, human beings are most unlikely to achieve this goal unless they act on the basis of decisions about what should be done and how it is best to do it, the goal of making such decisions is also worthwhile and important. That is, in short, decisions that guide actions that have moral importance are themselves morally important, and so it is worthwhile and important that human beings have means for making decisions that are moral and effective.

The Vindicating Argument of the Second Step

I am now ready to lay out the second step of the master argument. It consists in the use of the principle of vindication, VP3, as one premise and three other premises which help instantiate the antecedent of VP3 in terms of theories of empirical justification and the goal about decision-making which requires them. This argument is:

IV.   Principle VP3: If (1) the adoption of a principle of kind K by human beings is required for them to achieve a goal G, (2) goal G is worthwhile and important for human beings, and (3) it is not reasonable, at t, for human beings to believe that it is not reasonable for them to adopt a principle of kind K, then it is reasonable, at t, for human beings to adopt a principle, P, of kind K, if it is more reasonable, at t, for human beings to adopt P than any other principle of kind K.

V.   The adoption of some principle for determining the reasonableness of those empirical statements that are epistemically relevant to decisions that face human beings (in short, the adoption of some theory of empirical justification adequate to human decisions) is required for human beings to achieve goal G_1 – in each situation that arises, to make a morally right decision about what to do in the situation, and a correct decision about the most effective and efficient way to do it.

VI.   Goal G_1 is worthwhile and important for human beings.

VII.   If it is not reasonable today for any human being to believe any version of moderate$_1$ skepticism about physical objects, the past, the future, and other minds, then it is not reasonable today for human beings to believe that it is not reasonable for them to adopt a theory of empirical justification.

Therefore

VIII.   If (1) it is not reasonable today for any human being to believe any version of moderate$_1$ skepticism about physical objects, the past, the future, and other minds, and (2) it is more reasonable today, for human beings to adopt, *T*, a theory of empirical justification that is adequate to human decisions, than any other such theory of empirical justification, then it is reasonable, today, for human beings to adopt *T*.

The preceding discussion has, I believe, shown that all three premises of the second step of the master argument are quite reasonable. Thus, unlike the first step where premise II remains unjustified, the second step is complete. But, of course, two more time-consuming steps have not even been begun. The first concerns that difficult task of finding a theory of empirical justification that will instantiate clause (2) of the antecedent of VIII. We know, of course, that III, from the first step, satisfies clause (1). The other step consists in showing that this theory of justification conflicts with moderate$_1$ skepticism.

THIRD STEP: TOWARD VINDICATING THE EXPLANATORY FOUNDATIONAL THEORY

In Chapter 7, I shall propose and develop a theory of empirical justification which I claim combines the best features of foundational theories with the best of those nonfoundational theories that stress justification by what is called 'explanatory coherence', while avoiding the faults of both. Because of this, and because, I maintain, no rival exceeds this theory's ability to determine the epistemic statuses of a wide variety of empirical statements, I shall argue that this theory, called the 'explanatory foundational theory' is at least as reasonable as any theory of empirical justification. Given that I have done this, the problem posed for me by the third step of the master argument will be to find some way to upgrade the epistemic status of this theory so it becomes more reasonable than its competitors and, thereby, instantiates clause (2) of intermediate conclusion VIII.

A Principle of Conservatism

I faced a comparable problem in an earlier work when I attempted to show that a certain metaphysical theory, which I named 'compatible commonsense realism', is the most reasonable metaphysical theory of perception and the external world.[16] I had already argued that it was at least as reasonable as its rivals, and, like now, needed a way to upgrade it to being the most reasonable theory of its kind. What I did there seems clearly relevant here. I invoked one version of a test often used to evaluate various sorts of theories, and often called a test of 'conservatism' or 'familiarity'. For example, when considering tests for scientific hypotheses, Quine and Ullian say in favor of conservatism that "the less rejection of prior belief required, the more plausible the hypothesis – other things being equal'.[17] That is, prior belief affects the level of reasonableness of a theory, but only after everything else relevant has been taken into account. I shall discuss this and other 'nonevidential' tests of conservatism for explanatory theories in greater detail in Chapter 8, but let me here concentrate on the closely related principle I previously used to compare the reasonableness of metaphysical theories. In slightly altered and improved form, it is:

> CP.   *If* (1) it is at least as reasonable, at t, for human beings to believe (adopt) a theory, T_1, of kind K, as to believe (adopt) T_2 of kind K, and (2) T_1 is consistent with [appreciably] more pretheoretical, commonly [and firmly] accepted beliefs of mankind than T_2, *then* it is more reasonable, at t, for human beings to believe (adopt) T_1 rather than T_2.[18]

As stated, CP agrees with the Quine-Ullian test in having certain beliefs affect reasonableness only as a last resort. However, this principle may have greater scope than theirs, because it applies to any two theories of the same kind, no matter what kind they are. But Quine and Ullian discuss their principle only in the context of scientific explanatory theories. So CP applies, among others, to scientific theories, metaphysical theories, theories of justification, and ethical theories. But it surely is debatable whether such a principle should have so wide a scope. For example, in Chapter 8 I shall question its applicability to explanatory theories. Nevertheless, I do believe that I was correct in applying it to metaphysical theories, and that its application to theories of empirical justification is fully justified.

I argued previously, when considering metaphysical theories only, that what human beings accept commonly and – let me add here – with a high degree of firmness yet without any benefit of general theory, deserves some special, but perhaps quite meager, epistemic consideration. It would be quite dubious to classify all such beliefs as reasonable. But, as Quine and Ullian agree, they deserve, at the very least, preference over what, on the basis of everything else relevant, is, at most, as reasonable as they are. As we have seen emphasized by Hume, we human beings, when not philo-sophizing, are quite fully persuaded of and, indeed, often unable to resist belief in 'both an external and internal world'. Surely, if no theory of empirical justification is more reasonable for us to believe than one that yields the reasonableness of these beliefs we find ourselves believing so strongly, then it is more reasonable for us to believe that theory which confers reasonableness on those beliefs than any of the theories which do not. Thus, I conclude, we are justified in applying CP to theories of empirical justification. But, of course, we also must find some way to justify the appropriate instantiation for 'T_1' in the antecedent of CP.

Preview of the Explanatory Foundational Theory as Most Reasonable Because Conservative

At this early stage in the discussion, I can do little more than state which theory of empirical justification instantiates the antecedent of CP. It will only be after Chapter 7, where I develop the explanatory foundational theory in detail, that I shall be ready to argue that it is as reasonable as any theory of justification which provides the means for achieving the goal of making moral decisions, effectively and efficiently. I can note here, however, that it will be no objection to this claim about the comparative reasonableness of this theory that it is surely more reasonable to use merely deduction to justify empirical statements. It is quite clear now, and will become even more evident as we proceed, that a theory of empirical justification that limits all justification to deductive inference will fail repeatedly to provide means for making the required decisions. More is needed, indeed, I shall maintain, even more than deduction supplemented by enumerative induction. We shall also need 'hypothetical induction', that is, 'inference to the best explanation'. In effect, this is what, in greater detail, will be provided by the explanatory foundational theory.

In order to use CP to conclude that the explanatory foundational theory is the most reasonable for us to accept now, I must also show that it is consistent with appreciably more pretheoretical, commonly and firmly accepted beliefs of mankind than any rival that is otherwise as reasonable as it is. It is, again, clear that I can do this only after I have the theory available in detail and examine its consequences about which statements are acceptable in a variety of situations. In this case, we must wait until after Chapter 9, where the theory is applied to several specific situations. But, a short preview may be of some help.

The situation in which we shall find ourselves at the end of Chapter 9 will resemble that one we have found confronting the attempts to vindicate the straight rule for enumerative induction. On the assumption, which is clearly debatable, that it has been established that the straight rule is at least as reasonable as any rival, and more reasonable than all rules that are not asymptotic, the crucial question is whether we can eliminate all other asymptotic rules because they conflict with more of our pretheoretical beliefs than does the straight rule. It seems reasonable that infinitely many asymptotic rules would be eliminated in this way, but it is far from clear that this would rid of us of all of them. How to handle any that remain would, therefore, be one crucial remaining problem. We shall find that a somewhat similar problem will confront the explanatory coherence theory, but I hope to show that certain restrictions that will be built into the theory will solve it.

Another most serious and perplexing unsolved problem severely hinders the vindication of the straight rule. It is what Goodman calls the "new riddle of induction", and it arises because, unless some sort of restriction is placed on the applicability of the straight rule, it yields results that clearly conflict.[19] Furthermore, some of these results also conflict with our pretheoretical beliefs, so the straight rule not only has implausible consequences, but also is not fully consistent with these beliefs. Both of these problems also face the explanatory foundational theory. However, I find that the second problem confronts all the theory's most plausible competitors. Thus, as I shall argue, none of the consequences of theories that conflict with our common beliefs, because of the new riddle, need be considered in determining which of two theories is consistent with more of these beliefs, because all of the most reasonable theories are equally blighted. This, of course, does not dispel the first problem, but I hope to show how, because of built-in restrictions, the explanatory foundational theory avoids yielding conflicting results.

The Argument of the Third Step

We are ready to formulate the argument of the third step. It consists in three premises, one of which I claimed to have justified here, namely, CP restricted to theories of empirical justification, and two whose justification lies somewhere ahead of us. The argument is:

IX.   Principle CP1: *If* (1) it is at least as reasonable, at t, for human beings to adopt one theory of empirical justification, T_1, as to adopt another one, T_2, and (2) T_1 is consistent with appreciably more pretheoretical, commonly and firmly accepted beliefs of mankind than T_2, *then* it is more reasonable, at t, for human beings to adopt T_1 rather than T_2.

X. It is at least as reasonable, today, for human beings to adopt the explanatory foundational theory as any other theory of empirical justification that is adequate for human decisions.

XI. For any theory of empirical justification, T, that is adequate for human decisions, either the explanatory foundational theory is consistent with appreciably more pretheoretical, commonly and firmly accepted beliefs of mankind than T is, or it is more reasonable, today, for human beings to adopt the explanatory foundational theory rather than T.

Therefore

XII. It is more reasonable, today, for human beings to adopt the explanatory foundational theory than any other theory of empirical justification that is adequate for human decisions.

It is clear that we have much to do before completing the third step because of the huge task required to justify premises X and XI. But it is worth noting that when that task is finished, and we have also justified premise II of the argument in the first step, then the conclusions of the first three arguments, namely, III, VIII, and XII, will be justified, as well as what is simply deductively derivable from them. Consequently, at that point the following important intermediate conclusion, which follows from III, VIII, and XII, will be justified:

XIII. It is reasonable, today, for human beings to adopt the explanatory foundational theory of empirical justification.

This leads directly to the fourth and last step in the extended argument against weak$_2$-moderate$_1$ skepticism.

FOURTH STEP: INCOMPATIBILITY OF THE EXPLANATORY FOUNDATIONAL THEORY AND MODERATE$_1$ SKEPTICISM

The fourth step can be stated and discussed here quite briefly, but, like all steps but the second, it has premises whose justification must await the end of our examination. The conclusion of this last step, and thus the final conclusion of this refutation of weak$_2$-moderate$_1$ skepticism is that it is unreasonable for us to believe any of the three relevant versions of moderate$_1$ skepticism. The reason for this is twofold: as the first step shows, it is not reasonable for us to believe any of these moderate$_1$ skepti-

cal theses; and the theory of empirical justification that it is now reasonable for us to adopt has consequences that contradict all three skeptical
theses. Because of this, it is certainly reasonable for us to accept these
consequences, and so it is unreasonable for us to accept the skeptical
theses. More precisely, the argument is:

XIII.   As above.
XIV.   The explanatory foundational theory has consequences that
         contradict all forms of moderate$_1$ skepticism about physical
         objects, the past, the future, and other minds.
III.   As in XV, clause (3) below.
XV.   *If* (1) it is reasonable, today, for human beings to adopt a
         theory of empirical justification, *T*, and (2) *T* has consequences
         that contradict all forms of moderate$_1$ skepticism about phys-
         ical objects, the past, the future, and other minds, and (3) it is
         not reasonable, today, for any human being to believe any of
         these forms of moderate$_1$ skepticism [conclusion III], *then* it is
         unreasonable, today, for any human being to believe any of
         these forms of moderate$_1$ skepticism.

Therefore

XVI.   It is unreasonable, today, for any human being to believe any
         form of moderate$_1$ skepticism about physical objects, the past,
         the future, and other minds (that is, weak$_2$-moderate$_1$ skepti-
         cism about physical objects, the past, the future, and other
         minds is false).

The fourth step adds only two new premises to our previous stock, because
III and XIII are previous conclusions. The preceding brief discussion of
XV is, I find, enough to justify it, but XIV cannot even be considered
until the end of Chapter 9, where the explanatory foundational theory
will be applied in specific situations and its consequences for skepticism
derived.

CONCLUSION: REFUTATION OF WEAK$_2$-MODERATE$_1$ SKEPTICISM

I have, in one sense, completed the master argument of the book, but it
is clear it is not finished. It will be with us throughout the rest of the book,
where at all times our discussions and examinations will be relevant to
one or more of those four premises yet to be justified. These are, in sum-

mary: from the first step, premise II which concerns attempts to establish moderate$_1$ skeptical theses; from the third step, premise X according to which the explanatory foundational theory is as reasonable as any of its rivals, and premise XI which compares theories regarding reasonableness and consistency with pretheoretical beliefs; and from the last step, premise XIV which is stated above. We have, then, completed the two main tasks of this chapter: to lay out the master argument, and to justify all the premises we can at this early stage of the examination. The result has been that, at this point, seven of the ten premises are justified (I, IV, V, VI, VII, IX, and XV), including all three in the argument of the second step. So three steps remain to be completed. Completion of the first requires me to uncover and perfect the best skeptical arguments available. I shall start that search in the next chapter.

POSTSCRIPT ON SKEPTICISM ABOUT INDUCTION

The full master argument is now before us, but since I previously mentioned that one helpful side effect of its refutation of weak$_2$-moderate$_1$ skepticism about physical objects, the past, the future, and other minds is the refutation of skepticism about induction, I wish to conclude this chapter by extending the master argument so it provides that refutation. As hinted previously, and as we shall see in detail later, the reasonableness of the explanatory foundational theory implies the reasonableness of hypothetical induction, and that implies the falsity of skepticism about induction (the thesis that it is never reasonable for any human being to adopt any form of induction). So to achieve this refutation, we need only add two new premises to the master argument:

VXII. If it is reasonable, today, for human beings to adopt the explanatory foundational theory, then it is reasonable today for them to adopt hypothetical induction.

XVIII. If it is reasonable, today, for human beings to adopt hypothetical induction, then it is false that it is never reasonable for any human being to adopt any form of induction (that is, skepticism about induction is false).

These two premises conjoined with conclusion XVI yield what is desired:

XIX. Skepticism about induction is false.

Furthermore, because premise XVIII is clearly true, and the master argument justifies XVI, the only new task that this extension of the argument adds to our list is the justification of XVII. But once we see the details of the explanatory foundational theory, it will be easy to achieve that. Of course, this will not dispel skepticism about other particular forms of induction, such as enumerative induction, but, as I shall note briefly in the concluding chapter, not only will the justification of the explanatory foundational theory lessen the impact of that form of skepticism appreciably, it will also, I believe, help provide a new approach to its refutation.

NOTES

[1] H. Feigl, 'Validation and Vindication: An Analysis of the Nature and the Limits of Ethical Arguments', in W. Sellars and J. Hospers (eds.), *Readings in Ethical Theory*, New York: Appleton-Century-Crofts, 1952, p. 674.

[2] *Ibid.*, p. 675.

[3] *Cf.* W. Salmon, 'The Justification of Inductive Rules of Inference', in I. Lakatos (ed.), *The Problem of Inductive Logic*, Amsterdam: North-Holland Publishing, 1968, pp. 34–35.

[4] W. Sellars, *Philosophical Perspectives*, Springfield, Ill.: Charles C. Thomas, 1967, p. 410.

[5] H. Reichenbach, *The Rise of Scientific Philosophy*, Berkeley: University of California Press, 1951, p. 245.

[6] See H. Reichenbach, *Experience and Prediction*, Chicago: University of Chicago Press, 1938, sections 39, 42.

[7] See W. Salmon, 'On Vindicating Induction', in H. Kyburg and E. Nagel (eds.), *Induction: Some Current Issues*, Middletown, Conn.: Wesleyan University Press, 1963, pp. 27–28.

[8] See W. Salmon, 'Vindication of Induction', in H. Feigl and G. Maxwell (eds.), *Current Issues in the Philosophy of Science*, New York: Holt, Rinehart and Winston, 1961, pp. 250–255.

[9] Salmon, 'The Justification of Inductive Rules of Inference', p. 37.

[10] See I. Hacking, 'One Problem About Induction', in I. Lakatos (ed.), *op. cit.*, pp. 44–51; and, for Salmon, 'Reply' in that volume, pp. 89–90.

[11] See G. Harman, 'The Inference to the Best Explanation', *Philosophical Review* **74** (1965), 88–95.

[12] For this problem, see I. Hacking, 'Salmon's Vindication of Induction', *Journal of Philosophy* **62** (1965), 263.

[13] Sellars *op. cit.*, p. 409.

[14] My latest discussion of a method for justifying metaphysical theories is in my 'Reference and Ontology: Inscrutable but Not Relative', *Monist* **59** (1976), 353–356.

[15] R. Carnap, *Logical Foundations of Probability*, 2nd ed., Chicago: University of Chicago Press, 1962, pp. 246–247.

[16] See J.W. Cornman, *Perception, Common Sense, and Science*, New Haven, Conn.: Yale University Press, 1975, *passim*.

[17] W. Quine and J. Ullian, *The Web of Belief*, New York: Random House, 1970, p. 44.
[18] *Cf.* Cornman, *Perception, Common Sense, and Science*, p. 32, principle P3. The brackets contain the improvements.
[19] For a discussion of the new riddle as applied to principles of induction, see Salmon, 'On Vindicating Induction', pp. 33–40.

PART I

SKEPTICISM AND THE FOUNDATIONS
OF JUSTIFICATION

CHAPTER 2

SKEPTICISM AND A FOUNDATION OF CERTAINTY

The main task of Part I is to evaluate arguments for three instantiations of the skeptical schema which I have called 'skeptical thesis M_1S_i', that is, 'moderate$_1$ skepticism about ϕ's.' The first thesis to be considered is:

M_1S_1.   It is not epistemically reasonable at any time, t, for any human being, s, to believe a statement *if* it entails either (a) the existence of some particular physical object at t, or (b) the occurrence of some particular event before t, or (c) the occurrence of some particular event after t, or (d) the existence of mental phenomena of a being other than s, at any time.

Our prime reason for attempting this task is to justify premise II of the master argument which states that it is reasonable today for human beings to believe that the most plausible attempts to justify each skeptical thesis, M_1S_1 through M_1S_3, fail. As previously mentioned, the way to do this without begging any questions against any relevant skeptic, is for one person to present and refute in one document the best arguments for each M_1S_i that he can find. This is what I plan to do throughout Part I and beyond.

There are many extant skeptical arguments, and so it may seem to be a huge task to sift out and then evaluate the best of them. Fortunately, however, the great majority of them concern weak$_1$ skepticism rather than moderate$_1$ skepticism. That is, they are aimed to show that no human beings ever know whether or not there are ϕ's, rather than to deny it is reasonable for a human to believe there are ϕ's. This is an important difference, because the premises usually used to establish weak$_1$ skepticism are of dubious value for justifying moderate$_1$ skepticism. Consider, for example, two very recent skeptical arguments. Lehrer proposes an argument whose first premise is: if a man knows for certain that something is true, then there is no chance that he is wrong in thinking it to be true, that is, it is false that "the objective unconditional probability of his being wrong is greater than zero".[1] His second is: "For any contingent statement, there is always some chance that one is wrong in thinking it to be true, . . . [This] says that whatever contingent statement one thinks is

25

true, the probability that one is wrong is greater than zero".[2] Of course, this yields a skeptical conclusion, namely, that no contingent statement is known with certainty. But clearly, this does not justify M_1S_1. Indeed, it is relevant to weak$_1$ skepticism only if knowing implies knowing with certainty. But it is quite debatable whether or not that implication holds.

A similar argument is proposed by Unger. He claims to have defended skepticism by showing that:

each of two propositions deserves, if not our acceptance, at least the suspension of our judgment:

That, in the case of every human being, there is hardly anything, if anything at all of which he is certain.

That (as a matter of necessity), in the case of every human being, the person knows something only if he is certain of it.[3]

As it stands, this argument is no more relevant to moderate$_1$ skepticism than Lehrer's argument. Unger, however, thinks he can show that if it is reasonable for someone, s, to believe that there are ϕ's, then there is some proposition, p, such that s knows that p.[4] If he is correct in this, then if nothing is known, then nothing is reasonable. The crucial premises in his argument for this last thesis are that something is reasonable for s, only if s has a reason for it, and something is a reason for s, only if he knows it. But two implications of his premises are debatable. Not only is it not clear that p is a reason for q only if it is true that p, it is surely dubious that p is a reason for q only if p is certain. Indeed, even if what I shall call 'traditional' foundationalism is correct and foundational or basic evidence must be certain, this does not require that all evidence and all reasons are certain. But let us put aside the final disposition of this premise until Chapter 3 when we examine the claim that acceptability requires certainty. If that claim proves to be dubious, as I shall argue, then we can reject at least one of Unger's premises: either the premise that knowledge requires certainty, or the claim that reasonableness requires knowledge of reasons.

TRADITIONAL FOUNDATIONALISM AND SKEPTICISM

The history of arguments for skepticism is primarily the history of arguments about knowledge. Accordingly, rather than search for the most plausible attempts to justify M_1S_1, I shall attempt to arrive at the most plausible argument in its favor by a series of steps, each of which strengthens a previously refuted proposal. I shall begin with an argument based primarily on two premises widely accepted by many skeptics and nonskeptics since the time of Descartes. Indeed, it has been the acceptance of these claims that has made it so hard for their believers to avoid skepticism, in spite of constant effort. Both premises are essential to what I have called the 'traditional' foundational theory of justification. One is a principle approximated in C.I. Lewis's slogan, "If anything is to be probable, then something must be certain".[5] The second limits certainty to reports about what is supposedly given in sensory experience, and reports of psychological attitudes.

Explication of Lewis's Principle

Lewis's slogan can be stated somewhat more precisely as follows:

L1.   If anything is highly credible [that is, (epistemically) acceptable], then something is certain.

Note that I have replaced the term 'probable' by 'highly credible', where I take 'x is highly credible' to be short for 'x is more credible than its denial.' And the latter is synonymous with 'x is more reasonable than its denial.' I also shall use the following definition:

D1.   Statement, p, is (epistemically) acceptable for person, s, at time, $t =_{df}$. The credibility of p for s at t is high.

This definition explains the parenthetical remark in L1. I have made these replacements in L1 in order not to beg any questions in the ensuing discussion about the relationships between epistemic terms (such as 'credible', 'reasonable', and 'acceptable') and 'probable' as a term in probability theory which need not be given an epistemic interpretation. Indeed, as we shall see in Chapter 3, some of the major problems that arise in evaluating arguments for or against Lewis's principle center on the viability of claims about these relationships. In order to facilitate these evaluations, I use a quantitative technical term 'degree of credibility for a person, s, at a time, t'. The main function of this term is to help bridge the gap between qualitative epistemic terms like 'acceptable' and 'certain' and the quantitative concepts of probability theory in a way that begs no questions about how to interpret probability, and avoids problems, such as the lottery paradox.

I have interpreted Lewis's slogan in terms of principle L1, but there are reasons to revise it further. One objection to it is that it is somewhat plausible to hold that some statements – for example, 'This is my hand' – are what I shall call 'initially' or 'noninferentially' acceptable for someone at some time, and so their 'initial' credibility is high. But this does not imply

that any statement is certain. The point of this objection is that principle
L1 is false if some statements are merely initially acceptable, because a
statement is initially acceptable in the sense given by the following definition:

> D2.   Statement, p, is initially acceptable for a person, s, at a time,
> $t =_{df}$. p is acceptable for s at t, and it is false that p would be
> acceptable for s at t only if some other statement or set of
> statements should justify it (that is, increase its credibility
> enough to be acceptable) for s at t.

Note that D2 allows that something other than statements – for example,
a certain experience – is needed to justify a statement if it is to be initially
acceptable. Should a statement that is acceptable for s only if he has a certain sort of experience be called initially acceptable? We could then change
D2 so that it says that a statemtnt is initially acceptable only if nothing of
any sort is needed to justify it. I propose, however, that we should leave
D2 unchanged, because I believe that the view that a statement is initially
acceptable only if *nothing* at all is needed to justify it, is too strong a requirement for initial acceptability. What is required by D2 is strong
enough.

Nothing in D2 required anything to be certain. Nevertheless, the preceding objection to L1 can be rebutted and L1 shown to be true by pointing
out that a statement, p, is certain if it has a probability of 1, given tautological evidence – that is, let us say, if $\Pr(P/T) = 1$. And so at least
simple tautologies are certain, and version L1 of Lewis's principle is correct. This reply gives reason to accept L1, but both the objection and reply
show L1 does not capture what Lewis intended. He is interested in contingent, empirical statements rather than tautologies. Furthermore, Lewis
might seem to agree that some statements (for example, some of a person's
memory statements) are sometimes initially acceptable for a person. The
acceptability of these statements does not require certainty.[6] Lewis would
want his principle to concern 'inferentially' acceptable statements, that is,
statements that are acceptable but would not be acceptable should no
other statement justify them. Let us, then, replace L1 by:

> L2.   If an empirical statement, p, is *inferentially* acceptable for
> person s at time t, then some empirical statement is certain
> for s at t.

Even L2 is not accurate. It is clear that foundationalists such as Lewis wish to claim something about the relationship between a statement that is inferentially acceptable and the empirical evidence that renders it acceptable. The claim is that such evidence, or at least some crucial part of it must be certain. We can, therefore, improve on L2 by using:

L3.   If an empirical statement, p, is inferentially acceptable for s at t, then p is probable at t relative to e, which is s's (total) empirical evidence for p at t and e is certain for s at t.

Principle L3 captures one basic tenet of what I shall call the 'Cartesian' species of traditional foundationalism. However, L3 may not capture Lewis's own view, because it may be he would allow some memory reports to be included in evidence, even though they are not certain but only initially acceptable. Let us, then, make one last amendment to capture one thesis of what I shall call the 'Lewisean' species of the traditional view:

L4.   If an empirical statement, p, is inferentially acceptable for s at t, then p is probable at t relative to e, which is s's (total) evidence for p at t, and which contains at least one empirical statement that is certain for s at t.

Notice that L3 entails L4, but the converse is false. Indeed, L4 is one minimal requirement for any theory that I shall call 'traditional'.

A Second Foundational Premise: Only Basic-Reports Are Certain

The second premise of traditional foundationalism, which also proves helpful to a skeptic, is that an empirical statement is initially certain only if it is what I shall call a 'basic-report', that is, either a 'given-report' or a 'report of psychological attitude'. Given-reports are those sentences that describe and only describe what Lewis calls "the given", that is, "the direct and indubitable [present] content of experience".[7] I shall assume, for ease of discussion, that a sentence is a given-report if and only if it meets one of two conditions. First, either it or its denial is transformable into an intentional sentence of the form 'I am *now* having an experience of x', where substituends for 'x' are limited to certain phenomenal terms (e.g. 'pain' and 'itching'), observation-terms (e.g. 'something white' and 'a tree'), and certain topic-neutral terms (e.g. 'object' and 'event').[8] Second, it is logically equivalent to a conjunction or the denial of a conjunction of reports that meet the first condition. According to my stipulations, then, 'I am now having an experience of an electron' is not a given-report, because 'electron' is not an observation, phenomenal, or topic-neutral term.

And although 'I am now having an experience of a rock' is a given-report, it is an intentional sentence and so does not entail the existence of a rock.

Reports of psychological attitudes are characterized by the same two clauses that define 'given-report' except that the required form for the relevant 'nonmolecular' basic-reports is 'I am now x-ing ϕ', where substituends for 'x' are terms for psychological attitudes, whether cognitive (such as 'believe', 'think', 'doubt', and 'entertain'), or conative (such as 'desire', 'hope', 'detest', 'admire', 'love', 'strive', 'choose', and 'try').[9] And substituends for 'ϕ' include not merely propositional clauses, that is, clauses of the form 'that p', but also phrases that produce sentences expressing nonpropositional psychological attitudes. Some examples are phrases, such as 'about skepticism' as in 'I am now thinking about skepticism', or names of entities, such as 'Jones' as in 'I am now loathing Jones'.

SKEPTICAL ARGUMENT I: NO FOUNDATION OF CERTAINTY

As I have viewed a traditional foundationalist, his centuries-old problem has been to find some way to avoid skepticism without surrendering either of his two basic premises. In fact, it has often been thought that we must maintain those premises to avoid skepticism, but, on the other hand, there is no way to extend justification beyond basic-reports if neither premise is rejected. This second horn of this dilemma for traditional foundationalism is the source of our first attempt to state the most plausible argument for M_1S_1. This skeptical argument combines the two basic premises of traditional foundationalism with another very like one of those we have seen offered by Lehrer, namely, that no contingent, empirical statements – not even basic-reports – are epistemically certain for anyone at any time. This provides us with the following argument that I shall call 'skeptical argument I'. It begins with L4, which is common to all traditional theories, and proceeds as follows:

I.1.   If an empirical statement, p, is inferentially acceptable for s at t, then p is probable relative to e, which is s's (total) evidence for p at t, and which contains at least one empirical statement that is certain for s at t (L4).

I.2.   An empirical statement is certain only if some basic-report is certain.

I.3.   No basic-reports are certain.

Therefore

I.4.   No empirical statement is inferentially acceptable for anyone at any time.

This, of course, is not enough to justify M_1S_1, because it allows nonbasic-statements to be initially acceptable. But the crucial additional step is achieved in a way that Cartesian foundationalists would approve, namely, by limiting initially acceptable statements to basic-reports. Argument I continues, then, as follows:

I.5.   An empirical statement is initially acceptable only if it is a basic-report.

I.6.   If a statement is neither initially nor inferentially acceptable, it is not acceptable.

Therefore

I.7.   No 'nonbasic' statement (that is, an empirical statement that is neither a basic-report nor an 'eternalized' version of a basic-report) is acceptable for anyone at any time.

I.8.   If I.7 is true, then M_1S_1 is true (that is, roughly, it is never reasonable for any human being to believe that there are physical objects, past events, future events, or mental phenomena of others).

Therefore

I.9. M_1S_1 is true.

It is clear which premise any traditional foundationalist would attack. It is I.3. Although he would limit initial certainty to basic-reports, he would insist that at least some of them are certain, indeed, initially certain. A crucial question, then, is how to adjudicate this disagreement between a skeptic and a traditional foundationalist. One way, which should find approval by a skeptic, is to propose a thesis that provides a sufficient condition for when a basic-report is certain for someone, and then see whether it, or some amended version of it, avoids refutation. If some such thesis survives all these attacks, then we can conclude that I.3 is not reasonable, and so no argument with it as a premise justifies its conclusion. If none of these theses survive, then let us agree with those skeptics who find I.3 acceptable. I propose that we begin by concentrating on those basic-reports that are given-reports. I suggest this, because most debate relevant to our interest here has centered on given-reports. And let us begin by examining the following hypothesis:

> H1.   All given-reports that a person understands and believes with certainty are initially certain (epistemically).

THESIS H1 AND THE PROBABILITIES OF GIVEN-REPORTS

Reichenbach offers an objection to thesis H1 but he never lays it out very clearly. He bases his objection primarily on four claims. First, "Any phenomenal sentence is capable of being tested in terms of other such sentences; and though the other sentences cannot completely verify, or falsify, the given sentence, they can verify it, or falsify it, to a high degree". Second, the probability of a given-report is often low relative to the totality of other given-reports. Third, "A sentence system relative to which, on further extension, the probability of some individual sentence a goes to zero, is deductively, but it is not inductively consistent". Fourth, "For our system of knowledge we require inductive consistency, because this system cannot be constructed by deductive inferences alone but is based on inductive inferences." He concludes from this that "phenomenal sentences cannot be absolutely certain".[10]

I find that I must do considerable reconstruction in order to formulate this argument clearly enough for careful examination. The main problem is to understand what Reichenbach means by "inductive consistency". My best guess is the following:

> D3.   Probability statements $p_1, p_2, ..., p_i$, whether absolute, $\Pr(q) = n$, or conditional, $\Pr(q/r) = m$, are inductively consistent $=_{\mathrm{df}}$. The conjunction formed by $p_1, p_2, ..., p_i$ and the axioms of the probability calculus are deductively (logically) consistent.

Here '$\Pr(q) = n$' means that the probability of $q = n$, and '$\Pr(q/r) = m$' means that the conditional or relative probability of q, given $r = m$. Consider, for example, three probability statements: '$\Pr(p) = 1$', and '$\Pr(q) = 1$', and '$\Pr(p/q) = 0.5$'. These three are inductively inconsistent because when conjoined with two theorems of the probability calculus they imply a contradiction. One theorem is the rule of elimination:

> T1. $\Pr(p) = [\Pr(p/q) \times \Pr(q)] + [\Pr(p/\bar{q}) \times \Pr(\bar{q})]$.

The seond is:

> T2. $\Pr(q) + \Pr(\bar{q}) = 1$.[11]

Argument Against Thesis H1: *Inductively Inconsistent Given-Reports*

We can use the two preceding theorems to construct a Reichenbach-like objection to thesis H1. To do so, let us use just two given-reports, namely, a = 'I am now having a visual experience of holding something large and heavy'; and b = 'I am *not* now having a tactual experience of something large and heavy'. It would seem that it is improbable that a is true of some-one, s, at time t, given that b is true of s at t. That is, let us say, $\Pr(Tast/Tbst) < 0.5$. Here '$Tast$' is what I shall call 'the version of basic-report a, that is *eternalized* to s at t"', because although the truth-value of a varies with persons and times, the truth-value of '$Tast$' does not vary. There are two ways to construe '$Tast$', and I shall use both. The first is to make a 'semantic ascent' and read it as 'a is true of s at t'. The second is to replace the terms 'I' and 'now' in report a by 's' and 'at t', respectively. The eter-nalized result is, 'At t, s is having a visual experience of holding something large and heavy'. (Note: where the internal structure of a sentence of the form '$Tpst$' is irrelevant, I shall often replace it by 'Tp'.) Let us also assume that, as Reichenbach holds, if at t, a statement, p, is certain, then $\Pr(Tp)$ = 1, We then have the following argument:

(1) $\Pr(Tast/Tbst) < 0.5$.
(2)   T1 and T2.

Therefore

(3)   Either $\Pr(Tast) \neq 1$, or $\Pr(Tbst) \neq 1$ [and so it is inductively inconsistent that $\Pr(Tast) = 1$, $\Pr(Tbst) = 1$, and $\Pr(Tast/Tbst) < 0.5$].

(4)   At a time, t, s understands and believes with certainty the given-reports a and b.

(5)   If a given-report, p, believed by s at t, is certain, then $\Pr(Tpst)$ = 1.

Therefore

(6)   Given-reports that a person understands and believes with certainty are not certain.

I do not know whether I have captured what Reichenbach intended. One change I have made should be noted, however. I have used only given-report b instead of "the totality of other phenomenal sentences" that Reichenbach mentions. One reason for this is to avoid the question of whether a totality of sentences is certain at one time, t, if each of its members is certain at some time or other. Of course, we could restrict this totality to just those phenomenal sentences that the person uses to report his experiences at t. But I find that picking the latter totality adds nothing to the argument. Thus I use b for simplicity.

If we make the reasonable assumption that at some time someone understands and believes with certainty two given-reports, where the probability of one of them, given the other, is low, then it is reasonable to accept premises (1) and (4) as plausible proxies for statements about that pair. It might be objected, however, that in *every* case in which the antecedent of H1 is met for *any* pair of given-reports, x and y, of a person, s, $Pr(Txst/Tyst) = 1$. Consequently, premise (1) is false. Indeed, if we relativize probability functions to persons, as I shall suggest later, there is some plausibility to the proposal that $Pr_s(Tast/Tbst) = 1$, but for a person, u, who is not s, $Pr_u(Tast/Tbst) < 0.5$.[12] Unfortunately, an evaluation of this reply depends on a decision of which interpretation is to be given to the probability functions involved. If, as Reichenbach would propose, the value of $Pr(Tast/Tbst)$ is determined by the limit of the relative frequency of times when a is true of a person among times when b is true of that person, then its value seems to be quite low, whether or not relativized to s. This would also seem to be true for many nonsubjective interpretations of probability, such as Lewis's own view that conditional probability statements are to be construed as stating estimates of relative frequencies, based on the available data.[13] Because of this, I believe we should, for our present purposes, grant Reichenbach premise (1).

Surely premise (2) is acceptable, and we are considering here only what I shall call 'probability' senses of 'certain', that is, senses entailing a probability of 1. For such senses, (5) is true. Therefore, we should grant the soundness of the argument, if it is valid. And it is valid for the conclusion that defeats thesis H1. But, contrary to what Reichenbach seems to think, it does not succeed in refuting what he calls "Lewis's thesis", that is, the thesis that some given-reports are certain.[14] This is, of course, the thesis directly relevant to premise I.3. Reichenbach fails to refute it, because what the argument yields is:

(6a)   Some given-reports that a person understands and believes with certainty are not certain.

And while this is inconsistent with thesis H1, it is consistent with "Lewis's thesis". And, surely, Lewis needs only the existential thesis for his foundational view of empirical justification. Of course, if, as the preceding argument concludes, not all given-reports are certain, then Lewis and other traditional foundationalists have the task of uncovering the conditions which are sufficient for someone's own given-reports to be certain for him. That is, he should try to replace H1 by an alternative that provides an acceptable sufficient condition for the certainty of a given-report, and, thereby, justifies the rejection of premise I.3.

Before trying to find a viable replacement for H1, I would like to consider an attempt to use the preceding argument to conclude that no given-reports are certain. If successful, this would be a major step toward the justification of I.3. It might be claimed that the preceding argument shows that it is possible that the probability that any given-report is true of s at t is low, because for any one of them, p, there is another one, q, such that $Pr(Tp/Tq) < 0.5$, and it is possible that at t someone understandingly and firmly believes a report consisting of p and q. Consequently, because, according to this objection, certainty requires the impossibility of low probability, no given-reports are certain and "Lewis's thesis" is false. But this requirement for certainty is too strong. No foundationalist need adopt it, for even if the probability of a logically contingent statement is 1, it is nevertheless possible that it is low, as the preceding argument shows. If all justification is erected on a foundation of statements each of whose probability is actually 1, then it can be derived that the probability of any nonfoundational statement equals its conditional probability given the foundational statements. To require it to be *necessary* that the probabilities are not low does not affect this derivation, and it does eliminate many prime candidates for certainty. We are, then, justified in rejecting this objection to "Lewis's thesis".

THESIS H2 AND INDUCTIVE CONSISTENCY

With thesis H1 in doubt but the preceding objection to "Lewis's thesis" defeated, it seems plausible to amend thesis H1 so that any given-report it finds certain is inductively consistent with the rest of s's present given-reports, and also, of course, his other present basic-reports such as, 'I am now believing that I am holding something small and light'. We can now formulate the following replacement for H1:

H2.   Any given-report, p, is initially certain for a persons s, if (a) s understands and believes p with certainty at time t, and (b) 'Pr($Tpst$) = 1' is inductively consistent with the probabilities (both absolute and conditional) of his own basic-reports that he understands and believes with certainty at t.

If thesis H2 is acceptable, then s need only consider the set of basic-reports he understands and firmly believes at t. If p is one of these and the statement that $\Pr(Tp) = 1$ is inductively consistent with corresponding absolute probabilities for the other members of this set, such as q, and the relevant conditional probabilities, such as $\Pr(Tp/Tq)$, then p is certain for s. Of course, however, if, as stated by the objection to the previous premise (1), both $\Pr(Tp)$ and $\Pr(Tq)$ must be calculated individually in order to determine conditional probabilities such as $\Pr(Tp/Tq)$, then these conditional probabilities are of no use in testing $\Pr(Tp)$ and $\Pr(Tq)$ for inductive consistency. As a result, no inductive inconsistencies would arise, and thesis H2 would reduce, in effect, to thesis H1. That is, a person could ignore his other present basic-reports, as well as all his basic-reports about other times, and all nonbasic statements, when deciding whether a particular given-report is certain for him.

OBJECTIONS TO THESIS H2: REFUTATION BY FUTURE GIVEN-REPORTS

There are three plausible sorts of ways to attack thesis H2. The first is to claim that some future basic-reports must be considered at present in order to guarantee the certainty of a present given-report. The second is that some present (perhaps future also) nonbasic statements are relevant to whether a present given-report is certain. The third is that no empirical statement meets one necessary condition for certainty, even given that it satisfies the antecedent of H2.

The Impossibility of Error and Future Given-Reports

Goodman provides an example of the first sort of attack on H2 when he argues that some future given-reports conflict with present ones, and this shows that given-reports are not certain, even when the antecedent of thesis H2 is met. He argues that my judgments about my own immediate experience are "often withdrawn for good reason", and so are not certain. He considers a particular case:

The judgments I made a few moments ago that a reddish patch occupies the center of my visual field at the moment will be dropped if it conflicts with other judgments having a combined stronger claim to preservation. For example, if I also judged that the patch occupying the same region an instant later was blue, and also that the apparent color was constant over the brief period covering the two instants, I am going to have to drop one of the three judgments; and circumstances may point to the first as well as to either of the others.[15]

A Goodman-like Argument Against Hypothesis H2. To reconstruct Goodman's argument, let us use c = 'I am now having an experience of only one color – red'; d = 'I am now having an experience of only one color – blue'; and f = 'I am now having an experience of a color that is the same color that I experienced a moment ago'. One Goodman-like argument is the following:

(1)   At a time, t_1, a person, s, understands and believes with certainty given-report, c, about his own present visual experience, and a moment later at t_2 he understands and believes with certainty report, (d-and-f), about his own present experience.

(2)   If (1), then either the report at t_1 or the report at t_2 is false.

(3)   Statements c, d, and f are given-reports.

(4)   If (1), (2), and (3), then it is possible that at t_2, s is mistaken in believing c was true of him a moment ago at t_1.

(5)   If a given-report, p, is certain for someone at a time, t, then it is not possible that there is a time after t when he is mistaken about p.

Therefore

(6)   Given-report, c, is not certain for s at t_1.

Of course, it is clear that this argument, like the previous one, does not disprove "Lewis's thesis". However, if sound, it does provide additional reason to reject the claim that all given statements are certain, and, more importantly, it also disproves thesis H2 about when a given-sentence is guaranteed to be certain.

Let us grant premise (1) on the grounds that it is true for at least some three statements like c, d, and f, and so we can use these three to illustrate the point. Premise (2) is clearly acceptable, but (3), (4), and (5) should be examined. The only objection I have found to (3) is that f is not a given-report, and thus not a basic-report, because it is not exclusively about s's present sensory experience.[16] It concerns, in part, s's experience of a moment ago. If this objection stands, then not only would the argument fail, but a foundationalist who adopts thesis H2 could require that s reject f

rather then either c or d. I shall not become further embroiled in the difficult problem of deciding which phenomenal statements are given-reports. I shall say only that it seems to be no more reasonable for s at t_2, to reject f, that concerns an experience of only a moment ago about which he feels certain at t_2, than to reject c, about which he may no longer feel certain. Of course, it might be argued that no one should ever reject a given-report for a nonbasic statement, no matter how confident he feels about the latter, but I have found no reason to believe this. Let us, then, tentatively accept (3).

Certainty and the Impossibility of Error. We are left with the task of evaluating premises (4) and (5). To do so adequately we must unpack somewhat the relevant sense of the impossibility of error. I believe that the following rough definition will do for our purposes:

> D4.   It is impossible that s is (nonverbally) mistaken about $p =_{df}$. It is impossible that s understands what it is for p to be true and for p to be false, and s believes p to be true but p is not true; and it is impossible that s understands what it is for p to be true and for p to be false, and s believes p to be false but p is not false.

As stated, D4 shows that it is reasonable to accept premise (4). If (1) and (2) are true, then c, d, or f is false of s at the appropriate time. But if (3) is true, then none of the three is more likely to be immune from being false than either of the other two. Consequently, it is reasonable to conclude that it is possible that each one is false at its appropriate time, regardless of what s understandingly believes at t_2. Let us accept (4) then.

Statement (5) is the most debatable premise in the argument. Goodman clearly accepts it, because he says:

We are talking of knowledge without possibility of error – or, in practice, of judgment immune to subsequent withdrawal for cause. I cannot be said to be certain about what occurs at a given moment, even at that moment if I may justifiably change my mind about it at a later moment.[17]

Here Goodman would seem to agree that (5) is true by definition. Indeed, it might be thought that (5) is true by definition D4 for any sense of 'certain' that entails the impossibility of error. But this is true only for a strong interpretation of D4, namely, that it is impossible for s to be mistaken about p at t only if it is impossible that, *at t and later*, s understandingly believes that p is (true, false) of himself at t, but nevertheless, p

is not (true, false) of s at t. Another, weaker interpretation has as its necessary condition that it is impossible that, *at the time t*, s understandingly believes that p is now (true, false) of himself, but p is not (true, false) of s at t. This allows it to be impossible for s to be mistaken about p being (true, false) at t, even if he is mistaken about p at some time after t when he comes to think p was (false, true) of himself at t.

Surely, the stronger requirement is too strong to be made true by definition of any plausible sense of 'certain' because of many circumstances that often arise years in the future. Often, at t_3, years after t_1 when a person used a given-report, p, to report a present experience, he understandingly and firmly believes that p was true of him at t_1. But it is clearly possible that at t_3 his understanding belief about p is mistaken. Yet no plausible sense of 'certain' should entail the impossibility of this situation arising in the remote future. Indeed, I would claim that present certainty can allow actually mistaken beliefs in the remote future. Consequently, D4 should be taken in the weaker sense.

With (5) not true by definition for any plausible sense of 'certain', we can ask how (5) is to be justified. One way – the best I have found – is to conjoin the somewhat plausible claim:

(7)   Certainty at t implies the impossibility of mistake at t,

with:

(8)   Impossibility of mistake at t implies the impossibility of mistake forever after t.

But, even if we grant that there is a plausible sense of 'certain' that makes (7) true, (8) seems no more plausible than (5) itself.

The case that defeated the use of the strong interpretation of D4 to unpack (5) can also be used to cast some doubt on (5) and (8). For this task, however, we must do more than show that present certainty, which entails the present impossibility of error, does not entail the future impossibility of error. Both (5) and (8) can be viewed as logically contingent claims. Nevertheless, it is plausible to argue that if we assume that there are cases of certainty that entail only the *present* impossibility of error, then some of these are also cases where there is possibility of error in the remote future. If it be objected that this argument is question-begging, I think that little can be said except that, as contingent and far from obvious, both (8) and (5) require some support and there seems to be none. The best hope for support is to argue that all plausible foundational theories require

(5), but I find no reason to believe that claim. I conclude, therefore, that there is a sense of 'certain' that entails the present impossibility of error for which it is plausible that thesis H2 avoids refutation by the preceding Goodman-like argument.

A Minimum Truth-Entailing Sense of Certainty and Future Given-Reports

There is, however, a way to use the first three premises of the preceding argument to show that thesis H2 does not guarantee certainty for given-reports in any sense of 'certain' that entails truth, such as the preceding one that implies the imposssbility of mistake. A minimum truth-entailing sense would seem to be one where a given-report, p, being certain for s at t entails that p is, as a matter of fact, true of him at t.[18] But Goodman's example is a case where c, d, and f meet the antecedent of H2, and so are certain for s by H2, but either c is false of s at t_1, or either d or f is false of s at t_2. So, at least one of these reports is not certain for s in this minimum truth-entailing sense because of given-reports about some other time. And, of course, this is also true for all other truth-entailing senses. Consequently, contrary to H2, understanding belief and inductive consistency at present is not sufficient to guarantee for s the truth of his own present given-reports. For certainty that entails truth, the given-reports with which a given-report is inductively consistent should at least include those that s believes true of himself just before now and those just after now. But just how much of the past and future should be considered is a difficult question for which I know of no answer.

Reasonableness Senses of Certainty and Future Given-Reports

The difficulty of answering the preceding question, coupled with the fact that the inductive consistency of the given-reports that a person understandingly and firmly believes at one time does not guarantee certainty in any truth-entailing sense, gives reason to search for some other sense of 'certain' that is adequate to the needs of plausible foundational theories. Although I have interepreted Goodman as concerned with a truth-entailing sense of certainty, he also seems to be interested in a quite different sense. Indeed, in the previous quotation, Goodman seems to equate the impossibility of error with immunity from future grounds for rejection. But, given something like D4, the two are clearly different. The present and future guarantee of truth for a statement by present understanding belief is not a guarantee that it is never made unreasonable by new evidence in the future. If, at t, p is true of s at t, then forever after t, p is true of s at t.

But none of this implies that, forever after t, it is reasonable for s to accept that p is true of him at t. To see the difference, let us use another rough definition:

DS.   It is impossible that it is unreasonable for s to believe that $p =_{df}$. It is impossible that there is evidence, e, such that e and s's understandingly believing that p conjointly make it not reasonable for s to believe that p.

A sense of 'certain' that entails maximum reasonableness (rather than truth or some probability), I shall call a 'reasonableness' sense. DS would help unpack certain reasonableness senses of 'certain'. However, DS is, like D4, ambiguous regarding time. It can be interpreted to require that it is impossible that there is any time after t at which some evidence, e, and s's understanding belief that p was true of him at t make it false that p is reasonable for him. A weaker requirement is that it is impossible that, *at the time t*, s understandingly believes p, but this understanding belief together with e make it false that p is reasonable for s at t. Again, like D4, it is implausible to make the stronger requirement true of 'certain' by definition. As previously discussed, it seems possible that there are many cases where at t, p is certain for s in the weak sense, and that many years after t he understandingly maintains that p was true of him at t but his memory is so dim and so much contrary evidence has arisen in the interval that it is unreasonable for him to believe that p was true of him long ago at t. Let us, then, consider certainty that meets only the weak sense of D5, and see whether we can devise a sound Goodman-like argument concerning it.

A Goodman-like Argument Against Thesis H2 for Reasonableness Senses. We cannot merely transform the preceding Goodman-like argument concerning truth-entailing senses of 'certain' into a plausible one concerning reasonableness senses. I propose the following, however, as one of the most plausible versions:

(1a)   At a time t_1, s understands and believes with certainty given-report, c, about his own present visual experience, and, a moment later at t_2, s understands and believes with certainty given-report, (d-and-f), about his own present experience.

(2a)   If (1a), then either s's given-report at t_1 or his given-report at t_2 is false.

(3a)   If (1a) and the consequent of (2a) are true, then at t_2, it is unreasonable for s to believe his given-report at t_1 and his given-report at t_2.

(4a)   If at t_2, it is unreasonable for s to believe both of these reports, then at t_2, it is reasonable for him to believe c was false of him at t_1.

Therefore

(5a)   At t_2, it is reasonable for s to believe that given-report c was false of him at t_1.

(6a)   If (5a), then it is possible that (5a).

(7a)   If a given-report, p, is certain for someone at a time, t, then it is not possible that there is a time after t when it is reasonable for him to believe that p was false of him at t.

Therefore

(8a)   Given-report, c, is not certain for s at t_1 (contrary to H2).

I believe that for our purposes we can grant all premises except (7a) which is, of course, the crucial one.

We have concluded that (7a) is not definitionally true by D5 for reasonablness senses of 'certain'. Like the corresponding premise of the preceding argument, (5), Goodman seems to accept (7a). But again it is unclear how it is to be justified once its being true by definition is rejected. Furthermore, just as the previous attempt by the previous (7) and (8) fails, so the corresponding attempt fails in the present case. That is, even if we can accept:

(9a)   Certainty of p at t implies the necessity of the reasonableness of p at t,

there is no reason to accept:

(10a)   The necessity of the reasonableness of p at t implies that, for ever after t, it is impossible that the denial of p is reasonable.

Indeed, I find (10a) even less plausible than the corresponding previous premise (8): 'Impossibility of mistake at t implies the impossibility of mistake forever after t'.

Pure reasonableness senses of 'certain' are purely epistemic without any implications about the conditions in which the statements that are certain are either true or false. And, as for other non-truth-entailing epistemic terms such as 'plausible' and 'acceptable', what is reasonable at one time often becomes quite unreasonable at some future time. This is because what is reasonable or unreasonable at a time depends in part on what evidence is available then. But what evidence is available often changes over time. Consequently, what is actually reasonable or unreasonable changes also. It seems that this should also be true of what is necessarily reasonable at a certain time, and, *a fortiori*, of any sense of 'certain' that entails that necessity. Because of this, I conclude that neither the present (7a) nor (10a) is plausible, and so the second version of the Goodman-like argument fails as did the first.

It might be objected that the preceding argument can survive the rejection of (7a), because (7a) and (6a) can be dropped in favor of a premise that is much more plausible than (7a):

(11a)   If a given-report, *p*, is certain for someone at *t*, then, *as a matter of fact*, it is false that there is a time after *t* when it is reasonable for him to believe that *p* was false of him at *t*.

But (11a) is refuted by an example like those I urged against (7a) and, previously, (5). Assume there is a large group of reports, each of which is certain for someone at *t*, in a sense that implies it is necessary that the report is reasonable for the person at *t*. It is quite plausible that at least one of these fails to remain reasonable for the appropriate person at some time in the distant future, because overwhelming contrary evidence has accumulated and the person is no longer sure about what he experienced at *t*. So the actual future reasonableness of believing *p* to be false, like the mere possibility of this future reasonableness, fails to show that *p* is not certain now.

Probability Senses of Certainty and Future Given-Reports

It might be thought that Goodman's objection can be recast as a variation of Reichenbach's concerning probability senses of 'certain'. That is, it might be argued that $\Pr(Tc/Td \cdot Tf) < 0.5$, and so either $\Pr(Tc) \neq 1$ or $\Pr(Td) \neq 1$ or $\Pr(Tf) \neq 1$. Consequently, contrary to thesis H2, at least one given-report is not certain in Reichenbach's sense at the time it is made because of the probability of a given-report concerning a different time. But this argument is unsound. Another hypothesis conjoins at least as plausibly with the premise. That is, for time t_1, $\Pr_1(Tcst_1) = 1$, and so $\Pr_1(Tdst_2) \neq 1$, or $\Pr_1(Tfst_2) \neq 1$. For t_2, on the other hand, $\Pr_2(Tdst_2) = 1$, and $\Pr_2(Tfst_2) = 1$, and so $\Pr_2(Tcst_2) \neq 1$. Indeed, this is the hypothesis I would urge. It might be objected that probabilities should not be relativized to times, but, as we have seen concerning epistemic concepts, the

absolute probability of a statement changes as the evidence for the statement changes over time. And this is true of probabilities anywhere in the
spectrum from 0 through 1, even if a probability of 1 is reserved for analytic statements. Some of these – perhaps very complicated – might well
have a probability of less than 1 relative to the evidence available at some
time, where the probability of the evidence is 1. Relevant here is what
has been called "probability kinematics", that is, the study of how probabilities should change as evidence changes.[19] It should be noted, however,
that at present it is unclear how to decrease the probability of a statement,
p, after t, in a rational way, when $\Pr_t(p) = 1$.[20] Nevertheless, I think that
procedures can be developed to accommodate these cases. Consequently,
I see no reason to think that Goodmanian future low probabilities pose a
threat to thesis H2 for probability senses of 'certain'.

OBJECTION TO THESIS H2 :
NO PRESENT GUARANTEE OF FUTURE REASONABLENESS

We are almost ready to conclude that no argument involving the future
succeeds against thesis H2 for the most plausible non-truth-entailing senses
of 'certain'. But before doing so, I wish to consider an objection of the
sort that no empirical statement meets a necessary condition for certainty.
Thus no basic-reports of any sort are certain, as skeptical premise I.3
states. It goes as follows. First, a sentence, p, is certain (in any sense) for
s at t, only if it is reasonable at t for s to believe that p will remain reasonable for him forever after t. But, second, even given H2, this is not reasonable at t for any empirical statement, p, because, at t, s has no way to justify
that for any time after t, p will be reasonable relative to the evidence that
is available at that later time. Note, incidentally, how this second objection differs from the first. While the first requires truth, or, *in the future*,
maximum reasonableness or probability of 1 for p, the second requires only
the *present* reasonableness of the claim that p will remain reasonable in
the future.

If sound, the preceding argument is devastating for any foundationalist
seeking certainty. But I contend that the argument is not sound for any
plausible sense of 'certain', because no such sense implies what the argument requires of certainty. There is, however, a similar claim that it is
plausible to require. That is, at t, when p is certain for s, it is reasonable
for s to believe that p is reasonable, given the conjunction of his present
understanding belief that p and any future evidence. In other words, p is

certain for s at t, only if no statement of future evidence taken with his present understanding belief defeats, *at the time t*, the justification of p by this present understanding belief. I find this second, but not the first, requirement for certainty to be plausible, because while s's present evidence about his present experience should be strong enough to resist defeat now, this is not true of the future. This evidence loses its relative strength as time passes. Once the present moment has passed, and p is no longer a report about s's present experience, then his believing this report loses any special epistemic status it had for him at the time he understandingly and firmly believed he was having the experience. And once it loses that status, even his strong belief that p is true of him at t is much more easily defeated. Thus it may not be reasonable for s to expect p to remain reasonable for him in the future. But any later defeat by evidence because of this later change of status of s's belief gives s no reason to think that his understanding and firm belief at t is defeated at t by that same evidence, or that p is not certain for s at t while his belief has its original epistemic status. We can, therefore, reject this last attempt to use future situations to refute present claims about what is certain in plausible senses of 'certain'.

I have concluded that it is plausible to think that present given-reports are certain in plausible reasonableness senses for a person at the present, even if they are not reasonable for him in the future, and even if it is not reasonable at present for him to expect them to be reasonable for him in the future. I would claim the corresponding conclusion is true of Reichenbach's probability sense of 'certain'. It might seem, then, that I can also conclude that if a person, at t, seeks to discover whether a present given-report about himself is certain in a plausible non-truth-entailing sense, then he needs to consider the plausibility or probability of the report relative to a statement, q, only if, at t, q is also one of his own present basic-reports. But this conclusion, which favors thesis H2, would be premature. Although we have found it reasonable for the person to ignore future probability and reasonableness, we have not yet considered the second type of objection to see whether there might be some nonbasic statements about the present that he should consider.

OBJECTION TO THESIS H2: REFUTATION BY PRESENT NONBASIC STATEMENTS

One way to construct an objection involving present nonbasic sentences is to use the previous $a =$ 'I am now having a visual experience of holding something large and heavy'; and to consider one of s's present observation-reports, such as $g = $ 'I am now holding a small, light object'. Surely, $\Pr_t(Ta/Tg) < 0.4$, and so, it might be argued, for at least some time, t, $\Pr_t(Ta)$ is low, even when a satisfies H2, because $\Pr_t(Tg)$ is high. Thus, contrary to H2, not only is a not certain at t in Reichenbach's probability sense, but it is also not certain in any plausible reasonableness sense, because if $\Pr_t(Ta)$ is low, then it is not reasonable for s to accept a at t. For example, if we assume that $\Pr_t(Tg) = 0.9$, then we can derive that $\Pr_t(Ta) < 0.5$, and also that it is not reasonable for s to accept a at t.

One reply to this objection focuses on the fact that the objection depends on the assumption that the probability of g being true of s at t is high even when it conflicts with the claim that $\Pr_t(Ta) = 1$. But a defender of thesis H2 can begin a rebuttal by noting that g is one of s's observation-reports, and so it entails that a physical object is perceived by s. But a is one of s's basic-reports, and so it has no such entailment. Then he can argue that we should not use the assumption that $\Pr_t(Tg)$ is high to conclude that $\Pr_t(Ta) \neq 1$, unless $\Pr_t(Tg)$ can be established to be high on the basis of some basic-report that s understandingly and fully believes at t. If it is not established in this way, then it is more reasonable to claim $\Pr_t(Ta) = 1$ if a satisfies H2, and, assuming, $\Pr_t(Tg/Ta)$ is low, conclude that $\Pr_t(Tg)$ is low.

On the other hand, if there is a basic-report, r, that s understandingly and firmly believes at t and $\Pr_t(Tg/Tr)$ is high, then it might seem that we should conclude that $\Pr_t(Ta) < 1$. It is possible, however, that $\Pr_t(Tg/Tr)$ is high and $\Pr_t(Ta/Tr) = 1$, and so, according to our defender of H2, what is crucial for discovering the value of $\Pr_t(Ta)$ is not $\Pr_t(Ta/Tg)$ but rather $\Pr_t(Ta/Tr)$, or more generally, $\Pr_t(q/Tr)$, for every r that is a basic-report which s fully and understandingly believes at t, and any q at all. So, whether or not absolute probabilities of observation-reports and other nonbasic sentences are established by basic-reports, none needs to be considered in discovering whether or not a basic-report that meets the antecedent of H2 for s at t is certain for s at t. Therefore, if this defense is sound, observation-report g raises no problem for H2.

There is a general principle that, if reasonable, helps justify the preceding reply to the third objection to H2. We can arrive at it by beginning with H2 and replacing 'p is initially certain for s at t' by '$\Pr_t(Tpst) = 1$'. Then we can clarify the probability relationships described in clause (b) of H2 by specifying more precisely just what sort of inductive inconsistencies are necessary for the probability of a given-report that has been eternalized to s at t to be less than 1 for s at t. Finally, because given-reports are not epistemically different from other basic-reports, we should generalize the principle so it applies to all basic-reports. What results is:

G.   For any basic-report, p, if s understands and believes p with certainty at t, then $Pr_t(Tpst) \neq 1$ only if for some true statements of the form '$Pr_t(q/Trst) = n$', where 'r' is a basic-report that s understands and believes with certainty at t, the following is inductively inconsistent: '$Pr_t(Tpst) = 1$ and $Pr_t(Trst) = 1$ and $Pr_t(q/Trst) = n$'.

Notice that thesis G does not imply that all probabilities of empirical sentences 'originate' from those of given-reports. Thus G is consistent with foundational views of justification that, unlike the traditional view, do not require that there always be a basic-report at the base of every empirical justification. It is also consistent with many nonfoundational views. This is because, even assuming the requirement of inductive consistency as we should, G allows any probability of a nonbasic statement to be ascertained without consideration of those for all basic-reports. It only requires that the resulting probabilities be inductively consistent with the relevant one for basic-reports. Consequently, the use of G in the reply is not to be rejected on the grounds that its use is question-begging because it assumes that a foundation of basic-reports is required for any empirical justification. It might be claimed, however, that the use of G in this argument is question-begging for a different reason. It implies that whenever a change in probabilities must be made over time to avoid an inductive inconsistency that involves a basic-report and a nonbasic sentence which is not supported by a basic-report, it is the probability of the nonbasic sentence that must be adjusted — assuming the inductive consistency requirement and the constancy of the relevant conditional probabilities. Now it is difficult to decide whether this use of thesis G is question-begging in this way. I believe, however, that I have indicated that G is at least plausible enough to cast doubt on the assumption required by this first objection to thesis H2 from nonbasic sentences. Of course, we may come to find G implausible later, because reasons to reject G may materialize if certain foundational or nonfoundational views that are inconsistent with G come to be developed and are shown to be reasonable. But that does not affect the present use of G to rebut this objection from observation-reports. Furthermore, the explanatory foundational theory, which I shall develop in Chapter 7 and then defend as the most reasonable, is consistent with G.

The fourth objection to H2 is also aimed at the claim that nonbasic sentences are irrelevant to the assignment of certainty to basic-reports. Furthermore, it might be claimed, it is an objection that is consistent with thesis G that is so vital to the reply to the last objection, and also with any sort of foundational or nonfoundational view of justification. The objection assumes that at time t, science has reached the stage where it has a set of psychophysical laws that have been universally confirmed by repeated, rigorous tests, and where it has an acceptable theory that explains exactly these laws. Let us assume that one of these laws is $L =$ 'Someone has an experience of pain if and only if c-fibers in his central nervous system are firing'. We then imagine a situation in which a team of scientists carefully examines s at t and unanimously concludes $J =$ 'None of s's c-fibers are firing at t'. But, at t, s states given-report $k =$ 'I am now having an experience of intense pain'. According to this objection, $\Pr_t (L \cdot J) > \Pr_t(Tk)$. Thus $\Pr_t(Tk) \neq 1$, and k is not certain for s at t, even if at t he understandingly and firmly believes k. Consequently, if this situation arises at t, then at t, given-report k is not certain for s, in either Reichenbach's probability sense of 'certain' or in any plausible reasonableness sense of 'certain'. Therefore, contrary to thesis H2, it is false that a sufficient condition for present certainty need not include anything about nonbasic sentences about the present. Furthermore, this situation allows that both L and J are highly probable only if some basic-reports are at the base of their justification. So, the reply to the preceding objection based on G does not apply here.

One way to begin a reply is to point out that G is imprecise as stated, and that the preceding objection is inconsistent with G in its intended sense, namely:

G1.   For any basic-report, p, if s understands and believes p with certainty at t, then the probability, for s at t, that p is true of him at t does not equal 1, that is, $Pr_{s,t}(Tpst) \neq 1$, only if for some true statements of the form '$Pr_{s,t}(q/Trst) = n$', where 'r' is a basic-report that s understands and believes at t, the following is inductively inconsistent: '$Pr_{s,t}(Tpst) = 1$ and $Pr_{s,t}(Trst) = 1$ and $Pr_{s,t}(q/Trst) = n$'.[21]

Given Gl, s can plausibly claim that $Pr_{s,t}(Tk) = 1$, and plausibly deny $(L \cdot J)$, given G1 and one assumption, namely, that, as is often the case, '$Pr_{s,t}(Tk) = 1$' is inductively consistent with equally high probabilities for the other eternalized basic-reports that s believes understandingly and firmly at t. This requires that the probability for s at t, of $(L \cdot J)$ not be high relative to these basic-reports. But that would often be true. Of course, it may be quite reasonable for the scientists to accept $(L \cdot J)$ and reject that k is true of s at t, because of some of their own basic-reports. But since we are considering only what is certain for s at t, no problem is raised by the fact that these scientists should accept something else. It is plausible that a sentence, p, is certain for s at t, but its denial is reasonable for someone else at t, especially on the plausible assumption that, at t, s has a unique, epistemically overriding relationship to what he reports using p. Thus, this objection can be rejected for the same reason as the preceding one.

There is, however, a modification of this fourth objection that we should consider. It requires that we change the preceding situation so that there is just one scientist who makes the tests on s, namely, s himself. This is the case of the autocerebroscope.[22] Let us assume here that one of s's conjunctive basic-reports, p, consists of a given-report about his own present experience of a cerebroscope and also a basic-report to the effect that he fully believes L to be highly confirmed and scientifically explained. Furthermore, it seems plausible that $Pr_{s,t}(L \cdot J/Tp) > 0.5$. In this situation, where $Pr_{s,t}(L \cdot J/Tk) = 0$, we can derive that if $Pr_{s,t}(Tk) = 1$, then $Pr_{s,t}(Tp) = 0$, and that if $Pr_{s,t}(Tp) = 1$, then $Pr_{s,t}(Tk) \leqslant 0.5$. Thus, surely, either k or p is not certain for s at t. It is clear, however, that this conclusion raises no problem for the thesis H2 because '$Pr_{s,t}(Tkst) = 1$' is inductively inconsistent with '$Pr_{s,t}(Tpst) = 1$' conjoined with the preceding conditional probability sentences. And, we are assuming, p and k are basic-reports that, at t, s understandingly and fully believes. Thus k does not satisfy the antecedent of H2, and this modification of the fourth objection to thesis H2 fails as did the original version.

A FIFTH OBJECTION TO THESIS H2: STRICT COHERENCE
AND PROBABILITY OF 1

There is one last objection to thesis H2 that we should consider. It is of
the third sort and is based on the view that any rational probability or
credence function should be 'strictly coherent'. That is, following Carnap,
a function *Cr* is *strictly coherent* just in case it satisfies the basic axioms of
the probability calculus and "there is no (finite) system of bets in accordance with *Cr* on molecular [or atomic] propositions such that the
result is a net loss in at least one [logically] possible case, but not a net
gain in any possible case".[23] The idea is that it is irrational to bet where it
is impossible to win but possible to lose. One such case is where someone
puts up the whole stake in a bet when it is logically possible that he lose.
Such bets should be epistemically prohibited because irrational, and
strictly coherent functions do that. But, as has been shown, if a probability function is strictly coherent, then for any molecular or atomic statement, p, $\Pr(p) < 1$ if the denial of p is possible, And since the denial of any
empirical statement, including each basic-report, is possible, then no basic-
report has a probability of 1, even if H2 is satisfied. And, as a result, no
basic-report has maximum reasonableness. Consequently, as skeptical
premise I.3 states, no basic-report is certain at any time for anyone, either
in a probability sense or a reasonableness sense.[24]

Is this objection sound? Let us agree that it is not ideally rational to
bet in accordance with a probability function that requires you to put up
the whole stake of a bet when it is logically possible you are mistaken.
Nevertheless, it is not clear it is unreasonable to assign a probability of
1 to certain logically contingent claims, such as $E =$ 'Elsie the cow will
not jump over the moon from the earth today'. That is, although it may
not be ideally rational to put up the whole stake when betting on claim E,
it would also seem not to be ideally rational to put up any of the stake
when betting against that claim. But if all this is true of what is ideally
rational, and we agree with Carnap about strict coherence, then function *Pr* is ideally rational only if $\Pr(E) < 1$ and $\Pr(\bar{E}) = 0$. But this is a
contradiction.[25] One way to avoid this is to interpret 'possible' in the definition of 'strictly coherent' as 'causally possible' rather than 'logically
possible'. Then $\Pr(E) = 1$ and $\Pr(\bar{E}) = 0$. Of course, it is not clear this
would allow all given-reports that meet H2 to have a probability of 1.
However, another plausible interpretation of 'possible' is 'epistemically
possible', where something is epistemically possible just in case its denial

is not epistemically certain. And such an interpretation allows some basic-reports to have probabilities of 1. Regardless of whether the Carnapian interpretation of strict coherence should be rejected, however, the preceding discussion shows there is doubt about whether it should be accepted. Consequently, this fifth and last objection to thesis H2 does not justify rejecting H2.

CONCLUSION ABOUT THESIS H2 AND PROPOSALS CONCERNING CERTAINTY

I believe that I have examined the strongest arguments against thesis H2. Because we have been able to refute these arguments, I conclude that there is some reason to accept thesis H2, that is, when H2 is modified in accordance with G1 so it concerns what is certain for a person at a time, and the relevant probabilities of basic-reports for that person at that time. This gives us:

H3. Any basic-report, p, is initially certain for a person s, at time t, if (a) s understands and believes p with certainty at t; and (b) for all true sentences of the form '$\Pr_{s,t}(q/Trst) = n$', where 'r' is a basic-report that s understands and believes with certainty at t, the following is inductively consistent: '$\Pr_{s,t}(Tpst) = 1$ and $\Pr_{s,t}(Trst) = 1$ and $\Pr_{s,t}(q/Trst) = n$'.

It might be objected, however, that it would be premature to accept H3 before considering whether there is a plausible sense of 'certain' for which thesis H3 is acceptable. Obviously, as we have seen, no truth-entailing sense will do, but I would like to propose that there is at least one plausible probability sense of 'certain' for which H3 is true. In this sense, an empirical sentence, p, is certain for s at t, just in case $\Pr_{s,t}(Tpst/Test) \times \Pr_{s,t}(Test) = 1$, where e is s's evidence for p at t. And we can characterize initial certainty for this probability sense as follows:

D6. Empirical sentence, p, is *initially certain* for s at $t =_{df}$. p is certain for s at t – (and so $\Pr_{s,t}(Tpst) = 1$ – and it is false that $\Pr_{s,t}(Tpst)$ would equal one only if some *other* statement, e, were s's evidence for p at t such that $\Pr_{s,t}(Test) = 1$ and $\Pr_{s,t}(Tpst/Test) = 1$.

That is, roughly, p is certain for s at t, and it is false that p would be certain for s at t only if s had some other evidence that justifies p sufficiently to be certain for s at t. Furthermore, if it is plausible to accept H3, definition D6, and the principle:

R1.   If $Pr_{s,t}(Tpst) = 1$, then nothing is more reasonable for s at t
         than p,

then (a) and (b) of H3 imply not only that $Pr_{s,t}(Tpst) = 1$, but also that
whatever is initially certain in the preceding probability sense is also
initially certain in a reasonableness sense. This is, I believe, plausible for
basic-reports. Indeed, R1 is clearly true, if probability is given an epistemic
interpretation such as one where $Pr_{s,t}(p) = n$ just in case n equals the
degree of confirmation of p for s at t.

CONCLUSION ABOUT SKEPTICAL ARGUMENT I

Having found H3 acceptable, we can use it to refute premise I.3 of the
first skeptical argument. We need only justify that some basic-reports meet
the antecedent of H3. This would allow us to infer that some basic-report
is certain for some person at some time, contrary to I.3. This can be
achieved, I assume, by practically anyone who is now reading this book.
He need only use given-report, p = 'I am now having an experience of
something white'. For me, and, I would guess, for many of the others, the
only other basic-report that I believe now (at t_n) which is inductively relevant to p, is r = 'I am now believing that I am seeing a white page'. But,
I maintain, r raises no problem for the claim that $Pr_{c,n}(Tpcn) = 1$, because
'p' satisfies H3. It is true that this requires that $Pr_{c,n}(Tpcn) = Pr_{c,n}(Tpcn/$
$Trcn) = Pr_{c,n}(Trcn/Tpcn) = 1$, but, although I have no way to establish
these equalities, they seem quite reasonable, given the situation in which
I (c = Cornman) find myself now. So, it seems quite reasonable to conclude that given-report, p, is certain for anyone when he looks at this page,
if he meets the preceding description as I do now, and if he also understands and believes r with certainty, as I do now. Consequently, it is now
reasonable for me, and for anyone else for whom r is certain at some time,
to reject premise I.3 of skeptical argument I. Of course, similar situations
for myriads of other basic-reports would justify the same conclusion for
anyone in those situations.

Anyone who has found himself at some time in a situation like the one
described above has had reason to reject premise I.3. I shall assume from
here on, for ease of discussion, that some such situation has arisen at
least once for each person. Of course, I have not justified this generalization. If that proves bothersome to someone, then let him assume that my
subsequent discussion is aimed only at those of whom this is true. If he

should be one of the others, I am afraid that there is little I can do to justify the rejection of I.3 for him.

SKEPTICAL ARGUMENT II: INFERENTIAL ACCEPTABILITY REQUIRES CERTAINTY

Skeptical argument I should be rejected, because at least one of its premises is unreasonable. Unfortunately, however, a skeptic who wishes to justify thesis M_1S_1 is far from defeated. He can emphasize that anyone who accepts principle L3 or L4 stresses not merely certainty, but especially *initial* certainty. And any plausible version of foundationalism requires one quite general principle relating inferential and initial certainty, namely:

FP1   If all initially certain empirical statements are of kind K, and some empirical statement of kind L is inferentially certain for s at t_1, then some empirical statement which is of kind L is certain for s at a time, t_2, relative to a set of statements of kind K, each of which is certain for s at t_2.

Later, in Chapter 7, I shall show that FP1 is true for any plausible form of foundationalism. For now, let me indicate why this is so by assuming that foundationalism is true and, for example, that the initially certain empirical statements are basic-reports. Something is inferentially certain for s at t_1 only if it meets two conditions. First, it is certain relative to s's evidence, and, second, s's evidence is certain for him at t_1. This particular evidence need not be *initially* certain for s at any time, but, for any plausible foundational theory, any evidential chain of inferentially certain statements leads to a set of statements all of which are initially certain. So, if some nonbasic statement is inferentially certain, then, on the preceding assumptions, either it or some other inferentially certain statement is certain relative to evidence, e, that is comprised solely of basic-reports. This evidence, e, need not consist entirely of initially certain basic-reports; some of them may be only inferentially certain. But somewhere in any evidential chain of inferentially certain nonbasic statements there must be at least one of these, p, such that s's evidence for p at some time t_2, perhaps earlier than t_1, consists solely of basic-reports that are certain. Thus FP1 is true, if some plausible foundational theory is true.

Principle FP1 can be used with the Cartesian tenet, L3 to provide a second argument for M_1S_1 that avoids the previous objection to argument I. The crux of the first part of this new argument – skeptical argument

II – is that no nonbasic statements are initially certain, and none is either certain or probable relative to basic-reports. It follows from this, with L3 and FP1, that no nonbasic statements are inferentially acceptable. That is, more precisely:

II.1.   Principle FP1.
II.2.   An empirical statement is initially certain only if it is a basic-report.
II.3.   No nonbasic statement is certain relative to any set of basic-reports.

Therefore

II.4.   No nonbasic statement is inferentially certain.
II.5.   No statement is certain if it is neither initially nor inferentially certain.

Therefore

II.6.   No nonbasic statement is certain.
II.7.   No nonbasic statement is probable relative to any basic-report.

Therefore

II.8.   No nonbasic statement is probable relative to an empirical statement that is certain.
II.9.   Principle L3.

Therefore

II.10.   No nonbasic statement is inferentially acceptable.

Once II.10 is derived, argument II proceeds as I did, with premises I.5, I.6, and I.8, to reach the conclusion that M_1S_1 is true (I.9).

I find only two ways for a foundationalist to rebut this first part of argument II: attack premise II.7 or II.9, which is principle L3. Premise II.5 is clearly true and, although II.2 is worth debating, I believe it is quite reasonable and will not consider it here. However, later, in chapters 4 and 5, some points will be raised that support it. And, as argued above, premise II.1 is essential for a plausible foundational theory. I shall consider a relative of II.7 later in chapters 4 and 5 when I consider the claim that there are observation-reports and memory-reports which are probable relative to basic-reports. If this claim should prove reasonable, then we will have reason to reject II.7. This would not, of course, affect its kin, II.3, which I find to be quite plausible, because it concerns certainty rather than probability. However, issues relevant to II.3 will also be discussed in chapters 4 and 5.

What I propose to do next in Chapter 4 is evaluate the Cartesian premise, L3. I shall do it, however, by concentrating primarily on the principle it entails, L4. If, as I hope to show, L4 and, thereby, L3 prove to be implausible, then not only would skeptical arguments I and II be rebutted, but traditional foundationalism – whether Cartesian, Lewisean, or some other species – would also be refuted. Then the way would be opened for the flourishing of a wide variety of theories – both foundational and non-foundational – that are not based on 'the given' or the initially certain.

NOTES

[1] K. Lehrer, 'Skepticism and Conceptual Change', in R. Chisholm and R. Swartz (eds.), *Empirical Knowledge*, Englewood Cliffs, N.J.: Prentice-Hall, 1973, p. 52.

[2] *Ibid.*, p. 51.

[3] P. Unger, 'A Defense of Skepticism', *Philosophical Review* **80** (1971), 216.

[4] See P. Unger, 'Two Types of Skepticism', *Philosophical Studies* **25** (1974), 77–96.

[5] C. I. Lewis, *An Analysis of Knowledge and Valuation*, La Salle, Ill.: Open Court, 1946, p. 186.

[6] *Ibid.*, p. 334. However, Lewis talks of *prima facie* credibility, and says that it "may be dispelled and give way to improbability" (p. 355). Such a notion seems different from what I call 'initial' and 'noninferential' acceptability.

[7] C. I. Lewis, 'The Bases of Empirical Knowledge', in Chisholm and Swartz (eds.), *op. cit.*, p. 137.

[8] I have characterized observation terms, phenomenal terms, and topic-neutral terms in *Materialism and Sensations*, New Haven, Conn.: Yale University Press, 1971, pp. 69, 81, and 8 respectively.

[9] *Cf.* R. Chisholm, *Theory of Knowledge*, 2nd ed., Englewood Cliffs, N.J.: Prentice-Hall, 1977, p. 33.

[10] H. Reichenbach, 'Are Phenomenal Reports Absolutely Certain?' *Philosophical Review* **61** (1952). Reprinted in Chisholm and Swartz (eds.), *op. cit.*, pp. 354–356.

[11] One set of axioms for the probability calculus is the following: P1: $\Pr(p/e) > 0$; P2: $\Pr(e/e) = 1$; P3: $\Pr(p/e) + \Pr(\bar{p}/e) = 1$; P4: If $(p \cdot e)$ is possible, then $\Pr(p \cdot q/e) = \Pr(q/p \cdot e) \times \Pr(p/e)$. I have adopted these from R. Carnap, 'A Basic System of Inductive Logic', in R. Carnap and R. Jeffrey (eds.), *Studies in Inductive Logic and Probability*, Berkeley: University of California Press, 1971, p. 38.

[12] This might be one way to interpret Lewis's reply to Reichenbach that "there is no requirement of consistency that is relevant to protocols", in Lewis, 'The Given Element in Empirical Knowledge', *Philosophical Review* **61** (1952). Reprinted in Chisholm and Swartz (eds.), *op. cit.*, p. 369.

[13] See Lewis, *An Analysis of Knowledge and Valuation*, pp. 303–306.

[14] Reichenbach, *op. cit.*, p. 351.

[15] N. Goodman, 'Sense and Certainty', *Philosophical Review* **61** (1952). Reprinted in Chisholm and Swartz (eds.), *op. cit.*, p. 361.

[16] Lewis would seem to claim that f is not a given-report. See *An Analysis of Knowledge and Valuation*, p. 136.

[17] Goodman, *op. cit.*, p. 361.

[18] What I call 'truth-entailing' senses of 'certain' are called 'truth-evaluative' senses by R. Firth in 'The Anatomy of Certainty', *Philosophical Review* **76** (1967). Reprinted in Chisholm and Swartz (eds), *op. cit.*, pp. 207–208.

[19] For example, see R. Jeffrey, *The Logic of Decision*, New York: McGraw-Hill, 1965, ch. 11.

[20] Consider, for example, that if $Pr_t(p) = 1$ and the only way to change probabilities is by conditionalization – either 'strict' or 'generalized' – from the probabilities at t, then the probability of p will always remain 1. However, because the probability before t of a given-report being true of s at t is less than 1, conditionalization from such earlier times does allow its probability after t to be less than 1. Furthermore, conditionalization requires 'rigidity', that is, the relevant conditional probabilities do not change over the relevant time. But, as conditionalization itself shows, some conditional probabilities do change See, for example, W. Harper and H. Kyburg, 'The Jones Case', *British Journal for the Philosophy of Science* **19** (1968), 247–251. Indeed, I would claim that $Pr_1(Tcst/Tqst_2) \neq Pr_2(Tcst_1/Tqst_2)$, if q is a given-report about s at t_2, and $Pr_2(Tcst_1) = 1$ and $Pr_2(Tqst_2) = 1$ are inductively inconsistent. Assume that q is certain for s at t_2. Then $Pr_2(Tcst_1) = Pr_2(Tcst_1/Tqst_2) \neq 1$. But, assuming c is certain for s at t_1, $Pr_1(Tcst_1) = Pr_1(Tcst_1/Tqst_2) = 1$. For 'strict' and 'generalized' conditionalization, see P. Teller, 'Conditionalization and Observation', *Synthese* **26** (1973), 218–258.

[21] If someone complains that probabilities should not be relativized to persons, I shall not debate him here. Rather I refer him to Chapter 5 where I adopt an epistemic construal of probability which it is plausible to relativize to persons. For such relativizing, see also R. Carnap, 'Inductive Logic and Rational Decision', in Carnap and Jeffrey (eds.), *op. cit.*, pp. 13–19.

[22] See P. Meehl, 'The Compleat Autocerebroscope', in P. Feyerabend and G. Maxwell (eds.), *Mind, Matter and Method: Essays in Honor of Herbert Feigl*, Minneapolis: University of Minnesota Press, 1966, pp. 103–181, especially section 1.

[23] Carnap, *op. cit.*, p. 15; see also pp. 101–102, 111–114.

[24] See K. Lehrer, *Knowledge*, Oxford: Oxford University Press, 1974, pp. 150–151, for a similar claim.

[25] For a similar discussion of strict coherence, see W. Harper, 'Rational Belief Change, Popper Functions, and Counterfactuals', *Synthese* **30** (1975), 221–262.

CHAPTER 3

SKEPTICISM AND ACCEPTABILITY WITHOUT CERTAINTY

As stated in the last chapter, a premise that is basic both to traditional foundationalism and to skeptical arguments I and II, is approximated by Lewis's slogan: "If anything is to be probable, then something must be certain". I have explicated this finally as principle L4 for Lewis, and it became premise I.1 in the first skeptical argument. For a Cartesian, however, it became L3 which was used as premise II.9 in the second argument. The former, which is our primary concern here, is once again:

L4.   If an empirical statement, p, is inferentially acceptable for s at t, then p is probable relative to e, which is s's (total) evidence for p at t, and which contains at least one empirical statement that is certain for s at t.

Our present task is to evaluate reasons for or against L4 in order to discover whether we are justified in rejecting it and, as a result, both forms of traditional foundationalism and the two previous skeptical arguments. In order to help these evaluations, I shall begin by using definition D1 and making two assumptions that I believe even the most demanding skeptics would grant. In each case I shall use a quantitative technical term about the degree of credibility of a statement for someone at some time. As I mentioned previously, the main function of this epistemic term will be to help bridge the gap between the qualitative epistemic terms, 'acceptable' and 'certain', and the quantitative concept of probability. As stated before, according to D1, a statement, p, is acceptable for a person, s, at a time, t, just in case the credibility of p for s at t is high. That is, as I shall abbreviate it:

D1. $A_{s,t}(p)$ just in case $Cr_{s,t}(p) > 0.5$.

The first assumption proposes, in accordance with certain conclusions of the last chapter, that maximum credibility is a necessary condition of certainty. That is:

A1.   If $C_{s,t}(p)$, then $Cr_{s,t}(p) = 1$.

In order to calculate levels of credibility, we need to use the calculus of probability. Thus we need to find appropriate relationships between $Cr_{s,t}(p)$ and the probability of p. Indeed, this search will constitute a major part of our evaluations of reasons for Lewis's principle. There is, however, one such relationship we shall assume here; the problem will be to find others. Let us assume that if the credibility of p for s at t is greater than 0.5, then so is the probability for s at t of p, given s's total evidence at t. That is, more generally, for any n, where $0 < n < 1$:

A2.   If e is s's (total) evidence for p at t, and $Cr_{s,t}(p) > n$, then $Pr_{s,t}(p/e) > n$.[1]

Taken together, A1 and A2 imply that if p is certain for s at t, then the probability of p, for s at t, given s's total evidence at t is 1. I am, then, using what in Chapter 2 I called a 'probability' sense of 'certain'. Such a sense, which I used to interpret thesis H3, and which I find to give the most plausible interpretation of Lewis's principle, should be contrasted with what I called 'truth-entailing' senses, and 'reasonableness' senses. However, if, as some people claim, a probability of 1 entails truth, then we would also be considering a truth-entailing sense. And, if, as I claimed is plausible, a probability of 1 entails maximum reasonablenss, then we would also have a reasonableness sense of 'certain'. Nevertheless, for our present purposes, I shall not assume that either entailment holds. Indeed, I shall continue to make the controversial assumption that a probability of 1 does not imply truth.[2]

REASONS FOR AND AGAINST PRINCIPLE L4: LEWIS VS. GOODMAN

Is there any reason to accept Lewisean principle L4? Lewis thinks there is:

Proximate grounds of the probable or credible need not be certain: it will be sufficient if these are themselves genuinely credible. If '*P*' is credible on ground '*Q*', then the credibility of '*Q*' assures a credibility of lesser degree than if '*Q*' were certain. But if the credibility of '*P*' rests on '*Q*', and that of '*Q*' on that of '*R*', and so on; and if in this regress we nowhere come to rest with anything that is certain; then how can the credibilities spoken of be assessed at all or be genuine; since each in turn is relative to a ground, and no ultimate ground is given?[3]

This argument is, in effect, that the only thing that stops a regress which would result in nothing being credible (acceptable) is some evidence that is given and, therefore, certain. But it is clear that, as Goodman suggests, the regress is also stopped by evidence that is at least initially credible or acceptable:

Now clearly we cannot suppose that statements derive their credibility from other statements without ever bringing this string of statements to earth. Credibility may be transmitted from one statement to another through deductive or probability connections; but credibility does not spring from these connections by spontaneous generation. Somewhere along the line some statements, whether atomic sense reports or the entire system, or something in between, must have initial credibility. . . . All that is indicated is credibility to some degree, not certainty.[4]

Goodman is surely right about Lewis's regress argument. It shows at most that inferential acceptability requires initial acceptability. But is he also right in concluding that having probable knowledge "implies no certainty but only initial credibility"?

Goodman and Lewis agree that if anything is inferentially acceptable (credible), then something is acceptable relative to something that is at least initially acceptable. They disagree about whether anything is inferentially acceptable if nothing is certain. There is some reason to think that Goodman is right. To see this, let us first make the plausible assumption that one conjunct of a sufficient condition, C, for p being inferentially acceptable but not certain for s at t is that the probability of p for s at t, given e, which is s's evidence for p at t, times the probability of e for s at t, is greater than some minimal level but less than 1. That is, there is a minimum $n < 1$, such that $\Pr_{s,t}(p/e) \times \Pr_{s,t}(e) > n$. But no matter how close this n is to 1, it is possible that $\Pr_{s,t}(p/e) < 1$ and $\Pr_{s,t}(e) < 1$ and $\Pr_{s,t}(p/e) \times \Pr_{s,t}(e) > n$. So this one conjunct of a sufficient condition for inferential acceptability does not imply $\Pr_{s,t}(e) = 1$. Consequently, on the further assumption that when this conjunct is removed from conjunctive sufficient condition, C, what remains does not imply that $\Pr_{s,t}(e) = 1$, it is somewhat reasonable to claim that the full C does not imply that $\Pr_{s,t}(e) = 1$. It is also reasonable, then, that p being inferentially acceptable for s at t does not imply that $\Pr_{s,t}(e) = 1$.

So far, however, the objection applies to Cartesian principle L3, but not to L4. Although L3 requires that s's (total) evidence at t is certain, L4 allows there to be cases where s's evidence itself is merely acceptable. According to L4, inferential acceptability requires that at least one empirical member of e has a probability of 1. But if $\Pr_{s,t}(e)$ can be less than 1, then it does not seem that any of its conjuncts need have a probability of 1. Assuming the conjuncts are independent, it is only required that the product of their probabilities is $Pr_{s,t}(e)$. And, where $Pr_{s,t}(e) < 1$, none of e's conjuncts need have a probability of 1. Consequently, it seems plausible to agree with Goodman and reject not only version L3 but also version L4 of Lewis's principle.

How could someone reply to the preceding objection? I think that there are only two sorts of defense that have any chance of success. The first is to attack the unsupported assumption that there is a sufficient condition for the inferential acceptability of p for s at t which does not imply that the probability of s's evidence, e at t is 1. The second is to argue that if none of the conjuncts of e have a probability of 1, then $Pr_{s,t}(e)$ will not be high enough to allow $Cr_{s,t}(p)$ to be greater than the minimal level required for the acceptability of p. In what follows, I shall examine what I have found to be the strongest argument of each of these two sorts, and will briefly examine and reject one other less plausible argument which also has some appeal.[5] If these arguments fail, then, I believe, Goodman will have provided us with enough reason to reject principle L4 (and also L3), at least given our present evidence.

FIRST ARGUMENT: CREDIBILITY EQUALS PROBABILITY RELATIVE TO EVIDENCE

As far as I have found, all attempts of the first sort to defend Lewis's principle stress the importance of the relationship of what is inferentially acceptable, p, to the evidence, e, that makes p acceptable for s. And, surely, in some way or other, the degree of credibility of p for s is dependent on the probability of p for s at t, given s's evidence for p; that is, $Cr_{s,t}(p)$ depends on $Pr_{s,t}(p/e)$. Indeed, it might be argued that the credibility of p for s at t equals the probability of p for s at t, given s's evidence, e, for p at t. And this is because e is the sole evidence upon which s bases his justification of p. But, given definition D1, p is inferentially acceptable for s at t only if the credibility of p for s at t is greater than 0.5, and, it might be argued, this credibility equals $Pr_{s,t}(p/e)$ only if the probability, for s at t, of e is 1. Consequently, p is inferentially acceptable for s at t only if, at t, s's evidence, e, has a probability of 1, that is, e is certain for s at t. More perspicuously, this argument goes as follows:

(1)   If p is inferentially acceptable for s at t, then $Cr_{s,t}(p) > 0.5$ but $Cr_{s,0}(p) < 0.5$ (that is, the *initial* credibility of p for s at t is not high).

(2)   If p is an empirical statement and $Cr_{s,t}(p) > 5$, but $Cr_{s,0}(p) <$
0.5, and e is s's (total) evidence for p at t, then $Cr_{s,t}(p) =$
$Pr_{s,t}(p/e) > 0.5$.

(3)   If e is s's evidence for p at t, and $Cr_{s,t}(p) = Pr_{s,t}(p/e) > 0.5$,
then $Pr_{s,t}(p/e) > 0.5$ and $Pr_{s,t}(e) = 1$.

(4)   If e is s's evidence for p at t, and $Pr_{s,t}(p/e) > 0.5$ and $Pr_{s,t}(e) =$
1, then p is probable relative to e, which is certain for s at t.

Therefore

(5)   If p is an empirical statement that is inferentially acceptable
for s at t, and e is s's (total) evidence for p at t, then p is probable for s at t relative to e, which is certain for s at t.

If sound, the preceding argument establishes both principles L3 and L4,
and thus defeats the preceding arguments against these principles by showing that certainty of evidence must be implied by any sufficient condition
for inferential acceptability. We can accept premises (1) and (4). The consequent of (4) merely unpacks the antecedent of (4), when taken with the
plausible assumption that e is certain for s at t, if e is part of s's evidence at
t and $Pr_{s,t}(e) = 1$. Premise (1) follows from the previous characterization
of inferential acceptability. However, neither (2) nor (3) is clearly plausible.

How might someone justify premise (3)? I believe that it can be supported by the plausible claim that the probability of someone's evidence,
e, for a statement, p, should affect the credibility of p for him in such a way
that if $Pr_{s,t}(e) < 1$, then $Cr_{s,t}(p) < Pr_{s,t}(p/e)$. One reason for this is that
$Cr_{s,t}(p)$ should be no greater than the probability of s's evidence for p at
t times the probability of p relative to that evidence, because p's credibility
for s at t depends completely upon his evidence, e, and the support e gives
p. This justification of (3), then, uses a new assumption, namely:

A3.   If e is s's evidence for p at t, then $Cr_{s,t}(p) \leqslant Pr_{s,t}(p/e) \times$
        $Pr_{s,t}(e)$.

Then the argument for (3) is:

(6)   A3.

Therefore

(7)   If e is s's evidence for p at t, and $Pr_{s,t}(e) < 1$, then $Cr_{s,t}(p) <$
$Pr_{s,t}(p/e)$.

(8) $0 \leqslant Pr_{s,t}(e) \leqslant 1$.

Therefore

(3)   If e is s's evidence for p at t, and $Cr_{s,t}(p) = Pr_{s,t}(p/e) > 0.5$,
         then $Pr_{s,t}(p/e) > 0.5$, and $Pr_{s,t}(e) = 1$.

Here (8) is a theorem of the probability calculus, and so it is clearly acceptable. Thus only A3 is open to doubt. Let us accept it provisionally, however, at least until we examine additional proposed assumptions.

An Argument for Premise (2): *Strict Conditionalization*

The major problem for the first argument concerns premise (2) and the question of whether $Cr_{s,t}(p) = Pr_{s,t}(p/e)$, where e is s's evidence for p at t. However, there is a widely accepted requirement for rational change in credibility over time that might seem to be what is needed for this purpose. This requirement, which is called the principle of strict conditionalization, can be stated as relating the inferential credibility of p at a time, t, to certain 'initial' probabilities at time, t_0, when s has only tautological evidence. Here $Pr_{s,0}(p) = Pr_{s,0}(p/T)$, that is, $Pr_{s,0}(p)$ equals the probability of p for s at the time taken to be t_0, given tautologous evidence. The principle can be stated as follows:

A4.   If e is s's evidence for p at t, then $Cr_{s,t}(p) = Pr_{s,0}(p \cdot e)/Pr_{s,0}(e)$.[6]

We can now use A4 to argue as follows:

(9)   A4, and if p is inferentially acceptable for s at t, then $Cr_{s,t}(p) > 0.5$.

(10) $Pr_{s,0}(p \cdot e)/Pr_{s,0}(e) = Pr_{s,0}(p/e)$.

(11) $Pr_{s,0}(p/e) = Pr_{s,t}(p/e)$

Therefore

(2)   If p is an empirical statement and $Cr_{s,t}(p) > 0.5$, but $Cr_{s,0}(p) < 0.5$, and e is s's evidence for p at t, then $Cr_{s,t}(p) = Pr_{s,t}(p/e) > 0.5$.

It is clear that, even with its wide acceptance, principle A4 deserves close scrutiny, but so also does (11). Premise (11), which is called the 'rigidity assumption', has been claimed to be false, because whenever certain sorts of conceptual changes occur between time t_0 and the time t, the conditional probabilities are not equal. This is clearly true for the logical interpretation if the language is enriched between the two times by certain additions of predicates.[7] It might be objected, however, that any such conceptual changes result in p and e becoming different statements. Thus the rigidity assumption, when taken to concern statements, is not refuted by conceptual changes. But let us not debate this complex issue. Rather, let us assume that the rigidity assumption is correct, or, at least, restrict the argument to the many, many cases where it does hold.

Rejection of the Principle of Strict Conditionalization. Principle A4 is widely accepted, but I find reason to doubt it. We can use a theorem of the probability calculus, which we have seen before, to help show this, namely:

T1. $\quad \Pr(p) = [\Pr(p/e) \times \Pr(e)] + [\Pr(p/\bar{e}) \times \Pr(\bar{e})]$

Unless $\Pr(e) = 1$, $\Pr(p/e) \times \Pr(e) < \Pr(p/e)$, and sometimes the addition of $\Pr(p/\bar{e}) \times \Pr(\bar{e})$ will not bring $\Pr(p)$ up to $\Pr(p/e)$. This may be because $\Pr(p/\bar{e})$ is very low. So, sometimes, $\Pr(p) < \Pr(p/e)$. Indeed, by T1, $\Pr(p) = \Pr(p/e)$, only if $\Pr(p/\bar{e}) = \Pr(p/e)$, or $\Pr(e) = 1$. But surely, as A3 requires, $\mathrm{Cr}_{s,t}(p) \leqslant \Pr_{s,t}(p)$. Therefore, given (11), as seems needed if A4 is to be reasonable, sometimes $\mathrm{Cr}_{s,t}(p) < \Pr_{s,0}(p/e)$, contrary to the universal claim of A4.[8]

Another Argument for Premise (2): *Assumption A3 Strengthened*

Assumption A3 allows $\mathrm{Cr}_{s,t}(p)$ to be less than $\Pr_{s,t}(p/e) \times \Pr_{s,t}(e)$, but perhaps they should be equal. That is, since e is s's total evidence for p at t, it might be argued that there is no reason for any $\mathrm{Cr}_{s,t}(p)$ to be less than $\Pr_{s,t}(p/e) \times \Pr_{s,t}(e)$. Lewis, for example, might be implying such a claim when he says,

To assess the probability of a statement, its probability relative to its ground must be multiplied by the probability of its own ground, and so on.[9]

Lewis, as we have already seen, is worried about regress, but that is not our immediate concern. It is his view about what $\mathrm{Cr}_{s,t}(p)$ equals that is at issue, and he could be taken to hold that $\mathrm{Cr}_{s,t}(p) = \Pr_{s,t}(p/e_1) \times \Pr_{s,t}(e_1)$, and, more generally, $\mathrm{Cr}_{s,t}(e_n) = \Pr_{s,t}(e_n/e_{n+1})$, where e_{n+1} is 'the ground' for e_n. That is, he may accept:

A5. $\quad$ If e is s's evidence for p at t, then $\mathrm{Cr}_{s,t}(p) = \Pr_{s,t}(p/e) \times \Pr_{s,t}(e)$.

Assumption A5 might be used to argue as follows. $\mathrm{Cr}_{s,t}(p) = \Pr_{s,t}(p/e)$, because $\mathrm{Cr}_{s,t}(p) = \Pr_{s,t}(p)$ and the latter equals $\Pr_{s,t}(p/e)$ because of A5 and T1. That is, by T1, $\Pr(p) = \Pr(p/e) \times \Pr(e)$, as A5 requires, only if

$\Pr(p/\bar{e}) \times \Pr(\bar{e}) = 0$. And that is true only if $\Pr(\bar{e}) = 0$. Consequently, $\Pr(e) = 1$, and $\mathrm{Cr}_{s,\,t}(p) = \Pr_{s,\,t}(p/e)$. In more detail, this argument is:

(12)   A5.
(13)   If $\Pr_{s,\,t}(p) = \Pr_{s,\,t}(p/e) \times \Pr_{s,\,t}(e)$, then $\Pr_{s,\,t}(p/\bar{e}) \times \Pr_{s,\,t}(\bar{e})$
        $= 0$.
(14)   If $\Pr_{s,\,t}(p/\bar{e}) \times \Pr_{s,\,t}(\bar{e}) = 0$, then $\Pr_{s,\,t}(\bar{e}) = 0$.
(15)   If $\Pr_{s,\,t}(\bar{e}) = 0$, then $\Pr_{s,\,t}(e) = 1$.
(16)   If $\Pr_{s,\,t}(e) = 1$, then $\Pr_{s,\,t}(p) = \Pr_{s,\,t}(p/e)$.
(17) $\mathrm{Cr}_{s,\,t}(p) = \Pr_{s,\,t}(p)$.

Therefore (2).

In the preceding argument, if A5 is acceptable, then only (14) and (17) seem to require defense. But, as stated, (14) is clearly false, because $\Pr(p/\bar{e})$ $\times \Pr(\bar{e}) = 0$ if $\Pr(p/\bar{e}) = 0$, no matter what $\Pr(\bar{e})$ is. It might be replied, however, that this objection fails if in (14) p is restricted to contingent statements, because the following is true:

(18)   For *any* compatible, empirical statements, a and b, $\Pr_{s,\,t}(a/b)$
        > 0.

Then, because all empirical statements are contingent, we can derive:

(14a)   For any compatible, empirical statements, a and b, if $\Pr_{s,\,t}(a/b)$
        $\times \Pr_{s,\,t}(b) = 0$, then $\Pr_{s,\,t}(b) = 0$.

And, on the assumption that $(p \cdot \bar{e})$ is consistent, (14a) can be substituted for (14) in the argument for (2) with no ill effects, because (2) considers only empirical statements.

Premise (18) *and Strict Coherence.* Premise (18) is widely accepted, but I find it to be quite debatable. It is false for a theory that interprets probability as the limits of relative frequencies, and it seems false for a subjectivist theory that equates probability with degrees of actual belief of actual people. It is only for certain versions of a logical interpretation or, more generally, any theory that requires Carnap's version of 'strict coherence', that (18) is a theorem.[10] But, as I argued in Chapter 2, it is surely questionable whether a probability function that is to be an integral part of a theory of when a statement is acceptable needs to be strictly coherent. That is, it might be that a person is an ideally rational better, only if the probabilities he assigns to statements do not allow there to be any finite set of bets in accordance with those probabilities for which it is not logically possible he wins something from that set of bets, but it is logically possible he loses something. Nevertheless, I argued in Chapter 2 that there is no reason to think that a person is rational in accepting a statement, p, only if he uses a strictly coherent probability function to assign a probability to p. Indeed, I claimed it unreasonable to assign a probability of 1 to a statement only if it is logically necessary. Similarly, I find it implausible to claim $\Pr(a/b) = 0$ only if a and b are logically inconsistent. Consider the conditional probability that Elsie will jump over the moon, given that Elsie is a cow. The conjunction of these two sentences is clearly causally impossible. Thus it is irrational to put up any of the stake for a 'conditional' bet on Elsie jumping over the moon, conditional on Elsie being a cow, because such a bet is won only if this conjunction is true. So it surely seems that this conditional probability equals zero even though the two sentences are logically consistent.

I claim, then, that (18) is too debatable to support (14a). It should be noted, however, that relying on strict coherence to justify (18) will not save the preceding argument for (2). Strict coherence also requires that no contingent statement has an absolute probability of zero. Consequently, strict coherence requires that for any compatible, contingent statements, a and b, $\Pr(a/b) \times \Pr(b) \neq 0$. But, because there are cases where the antecedent of A5 is true, is follows with A5, (13), and (17), that in *some* cases $\Pr_{s,\,t}(p/\bar{e}) \times \Pr_{s,\,t}(\bar{e}) = 0$, contrary to strict coherence. As a result, we can conclude that if strict coherence is not required, premises (14) and (14a) are quite dubious, but if it is required, then some other premise should be rejected. In either case, premise (2) remains unsupported.

It is worth noting that *if* both A5 and (17) are plausible but strict coherence is not, then we can reject (14) and (14a) for:

(14b)   If $\Pr_{s,\,t}(p/\bar{e}) > 0$ and $\Pr_{s,\,t}(p/\bar{e}) \times \Pr_{s,\,t}(\bar{e}) = 0$, then $\Pr_{s,\,t}(\bar{e}) = 0$,

and conclude:

(2a)   If p is an empirical statement and e is s's evidence for p at t, and $\Pr_{s,\,t}(p/\bar{e}) > 0$, and $\Cr_{s,\,t}(p) > 0.5$ but $\Cr_{s,\,0}(p) < 0.5$, then $\Pr_{s,\,t}(p) = \Pr_{s,\,t}(p/e)$.

And this allows us to infer:

(5a)   If p is an empirical statement that is inferentially acceptable for s at t, and e is s's empirical evidence for p at t, and $\Pr_{s,\,t}(p/\bar{e}) > 0$, then e is certain for s at t.

Of course, this would not establish either version L3 or L4 of Lewis's principle, but it would allow us to infer that both versions are correct for the many cases where we know that $\text{Pr}_{s,t}(p/\bar{e}) > 0$. But the crucial question is whether it is reasonable to use both A5 and (17) to justify (2).

Assumption A5 *and the Absolute Probability of the Evidence.* Let us continue to assume that strict coherence is not required for justification. Given this assumption, it may seem that A5 is acceptable. Furthermore, there is a quite reasonable thesis that might seem to support A5, namely:

(19)   If e is s's empirical evidence at t, then $\text{Pr}_{s,t}(e)$ is the only absolute probability that s needs to derive that $\text{Cr}_{s,t}(p) = n$.

But what yields A5 with (19) is dubious, that is:

(20)   If $\text{Pr}_{s,t}(e)$ is the only absolute probability that s needs to derive $\text{Cr}_{s,t}(p) = n$, then $\text{Cr}_{s,t}(p) = \text{Pr}_{s,t}(p/e) \times \text{Pr}_{s,t}(e) = n$.

Premise (19) is reasonable because we should not require that someone base his justification on evidence that is not available. Thus, of absolute probabilities, only $\text{Pr}_{s,t}(e)$ need be considered to calculate $\text{Cr}_{s,t}(p)$. But this does not show that no conditional probability, except $\text{Pr}_{s,t}(p/e)$, is relevant. Because of many cases where the fact that $\text{Pr}_{s,t}(p/\bar{e}) > 0$ is available to s, it seems somewhat reasonable to claim that if (17) is true, then $\text{Cr}_{s,t}(p) \neq \text{Pr}_{s,t}(p/e) \times \text{Pr}_{s,t}(e)$ in these cases because, instead:

A6. $\text{Cr}_{s,t}(p) = \{[\text{Pr}_{s,t}(p/e) - \text{Pr}_{s,t}(p/\bar{e})] \times \text{Pr}_{s,t}(e)\} + \text{Pr}_{s,t}(p/\bar{e})$.

This results from substituting '$1 - \text{Pr}(e)$' for '$\text{Pr}(\bar{e})$' throughout T1, and assuming (17). Here the only absolute probability s needs to calculate $\text{Cr}_{s,t}(p)$ is $\text{Pr}_{s,t}(e)$, but $\text{Cr}_{s,t}(p) \neq \text{Pr}_{s,t}(p/e) \times \text{Pr}_{s,t}(e)$. Thus, on the assumption that (17) is true, (20) is false and this argument for A5 fails.

The preceding objection to (20) is also an objection to A5. That is, given T1 and (17), there are cases where $\text{Cr}_{s,t}(p) > \text{Pr}_{s,t}(p/e) \times \text{Pr}_{s,t}(e)$ because $\text{Pr}_{s,t}(p/\bar{e}) > 0$ and $\text{Pr}_{s,t}(\bar{e}) > 0$, and both of these probabilities as well as evidence, e, are available to s at t. Thus, in these cases the antecedent of A5 is true, but its consequent is false. This is also true of A3, incidentally, which previously had seemed quite reasonable.

The preceding reason to reject A3 and A5 depends on transforming T1 into A6. This is legitimate if premise (17) is acceptable. Some people, such as subjectivists, who claim that there are many equally rational probability functions, would reject (17). This is, of course, quite different from rejecting the weaker thesis that credibility functions are probability functions. However, if only this weaker thesis, which I find quite plausible, is true, then A3 or even A5, rather than A6, might still be true. That is, even if each credibility function is governed by the probability calculus, there is still the question of how a certain credibility function is related to some other probability function. But we need not answer this question at this point, because the preceding discussion shows that if either A3 or A5 is acceptable, as is not implausible, then (17) and A6 should not be accepted. Consequently, without deciding whether to accept A5 or (17), we can conclude that no argument which uses both A5 and (17) as premises is sound. Thus neither (2) nor (2a) is justified by the preceding arguments.

I know of no arguments for conclusions (5) and (5a) that are more likely to succeed than those we have just rejected. So, with their rejection, we can conclude that there is no reason for claiming that in all cases inferential acceptability requires evidence that is certain. Consequently, because of the *prima facie* plausibility of the preceding argument from Goodman against version L3 of Lewis's principle, we have reason to reject L3, at least provisionally, as well as skeptical argument II, and the first sort of defense of L4. Obviously, this does not show L4 to be implausible, because it has not yet been shown that the second sort of defense fails.

SECOND ARGUMENT: THE PROBABILITY OF CONJUNCTIVE EVIDENCE

The second sort of defense of principle L4 states that at least one empirical conjunct of s's evidence, e, must have a probability of 1, if $\Pr_{s,t}(e)$ is to be high enough to make the credibility of p for s at t greater than 0.5. Nothing we have found clearly acceptable so far requires that there is a minimum level for $\Pr_{s,t}(e)$, if $\mathrm{Cr}_{s,t}(p) > 0.5$. Nevertheless, it seems reasonable to require that s's evidence for p be probable, and, by A2, that p is probable, given this evidence. That is, more generally:

A7.   If e is s's evidence for p at t, and $\mathrm{Cr}_{s,t}(p) > n$, then $\Pr_{s,t}(p/e) > n$ and $\Pr_{s,t}(e) > n$.

It might be objected, however, that if I am right in rejecting A4 (the principle of strict conditionalization), then it need only be required that, as A2 states, $\Pr_{s,t}(p/e) > 0.5$, if $\mathrm{Cr}_{s,t}(p) > 0.5$. That is, high credibility of p for s requires only that p is probable, given s's evidence e. Not even the rejected A4 puts as strong a requirement on high credibility as does A7 which requires $\Pr_{s,t}(e) > 0.5$.

It is true that A7 is stronger than A4 in the respect that while both require that $\Pr_{s,t}(p/e) > n$, A7 also requires that $\Pr_{s,t}(e) > n$. But A4 is stronger than A7 in another way, because it requires that $\mathrm{Cr}_{s,t}(p) = \Pr_{s,t}(p/e)$, and it is this requirement that we found implausible. Furthermore, the additional requirement of A7 seems needed. If the probability of the evidence someone uses is very low (for example, where $e =$ 'Last night God told me that the world will end next Wednesday', and $p =$ 'The world will end next Wednesday'), then although $\Pr_{s,t}(p/e)$ is very high, $\mathrm{Cr}_{s,t}(p)$ would seem to be very low, because the probability of the evidence, e, which is used to justify p, is so very low. It seems plausible, then, to require that both $\Pr_{s,t}(p/e)$ and $\Pr_{s,t}(e)$ be high, and so I propose that we accept A7.

It might be argued that there is a stronger reason to accept A7, because it is implied by another quite reasonable principle:

A8.   If e is s's evidence for p at t, and $\mathrm{Cr}_{s,t}(p) > n$, then $\Pr_{s,t}(p/e) \times \Pr_{s,t}(e) > n$.

Now I am somewhat inclined to think A8 is acceptable, in part because I tend toward accepting A3 which is equivalent to A8, and A5 which implies both of them. But this is also because it does not seem reasonable that p is credible where $\Pr_{s,t}(p/e)$ and $\Pr_{s,t}(e)$ each barely exceed 0.5, but their product is less than 0.26. Unfortunately, however, I know of no viable way to justify my inclination that does not require embedding A5 or A8 in what turns out to be the best theory of justification. This, in fact, is what I shall propose later. The only other reason I can find that has any plausibility is that $\Pr_{s,t}(p/e) \times \Pr_{s,t}(p) = \Pr_{s,t}(p \cdot e)$, and p is acceptable and so highly credible for s at t, only if it is acceptable for s to add p to his evidence at t. But such an addition is highly credible for s at t, only if the conjunction of p and e is probable for s at t. What results is A8 for $n = 0.5$. But if one such instantiation of A8 is justified, then it is reasonable to accept it for any n, where $0 \leqslant n \leqslant 1$.

The preceding argument has some appeal, but I believe it results from conflating two senses of 'p is acceptable'. One sense is 'p is (epistemically) worthy of belief', and the other is 'p is (epistemically) worthy of use as evidence'. Throughout the preceding discussions we have been concerned with only the first sense. I have assumed, through definition D1, that p is acceptable for s, that is, worthy of s's belief, only if p is highly credible for s. But it is surely quite questionable – even dubious – to claim that p is worthy of belief only if it is acceptable to use p as evidence to justify other statements. For example, it has been argued that it is acceptable to use p as evidence only if p is more probable than any statement with which it competes.[11] But while this may be a plausible requirement for what is acceptable as evidence, it is too strong for what is acceptable as (worthy of) belief. It would result, for example, in it not being acceptable for me now, today, that I will not win anything in next year's Pennsylvania lottery, because the probability of this is no greater than its competitors about other ticket holders not winning. But surely this is epistemically worthy of belief.[12] Consequently, I think we should not use the preceding argument to justify A8 for acceptable belief. Thus, at present, A8 is of no help to us in justifying A7, and we shall have to rely on the first, weaker reason for adopting A7. Nevertheless, A8 seems clearly reasonable when adapted to acceptability as evidence, and I shall return to it when examining one last argument for principle L4.

Assumption A7 *and the Low Probability of Conjunctive Evidence*

One way to formulate an argument for principle L4 that uses a species of A7 is to find a way to show that the probability of evidence for an empirical statement that is not initially certain is low, if none of its conjuncts has a probability of 1. This implies that the evidence, e, for any inferentially acceptable statement, p, is a conjunction. But it is surely debatable whether any evidence a person has for each statement that is inferentially acceptable for him is conjunctive. We need not assume this, however. We need only assume that any inferentially acceptable statement (even one that is probable given a statement that is acceptable but not initially acceptable as evidence) is also probable given a statement that is initially acceptable as evidence. That is, it is probable given what we can call 'foundational' evidence, as the following modification of A7 states:

A7a. If f is s's foundational evidence for p at t, and $Cr_{s,t}(p) > n$ then $Pr_{s,t}(p/f) > n$ and $Pr_{s,t}(f) > n$.

This allows someone to use inferentially acceptable statements as evidence if they have already been found to be acceptable as evidence, while requiring that no such justification of p for s succeeds if $Pr_{s,t}(p/f) \leqslant 0.5$.

Let us now consider a physical-object statement, p. According to the present argument, f, which is s's foundational evidence at t for p, consists in a large conjunction of his own basic-reports, b_1 through b_n. Furthermore, let us assume, the probability of each of many of these, b_1 through b_n, is independent of any conjunction of the other conjuncts of f. Consequently, the probability of f for s at t is no greater than the product of the absolute probabilities for s at t, of b_1 through b_m. But because m is large, $\mathrm{Pr}_{s,t}(f) < 0.5$ if the probabilities of b_2 through b_m are less than 1. Therefore, by D1 and A7a, for at least any physical-object statement, p, it is inferentially acceptable for s at t only if p is probable for s at t relative to some of s's foundational evidence, f, which contains at least one empirical conjunct that has a probability of 1 for s at t. But then, because that conjunct is part of s's evidence at t, it is certain for s at t. Thus, principle L4 is correct – at least for physical-object statements.

The preceding argument is very complex. Let me lay out its skeletal premises, and then flesh it out by an informal discussion of any premises that are debatable.

(1)   If p is a physical-object sentence, and f is s's foundational evidence for p at t, and $\mathrm{Pr}_{s,t}(p/f) > 0.5$, then f is a conjunction of basic-reports, b_1 through b_n, where n is large, and the probability for s at t of each of many conjuncts of f (b_1 through b_m) is independent of every conjunction of other conjuncts of f.

(2)   If the consequent of (1) is true, then $\mathrm{Pr}_{s,t}(f) \leqslant \mathrm{Pr}_{s,t}(b_1) \times \mathrm{Pr}_{s,t}(b_2) \times \ldots \times \mathrm{Pr}_{s,t}(b_m)$.

(3)   If $\mathrm{Pr}_t(f)$ is no greater than the product of many numbers, and each number is less than 1, then $\mathrm{Pr}_{s,t}(f) \leqslant 0.5$.

Therefore

(4)   If p is a physical-object statement, and f is s's foundational evidence for p at t, and $\mathrm{Pr}_{s,t}(p/f) > 0.5$, and the probability, for s at t, of each empirical conjunct of f is less than 1, then $\mathrm{Pr}_{s,t}(f) \leqslant 0.5$.

(5)   Definition D1 and assumption A7a.

Therefore

(6)   If p is a physical-object statement that is acceptable for s at t, then p is probable for s at t, given some of s's evidence at t, which contains at least one empirical statement that has a probability of 1 and so is certain for s at t.

Of the four premises, (2) is the only one that is clearly true. We can see this by realizing that if $f = b_1 \cdot b_2 \cdots b_n$ then, because $\mathrm{Pr}_{s,t}(f) = \mathrm{Pr}_{s,t}(b_1 \cdot b_2 \cdots b_n)$, the following is true by the probability calculus:

$$\Pr(f) = \Pr(b_1) \times \Pr(b_2/b_1) \times \Pr(b_3/b_1 \cdot b_2) \times \ldots \times \Pr(b_n/b_1 \cdot b_2 \cdots b_{n-1}).$$

And if $\Pr(p)$ is independent of q, then $\Pr(p/q) = \Pr(p/T) = \Pr(p)$, where T is any tautology. So, as premise (2) states, if the consequent of (1) is true, then $\Pr(f)$ is no greater than the product of the absolute probabilities, for s at t, of b_1 through b_m.

D1 is an acceptable definition, and so premise (5) is reasonable if assumption A7a is. And it is at least somewhat reasonable, because its requirement of the need for foundational evidence to justify statements has some initial plausibility. Nevertheless, without developing a complete theory of the requirements for extending evidence beyond foundational evidence, there is no way to decide about this assumption. And, because I shall not even finish this task by the end of the book, let me merely mention here that A7, which is a weaker principle governing acceptable belief, makes the argument invalid, but seems to be about as plausible as an assumption as A7a. Unlike A7a, A7 does not require that everything acceptable be probable relative to *foundational* evidence. Given that we have no available way to choose one, or both, or neither of these principles, we can only conclude here that premise (5) remains debatable, and so we cannot determine whether the argument that uses (5) is sound. If, however, only this were to keep us from concluding that the argument is sound, we should not dismiss it as unsound; its status would be merely undecided.

Premise (1) *and Basic Evidence as a Conjunction of Basic-Reports.* Premise (1) is clearly both crucial and dubious. It has three implications where it can be attacked: (a) the empirical, foundational evidence for any physical-object statement is a conjunction of basic-reports; (b) there are many conjuncts in each of the conjunctions that constitute foundational evidences; and (c) the probabilities of a large proportion of these conjuncts are independent of every conjunction of other conjuncts. Furthermore, it seems that (b) is reasonable only if (a) is. If foundational evidence is not restricted to basic-reports, then it is reasonable to include some physical-object statements, such as observation-reports. And if this is allowed, then it seems that many inferentially acceptable statements would require only a few initially credible physical-object statements as the foundational evidence relative to which they are probable. So, a negative decision about (a) is doubly decisive. As in the preceding case, however, we cannot decide about (a) without developing a theory of foundational evidence, which will not be done until later in the book. We can, however, justify rejecting (1) even if we assume (a) is true: let us, then, grant (a) for present purposes, and consider (b) and (c).

As discussed somewhat in Chapter 2, I find it plausible that in many cases the probabilities of a large percentage of basic-reports that are conjuncts in any foundational evidence that justifies a physical-object sentence are independent of the other conjuncts. This is because such phenomenal statements include those that concern only the sensory experience of one sense modality, and in many cases it is plausible to consider the probability of each of these to be independent of all those involving only other sense modalities. But, as pointed out in Chapter 2, it is far from clear this is true in all cases. Nevertheless, let us also grant (c) here. The obvious problem for premise (1) is that, contrary to clause (b), it is not reasonable to think that a large number of basic-reports are needed. An example will illustrate my reason for this. Assume that $p = $ 'There is a large, heavy object in my hands now'. Also let $b_1 = $ 'I am now having a tactual experience of something large and heavy in my hands'; let $b_2 = $ 'I am now having a visual experience of my holding something large and heavy in my hands'; and let $b_3 = $ 'I am now believing that I am now holding something large and heavy in my hands'. It seems somewhat plausible to suppose that $\mathrm{Pr}_{s,t}(p/b_1 \cdot b_2 \cdot b_3) > 0.5$, and that no other basic-reports are relevant to the probability of p for s at t. Furthermore, it may well be that the probabilities of b_1, b_2, and b_3 are quite high, although less than one, for s at t. So, even if we make the false assumption that each of these basic-reports is independent of the other two, we get the result that $\mathrm{Pr}_{s,t}(b_1 \cdot b_2 \cdot b_3) > 0.5$. Of course, it might be objected that it is wrong to assume that $\mathrm{Pr}_{s,t}(p/b_1 \cdot b_2 \cdot b_3) > 0.5$, either because this probability is not high, or because no physical-object statement has a determinate probability, given only basic-reports. I shall answer the first objection only by making two points. First, the preceding example does have some plausibility. Second, in Chapter 5, I shall argue in much more detail that in some situations a particular observation-report is probable for s at t, given a specific set of four basic-reports. But the addition of one more basic-report does not affect the present point. The second objection seems quite implausible to me. But even if it were correct, it would refute (a) and destroy the argument in a different way. So, barring that unhelpful reply, the preceding examples give some reason to conclude that (b) and thereby (1) are implausible.

It might be suggested that (1) can be saved by amendment, because, in spite of the previous example involving only three basic-reports, some more are needed to make p probable. Assume that, like my example in Chapter 5, at least four are needed. If the probability of none of four or more independent basic-reports is greater than 0.8, then the probability of their conjunction equals the product of their probabilities which is less than 0.5. It might be suggested, then, that we amend premise (1) so it concerns only four or more independent conjuncts rather than a large number. Premise (1), as amended, is more plausible than the original version, but even if the amended version is granted, the change results in a problem for premise (3). Changing (1) requires a change in (3) to preserve the validity of the inference to (4), and this makes (3) clearly false. Even unamended, (3) is false. No matter how large m is, there are cases where the product of m numbers, each less than 1, is greater than 0.5. But when (3) is amended so it concerns only four numbers it is clearly false. And if it is amended further so it states that each number is *significantly* less than 1 (perhaps no more than 0.8), then, although (3) is true for 0.8, we cannot conclude (6) but only that the probability of at least one conjunct in the evidence for p is not significantly less than 1 (in this case, it is 0.8 or greater). But this will not allow us to infer that some conjunct is certain. I conclude, then, even with (a) assumed, this argument fails to justify version L4 of Lewis's principle. And I know of no argument of this sort that is more plausible.

THIRD ARGUMENT: A REQUIREMENT FOR ADDING STATEMENTS TO EVIDENCE

I have been able to find only one other argument for Lewis's principle that is even remotely plausible. I wish to discuss it briefly to show where it fails. Whereas the preceding argument concerns conjunctive evidence synchronically, the present one considers the diachronic process of adding new statements as evidence to previous evidence. This argument relies on a principle corresponding to A8 that applies to acceptability as evidence, namely:

A9. If it is acceptable for s to add statement p to his evidence, e at t, then $\mathrm{Pr}_{s,t}(p \cdot e) > 0.5$.

Given A9, then whenever it is acceptable for s to add a statement, p_n, to his evidence at t only if another statement, p_{n-1}, is already part of s's evidence at t, and this is true for every p_i from p_1 through p_n, then it follows that it is acceptable for s to add p_n to his evidence at t, only if $\Pr_{s,t}(f \cdot p_1 \cdot p_2 \ldots p_n) > 0.5$. This is because f is s's foundational evidence, and so at t, s's evidence, e, is $(f \cdot p_1 \cdot p_2 \ldots p_{n-1})$. But according to the present argument, if f is not certain, and for any $i \leqslant n$, $\Pr_{s,t}(p_i/f \cdot p_1 \cdot p_2 \ldots$ $p_{i-1}) < 1$, then there is an $m \leqslant n$ such that $\Pr_{s,t}(f \cdot p_1 \cdot p_2 \ldots p_{m-1}) \times$ $\Pr_{s,t}(p_m/f \cdot p_1 \cdot p_2 \ldots p_{m-1}) < 0.5$. That is, $\Pr_{s,t}(f \cdot p_1 \cdot p_2 \ldots p_m) < 0.5$. Thus it is not acceptable for s to add p_m or p_n to his evidence at t. For example, if $\Pr_{s,t}(p_1/f) = 0.8$, and $\Pr_{s,t}(f) = 0.9$, then $\Pr_{s,t}(f \cdot p_1) = 0.72$. Then if $\Pr_{s,t}(p_2/f \cdot p_1) = 0.8$, and $\Pr_{s,t}(p_3/f \cdot p_1 \cdot p_2) = 0.8$, then $\Pr_{s,t}(f \cdot p_1 \cdot$ $p_2 \cdot p_3) < 0.47$. Consequently, there comes a time when someone uses exactly the same procedure to show it is acceptable to add p_m to his evidence that he used for p_{m-1}, but, because of A9, it is acceptable to add p_{m-1} but not p_m. And it is unreasonably arbitrary that a procedure that is successful through p_{m-1}, should suddenly fail for p_m. Therefore, concludes this argument, a person's basic evidence is certain if any p_i is inferentially acceptable for him.

If sound, the preceding argument establishes not only principle L4 but also the thesis that inferential acceptability requires basic evidence that is certain. But it is not sound, because $\Pr_{s,t}(f \cdot p_1 \ldots p_i)$ can be high when the probabilities of the conjuncts of b are high but less than 1, and, for all $i \leqslant n$, $\Pr_{s,t}(p_i/f \cdot p_1 \cdot p_2 \ldots p_{i-1}) < 1$. This is true even when n is very large. No matter how large n is, there are n numbers each less than 1 with a product greater than 0.5. Thus the argument is invalid. It also fails because it is unreasonable to think that in actual cases n is very large. Thus it is even more unlikely that for some $m \leqslant n$ in actual cases, $\Pr_{s,t}(f \cdot p_1 \cdot$ $p_2 \ldots p_m) < 0.5$, if no empirical probabilities are 1.

It might be suggested that there is another reason to reject the argument, namely, A9 is dubious. However, although I am unsure about A9, I know of no reason to reject it. Consequently, the issue of its status, like some of the other previously mentioned issues, will be resolved only after a satisfactory theory of evidence is developed.

CONCLUSION: INFERENTIAL ACCEPTABILITY DOES NOT REQUIRE CERTAINTY

I have tried to discover an argument in favor of some version of Lewis's principle that outweighs the reason for rejecting the principle that I constructed from Goodman's suggestion about initial credibility. I quickly rejected Lewis's own argument because it does not show that certainty is required for inferential acceptability, but, at best, it justifies that some initially acceptable statements are needed. I then tried to show that none of the three most plausible arguments I have found succeed in overriding the Goodman-like reason. Consequently, I conclude that we should, at least at present, reject all versions of Lewis's principle. Inferential acceptability might well require some sort of initial credibility, but, based on our present evidence, there is no reason to think it requires certainty. We can, then, reject principle L4, and, of course, L2 and L3 as well. Furthermore, we can now also dispose of Unger's argument for moderate₁ skepticism that was discussed in Chapter 2, because we have reason to reject its implication that reasonableness, or acceptability, requires reasons that are known with certainty and so are certain.

It should be noted that my conclusion is tentative. This is because there is one sort of reason for a version of Lewis's principle that we have not yet examined, namely, that it is a necessary part of the most reasonable theory of evidence. But this lack of examination results from lack of theory. So, until such a theory is developed, my conclusion is justified. I shall, however, present and defend, in Part II, a foundational theory which utilizes but does not require basic-reports that are certain. If I succeed in that, then, when those results are coupled with the present ones, the conclusion need no longer be tentative.

SKEPTICAL ARGUMENT III:
NOTHING NONBASIC IS PROBABLE RELATIVE TO BASIC-REPORTS

Principle L4 is premise I.1 of skeptical argument I, and L3 is premise II.9 of argument II. So, with our tentative rejection of L3 and L4, we have another reason to reject argument I and our first reason to reject II. We also have, of course, reason to reject traditional foundationalism, as I have described it, because it also requires L4. But it is now easy to see that, despite the claims of some philosophers, a refutation of traditional foundationalism is not sufficient to refute all forms of foundationalism. Indeed, the preceding discussion can easily lead us to imagine a foundational theory that proposes initial acceptability as the base of justification, rather than initial certainty. For such a theory, indeed, for any plausible foundational theory, as we shall see more clearly in Chapter 7, there is a principle that relates inferential and initial acceptability in a way that corresponds to the relationship between inferential and initial certainty that is stated by FP1. This new principle is:

FP2.   If all initially acceptable empirical statements are of kind K, and some empirical statement of kind L is inferentially acceptable for s at t_1, then some empirical statement which is of kind L, is probable for s at a time, t_2, relative to a set of statements of kind K, each of which is acceptable for s at t_2.

One, quick justification of the claim that FP2 is required for any plausible version of foundationalism parallels the justification at the end of Chapter 2 for FP1. In brief, the reason is that for any plausible foundational theory whatsoever, if all initially acceptable empirical statements are, for example, basic-reports, and if no nonbasic statement is probable relative to any set of acceptable basic-reports, then both initial and inferential acceptability would be restricted to basic-reports. This is because no nonbasic statements would be made inferentially acceptable by relationships to basic-reports, and there would be no other way for them to become inferentially acceptable. Thus only basic-reports would be acceptable.

The question now arises whether FP2 can be used in a sound argument to justify skeptical thesis M_1S_1. If so, then foundationalism, which, as we have seen, requires FP2, would lead to skepticism, and the only way to avoid skepticism would be to find a viable nonfoundational theory. Unfortunately, there is a quite simple way for a skeptic to use FP2 to establish M_1S_1. The first, crucial part of this argument – skeptical argument III – relies only on FP2 plus two premises from the previous arguments that we have not yet evaluated, namely, I.5 and II.7. This new first part goes as follows:

III.1.   An empirical statement is initially acceptable only if it is a basic-report (1.5).
III.2.   No nonbasic statement is probable relative to any set of basic-reports (II.7).
III.3.   Principle FP2.

Therefore

III.4.   No nonbasic empirical statement is inferentially or initially acceptable for anyone at any time (II.10).

The rest of the argument proceeds, by means of premises I.6 and I.8 to conclude, as before, that M_1S_1 is true (I.9), and so it is never reasonable for any human to believe that there are physical objects, past events, future events, or mental phenomena of others.

Once argument III has been formulated, it can easily be seen that, unless all forms of foundationalism should be rejected, the only way to avoid the skeptical conclusion that M_1S_1 is true is to show that either premise III.1 or III.2 is not plausible. Plausible foundational theories require principle FP2 and the other two premises – I.6 and I.8 – are unassailable. The task of the next two chapters is to examine premises III.1 and III.2. I propose to approach this task by considering those nonbasic statements which I find most likely to justify the rejection of each premise, namely, observation-reports (such as, 'I am now seeing my hand'), and memory-reports (such as, 'I now remember that I saw my hand a short while ago'). Many people, such as G. E. Moore, would claim that the preceding example of an observation-report is certain, and, moreover, I would assume, initially certain. Others, such as Lewis may well take some memory-reports to be initally acceptable. If either of these claims is justified, then III.1 should be rejected.

Of course, we may find no way to justify that some report of one of these two kinds is initially acceptable for someone at some time. Then premise III.1 would survive our attack. But we still might be able to show that some of these reports are inferentially acceptable because justified by basic-reports. Perhaps, for example, 'I am now seeing my hand' being true of s at t, is probable, for s at t, relative to 'I am now having visual experience of my hand, and I now believe that I am now seeing my hand' being true of s at t. Perhaps, also, the second, conjunctive basic-report meets the antecedent of thesis H3 for s at t, and so it is certain for s at t. Under those conditions, it is somewhat plausible to claim that the observation-report, 'I am now seeing my hand', is inferentially acceptable for s at t. If so, then premise III.2 would be unreasonable and should be rejected. But if this and all other observation-reports, and also all memory-reports, fail to provide a way to rebut III.1 or III.2, then we should conclude that both skeptical premises are acceptable. Surely, if neither of these two kinds of nonbasic statements falsifies either of the two premises, then no other kind does. And if these two premises survive our attack, then so does skeptical argument III, and we will have failed in our attempt to refute skeptical thesis M_1S_1.

NOTES

[1] It should be noted that D1 and A2 entail that if p is acceptable for s at t, then the probability, for s at t, of p, given s's total evidence, e, is high. It seems that some

would disagree with this. See, for example, I. Levi, *Gambling with Truth*, Cambridge, Mass.: MIT Press, 1967, pp. 96–98.

[2] For one view that probability of 1 implies truth, see R. Carnap's discussion of strict coherence in 'Inductive Logic and Rational Decision', in R. Carnap and R. Jeffrey (eds.), *Studies in Inductive Logic and Probability*, Berkeley: University of California Press, 1971, p. 15.

[3] C. I. Lewis, *An Analysis of Knowledge and Valuation*, La Salle, Ill.: Open Court, 1946, p. 333.

[4] N. Goodman, 'Sense and Certainty', in R. Chisholm and R. Swartz (eds.), *Empirical Knowledge*, Englewood Cliffs, N.J.: Prentice-Hall, 1973, pp. 362–363.

[5] The first two arguments were suggested to me by M. Pastin, 'C. I. Lewis's Radical Foundationalism', *Nous* 9 (1975), 407–420.

[6] For a defense of the principle of strict conditionalization, see I. Levi, 'Probability Kinematics', *British Journal of the Philosophy of Science* 18 (1976), 197–209. See also Carnap, *op. cit.*, pp. 15–19.

[7] For discussions of the effects of conceptual change on probabilities, see K. Lehrer, 'Induction and Conceptual Change', *Synthese* 23 (1971–1972), 215–220; and I. Niiniluoto and R. Toumela, *Theoretical Concepts and Hypothetico-Inductive Inference*, Dordrecht: Reidel, 1973, pp. 180–186.

[8] See R. Jeffrey, *The Logic of Decision*, New York: McGraw-Hill, 1965, pp. 153–161, for a discussion of strict conditionalization as a special case where $Pr(e) = 1$.

[9] Lewis, 'The Given Element in Empirical Knowledge', in Chisholm and Swartz (eds.), *op. cit.*, p. 372.

[10] See Carnap, *op. cit.*, pp. 15, 101–104, 111–116.

[11] For one definition of 'compete', see K. Lehrer, *Knowledge*, Oxford: Oxford University Press, 1974, pp. 193–198.

[12] To be sure, the specter of the lottery paradox appears here. But this paradox arises only where what Kyburg calls "the conjunction principle" applies; see H. Kyburg, 'Conjunctivitis' in M. Swain (ed.), *Induction, Acceptance, and Rational Belief*, Dordrecht: Reidel, 1970, p. 53. But I maintain that this principle applies at most to what is acceptable as evidence, and not to what is merely acceptable as belief.

CHAPTER 4

SKEPTICISM AND THE PROBABILITY
OF NONBASIC STATEMENTS (I): ON
SUFFICIENT CONDITIONS FOR
ABSOLUTE PROBABILITIES

The two tasks that confront us now are to examine the claims that no nonbasic statements are initially acceptable (premise III.1), and that none are probable relative to basic-reports (premise III.2). Although it may seem natural to consider first whether any nonbasic empirical statements are initially acceptable, I shall, instead, begin with the second claim, because points developed in evaluating it will also prove helpful in evaluating the first claim. It should be noted, incidentally, that a nonbasic statement that is probable relative to basic-reports may be initially acceptable rather than inferentially acceptable. What is important for distinguishing the two species of acceptability is that, as definition D2 states, initial acceptability of p requires, and inferential acceptability of p forbids, that p would be acceptable even if no other statement should justify it sufficiently to be acceptable. So if we discover that some nonbasic sentences are probable relative to basic-reports that are certain for someone at some time, we will not yet know whether they are initially or noninferentially acceptable. But, I would claim, we would know something more important; we would know that they are acceptable. Of course, we may find that no nonbasic statements are probable relative to basic-reports. Then, no nonbasic statements would be made inferentially acceptable by basic-reports, but, nevertheless, some might be initially acceptable and others inferentially acceptable because of them.

In order to evaluate premise III.2, that no nonbasic statements are probable relative to any basic-reports, we must first decide how we are to construe what it is for p to be probable relative to q. I believe we can unpack it in two different quite general ways. Either this phrase can be interpreted as stating a relationship in an argument between its premises and its conclusion, or it can be interpreted in terms of probability theory as $\Pr(p/q) > 0.5$. These two interpretations are importantly different. There is a conditional statement corresponding to any argument with its premises as antecedent and its conclusion as consequent. But $\Pr(p/q) > 0.5$ yields no such conditional. The importance of this difference will become clear as our discussion progresses. I propose to consider the first construal in this chapter, and the second in the next chapter.

According to the first construal, 'p is probable relative to q' expresses a relationship between premises and conclusion that can be replaced by conditionals, such as: 'If q is true, then p is probable', and 'If q is probable, then p is probable'. Similar arguments translate into statements like 'If q is true, then p is highly credible (that is, p is acceptable)', and 'If q is true, then p is confirmed (justified)'. Generally, two sorts of arguments have been thought to provide instances of the preceding conditionals: deductive and inductive arguments. Our strategy, then, will be to see whether either form of argument will warrant the required sort of inferences from basic-reports to nonbasic statements. In particular, we will begin by choosing the simplest form of observation-report as our nonbasic statement. If neither a deductive nor an inductive argument warrants our inferring such a report from premises that are basic-reports, and, sometimes, also analytic sentences, then we will have reason to accept premise III.2 for the first interpretation of 'p is probable relative to q'. The remaining task would then be to see what results are obtained when we use the second interpretation. And if one of these forms of argument warrants such an inference, then we will face the additional task of discovering whether these argument forms allow us to infer any other sorts of nonbasic statements from basic-reports.

ON BASIC-REPORTS ENTAILING NONBASIC STATEMENTS

The abundance of reasons that have been provided for rejecting the view known as 'analytical phenomenalism' can be used to justify the claim that no deductive argument form will warrant inferences from basic-reports to nonbasic statements. To see this, let us pick one of the most likely candidates as conclusion, namely:

(1)   I am now seeing a yellow object.

And let us be as generous as possible regarding what we allow to be included among the premises. It is clear we can allow any basic-report, and that includes any conjunction, disjunction, or negation of any basic-reports. We can also include any analytic sentences on the grounds that deductive validity with analytic statements would show that (1) is entailed by some basic-reports, and that is enough to justify that (1) is highly credible (acceptable), if the basic-reports are certain. Indeed, it would allow us to conclude that (1) is certain if the basic-reports are, and also that (1) is acceptable if the conjunction of these basic-reports (also a basic-report) is acceptable. On the other hand, however, if we find it reasonable to conclude that no basic-report, no matter how complicated, entails (1), then it is reasonable to conclude also that no basic-reports, even when conjoined with all analytic sentences, will yield any nonbasic sentence.

Our strategy is to try to uncover the basic-report that is most likely to yield (1). We can approach this task by beginning with:

(2)   I am now having an experience of something yellow, and I am now believing I am now seeing something yellow.

It is easy to show that (2) does not entail (1), by the strategy of finding another sentence of any sort for which it is clear that its conjunction with (2) does not entail (1). Then (2) does not entail (1). For this purpose, we need only:

(3)   I am hallucinating in a room containing nothing that is yellow.

The problem, of course, is that because of the possibility of hallucination as well as illusory experiences and perceptual relativity, no statement merely about present experience and belief guarantees veridical perception. Thus it would do no good to supplement (2) with:

(4)   I fully believe I am a normal perceiver in normal conditions who is not hallucinating but rather is having a veridical visual experience.

It is clear that the conjunction of (2) and (4) with (3) does not entail (1), because they are consistent with my now seeing nothing at all.

On Analyzing Physical-Object Statements by Subjunctive Conditionals

It is generally thought that subjunctive conditionals provide the best hope for yielding analyses of physical-object statements.[1] It might be suggested, then, that we should supplement (2) with the appropriate conditionals. But there are four reasons why this proposal fails. First, our present concern is not the analysis of a physical-object statement by any sort of sensation statement, but rather the derivation of at least one physical-object statement from some basic-report. And no subjunctive conditional is a basic-report, because, although a subjunctive conditional can be formed from a material conditional whose antecedent and consequent are both basic-reports, what results is not reducible to any conjunction or

disjunction of basic-reports. But, second, even if we liberalize our requirements and call such a conditional a basic-report, it is highly unlikely that
any helpful subjunctive conditionals would qualify as initially acceptable,
let alone initially certain. They would be, at best, inferentially acceptable or
certain, and the question of whether any of these conditionals is probable
relative to initially acceptable basic-reports would arise. And, I find, that
question is no less easily answered than its kin which we are currently
considering, that is, whether any nonbasic statements are probable relative
to basic-reports (in the less liberal sense).

The third reason is that the purpose of using subjunctive conditionals
in analyses of physical-object statements is not to help provide statements
that entail observation-reports, but rather to provide statements entailed
by physical-object statements that are not observation-reports, such as
'There is something yellow here'. This sentence does not entail that someone is having an experience, and so the best hope for a phenomenalistic
analysis of the sentence is a subjunctive conditional about what someone
would experience if certain facts were true of him. But (1) would seem to
entail that I am now having some visual experience, so there is no reason
to think that any conditional found in what entails (1) need be subjunctive.
This leads to the fourth and crucial reason. No eligible conditional – whether subjunctive or not – seems to be at all helpful in constructing a
basic-report that entails (1). Indeed, one way to see how hopeless it is to
search for any basic-reports that entail (1) is to consider a sentence involving a basic-report that may well seem to entail (1):

(5)   I am now having an experience of something yellow, and I am
          now a normal perceiver in conditions optimal for seeing the
          color of things.

Whether (5) entails (1) depends on how restrictively being normal and
being optimal are understood. If it is possible for a normal perceiver to be
in optimal conditions, and yet be fooled by a Cartesian malicious demon,
then (5) fails to entail (1). If this is not possible – perhaps because conditions are not optimal whenever such a demon is at work – then it seems
(5) would entail (1). But it seems clear there is no way to use basic-reports
to unpack a claim about my being in optimal conditions in such a way that
it makes it impossible that (5) is true and a Cartesian demon is at work. I
conclude, then, that it is extremely unlikely that any basic-report, no
matter how complicated, entails (1). As a result, we can also conclude that

it is very reasonable that no nonbasic statement is entailed by any basic-report, because, if any are, then (1) is.

On Probabilistic Analyses of Physical-Object Statements

It might be objected at this point that I have overlooked one quite different sort of sentence involving basic-reports, namely a probability statement. C. I. Lewis seems to have thought that physical-object statements are to be given phenomenalistic analyses by probability sentences rather than by subjunctive conditionals. I have argued elsewhere that this attempt fails.[2] What is relevant to our purposes can be reconstructed using the following sentences: L = 'A sheet of paper lies before me'; S = 'I just had a visual experience of a sheet of paper'; A = 'I tried to tear and believe I succeeded in tearing paper just now'; and E = 'I am now having a visual experience of torn paper'. If Lewis is right, then the statement that the probability of E, given S and A, is almost 1 – that is, '$\Pr(E/S \cdot A)$ is almost 1' – entails L.[3] But even if we grant that E, S, and A are basic-reports, and that a probability statement consisting only of basic-reports is itself a basic-report, this attempt fails. The entailment claim is false. The probability statement in its antecedent does not entail that anything exists, and so does not entail L. Indeed, the claim that the absolute probability of L is almost 1 does not entail L. And, on some interpretations of probability, not even '$\Pr(L) = 1$' entails L. So this reply fails to overturn our previous conclusion.

CONCLUSION: THE FAILURE OF DEDUCTIVE INFERENCE TO AVOID SKEPTICISM

The failure of the thesis that basic-reports entail nonbasic statements shows why what I have called the Cartesian species of traditional foundationalism leads to skepticism. This species requires not only a foundation of certainty as L3 specifies, but also that, of empirical sentences, only basic-reports are initially certain, and that the extension of knowledge beyond the foundation is by deductive inference alone. This last requirement is made in order to guarantee inferential certainty of what is known. Thus, on this Cartesian view, each of us must begin only with his own basic-reports and 'conceptual' truths as initial premises and try to extend his knowledge by deductive derivation. But we have just seen that justification, and so knowledge, is not extended to nonbasic statements from basic-reports by deductive inference. None of this, however, shows that foundationalism in general leads to skepticism. In fact, it does not even show this for everyone who requires only certainty at the foundation and extension of justification only where there is inferential certainty. If, as I would urge, such a person adopts a probability sense of certainty, and if, as I have argued, many basic-reports are initially certain, then this person can plausibly argue that whatever has a probability of 1, given what is initially certain for someone at some time, is certain for him at that time. So, if some nonbasic statements have a probability of 1, given certain basic-reports, and they are not initially certain, then they are inferentially certain. Similarly, as I shall argue in Chapter 5, if some nonbasic statement which is not initially acceptable, is probable, for s at t, given basic-reports of s which are certain for s at t, then the nonbasic statement is highly credible (acceptable) for s at t. Someone who argues in either of these ways would not be what I have called a 'Cartesian' traditional foundationalist. But he might be what I call a 'Lewisean' traditional theorist, that is, one who holds that inductive as well as deductive inferences can extend both certainty and acceptability.

ON ENUMERATIVE INDUCTIVE INFERENCES FROM BASIC TO NONBASIC STATEMENTS

Might some sort of inductive argument with only basic-reports and analytic sentences as premises yield that some nonbasic statement is probable? Generally, it is thought that there are two kinds of inductive argument where the premises are nonprobabilistic statements of fact and the conclusion is a probability statement. These can be called 'enumerative induction' and 'induction by analogy'. Unfortunately, it is not clear in either case just what the correct forms of these inductive inferences are. However, for our purposes, it is enough to approximate them and show where problems arise. Accordingly, I propose that we use Plantinga's explication of what he calls a "direct inductive argument" as our example of the form of enumerative inductive arguments. Plantinga says:

A direct inductive argument for S is an ordered pair of arguments of which the first member is a simple inductive argument *a* for *S*, and the second is a valid deductive argument one premise of which is the conclusion of *a*, the other premise being drawn from *S*'s total evidence.

And also:

A simple inductive argument for S is an argument of the following form:

Every *A* such that *S* has determined by observation whether or not *A* is *B* is such that *S* has determined by observation that *A* is *B*. Therefore, probably every *A* is a *B*.[4]

There are reasons why we should not take simple inductive arguments as imbedded in every enumerative inductive argument. One reason, noted by Plantinga, is that it does not accommodate arguments where only some fraction of A's, such as m/n, has been determined by observation (that is, by experiencing these A's) to be B's. In such a case, the conclusion would seem to be that, probably, m/n A's are B's. Another reason is that, as described by Plantinga, a simple inductive argument will allow someone to conclude that it is probable that all A's are B's, when, for example, he has intentionally limited his observation of A's to those that other people have told him are B's, as he desires. But regardless of these problems, I shall use the direct inductive argument form to illustrate why enumerative induction fails to warrant inference from basic-reports to a conclusion about the probability of some nonbasic statement. I do this because I find that whatever amendments might succeed in avoiding these problems would not affect the inability of enumerative induction to warrant the inferences that concern us.

It is easy to see why enumerative induction is no help for us. Consider again observation-report, (1). If I use a direct inductive argument to show it to be probable, I need something like the following as the conclusion of a simple inductive argument:

(6)   Probably, every (almost every) time when I have an experience of something yellow is a time when I am seeing something yellow.

Then with basic-report, (2), I can infer that it is probable that I am now seeing something yellow – (1). But in order to warrant the inference to (6) by a simple inductive argument, the following premise is needed:

(7)   Every (almost every) time when I have an experience of something yellow, such that I have determined by observation whether or not it is a time when I am seeing something yellow, is such that I have determined by observation that this, which is a time when I am having an experience of something yellow, is also a time when I am seeing something yellow.

And (7) is to be justified by a series of statements about me at present and in the past which are of the form:

(8)   The present time is a time when I having an experience of something yellow and have determined by observation that

this, which is such a time, is also a time when I am seeing something yellow.

The problem, of course, is that (8) is not a basic-report, because

(9)   I have determined by observation that the present time is a
         time when I am seeing something yellow,

is not a basic-report. And, as this argument for (1) by means of (7) and
(6) illustrates, any other direct inductive argument for (1) will have the
same flaw. In order to use any basic-report, whether simple like (2) or more
complicated, to derive that (1) is probable, the substitute for (6) must be
of the form:

(6a)   Probably, every (amost every) A is a B (where B = time when
         I am seeing something yellow).

And to get (6a) by means of a simple inductive argument we need the same
substituend for 'B' in any replacement for (7) and (8). But it is just that
substituend which keeps (7) and (8) from being basic-reports. Consequently, no direct inductive arguments, and, more broadly, no enumerative
inductive arguments which have only basic-reports and analytic sentences
as premises yield the conclusion that (1) is probable. So we can conclude
that the enumerative inductive arguments are no more helpful than
deductive arguments.

ON INDUCTION BY ANALOGY FROM BASIC TO NONBASIC STATEMENTS

It is now quite easy to see that induction by analogy fails for the same
reason as enumerative induction. I think it is fair to represent the form of
an analogical argument as follows:

(i)   Entities $o_1, o_2, \ldots, o_n$ have properties $P_1, P_2, \ldots, P_m$ in
         common.
(ii)   Entities $o_2, o_3, \ldots, o_n$ have property p_{m+1}.

Therefore

(iii)   It is probable that entity o_1 has property p_{m+1}.

The point here is that the more something is like a group of other things
in certain known respects, the more probable it is that it is also like them
in some additional, unknown respect. To make this argument form relevant to (1) we should rephrase (1) as:

(1a)   The present moment (o_1) is a time when I see something yellow (p_{m+1}).

Premise (i) need cause no problem because we can let properties p_1 through p_m be those ascribed in basic-reports. But premise (ii) is clearly not a basic-report, because it ascribes the property p_{m+1} to moments of time, o_2 through o_n, and no sentence stating that a moment has property p_{m+1} is a basic-report. So no analogical inductive argument succeeds.

HYPOTHETICAL INDUCTION AND INFERENCE FROM BASIC TO NONBASIC STATEMENTS

Have we completed the first task relevant to premise III.2, that is, the task of showing that no premise composed of basic-reports and analytic sentences yields a conclusion that some nonbasic statement is probable? We have, if we have encompassed all inductive arguments, and if, as is widely assumed, all arguments that justify their conclusions are either deductive or inductive. But there are those who would claim that neither condition is true. In the first place, there is supposed to be a form of inductive argument known variously as 'hypothetico-deductive argument', 'inference to the best explanation', and 'hypothetical inductive argument'. As Harman puts it:

In making an inference to the best explanation one infers, from the fact that a certain hypothesis would explain the evidence, to the truth of that hypothesis. In general, there will be several hypotheses which might explain the evidence, so one must be able to reject all such alternative hypotheses before one is warranted in making the inference. Thus one infers, from the premise that a given hypothesis would provide a "better" explanation for the evidence than would any other hypothesis, to the conclusion that the given hypothesis is true.[5]

Furthermore, according to Roderick Chisholm's critical cognitivist,

there are principles of evidence, other than the principles of induction and deduction, which tell us, for example, under what conditions the state we have called "thinking that one perceives" will *confer evidence*, or *confer reasonableness*, upon propositions about external things . . .[6]

We must, then, examine both the claim that there is a form of inductive inference we have overlooked, and the claim that there are epistemic principles that are neither deductive nor inductive.

In considering the problem of inferring what is indirectly evident from what is directly evident – a problem that parallels our present concern –

Chisholm claims that hypothetical induction, as well as deduction, enumerative induction, and induction by analogy are of no help. It is because of this, that he adopts 'critical cognitivism' which proposes epistemic principles that are neither deductive nor inductive. He states his objection to hypothetical induction when discussing the problem of other minds, where the problem is not to infer the indirectly evident from the directly evident, but rather to infer something unobserved about a person's mental states from his observed behavior. Nevertheless, if sound, his objection is easily transformable to apply to the problem of inferring what is nonbasic from what is basic.

Chisholm's Objection to the Use of Hypothetical Induction: How to Justify Bridge Laws

Chisholm considers an example of trying to use hypothetical induction to justify a claim about a person's state of depression or about his thoughts. He says,

The "hypothesis" that Jones is now depressed, or that he is thinking about a horse, will be put forward as the most likely explanation of certain other things we know – presumably, certain facts about Jones's present behavior and demeanor. But in order to construct an inductive argument in which the hypothesis that Jones is depressed, or that he is thinking of a horse, *is* thus to be confirmed, we must have access to a premise telling us what some of the consequences of Jones's depression, or some of the consequences of his thinking about a horse, are likely to be. And how are we to justify *this* premise if we are not entitled to make use of any information about Jones's depression or thoughts? The only possible way of finding the premise our hypothetical induction requires is to appeal to still another induction – this time an argument from analogy.[7]

And, of course, as Chisholm concludes, analogical induction will not help. We can add that neither deduction nor enumerative induction will help either. So, if Chisholm is right, hypothetical induction, either alone or combined with deduction and with other forms of induction, fails to solve the problem of other minds, And, for exactly parallel reasons, it fails to provide a way to infer the nonbasic from the basic.

Reply to Chisholm's Objection: What an Explanatory Hypothesis Includes. The weakness in Chisholm's argument against the use of hypothetical induction lies in his claim that the only way to justify the additional premise that relates the explaining hypothesis to what it explains is by some other form of induction. It is at this point that Kyburg attacks the argument. He does so by stating an example of how someone must use hypothetical induction to justify a nonbasic hypothesis such as H = 'There is a cat on the roof now'. This hypothesis is supposed to explain a basic-report such as O_1 = 'I am now taking there to be a cat on the roof now'. In order for the explanation to succeed, we need the additional statement relating H to some basic-report. Let us follow Kyburg[8] and use:

R.   If H (There is a cat on the roof during time interval Δt), then C (Practically always, when I take myself to be looking toward the roof during Δt, under what I take to be appropriate conditions of illumination and perspective and health, I take something to be a cat on the roof).

Here hypothesis C is a generalization from basic-reports, and let us agree with Kyburg, for now, that C is justified by enumerative induction from 'observed' instances, that is, from appropriate basic-reports. Then generalization C is explained by hypothesis H conjoined with R, and basic-report O_1 is explained by H and R and basic-report O_2 = 'I am now taking myself to be looking toward the roof, under what I take to be appropriate conditions of illumination and perspective and health'. Then on the assumption that H provides the best explanations of C and O_1, we can conclude, follwing Harman, that it is reasonable that H is true.

Chisholm's objection to this example, of course, is that even if we grant that H is justified in this way, H does not explain either C or O_1 unless R is justified, and there is no way to justify R by means of premises that are only basic-reports and analytic sentences. Kyburg's reply to this seems to be that C is an analytic consequence of H, and so R is analytic. Thus R need not be justified by deduction or induction, and, furthermore, it is allowed as a premise with basic-reports. Unfortunately, R is not analytic, nor is a related principle, P*, that Kyburg takes to be analytic. It is clearly possible that H is true and that a Cartesian malicious demon fools everyone when they look at this roof into believing that they see a dog, instead of a cat, on the roof, no matter what else they believe. Thus this way to avoid Chisholm's objection fails.

Nevertheless, Chisholm's claim about the justification of R is mistaken, as is his objection. To see this, let us assume that the relevant form of hypothetical induction is the following somewhat simplistic form:

(1)   Basic-reports, $b_1, b_2, \ldots, b_n$ are to be explained for s at t.
(2)   Hypothesis, T, explains $b_1, b_2, \ldots, b_n$ better at t than any hypothesis that conflicts with T.

Therefore

(3)   It is probable, for s at t, that T is true.

This argument form clearly differs from any valid deductive form, the form of simple inductive inference, and the form of induction by analogy. Using this form, Chisholm would make his objection by letting $n = 1$, $b_1 = o_1$, and $T = H$. This leaves R unjustified. But his mistake is in failing to realize that an explaining hypothesis or theory can be interpreted to include both the theoretical postulates, such as H, and also the bridge laws or correspondence rules of the theory, such as R. Thus we can substitute (H-and-R) for T in the preceding argument form and thereby justify R as well as H by hypothetical induction.

A New Objection: No Way to Justify Which Hypothesis Is Best

Chisholm's objection fails, but another remains to be considered. Our present concern is whether some deductive or inductive argument form warrants inferences from premises that are either basic-reports or analytic to nonbasic conclusions. But it is dubious that any instantiations of premises (1) and (2) of the preceding argument form are basic-reports. So hypothetical induction will not provide the inferences we seek.

The premise of this objection is correct, but its conclusion does not follow from it. Another is needed to the effect that either premise (1) or (2) is not justifiable by deductive or inductive inference from premises that are either basic-reports or analytic. This additional premise is not trivial. It is at least possible that premise (1) is deducible from certain facts about a basic-report, such as that it is certain for someone at some time, which in turn, might be entailed by some sort of basic-report. And it may be that the characteristics that make H the best explanation are syntactical and logical features of sentences and so it is possible that the statement that H has these characteristics is analytic. We will be able to decide about this when, in chapters 7 and 8, we examine what I call 'nonevidential tests for explanatory systems'. But even if all these possibilities are true, more is needed to yield premise (2). The claim that a hypothesis is better than its rivals if it has these characteristics must be analytic. This also is possible, but I doubt that it is true. Indeed, it seems likely that much of what I just claimed to be possible is false. So, without delving into the many complex issues raised by these speculations, there is some reason, at this point, to think that at least premise (2) is not justifiable by any series of inferences, whether deductive or inductive, from premises which include only basic-reports and analytic sentences. So we have some reason to think that hypothetical induction, combined with deduction, enumerative induction, and induction by analogy, fails to provide the desired inferences. Of course, a more detailed examination and clarification of hypothetical induction, which will be started in Part II, may prove differently. But, for now, our best hope might seem to be to find a viable form of inference that is neither deductive nor inductive, because the three forms of induction we have examined seem to encompass all species of induction. This new search takes us to Chisholm's 'critical cognitivism'.

CHISHOLM'S EPISTEMIC PRINCIPLES AND INFERENCES
FROM DIRECTLY TO INDIRECTLY EVIDENT

What distinguishes critical cognitivism from its rivals, according to Chisholm, is that it alone proposes a set of epistemic principles in addition to deductive and inductive principles. As we can see from examining the nine examples Chisholm first proposed, there are three sorts of these epistemic principles. One sort provides a factual, nonepistemic sufficient condition for something being evident for a person, s, at a time, t. And since this condition concerns only what Chisholm calls "self-presenting states" for s at t, whatever is inferred to be evident by this sort of principle is what Chisholm calls "the directly evident", or, in my terminology, 'the initially certain'. One example of such a principle is H1, which was discussed in Chapter 2; another, stated by Chisholm, is:

Necessarily, for any S and any t, if S thinks at t that he perceives something that is red, then it is evident to S at t that he then thinks he perceives something that is red.[9]

An important difference between H3 and this example from Chisholm is that the latter but not the former allows different basic-reports to be directly evident when that implies an inductive inconsistency. It is this difference that would stop H3 from being a principle of this first sort, if probability is understood epistemically, because then inductive consistency, which is mentioned in the antecedent of H3, would be epistemic. Of course, if Carnap is right and all probability statements are analytic, then this would raise no problem for using H3 to infer conclusions from premises which are basic-reports and analytic sentences.

Epistemic principles of the second sort are the most important for our purposes, because they function to provide inferences from premises constituted solely of what is directly evident to conclusions stating that something is acceptable, reasonable, or evident. And, I suppose, what can be inferred as having one of these epistemic statuses by use of this second sort of rule, but not by use of the first, is indirectly or inferentially acceptable, reasonable, or evident. An example of this sort of principle is Chisholm's first formulation of his principle B, which is equivalent to:

> B.   If S believes that he is perceiving something to have a certain property F, then it is reasonable for S that he is perceiving something to be F, and that something is F.[10]

Notice that the antecedent of B concerns only a 'self-presenting state', or, linguistically, a basic-report, as is required by a principle that warrants inference from only basic-reports and analytic sentences to conclusions about the probability or epistemic status of nonbasic statements. Principle B, then, might well be the sort of principle we need to supplement deductive and inductive rules. However, as we shall see, Chisholm's own amended versions of B (approximately, B1 and B4) include an epistemic clause in their antecedents and so do not qualify as this sort of principle.

In both the first and second sorts of principles, the antecedent is supposed to be factual and nonepistemic, while the consequent is epistemic. But in principles of the third sort, both antecedent and consequent include epistemic claims, because they state that certain statements having a certain status affect the epistemic status of other sentences. Consider Chisholm's principle G:

> G.   If the conjunction of all those propositions e, such that e is acceptable for S at t tends to confirm h, then h has some presumption in its favor for S at t.[11]

Let us concentrate on principle B as a prime example of the sort of nondeductive, noninductive epistemic principle that, according to Chisholm, provides the desired link between the directly evident and the indirectly evident, the basic and the nonbasic. Our primary concern will be to judge whether it is reasonable to adopt a set of principles like B. Crucial to this decision will be the task of seeing whether B, or at least one of its amended versions, survives a series of purported counterexamples. Before doing this, however, it is worth considering briefly what semantic status Chisholm would assign to these principles. From his contrasting these principles with deductive and inductive rules, it would seem he would claim that they are rules of inference which warrant inferences that no deductive or inductive rules of inference warrant. But, as B illustrates, he states his principles in indicative form rather than as rules. Thus he might agree to their use as additional premises that, with the use of only deductive inference rules, allows the derivation of epistemic claims about nonbasic statements. I do not propose to speculate about which alternative Chisholm would accept. I wish merely to note one difference between the two, namely, that for the second alternative only, where the principles are premises, no argument involving B is an example of inferring something nonbasic from premises that are either basic-reports or analytic. But once we see that this can be easily avoided by construing the epistemic principles as rules of inference instead of premises, it no longer seems important for our purposes which way these epistemic principles are interpreted. What distinguishes a foundationalist who is a critical cognitivist from a traditional foundationalist is that the first, but not the second, allows epistemic principles of the preceding three sorts, none of which are either deductive or inductive rules of inference, or analytic sentences, or, as is clear, basic-reports.

Critical Examination of Epistemic Principle B

As stated, principle B is inadequate, as Heidelberger has shown. Assume that B has the form: 'If P, then Q and R'. Then Heidelberger's strategy is to discover a statement, T_1, such that P and T_1 do not imply either Q or R. So P implies neither Q nor R. Heidelberger creates his counterexample by letting F be the property of being yellow, and $T_1 = $'s knows at t that U', where $U = $ 'There is a yellow light shining on the object s sees, a moment ago there was no colored light shining on the object, and at that time s perceived the object to be white'. Surely, given that s knows all this, it is at least not reasonable for him that he is perceiving something yellow or that something is yellow, regardless of whether he now believes that he is now perceiving something to be yellow. So B must either be amended or abandoned.[12]

Examination of Chisholmian Amendments to B

Chisholm later agreed with Heidelberger's criticism of B and proposed an amendment to avoid the preceding counterexample. His idea is to propose a statement to be conjoined with P in the antecedent of B that is not true in the situation envisioned by Heidelberger. The problem, as Chisholm sees it, is that at times, something, which is known by s and thus evident to s, makes it not reasonable that s is perceiving something yellow. He wants, then, to add to the antecedent of B that anything, e, that is evident to s at t would, when taken with just his perceptual belief, p, confirm or make reasonable, for s at t, that he perceives something to be yellow. What results can be closely approximated in our terms by:

B1.   *If* (i) s believes at t that he is perceiving something to have property F, and (ii) for any statement, e, that is evident for s at t, if the conjunction of (i), and e, and what it entails should be exactly what is evident for s at t, then it would be reasonable (acceptable) for s at t, that s is perceiving something to be F, *then* it is reasonable, for s at t, that he is perceiving something to be F, and that something is F.[13]

If we let e be U which, according to T_1, s knows, then, supposedly, U is evident to s, and so it falsifies (ii) and the antecedent of B1 is not satisfied. Thus the preceding example does not counter B1.

Unfortunately, this reply fails. Assume that T_1 is false because U is not evident to s, but it is merely reasonable, that is, assume T_2 = 'It is reasonable but not evident, for s at t, that U'.[14] Then neither U nor, we can assume, any other statement falsifies (ii). So B1 yields that it is reasonable for s at t that he perceives something to be yellow. But that is surely quite dubious, because of U which is reasonable but not evident for s at t. Perhaps we should replace B1 by B2 whose clause (ii) applies to anything reasonable for s at t. But then we can replace T_2 by T_3 = 'It is not reasonable for s at t that U'. And the preceding objection to B1 can be adapted to refute B2, if T_3 is plausible, as an elaboration of our story will show. Assume that U is true, but s has conveniently forgotten about a moment ago and refuses to allow the many people who have been with him to tell him their views, which are unanimously that the object is white and the light is now yellow. In short, he forgets what is epistemically bothersome, and intentionally keeps himself from easily obtainable evidence. Consequently, U is not reasonable for s at t because he lacks the evidence that would make it reasonable. So U does not falsify clause (ii) of B2, and, assuming nothing else does either, B2 warrants the conclusion that it is reasonable for s at t that he is seeing something to be yellow. But this is not reasonable for him at t because of his convenient mental lapse and obstinate refusal to receive easily obtainable evidence that would make U reasonable, perhaps even evident, for him. Thus B2 should be rejected as were B and B1.

The obvious move at this point is to descend farther down the epistemic scale to where we form B3 by having its clause (ii) apply to any statement that is not unreasonable (unacceptable) for s at t. Then a new T_4 would have to state that U is unreasonable for s at t. But if that is true, then it might well seem that U has no effect on the confirmation of a statement for s at t, because what is unreasonable should not be used to show that something is not reasonable. So the fact that T_4 does not falsify clause (ii) of B3 may seem not to create a counterexample for B3. Perhaps, then, we can adopt B3 as one epistemic principle.

Unfortunately, some problems remain for B3. If that principle warrants our concluding that, in the preceding elaborated story about our obstinate person, s, U is unreasonable for s at t, then something unreasonable, given B3, might well be relevant to what is reasonable for s at t, and, as a result, would produce a counterexample to B3. In order to use B3 to show U is unreasonable for s at t, we need to continue the preceding story in such a way that B3 implies that the denial of U is reasonable. We can do this by describing s using the statement, V: 's believes at t that he is perceiving that there is one light shining on the object he sees, and it is not yellow'. Assume that if what is entailed by the conjunction of V with any statement not unreasonable for s at t should be exactly what is evident for s at t, then it would be reasonable, for s at t, that W ('s is perceiving that there is one light shining on the object he sees, and it is not yellow'). Then we can conclude, by B3, that it is reasonable for s at t that there is one light shining on the object he is seeing and it is not yellow. It follows from this that it is unreasonable for s at t that there is a yellow light shining on the object he is now seeing. But if a statement, p, is unreasonable for s at t, then so is p conjoined with anything else. Therefore, U is unreasonable for s at t. Thus, if B3 is correct, then, as before, U fails to falsify clause (ii) and so does not stop the inference that it is reasonable for s at t that he is perceiving something to be yellow. But, as noted previously, this is not reasonable for s at t because of U, s's convenient memory lapse, and his refusal to listen to relevant testimony. So, by warranting that U is unreasonable for s at t, B3 helps create a counterexample to itself.

I can think of one reply to this objection. It is based on an assumption which may be mistaken, namely, that if what is entailed by the conjunction of V with any statement not unreasonable for s at t is exactly what is evident for s at t, then the statement, W ('s is perceiving that there is one light shining on the object he sees and it is not yellow'), would be reasonable for s at t. Perhaps this assumption is false in the preceding story. It would be, if we could make one other assumption, that is, that every statement which is not initially acceptable for s at t and against which s has no evidence at t is as reasonable as its denial. Consider, then, Z: 'There is a malicious demon that causes most people to have false perceptual beliefs most of the time'. It seems clear that Z would not be initially acceptable for any person, and very few people, if any, would have evidence against Z. So, counting s among this vast majority, we can conclude that, because of Z, clause (ii) of B3 is not met for W in the preceding situation. Thus the objection fails.

The crucial question is whether Z, or some similar statement, qualifies as not unreasonable for s at t. I think it not unlikely that if we assume that lack of contrary evidence implies a statement is not unreasonable, then in any situation for any person, there is some statement that, like Z, stops clause (ii) of B3 from being met. If so, then there are no counterexamples to B3. But notice the price paid to avoid counterexamples. The antecedent of B3 is never met, and so B3 is of no value in extending reasonableness beyond the foundation of directly evident or initially acceptable statements. In short, B3 is useless as an epistemic principle if we assume there is always some statement like Z that is not unreasonable for s at t. But if we assume this is not true in every case, then I believe we can further describe the preceding situation so that no statement like Z stops the satisfaction of clause (ii) of B3 for W, and the previous counterexample reappears. Consequently, I conclude, either B3 is incorrect or it is useless, and so it, like its relatives, should be rejected.

I can think of another sort of amendment that Chisholm might make. Indeed, Chisholm's latest version embodies such a change. It is, once again, a change in clause (ii), but it differs from the previous three changes, as it should, because it is of no help to proceed farther down the epistemic scale to include any statement whose denial is not evident. Then, surely, something like Z would always falsify clause (ii). Instead, following Chisholm, we could require that nothing that is not unreasonable for s at t would make it reasonable, for s at t, that he is *not* perceiving something to be F. Would this help? To find out, let us form B4 from B3 by using the following, which approximates Chisholm's new clause:

(ii)   For any statement, e, that is not unreasonable for s at t, it is false that if what is entailed by e should be exactly what is evident for s at t, then it would be reasonable, for s at t, that s is *not* perceiving something to be F.[15]

Of course, if something like statement Z is not unreasonable for s at t, then Z would, if evident, make it reasonable for s that he is not perceiving something to be F. Once again, clause (ii) would never be satisfied, and

B4 would be useless. But, even if Z and its kin are unreasonable for s at t, this last change does not help extract Chisholm from the preceding objection to B3. Indeed, I find the previous example more telling against B4 than against B3. In that example, we imagined that the conjunction of V with anything not unreasonable, for s at t, would make reasonable, for s at t, that s is perceiving something to be yellow, if what is entailed by that conjunction should be exactly what is evident for s at t. But then we can assume that the only sentences that are both epistemically relevant to whether or not s is perceiving something to be F (yellow) and are also not unreasonable for s at t are statement (i), some given-report about something appearing yellow, and the sentences, including V, that make U unreasonable for s at t. But no conjunction of these sentences would make the claim that s is *not* perceiving something to be yellow reasonable for s at t, if what it entails should be exactly what is evident for s at t. So, again, by avoiding what would make U reasonable for him at t, s would be able to infer, by means of B4, that it is reasonable, for him at t, that he is perceiving something to be yellow. But, again, that would be incorrect.

CONCLUSION ABOUT CHISHOLMIAN EPISTEMIC RULES: NOT SATISFACTORY

Each counterexample we found to a principle of the form of B is constructed by finding a statement which, when conjoined with the antecedent of the principle, does not imply its consequent. Thus the antecedent does not imply the consequent. I tried repeatedly to adjust the antecedent to stop the series of counterexamples, but no amendment produced a usable and correct version. I believe that this failure results from the kind of amendment to B found in B1 through B4 coupled with the restrictions put on what is allowed in the antecedent and with what is said to be reasonable in the consequent.

The question immediately arises whether some different sort of amendment to B would be more fruitful. If not, then it would be reasonable to conclude that Chisholm's critical cognitivism fails to provide acceptable epistemic principles, in addition to those of deduction and induction, that warrant inferences from premises that are analytic or solely about what is directly evident or initially acceptable to conclusions about the reasonableness of some observation-report. Therefore, because, with one possible exception, we have found that no combination of deductive and inductive principles warrants such inferences either, we should also conclude that on the first interpretation of '*p* is probable relative to *q*', skeptical premise III.2 is true. That is, no nonbasic statement is probable relative to any basic-reports. This is because on the first interpretation, '*p* is probable relative to *q*' can be unpacked as a conditional which has *q* as antecedent, and, as consequent, a statement about the probability, credibility, or reasonableness of *p*. The one possible exception, to be discussed in more detail later, is hypothetical induction. If the difficulties previously mentioned for using this form of induction to infer what is nonbasic from what is basic can be overcome, then premise III.2 may be refutable, even given the first interpretation. If they are not overcome, as seems likely however, and no different sort of amendment to B succeeds, then the last hope for a foundationalist who wishes to refute III.2 is to find some viable principles that embody the second interpretation. And if he fails in that attempt, his only way to refute skeptical argument III is by attacking premise III.1: 'An empirical statement is initially acceptable, only if it is a basic-report'.

There are two ways we might proceed at this point. First, we can look for a different sort of amendment to or replacement for B which has the same form as B. Second, we can ignore, for the present at least, principles which have the same form as B, and consider those that utilize the second interpretation of '*p* is probable relative to *q*'. I propose to do the latter, in part because, as we shall see, it will help us uncover the most plausible principle with the form of B. This will be the task of the next chapter.

NOTES

[1] For a more detailed examination of subjunctive analyses of physical-object statements, see my *Perception, Common Sense, and Science*, New Haven, Conn.: Yale University Press, 1975, pp. 121–123.

[2] *Ibid.*, pp. 123–125.

[3] See C. I. Lewis, *An Analysis of Knowledge and Valuation*, La Salle, Ill.: Open Court, 1946, pp. 248–249.

[4] A. Plantinga, *God and Other Minds*, Ithaca, N.Y.: Cornell University Press, 1967, p. 251.

[5] G. Harman, 'The Inference to the Best Explanation', *Philosophical Review*, **74** (1965), 89.

[6] R. Chisholm, *Theory of Knowledge*, Englewood Cliffs, N.J.: Prentice-Hall, 1966, p. 62. I have quoted from the first edition because the relevant passage on p. 127 of the second edition 1977, seems to have an inadvertent omission.

[7] Chisholm, *Theory of Knowledge*, 2nd ed., p. 129.

[8] See H. Kyburg, 'On a Certain Form of Philosophical Argument', *American Philosophical Quarterly* 7 (1970), p. 233.

[9] R. Chisholm, 'On the Nature of Empirical Evidence', in R. Chisholm and R. Swartz (eds.), *Empirical Knowledge,* Englewood Cliffs, N.J.: Prentice-Hall 1973, p. 242.

[10] See Chisholm, *Theory of Knowledge*, 1st ed., p. 45.

[11] See Chisholm, *Theory of Knowledge*, 2nd ed., pp. 82–83.

[12] See H. Heidelberger, 'Chisholm's Epistemic Principles', *Noûs* 3 (1969), 73–75.

[13] See Chisholm, 'On the Nature of Empirical Evidence', p. 244.

[14] I believe that for Chisholm, 'h is reasonable' corresponds to 'h is beyond reasonable doubt'. Then 'h is certain' would mean that h is reasonable, and 'for every i, if accepting i is more reasonable for s than accepting h, then i is certain for s'. For the appropriate definitions, see *Theory of Knowledge*, 2nd ed., p. 135.

[15] See Chisholm, *Theory of Knowledge*, 2nd ed., p. 76. The definitions needed to unpack Chisholm's statement of the principle so it closely resembles B4 are on pp. 135–136.

CHAPTER 5

SKEPTICISM AND THE PROBABILITY OF NONBASIC STATEMENTS (II): ON SUFFICIENT CONDITIONS FOR CONDITIONAL PROBABILITIES

In the last chapter, we found reason to agree with premise III.2, that no nonbasic statements are probable relative to basic-reports, when 'p is probable relative to q' is interpreted as a conditional statement with a factual antecedent, q, and a consequent stating that p is probable, highly credible, or reasonable. Our procedure was to begin with Heidelberger's counterexample to Chisholm's epistemic principle, B, and Chisholm's attempt to avoid it, and then to show that Chisholm's amendments and others like it are also mistaken. Heidelberger also considered ways that Chisholm might change his principle to avoid objections.[1] One of his suggestions is that Chisholm use principles that, unlike B, are not conditional in form. That is, instead of proposing principles of the form:

> If q then it is (probable, acceptable, highly credible, reasonable, evident, certain) for s at t that p,

Chisholm might try one with the following form:

> q makes p (probable, acceptable, highly credible, reasonable, evident, certain) for s at t.

The latter sort, unlike the former, is consistent with the claim that it is false that if q and r, then p is (probable, acceptable, etc.) for s at t. Thus principles of the second sort avoid all the preceding counterexamples to Chisholm's B and its kin.

Heidelberger's suggestion takes us to the second interpretation of 'p is probable relative to q', namely, when it means '$\Pr(p/q) > 0.5$'. I shall read this as: 'The probability of p, *given* q, is greater than 0.5', or, identically, 'p is probable, *given* q'. I shall continue to use 'p is probable *relative* to q' as ambiguous, because it has two quite different interpretations. On this second interpretation, then, it is clear that the claim that p is probable relative to q is not falsified by the claim that p is not probable relative to q and r (that is, $\Pr(p/q \cdot r) < 0.5$), and so none of the previous problems for B arise. This is because it is a theorem of the probability calculus that $\Pr(p/q) = [\Pr(p/q \cdot r) \times \Pr(r/q)] + [\Pr(p/q \cdot \bar{r}) \times \Pr(\bar{r}/q)]$, and this allows $\Pr(p/q)$ to be much larger than $\Pr(p/q \cdot r)$. Nevertheless, the question remains whether, for $p =$ 'I am now perceiving something that is F', there is an appropriate q for which $\Pr_{s,t}(Tp/q) > 0.5$. If there is one, then we can adopt the second interpretation and reject skeptical premise III.2.

ON PRINCIPLES FOR INFERRING CONDITIONAL PROBABILITIES

I propose that we begin by looking for a principle of the following form:

> If e is s's evidence for p at t, and e has property G, then $\Pr_{s,t}(Tp/Te) > 0.5$.

That is, we should search for some characteristic of s's evidence, e, such that if e has the characteristic, then Tp is probable, for s at t, given Te. Although the preceding principle is a conditional and thereby allows us to detach its consequent when the antecedent is satisfied, the previous problems for B do not arise because the consequent states a relative probability rather than one that is absolute (for example, $\Pr(Tp) > 0.5$). Nevertheless, a problem that does not confront B does arise. As Heidelberger puts it regarding 'e makes p evident':

How, if we have assurance that a proposition has been made evident by a subjective proposition, can we pass on to saying that it is "absolutely evident"; that it is evident not merely with respect to this or that subjective proposition, but that it is evident *simpliciter*.[2]

The problem is, of course, that the use of principles that incorporate the second interpretation requires the discovery of principles of a quite different sort, namely, those that tell us when we can infer that p is evident (or acceptable) for s at t from the claim that p is evident (or acceptable), for s at t, given e. Let us, however, delay a discussion of this problem until after we examine some specific proposals for rules of the first sort.

Chisholm might propose that we can formulate the principle we desire merely by adapting his original B to the second interpretation of 'p is probable relative to q'. That is, he might propose something like:

BR1.   If $e =$'s believes at t that he is perceiving that something is F', then $\Pr(Tp/Te) > 0.5$ (where $p =$'s is perceiving that something is F').

However, for reasons like those discussed in Chapter 2, we should relativize the probability statement in BR1 to person s and time t, and also trans-form p and the sentence in set e into our preferred form for reports. And I propose that we add to set e what is considered to be foundational evidence for what Firth calls the "traditional empiricist theory of evidence", name-ly, some appropriate given-report.[3] One reason for this addition is, as Heidelberger notes, "that men are capable of believing almost anything, about what they perceive or remember no less than about anything else".[4] And, for added insurance, let us also require that s believe with certainty that he and the conditions relevant to perceiving something to be F are normal. A new candidate, which embodies all these changes and thus combines Chisholm's 'taking criterion' with the 'empiricist criterion', is:

BR2.   If $e = \{$'I now believe with certainty that I am now perceiving something that is F', 'I am now having an experience of some-thing that is F', 'I now believe with certainty that I and the conditions relevant to my seeing something to be F are nor-mal'$\}$, and $p =$ 'I am now perceiving something that is F', then $\mathrm{Pr}_{s,\,t}(Tpst/Test) > 0.5$.

Our immediate concern is to discover whether BR2 is acceptable as an epistemic principle. This raises two problems. The first is the problem of finding what is to count for or against BR2. It is far from clear how to show that something conjoined with the antecedent of BR2 does not imply the relative probability statement in its consequent. This is partly because of the general problem of how to assign numerical values to probabilities. This in turn is partly due to the second problem, namely, the problem of understanding the particular sort of probability statement found in BR2.

Brief Interlude on Interpreting Probability

It is clear that no frequency interpretation (whether a finitist or limit theory) will do, because there is no way to reconstruct sentences *Tpst* and *Test* as sets, such as the set of times p is true of s and the set of times e is true of s. These sentences concern a 'single case' concerning time t, and so there is no relative frequency which equals the number of times both are true divided by the number of times *Test* is true.[5] No propensity inter-pretation seems any more helpful. One problem is that all propensity interpretations I have found talk of kinds of experimental arrangements and kinds of outcomes, rather than particular ones, such as it being true of s at t that he is now perceiving something that is F.[6] But another is that, even if the first problem can be avoided, it seems quite implausible to construe the relative probability in BR2 as saying that 0.5 is less than the numerical value of the strength of the dispositional tendency of a particular conjunctive state of s (namely, the state of s's believing he is now perceiving something that is F, and s's having an experience of something that is F, and s's believing with certainty that he and the relevant conditions are normal) to result in the state of s's perceiving that something is F. Surely that first, subjective state has no tendency or power to produce a state of perceiving. If it be replied that this tendency is not to produce such a state but rather to be accompanied by it, then it is unclear anything more is said than that it is probable that this state of perceiving occurs when this 'subjective' state occurs. But then, of course, we have not been provided with an interpretation of probability.

Might Carnap's logical interpretation be what we want? To answer that, I must divide it into two other questions. The first is the question of whether we should follow Carnap in his reading, or unpacking of the phrase '$\mathrm{Pr}_{s,t}(p/e)$'. The second is whether Carnap's procedure for assigning numerical values to probabilities is what we want. Regarding the first question, we have available two pairs of exclusive readings: factual versus epistemic, and objective versus subjective. The frequency and propensity interpretations are factual and objective. Carnap's reading is objective and epistemic, as is brought out by his reading of probability function, C. He says, "I read '$C(H/E)$' as 'the degree of confirmation (or briefly 'the confirmation') of H with respect to E' (or: '. . . given E')".[7] This is clearly epistemic, and it is objective because, as I understand it, a 'reading' of probability is subjective only if it entails some factual description of a subjective state of persons. I propose we follow Carnap in this reading. Thus, throughout this book we are to understand '$\mathrm{Pr}_{s,t}(p/e) = n$' as 'the degree of confirmation of p, for s at t, given e, equals n'. And '$\mathrm{Pr}_{s,t}(p) = n$' is to be read as 'the degree of confirmation of p, for s at t, equals n'.

It is far from clear that Carnap's sort of answer to the second question should be followed. For one thing, it is quite debatable whether Carnap is right to construe statements of the form of '$C(H/E) = n$' as analytic because of the definition of the mathematical function C. It is also disputable how a sentence such as *Tesp* is to be incorporated into Carnap's theory. We need not, however, debate any of this here. We need only note that I shall follow Carnap's objective epistemic reading of probability statements, and that I shall use H3 to assign certain values, and, hopefully, some kin of BR2 to provide others. In this, of course, I depart from Carnap.

Procedure for Evaluating Principles for Inferring Conditional Probabilities

I believe enough has been done to dispel the second problem for critically evaluating BR2. But we must still consider the first problem which concerns finding a procedure for making this evaluation. How are we to do this, especially without a complete set of principles for assigning probabilities, both relative and absolute? The best approach, I find, is to proceed as follows. We know from probability theorem T1, as stated in Chapter 2, that:

$$\Pr_{s,t}(p) \geqslant \Pr_{s,t}(p/q) \times \Pr_{s,t}(q).$$

Thus we can arrive at what Heidelberger sought, namely, a statement about the absolute probability of p if we have a way to find the value of $\Pr(q)$. But I have already argued in Chapter 2 that principle H3 is acceptable. Thus we can conclude that for any basic-report, b, that satisfies the antecedent of H3, $\Pr_{s,t}(Tb) = 1$. So whenever the three statements in set e meet the antecedent of H3, then individually and conjointly 'their' probabilities for s at t equal 1 (*Note* that for ease of discussion, I often talk of the probability, for s at t, of a report, when, strictly speaking, I should talk of the probability, for s at t, of the report eternalized to s at t). As a result, whenever the antecedents of both H3 and BR2 are satisfied, then $\Pr_{s,t}(Tp)$ > 0.5, *provided that* BR2 is true. Therefore, if we can find a situation where both antecedents are met but it is unreasonable to conclude that the degree of confirmation of p, for s at t, is greater than 0.5 (or, as I shall say, p is highly confirmed for s at t), then we will have reason to reject BR2. This is how we shall test BR2.

Let us assume that the antecedents of H3 and BR2 are met by certain members of s's evidence set e_1, in a particular situation:

S1.(1) $e_1 = \{b_1^1, b_2^1, b_3^1\}$, where $b_1^1 = $ 'I now believe with certainty that I am now seeing something that is yellow', $b_2^1 = $ 'I am now having a visual experience of something yellow', and $b_3^1 = $ 'I now believe with certainty that I and the conditions relevant to my seeing something to be yellow are normal';

(2) at t, s understands and believes with certainty the conjunction of b_1^1, b_2^1, and b_3^1;

(3) for all true sentences of the form '$\Pr_{s,t}(q/Trst) = n$', where 'r' is a basic-report that s understands and believes with certainty at t, the following is inductively consistent: '$\Pr_{s,t}(Te_1st) = 1$, and $\Pr_{s,t}(Trst) = 1$, and $\Pr_{s,t}(q/Trst) = n$'.

The crucial question, then, is whether we can further elaborate the situation described above in such a way that it is clearly implausible that the degree of confirmation of observation-report p_1 ('I am now perceiving something that is yellow') for s at t, is high. One obvious way to begin is by injecting into the situation that irrationally obstinate person, s, with the conveniently poor memory, who, as we saw in Chapter 4, played havoc with B2 and its kin. Does he also provide a reason to object to BR2?

Objection to Principle BR2: *Refusing to Evaluate Rationally.* Our obstinate friend causes less of a problem for BR2 than he did for B through B4. This is because in situation, S1, which allows us to derive that p_1 is highly confirmed for s at t, Tp_1 is supposed to be probable relative to a set of basic-reports that are certain for s at t, and that include not only s's belief-report, b_1^1, but also his report about his visual experience and his conviction that everything relevant to his seeing color is normal. Nevertheless, s's refusal to listen to the testimony of others, and his convenient forgetting that just a moment ago he had an experience of the object before him as white, surely seem to require that we not conclude that p_1 is highly confirmed for s at t. This becomes even clearer, if we make, as I suggest we should, the following new assumption:

A10.   If e is s's evidence for p at t, and $\Pr_{s,t}(Test) = 1$, and $\Pr_{s,t}(Tpst/Test) > 0.5$, then p is acceptable (highly credible) for s at t.

My reason for assuming A10 is that if s's evidence e satisfies the antecedent of A10, then $\Pr_{s,t}(Te) = 1$ and so it follows that $\Pr_{s,t}(Tp) > 0.5$. And, importantly, this is derivable using only $\Pr_{s,t}(Tp/Te) > 0.5$ and the probability of s's evidence at t. That is, only what is available to s at t is needed to derive $\Pr_{s,t}(Tp) > 0.5$ from $\Pr_{s,t}(Tp/Te) > 0.5$, as would not be true if $\Pr_{s,t}(Tp) > 0.5$, but $\Pr_{s,t}(Tp/Te) \times \Pr_{s,t}(Te) < 0.5$. Given A10, p_1 is acceptable for our dogmatic believer, s. And that is implausible, especially if we emphasize that s is intentionally avoiding listening to those around him, and is trying hard not to remember the details of his experience a moment ago. We should, then, reject BR2 as we did B and its relatives.

An obvious move at this point is to specify more fully what is to be in s's evidence set if we are to produce a sufficient condition for Tp_1 being highly confirmed, and, according to A10, p_1 being acceptable, for s at t. What we would like to ensure is that s be trying to do everything within his power to receive and evaluate fairly all the available evidence that is relevant to p_1's being true of him at t. Let us, then, add a fourth basic-report to s's evidence set:

> b_4^1: 'I am now trying hard to evaluate rationally, and I believe I am now evaluating rationally, all evidence (including any about the past) now available to me that is relevant to my now seeing something to be yellow, or to my present visual perceptual conditions being normal, or to my canons of evidence being reasonable'.

Then with $e_2 = \{b_1^1, b_2^1, b_3^1, b_4^1\}$ and with situation S1 amended to include b_4^1 and e_2, we have situation S2. Note that I have included in b_4^1 a clause about trying hard to use reasonable canons of evidence. I added this because a person could be quite open and rational about everything except his own, irrationally idiosyncratic canons of evidence which he refuses to reconsider. For example, such a person might obstinately consider only 'direct' testimony from God to be evidence relevant to p_1. Thus he could meet all the other requirements of situation S2, and intentionally avoid the contrary testimony of others. Once again we would have a person for whom Tp_1 would not be highly confirmed at t, and p_1 would not be acceptable at t.

Is situation S2 sufficient for p_1 being highly confirmed for s at t? There is some reason to think it is. I say this in spite of the fact that it is still possible in situation S2 that, in spite of his understanding and firmly believing that he is trying to be rational and open, s may still be blocking out relevant evidence and fooling himself about the present observation conditions and the rationality of his canons of evidence. But the point behind S2 is that it is epistemically certain for s at t that he has the relevant beliefs and experiences, and that he is trying hard to be rational in obtaining and assessing evidence and in choosing his canons of evidence. I find nothing more we can ask of him at this time. In having the relevant beliefs, and in trying to be rational, he is doing everything in his power at this time. He seems to deserve the minor epistemic honors of having Tp_1 be probable, that is, highly confirmed for him at t, and p be acceptable for him at t.

There is, nevertheless, still one way this person might be irrational. We must rule out this possibility if we are to have a sufficient condition for p_1 being highly confirmed for s at t. It is clearly possible that although s fully believes that he is trying mightily to consider everything epistemically relevant to p_1, he overlooks one of his own basic-reports, b_5, which he understandingly and fully believes, and $Pr_{s,t}(Tp_1/Tb_5) < 0.5$. Then we could not invoke H3 in situation S2 to infer that evidence e_1 is certain for s at t. Even worse, I believe, is that we should not infer that p_1 is acceptable for s at t in S2, if we find such a basic-report that fits with situation S2. So if we find one, then S2 is not sufficient for p_1 being highly confirmed. Consider one adapted from the triad we used in Chapter 2 to formulate Goodman's objection to the certainty of given-reports:

> b_5^1: I now believe I remember that the object now before me looked and was white just a moment ago, and I am now having an experience of a color that is the same color that I saw a moment ago.

I find it plausible that $Pr_{s,t}(Tp_1 Tb_5) < 0.5$, that s fully believe b_5^1 in situation S2, and that, because of this, p_1 is not highly confirmed for s at t. Consequently, we must change clause (3) in the description of situation S2 so that it also requires that '$Pr_{s,t}(Tp_1/Te_1) > 0.5$' be inductively consistent with the appropriate probabilities, including absolute probabilities of 1 for all eternalized basic-reports that s understandingly and fully believes at t. What results is S3 whose third clause is:

(3)   each of the statements: '$Pr_{s,t}(Te_1 st) = 1$', and '$Pr_{s,t}(Tp_1 st/ Te_1 st) > 0.5$', is inductively consistent with the conjunction of '$Pr_{s,t}(Trst) = 1$' and all true statements of the form '$Pr_{s,t}(q/ Trst) = n$', where 'r' is a basic-report that s understands and believes with certainty at t.

I submit that S3 is sufficient for Tp_1 being probable, that is, highly confirmed for s at t. To bolster my claim, let me point out that S3 is only said to be sufficient for Tp_1 having a degree of confirmation greater than one half for the person s at the time t. This is a very weak claim. It requires no more than that the degree of confirmation of Tp for s at t is some miniscule amount greater than that of its denial, and it is compatible with p_1 being disconfirmed for s at all times other than t. Thus this claim implies no more than that S3 gives a minute edge in confirmation to Tp_1 over its denial for one person, s, at one time, t. This extremely weak claim seems quite plausible.

Proposal for a Principle for Inferring Conditional Probabilities: BR3

We have been testing epistemic principles of the form:

$$\text{If } R, \text{ then } Pr_{s,t}(Tp/Te) > 0.5,$$

where e consists of basis-reports and p is an observation-report. We have done this indirectly for each principle by describing a situation that instantiates its antecedent and also that of principle H3. Thus if both H3 and the principle we are testing are correct, then some observation-report is probable (highly confirmed) for some person at some time, whenever one situation instantiates the antecedents of both principles. I have argued that we may accept situation S3 as sufficient for Tp_1 being highly confirmed for s at t. Consequently, we should be able to extract from S3 a general principle of the above form that is also acceptable. We can do this by doing three things: first, replacing 'yellow' in b_1^1, b_2^1, b_3^1, and b_4^1 by the variable 'F', to form sentence vaiables, b_1, b_2, b_3, and b_4; second, substituting variable, p ('I am now perceiving something that is F') for p_1; and, third, removing from S3 what is required only for the instantiation of principle H3. What results is:

BR3.   *If* (1) $e = \{b_1, b_2, b_3, b_4\}$, *where b_1 through b_4 are basic-reports, and $p = $ 'I am now perceiving something that is F'; and* (2) *for all true sentences of the form* '$Pr_{s,t}(q/Trst) = n$', *where* 'r' *is a basic-report that s understands and believes with certainty at t, the following is inductively consistent:* '$Pr_{s,t}(Tpst/Test) > 0.5$, *and* $Pr_{s,t}(Trst) = 1$, *and* $Pr_{s,t}(q/Trst) = n$', *then* $Pr_{s,t}(Tpst/Test) > 0.5$ (*that is, p being true of s at t is highly confirmed, for s at t, given that the reports in e are true of s at t*).

I claim that the preceding discussion provides reason sufficient to warrant the acceptance of BR3. It might be thought, however, that this is mistaken, because not all substituends for 'F' are observation-terms, like 'yellow'. There are other substituends, such as 'constituted ultimately of electrons and quarks' for which BR3 is quite implausible. It should be remembered, however, that a sentence of the form of b_2 ('I am now having an experience of something that is F'), is a basic-report, only if it is a given-report; and it is a given-report, only if its substituend for 'F' is either a phenomenal term ('hurting'), or an observation term ('sweet'), or a certain sort of topic-neutral term ('interesting to me'). So the restriction on substituends for 'F' in b_2 is enough to rebut this objection.

I also claim it is clear that the antecedent of BR3 is often satisfied by someone. Consider a situation where no one is anywhere near s at t, and s has no beliefs or experiences at t, except for b_1^1 through b_4^1, that are at all relevant to the probability of p_1. This is often true when, for example, someone first notices the bright yellow color of a flower when walking alone through a wood while meditating. Because there are so many of these situations, it is reasonable to conclude that for some instantiations of 'e' and 'p', some sentences of the form $Pr_{s,t}(Tp/Te) > 0.5$ are true. Consequently, there is reason to reject premise III.2 ('No nonbasic statement is probable relative to any basic-report') of skeptical argument III, when the second interpretation of 'p is probable relative to q' is used. We are, then, justified in rejecting skeptical argument III, because it is clear by now that the second interpretation (namely, $Pr(p/q) > 0.5$) is viable for a foundationalist and provides counterexamples to III.2.

PROPOSAL FOR A PRINCIPLE FOR INEFRRING ABSOLUTE PROBABILITIES: B5

The preceding discussion and the conclusions we have drawn from it raise two questions we should consider. One question is whether, after our preceding examinations of epistemic principles that embody the second interpretation of 'p is probable relative to q', we have uncovered anything new which will help us decide whether III.2 is implausible for the first interpretation. It might seem that our method of testing BR3 by considering what follows from it and principle H3 when instantiated by situation S3 provides just the sort of principle we want, namely, one of the form: if q, then p is probable for s at t. And, of course, we do get a principle of that general form, which we can abbreviate as:

B5.   If situation S3 is met for any observation-term, 'F', and $p =$ 'I am now perceiving something that is F', then $Pr_{s,t}(Tpst) > 0.5$.

But note what is required for a principle to embody the first interpretation of 'p is probable relative to q' and also refute premise III.2. Such principles, like Chisholm's first version of B, have antecedents consisting of and only of basic-reports and analytic sentences. But the final amendment made to produce clause (3) of S3 includes the clause that a certain probability statement is inductively consistent. This clause is clearly not a basic-report, and it seems not to be analytic, because it seems possible that the statement is inductively inconsistent, unless, of course, all true probability statements and the probability axioms are analytic. Then what follows from them about inductive inconsistency would also be analytic. But, contrary to Carnap, I find it very implausible that '$Pr_{s,t}(p) = n$'

means that n is the degree of confirmation of p, for s at t, and is also analytic. So I believe we could conclude that the antecedent of B5, unlike that of B but like that of B_1 through B_4, contains a clause that is neither basic nor analytic. So, even assuming that B5 is true, it provides no counterexample to premise III.2 on the first interpretation of 'p is probable relative to q'.

Conclusion About Chisholm's Critical Cognitivism

We previously found nothing like principle B, with its antecedent restricted to basic statements and analytic sentences, to be a plausible epistemic principle. We just found principle B5 to be plausible, but only after what surely seems to be neither a basic-report nor analytic was included in its antecedent. It seems quite reasonable to conclude, then, that III.2 is correct for the first interpretation of 'p is probable relative to q'. We can also conclude that there is no acceptable replacement for principle B, whith its antecedent restricted as Chisholm's critical cognitivism requires. Thus Chisholm's cognitivism should also be rejected. So if, as Chisholm seems to think, rules like B are "essential to any adequate theory of evidence",[8] then there is no adequate theory of evidence, and skepticism triumphs. Another way to reach this same unhappy conclusion is to follow Chisholm again, when he says, "It would seem reasonable to conclude, therefore, that if the indirectly evident can be made evident by what is directly evident, then there are principles of evidence other than the formal principles of deductive and inductive logic".[9] But with the demise of Chisholm's version of critical cognitivism, it might seem that none of these additional, required principles are acceptable, and so no inference from the directly evident to the indirectly evident is warranted. If all this is right, then the prospects for avoiding skepticism are dim indeed. Yet, on the brighter side, we have just seen the refutation of the strongest argument we have yet developed for skeptical thesis M_1S_1 – roughly, 'It is never reasonable (acceptable) for any human to believe that there are particular physical objects, past events, future events, and mental phenomena of others'. At this point, then, it may well seem that neither skepticism nor its denial is reasonable.

REJECTION OF THESIS M_1S_1 AND A NEW ARGUMENT FOR A NEW
THESIS

The second question we should consider arises here. Can we devise a new argument for skeptical thesis M_1S_1 that avoids all the problems for rejected arguments, I, II, and III? To answer this question, we need to note four important points. First, as argued above, there are situations in which, by BR3, it is probable for someone, s, at a time, t, that he is now seeing something that is yellow, given basic-reports, b_1^1, b_2^1, b_3^1, and b_4^1 – that is, $\text{Pr}_{s,\,t}(Tp_1st/Te_1st) > 0.5$. Second, in many of these situations the conjunction of b_1^1, b_2^1, b_3^1, and b_4^1 meets the antecedent of H3 for this person at this time. Thus $\text{Pr}_{s,\,t}(Te_1st) = 1$, and $\text{Pr}_{s,\,t}(Tp_1st) > 0.5$. Third, eternalized observation-report, Tp_1st, entails that there is something yellow that s perceives at t, and so, by probability theorem T1, it is probable (highly confirmed) for s at t that there is a yellow object which he perceived at t. Fourth, using plausible assumption A10, we can conclude that it is acceptable for s at t that there is a yellow object which he is now perceiving. This result is inconsistent with thesis M_1S_1 which entails that no such claim about a perceived object is ever acceptable for human beings. It follows that M_1S_1 is false, and so we should abandon the search for an argument to justify it. This shows that our reasons for rejecting premise III.2 are of crucial importance. They constitute the first grounds we have found for rejecting what, until now, had been the skeptical thesis which shaped our whole inquiry.

Let us not overestimate the amount of success we have achieved in refuting M_1S_1. So far we have merely found a way to show it is sometimes acceptable for someone that there is a physical object that he is perceiving. If that is the best we can do, our success is severely limited, and a skeptic is far from defeated. Indeed, it is easy to construct a new skeptical thesis and an argument for it which grant us this very limited success, but absolutely no more. This revised skeptical thesis is:

M_1S_2.   It is not (epistemically) reasonable at any time, t, for any human being, s, to believe a sentence, if it entails either (a) the existence of some particular physical object that s is not perceiving at t, or (b) the occurrence of some particular event before t, or (c) the occurrence of some particular event after t, or (d) the existence of a mental phenomenon of a being other than s, at any time.

A strong argument for thesis M_1S_2 goes somewhat as follows. Except for what is entailed by sets of acceptable basic-reports and observation-reports, no nonbasic statements are probable relative (in either sense) to any such set of reports. But, at most, these reports are initially acceptable.

Consequently, by the previous foundational principle, FP2, none of these nonentailed, nonbasic statements is ever acceptable for anyone. Thus, of nonbasic statements, only what these conjunctions entail is ever acceptable for anyone. In more detail, we can lay out this fourth skeptical argument as follows:

IV.1.   An empirical statement is initially acceptable for a human being, s, at a time, t, only if it is a basic-report or an observation-report about s at t.

IV.2.   No nonbasic statement that is not entailed by a set of basic-reports and observation-reports is probable, for s at t, relative to any set of basic-reports and observation-reports about s at t that are acceptable for s at t.

IV.3.   Principle FP2 (if all initially acceptable empirical statements are of kind K, and some empirical statement of kind L, is inferentially acceptable for s at t_1, then some empirical statement which is of kind L is probable for s at a time, t_2, relative to a set of statements of kind K, each of which is acceptable for s at t_2).

Therefore

IV.4.   No nonbasic statement that is not entailed by a set of basic-reports and observation-reports is (initially or inferentially) acceptable for s at t.

IV.5.   If IV.4 is true, then M_1S_2 is true.

Therefore

IV.6. M_1S_2 is true.

Examination of the Premises of Argument IV

I can envision a foundationalist argument against each premise of argument IV, except IV.3 which I have argued is required for any plausible foundational theory. Nevertheless, I would maintain that IV.1 and IV.5 are correct, and so a foundationalist must attack IV.2 if he is to refute this argument for skeptical thesis M_1S_2. Premise IV.5 is rather easily seen to be quite reasonable by concentrating on three points. The first is, as previously noted, the failure of analytic phenomenalism to provide any conjunction of basic-reports that entails any physical-object statement at all. The second is the equally well documented failure of analytic behaviorism to help solve the problem of other minds by producing a set of physical-object statements that entail some psychological statement, such as a belief-statement or a given-report.[10] The third point is that no observation-report (such as, $p_1 = $ 'I am now seeing something yellow') entails, by itself, anything about times other than those when it is true. These points make it quite reasonable that no conjunction of basic-reports and observation-reports that are only about one person at one time entail any statement about something not perceived by that person at that time, including those about earlier times, later times, or minds of others. Consequently, we can accept that if intermediate conclusion IV.4 is true, then skeptical thesis M_1S_2 is true, because none of the statements that M_1S_2 finds not to be acceptable is entailed by any conjunction of basic-reports and observation reports. So premise IV.5 is plausible.

It might be objected, however, that although the first two points are correct, the third is mistaken. The observation-report, 'I am now seeing something yellow' does entail something about the past and the future because it entails 'There is a yellow object now' which, in turn, entails 'There was an object a few moments ago, and there will be an object a few moments from now'. But even if we grant the first entailment, which is debatable, the second is clearly mistaken. To see this, we need only conjoin that statement with the claim that some Cartesian-like demon creates the physical world just for those instants when 'I am now seeing something yellow' is true of someone. The resulting conjunction clearly does not entail that there was or will be an object either before or after any one of those moments. Consequently, 'There is a yellow object now' does not entail this either, and this objection fails. The third point, like the first two, seems clearly acceptable.

Examination of Premise IV.1: *No Observation-Reports are Initially Acceptable.* I find premise IV.1 plausible because it is entailed by III.1 ('An empirical statement is initially acceptable, only if it is a basic-report') and, as I shall argue, III.1 is plausible. I used IV.1 instead of III.1 only because it simplifies the argument somewhat. The best way to justify III.1 is by showing that no observation-reports are initially acceptable, and if none of them are, then no other nonbasic statements are. The crucial claim is clearly the first. As definition D2 states, a statement is initially (noninferentially) acceptable for someone, s, at time, t, just in case it is acceptable for s at t and it would be acceptable for s at t even if no other statement should justify it for s at t. Thus I claim that an observation-report, p, is not initially acceptable for s at t, if 'p' would be acceptable for s at t only if some other statement should justify p for s at t.

How am I to establish that first claim? It is clearly not enough to show, as was done previously, that $\Pr_{s,t}(Tp) > 0.5$ only if $\Pr_{s,t}(Tp/Te) > 0.5$, where e consists in initially certain statements for s at t. This is because $\Pr_{s,t}(Tp) > 0.5$ only if $\Pr_{s,t}(Tp/Te) > 0.5$, whenever $\Pr_{s,t}(Te) = 1$. So if, as I have argued, certainty of e for s at t implies $\Pr_{s,t}(Te) = 1$, then, even when p is *initially* acceptable, $\Pr_{s,t}(Tp) > 0.5$ only if $\Pr_{s,t}(Tp/Te) > 0.5$, whenever e is certain for s.

On the other hand, it is too much to require me to show that there is no sufficient condition for $\Pr_{s,t}(Tp) > 0.5$ that resembles the antecedent of H3, which I have argued is sufficient for the initial certainty of basic re-ports. If I had to establish this to justify III.1, then it is clear I would fail, because, as we have seen, B5 is of such a form (that is, 'If R, then $\Pr_{s,t}(Tp) > 0.5$'), and it is quite reasonable. Furthermore, an observation-report meets the antecedent of B5 just in case it meets the antecedents of BR3 and H3, and the joint truth of the antecedents of these two principles, taken with assumption A10, implies that relevant reports are acceptable for s at t. But this does not imply the reports are initially acceptable. So, although B5 may resemble H3, which provides a sufficient condition for initial certainty, it seems clear that inferential acceptability is not excluded by B5 and other similar principles.

To justify the claim that no observation-report is initially acceptable for anyone at any time, I shall argue that observation-report, p_1 ('I am now seeing something yellow'), is not acceptable for a person at any time when that person lacks evidence that justifies p_1 for s at t. To see this, let us com-pare two situations. In the first, s is agnostic at t about every empirical statement, including all basic-reports, except given-report, b_2^1 ('I am now having a visual experience of something yellow'), because of neurotic skepticism about everything but his own present experiences. He under-stands and believes b_2^1 with certainty. In the second situation, s is equally neurotic except that, instead of b_2^1, he understandingly and fully believes p_1. These situations highlight an important difference between those two formally similar epistemic principles, B4 and H3. In the first situation, b_2^1 is acceptable, because certain, for s at t, since there are no relevant basic-reports to create inductive inconsistencies for b_2^1. In the second situation, however, even if we assume no relevant inductive inconsistencies, we cannot infer that p_1 is acceptable for s at t, because we cannot infer for some set, e, of basic-reports, such as b_1^1 through b_4^1, either that e is certain for s at t, or that $Pr_{s,t}(Tp_1 \,/\, Te) > 0.5$. And so, we cannot infer that there is some set of basic-reports which justifies p_1 for s at t. In fact, in this situation, I believe we can draw the stronger conclusion that there is no set, e, of basic-reports which justify p_1 for s at t, because, with s being agnostic about all his basic-reports, none are acceptable for him at t. And, surely, a statement, p, justifies a statement, q, for s at t, only if p is acceptable for s at t.

So far I have only argued for the claim that in the second situation no basic evidence justifies observation-report, p_1, for s at t. We also need, of course, reason to think that no nonbasic evidence does the job either. We can provide this, I believe, by assuming that no relevant nonbasic statement, other than p_1, is acceptable for s at t, because of his amnesia about all past facts and relevant generalizations and theories, his neurotic skepticism about all observation-reports except p_1, and all given-reports. In this situation, then, it is reasonable to hold that s has no evidence which justifies p_1 for s at t. Furthermore, I maintain, in this situation, and in any other where a person lacks any such justifying evidence for an observation-report such as p_1, that report is not acceptable for that person at that time. Consequently, any observation-report would be acceptable for a person, s, at a time, t, only should s have evidence other than p, to justify the report for himself at t.

A Reply to Defense of Premise IV.1: *Some Observation-Reports Are Acceptable Without Evidence.* I find that the preceding argument justifies the claim that no observation-reports are initially acceptable. There is, however, one reply to my justification we should examine before moving on. This reply states that $Pr_{s,t}(Tp_1) > 0.5$ if, in the situation described above, basic-reports b_1^1 through b_4^1 are true of s at t, even when our skeptical friend, s, does not believe these basic-reports are true. But, because he does not believe them, in this situation s has no evidence relevant to p_1. Yet p_1 is acceptable for s at t, because it is probable, that is, highly confirmed for s at t. So, according to this reply, there are situations in which p_1 is acceptable for s when not justified by his evidence. That is, p_1 is sometimes initially acceptable for someone.

The best way I have found to rebut this reply is to confront it with a dilemma. Consider, for example, the conjunction of basic-reports b_1^1 ('I now believe that I am now seeing something yellow'), and b_2^1 ('I am now having an experience of something yellow'). Surely in the envisoned situation, p_1 ('I am now seeing something yellow') is no more reasonable for s at t than this true conjunction, even though s believes p_1 but not the conjunction. So, if this true conjunction is not acceptable for s at t – as I would argue because of s's agnosticism – then p_1 is also not acceptable for s at t. But if this conjunction is acceptable for s at t, in spite of his angosticism, then in this particular situation where there is so little else relevant to p_1 for s, the conjunction is s's evidence for p_1 at t. This implies that s has some evidence for p_1 at t, contrary to what is required for the reply to succeed. Therefore, either p_1 is not acceptable for s at t in this situation and the reply fails, or s has evidence for p_1 and the reply fails. So, this reply fails, and I know of no other more likely to succeed.

I believe I have justified the premise that no observation-reports are initially acceptable. If anyone still doubts this, he should still agree that the preceding discussion has shown it to be not unreasonable that no observation-reports are initially acceptable. Given this, I shall invoke the principle that in any attempt to 'refute' a skeptical thesis, any claim that is contrary to that thesis and is not itself initially acceptable, should be rejected if the available evidence does not make it reasonable. Thus, given our task here, we should reject the claim that some observation-reports are initially acceptable.

A Second Reply to Defense of IV.1: *The Initial Acceptability of Non-Observation, Nonbasic Statements.* I claimed earlier that if no observation-reports are ever initially acceptable for anyone, then no other nonbasic statements are. So, I conclude, premise III.1 ('An empirical statement is initially acceptable, only if it is a basic-report') and, thereby, IV.1 are reasonable. A foundationalist, then, must attack premise IV.2, if he is to refute skeptical argument IV, unless I an wrong to claim that a nonbasic statement is initially acceptable only if some observation-report is.

Only two sorts of nonbasic statements have any plausibility as candidates for being initially acceptable, once it is granted that no observation-reports are initially acceptable. These are memory reports and what I shall call 'observation-entailed' statements. The latter are empirical statements that are entailed by some observation-report, but do not entail any observation-report. For example, p = 'I am now seeing a yellow object here' entails but is not entailed by q = 'There is a yellow object here now'. I find it somewhat plausible that q has greater initial credibility than p, because when I have no evidence available at all, it would seem to be more reasonable for me to bet that there is a yellow object here now, than to bet that there is a yellow object here now which I am seeing. But I find no more reason to think that q is initially acceptable for someone than that p is. I say this because it seems to me that exactly those situations that are most likely to be sufficient for p's being initially acceptable for s at t are the situations that are most likely for this to be true of q, namely, those involving some perceptual experiences or beliefs relevant to something being yellow. Thus I find it to be plausible that q is initially acceptable for s at t only if p is also. But regardless of that point, it is clear, for reasons paralleling those given above for p, that when someone has absolutely no evidence for q, other than q itself, then q is not acceptable for him at that time. So q, like p, is not initially acceptable for anyone at any time.

Let us turn to memory-reports. In line with my preceding characterizations of other sorts of reports, I shall say that a sentence is a memory-report just in case it meets one of two conditions. First, either it or its denial is transformable into a sentence of the form, 'I am now remembering ϕ'. Here, substituends for 'ϕ' include anything, whether propositional or not, that produces a meaningful sentence, such as 'the Rose Window at Chartres', and 'that I saw the Rose Window at Chartres'. Second, it is logically equivalent to a conjunction or the denial of a conjunction of reports that meet the first condition.

There are various sorts of memory-reports, but I believe only one sort has any chance of being initially acceptable if observation-reports are not. For ease of discussion I shall concentrate on propositional memory-reports, namely, any whose substituend for 'ϕ' is of the form 'that P', and shall assume that each of these entails its own substituend for 'P'. One example is 'I am now remembering that I saw a yellow object a few moments ago', which entails 'I saw a yellow object a few moments ago'. These propositional memory-reports can be divided, for our purposes, into four sorts, which I shall call 'basic memory-reports', 'observational memory-reports', 'observation-entailed memory-reports', and 'nonexperiential memory-reports'. The first sort are memory-reports constructable from sentences of the form, 'I am now remembering that P, — ago'. Here the substituends for 'P' are limited to "past basic-reports", that is, sentences which are constructed by changing the tense of a basic-report from present to past (such as, 'I had an experience of a yellow object'). And temporal phrases (such as, 'a short while' and 'ten years') are to fill in the blank. Observational memory-reports differ from basic memory-reports only in that their substituends for 'P' are observation-reports put in past tense. And observation-entailed memory-reports are those whose substituends for 'P' are observation-entailed statements made past tense, if need be. All other propositional memory-reports are nonexperiential.

On the Acceptability of Basic Memory-Reports. Of these four kinds, it seems quite clear that only basic memory-reports have any chance of being initially acceptable, given that no observation-reports are. The most likely other candidates are observational memory-reports (such as, 'I am now remembering that I saw a yellow object a few moments ago'), and observation-entailed memory-reports (such as, 'I am now remembering that there was a yellow object a few moments ago'). But because neither the corresponding observation-report ('I am now seeing a yellow object') nor the corresponding observation-entailed report ('There is a yellow object now') is initially acceptable, neither of these memory-reports is initially acceptable. This pair of memory-reports clearly is no more initially credible than the observation-report or the observation-entailed report.

A Principle for Inferring Conditional Probabilities of Basic Memory-Reports. Basic memory-reports are the only remaining candidates for non-basic statements that are initially acceptable. I think it is clearly true that some of these are sometimes acceptable. Of course, as before, this does not prove them initially acceptable. To see the parallel, let us omit b_3 of BR3; replace b_1 by b_6 ('I now believe that I am now remembering that I had an experience of an F-object a short time ago'); and transform b_4 into a corresponding b_7 (briefly: 'I am now trying hard to evaluate relevant evidence rationally and I do believe I am doing so'). Then, also using b_2 ('I am now having an experience of an F-object'), we can devise a principle much like BR3, namely:

> BR4.   *If* (1) $e = \{b_2, b_6, b_7\}$, where b_2, b_6, and b_7 are basic-reports, and $m =$ 'I am now remembering that, a short time ago, I had an experience of something that is F; and (2) for all true sentences of the form '$\Pr_{s,t}(q/Trst) = n$,' where 'r' is a basic-report that s understands and believes with certainty at t, the following is inductively consistent: '$\Pr_{s,t}(Tmst/Test) > 0.5$, and $\Pr_{s,t}(Trst) = 1$, and $\Pr_{s,t}(q/Trst) = n$', *then* $\Pr_{s,t}(Tmst/Test) > 0.5$.

And, of course, given BR4, whenever evidence, e, satisfies the antecedent of H3, then $\Pr_{s,t}(Te) = 1$, $\Pr_{s,t}(Tm) > 0.5$, and, by A10, m is acceptable for s at t. But is m initially acceptable for s at t?

Conclusion About Premise IV.1: *It is Reasonable.* I claim that m has roughly the same epistemic status for s at t as we found for p ('I am now perceiving something that is F') when we examined principles BR3 and B5. That is, when s has evidence, such as b_1 through b_4, for p, and b_2, b_6, and b_7 for m, then p and m are acceptable for s at t. So, like BR3, principle BR4 is quite plausible. But when s has no relevant evidence for either p or m, then neither p nor m is acceptable for s at that time. I think that an argument paralleling the one concerning p also succeeds for m. This is especially true, given that conservative principle I invoked before that cautions us to reject claims opposed to skepticism, unless they are initially acceptable or have been justified. We should, then, accept the claim that no basic memory-reports, and so no memory-reports of any kind, are ever initially acceptable for someone. Consequently, we can at last conclude that if no observation-reports are initially acceptable, then no other nonbasic statements are. We can conclude this, because we have eliminated the last two candidates, namely, observation-entailed statements and memory-reports. So, because we have already established that no observation-reports are ever initially acceptable for anyone, we can conclude that premise III.1 ('An empirical statement is initially acceptable, only if it is a basic-report') and, then, IV.1 are reasonable.

Rejection of Premise IV.2 *and Thesis* M_1S_2: *The High Probability of Basic Memory-Reports.* We have not been able to defeat skeptical argument IV by falsifying premise IV.1. We have, however, justified two claims which are very important for our evaluation of argument IV and skeptical thesis M_1S_2. One of these warrants the rejection of premise IV.2 ('No nonbasic statement that is not entailed by a set of basic-reports and observation-reports is probable, for s at t, relative to any set of basic-reports and observation-reports about s at t that are acceptable for s at t'). This is the claim, which we can derive from BR4 and an instantiation of its antecedent, that $\Pr_{s,t}(Tmst/Test) > 0.5$. This claim is sometimes justified, because BR4 and some instantiations of its antecedent are justified. But it follows from this that some nonbasic statements are probable relative to a set of basic-reports, in the second sense of 'p is probable relative to q'. And, for some s and t, the members of this set clearly meet the antecedent of principle H3. So $\Pr_{s,t}(Test) = 1$, from which it follows that each of the members of e is acceptable for s at t. But, as is quite clear, no memory-report, such as m, is entailed by any conjunction of basic-reports and observation-reports about the present. Therefore, for some s and t, some 'nonentailed', nonbasic statement is probable, for s at t, relative to some basic-reports that are acceptable for s at t. So premise IV.2 and thus argument IV for thesis M_1S_2, should be rejected.

The second claim falsifies skeptical thesis M_1S_2 as well. It is the claim that follows from $Pr_{s,t}(Tm/Te) > 0.5$ and $Pr_{s,t}(Te) = 1$, given assumption A10, namely, that memory-report, m, is acceptable for s at t. This claim is justified because BR4 is plausible and sometimes, for some basic-memory reports, the antecedents of both BR4 and H3 are appropriately satisfied. But such memory-reports are about past events in the relevant sense, that is, they entail that some particular event occurred before now. So, contrary to M_1S_2, it is reasonable for some human being to believe at some time that some particular past events have occurred.

A FIFTH SKEPTICAL ARGUMENT FOR A THIRD SKEPTICAL THESIS

We are forced to reject argument IV and thesis M_1S_2, because of basic memory-reports, but it is easy to revise both so that little need be conceded by a skeptic. Premises IV.2 and IV.6 can be slightly adjusted to yield the conclusion that a new skeptical thesis, M_1S_3 is true. This requires a slight retrenchment from M_1S_2, because M_1S_3 grants that basic memory-reports are sometimes acceptable for some of us. But other than that slight concession, it agrees with M_1S_2. The only change we need to make in M_1S_2 to arrive at M_1S_3 is to replace clause (b) by one concerning those particular events occurring before now that are 'nonsubjective for s'. Here, roughly, an event, e, is nonsubjective for s if and only if the sentence, 'e occurs at t', entails a sentence that is not entailed by any basic-report whether or not eternalized to s at t. The new thesis, then, is:

M_1S_3. It is not (epistemically) reasonable at any time, t, for any human being, s, to believe a sentence, if it entails either (a) the existence of some particular physical object that s is not perceiving at t, or (b) the occurrence of some particular event before t that is nonsubjective for s, or (c) the occurrence of some particular event after t, or (d) the existence of a mental phenomenon of a being other than s, at any time.

It is easy to find a skeptical argument for M_1S_3. We need only modify argument IV slightly to create V. The only changes occur in premises IV.2 and IV.5 to form V2. and V.5. Premise IV.2 becomes:

V.2 No nonbasic statement that is not entailed by a set of basic-reports, observation-reports, and basic memory-reports is probable for s at t, relative to any set of basic-reports, observation-reports, and basic memory-reports about s at t that are acceptable for s at t.

This, with V.1 (that is, IV.1) and V.3 (that is, IV.3), yields:

V.4.   No nonbasic statement that is not entailed by a set of basic-reports, observation-reports, and basic memory-reports about s at t is acceptable for s at t.

And, with V.5 ('If V.4 is true, then M_1S_3 is true') we can derive:

V.6. M_1S_3 is true.

A skeptic who rejects M_1S_2 for M_1S_3 has sacrificed very little, because what M_1S_3 allows to be acceptable for s at t beyond what is permitted by M_1S_2 are statements solely about events before t that are subjective for s. Indeed, it is likely that M_1S_3 could be tightened somewhat to limit acceptable basic memory-reports to those that concern only the very recent past. But we need not worry about this restriction, because what will concern us about argument V is independent of whether M_1S_3 is amended to embody this restriction.

Argument V escapes all the objections that we have seen refute arguments I through IV, including the last objection aimed at IV.2. And, like premise IV.1 and IV.5 of argument IV, premises V.1 and V.5 are clearly acceptable. This leaves only V.2 and V.3 (principle FP2) open to attack, and only V.2 available for refutation by a foundationalist. This might not worry a foundationalist. He might think that V.2 can easily be refuted, because it allows observation-reports to be included in the evidence relative to which 'nonentailed' sentences are probable. *But*, he might argue, we have just seen that m is probable relative to $e = \{b_2, b_6, b_7\}$, when there are no relevant inductive inconsistencies. So, instantiations of a memory-report, such as m_1 ('I am now remembering that I saw a yellow object a moment ago'), would seem to be probable relative to an evidence set e_3, that consists in: first, p_1 ('I am now seeing something yellow') as a replacement for b_2; second, a relative of b_3 about normalcy of recent observation conditions; third, a replacement for b_6 which states s's belief about what he remembers; and, fourth, a replacement for b_7 which concerns s's evaluation of relevant evidence. That is, it seems clear that $Pr_{s,t}(Tm_1/Te_3) > 0.5$, in part because observation-report, p_1, is included in e_3.

Unfortunately for this foundationalist, a skeptic can grant him the preceding conclusion without being forced to surrender V.2. Premise V.2, like IV.2, denies that a nonbasic statement such as m_1 is probable relative to a set of reports each of which is *acceptable* for s at t. Nevertheless, it might be replied that we could further describe the relevant situation so, by H3, all relevant basic-reports are certain for s at t, and, by H3 and BR3, Tp_1 is probable for s at t. If all this were true, then we would indeed have a counterexample to premise V.2. However, three things should be noted at this point. First, we do not yet have a principle, like BR3 and BR4, that warrants the inference that $\mathrm{Pr}_{s,t}(Tm_1/Te_3) > 0.5$. Second, even if we should justify such a principle, we still would not have one, like B5, that permits the inference that $\mathrm{Pr}_{s,t}(Tm_1) > 0.5$, which is, of course, what would refute M_1S_3. Third, even if we should reject V.2 for this reason, that would only cause another slight retreat by skeptics to a safer thesis, namely, one that allows some "observation memory-reports" about the very recent past to be justified. And, at the present stage of our investigation, it is quite unclear how to expand the realm of the empirically acceptable beyond that.

FOREWORD TO AN EXAMINATION OF NONFOUNDATIONAL THEORIES

Given the preceding situation, a fresh tack might well seem to be what would best serve our purposes. I propose, accordingly, that for now we stop our present procedure which consists in our repeatedly attempting to refute skeptical arguments and force a series of retrenchments upon skeptics, while refraining from questioning those two principles, FP1 and FP2, that are crucial for any plausible foundational theory. Now is perhaps a good time to see whether theories that reject these two principles might produce a complete rout of skeptics, rather than merely their step-by-step retreat. Such theories are plausible, only if they are nonfoundational. Consequently, I propose that we switch our attention to the job of un-covering some viable nonfoundational theory of empirical justification that refutes skeptical argument V and, hopefully, skeptical thesis M_1S_3 as well. This confronts us with a large task which we must complete before returning to V and M_1S_3. We must distinguish, clarify, and evaluate the most plausible forms of nonfoundationalism. My approach to this will be to characterize and contrast the minimal versions of foundationalism and nonfoundationalism, and then to delineate and critically evaluate the main species and varieties of nonfoundationalism. That is the principal burden of the next chapter.

NOTES

[1] See H. Heidelberger, 'Chisholm's Epistemic Principles', *Noûs* 3 (1969), 75–78.

[2] *Ibid.*, p. 78.

[3] See R. Firth, 'Ultimate Evidence', *The Journal of Philosophy* 53 (1956); reprinted in R. Swartz (ed.), *Perceiving, Sensing, and Knowing*, Berkeley: University of California Press, 1976, pp. 486–496.

[4] Heidelberger, *op. cit.*, p. 81.

[5] For the frequency interpretation of probability and 'single cases', see W. Salmon, *The Foundations of Scientific Inference*, Pittsburgh: University of Pittsburgh Press, 1966, pp. 90–96.

[6] For examples of propensity interpretations, see K. Popper, 'The Propensity Interpretation of Probability', *British Journal for the Philosophy of Science* 10 (1959–1960), 25–42; and J. Fetzer, "A Single Case Propensity Theory of Explanation", *Synthese* 28 (1974), 171–198.

[7] R. Carnap, 'Inductive Logic and Rational Decisions', in R. Carnap and R. Jeffrey (eds.), *Studies in Inductive Logic and Probability*, Berkeley: University of California Press, 1971, p. 25.

[8] R. Chisholm, 'On the Nature of Empirical Evidence', in R. Chisholm and R. Swartz (eds.), *Empirical Knowledge*, Englewood Cliffs, N.J.: Prentice-Hall, 1973, p. 241.

[9] R. Chisholm, *Theory of Knowledge*, 2nd ed., Englewood Cliffs, N.J.: Prentice-Hall, 1977, p. 66.

[10] For reasons to reject analytical behaviorism, see my *Materialism and Sensations*, New Haven, Conn.: Yale University Press, 1971, pp. 132–140.

PART II

AN EXAMINATION OF NONFOUNDATIONAL THEORIES

CHAPTER 6

FOUNDATIONAL VERSUS NONFOUNDATIONAL THEORIES OF JUSTIFICATION

One of the staunchest defenders of a foundational theory of the justification of empirical statements is R. M. Chisholm. His defense consists primarily in elaborating his own particular version of foundationalism, giving examples of how his theory works, and arguing that the main foundational and nonfoundational alternatives to his theory are flawed. As we saw in Chapter 4, his version, which he calls 'critical cognitivism', differs from both species of what I dubbed 'traditional foundationalism'. Although he agrees with 'Cartesian' foundationalists that there must be 'directly evident' empirical statements at the base of justification and that all these statements are roughly what I call basic-reports, Chisholm disagrees with the Cartesian requirement that justification is to be extended from the directly evident only by deductive inference. On this point, he agrees with 'Lewisean' traditional foundationalists, because both of them allow extension of justification by enumerative induction. The crucial differences between Chisholm's theory and a Lewisean theory, as I have construed it, is that only the latter allows some empirical statements which are merely initially acceptable at the foundation, and only the former allows rules of inference that are neither deductive nor inductive.

We also found in Chapter 4 that there are reasons to doubt that any of the preceding three forms of foundationalism provides the means for avoiding epistemological skepticism. Neither deduction nor induction by either enumeration or analogy warrants any extension of justification from a foundation of basic-reports. In this, we agreed with Chisholm's evaluation of his foundational opponents. However, we also found no way to amend Chisholm's crucial epistemic principle, B, so it becomes both plausible and usable as an epistemic principle in Chisholm's theory. Thus Chisholm's own theory is seriously flawed. Because of all this, by the end of Chapter 4, there was some reason to doubt that foundationalism would provide a way to avoid skepticism. However, since then we have found reason to reject skeptical thesis M_1S_1 and M_1S_2, and have come to realize that there may be unexamined versions of foundationalism which avoid all the problems that plague the three theories already discussed.

I believe that the best way to begin a search for new, viable versions of foundationalism is to characterize the minimal thesis and then examine ways to amplify it to produce its varieties. Such a characterization will also help us begin to locate the main nonfoundational alternatives, by helping us focus on what is the minimal nonfoundational theory. Once we have isolated these two minimal theses, we will be ready to see clearly where objections apply and how effective they are. As a result, not only will we be able to discover whether some form of foundationalism avoids all the preceding problems, but we will also be better able to evaluate objections to nonfoundational theories – in particular, those that Chisholm raises in defense of his own theory against what he takes to be the main versions of nonfoundationalism. And, as a side benefit, we will be able to classify more precisely the theories of various philosophers, such as Quine and Sellars, who are all too quickly described as nonfoundationalists.

CHISHOLM'S THESIS AND MINIMAL FOUNDATIONALISM

Because we have considered Chisholm as one paradigm of a foundationalist, let us begin our search for a characterization of minimal foundationalism with a view he endorses that he calls 'thesis A':

A.   Every empirical statement, which we are justified in thinking that we know, is justified in part by some empirical statement which justifies itself.[1]

To see whether thesis A adequately characterizes minimal foundationalism, we should first interpret and then unpack two phrases: 'x justifies y in part', and 'x justifies itself'. In both cases, I shall assume the phrases are to be relativized to a person and a time. For our purposes throughout this book, I shall interpret the second phrase as 'x is initially acceptable', and use that term throughout the rest of the discussion. So we can unpack the second phrase using the previous definition, D2:

D2.   Statement, p, is initially acceptable (justifies itself) for a person, s, at a time, $t =_{df.} p$ is acceptable for s at t, and it is false that p would be acceptable for s at t only if some other statement or set of statements should justify it (that is, increase its credibility enough to be acceptable) for s at t.[2]

Note, once again, that D2 is consistent with the view that a sentence is initially acceptable (self-justifying) for a person only at times when certain conditions are met. That is, D2 does not require that a sentence be initially acceptable for someone under all conditions and at all times. As we saw previously, the crucial point is whether or not some other statement is needed to justify it for the person at that time. For example, it seems plausible to claim that the report, 'I am now having a visual experience of my holding something large and heavy', is initially acceptable for s at t only if it does not conflict with any other basic-report that s believes at t, such as 'I am not now having a tactual experience of something large and heavy'.

In order to unpack 'x justifies y in part', it is important to realize that 'z justifies y' is ambiguous. It may mean that the credibility of y is high *relative to* evidence z. Here 'relative to' is itself taken as ambiguous in the two senses discussed in the last two chapters. Or it may mean that the credibility of y is high relative to z and whatever is highly credible relative to z is acceptable. I propose to limit the use of 'z justifies y' to the second 'achievement' sense, and to use 'y is justified relative to z' as short for the first, 'conditional' sense. So 'z justifies y' entails that y is acceptable, but 'y is justified relative to z' does not entail this, but only that y is acceptable relative to z. Given all this, and also that x justifies y in part only if x is a needed part of something that justifies y, we have the following:

D7. x justifies y in part (at least) for person s at time $t =_{df}$. there is evidence, e (that is, a set of statements) which justifies y for s at t, and e would not justify y if it did not contain x either as an element or as a conjunct of a statement that is logically equivalent to an element.

We are almost ready to use D2 and D7 to replace A by a more precise attempt to formulate the minimal foundational thesis. But, first, one last point. We are interested here in the minimal thesis regarding the justification and acceptability of a statement, rather than one that concerns what is required for being justified in thinking that we know the statement. The latter may well require a stronger minimal thesis than the former. So, I propose that we replace 'which we are justified in thinking that we know' in A by 'which is acceptable for s at t'. Consider, then, the following substitute for A:

F1.   Any empirical statement, p, is acceptable for s at time t, *if and only if* either p is initially acceptable for s at t; or (i) some evidence, e, justifies p for s at t, and (ii) e contains some empirical statement, x, other than p, that is initially acceptable for s at t, and e without x does not justify p for s at t.

Unfortunately, F1 states neither a necessary nor sufficient condition for any foundational theory, and so it is not the minimal thesis. There are two reasons why it is not sufficient. First, on the assumption that F1 is a material bi-conditional, it would follow from universal skepticism about justification. But skepticism should not be allowed to imply the minimal thesis. Second, F1 allows some statement to be justified, and so acceptable, for someone without any recourse to initially acceptable statements. According to F1, a person need only have available *some* set of evidence for p that requires him to rely on an initially acceptable statement when using that set. But he need not use it to justify p. Such a situation is inconsistent with every foundational theory, because each one requires a person to have recourse to some initially acceptable statement at some stage of his justification. Let us replace F1 by:

F2.   Any empirical statement, p, would be acceptable for s at time t, *if any only if* it would be true that: either p is initially acceptable for s at t; or (i) some evidence, e, justifies p for s at t; and (ii) any evidence, e, that justifies p for s at t contains some empirical statement, x, other than p, that is initially acceptable for s at t, and e without x does not justify p for s at t.

Thesis F2 is stronger than F1, and, I believe, all theories that meet F2 are foundational. But I find that, like F1, some theories that fail to meet F2 are also foundational. Thus it is not the minimal view. The problem is that F2 requires that *every* set of statements, e, which justifies p for s, contains an initially acceptable statement. But there can be series of sets of statements, e_1 through e_n, where each e_i in the series justifies e_{i-1}, but only e_1 justifies p. Any foundational theory should require that *some* e_i in such a chain of justification for p contains an initially acceptable statement, but it need not require that e_1, the set that justifies p, contains such a statement.

To amend F2 appropriately, let us use the concept of "evidential series" characterized as follows:

D8. E is an evidential series (E-series) for $p =_{df}$. E is a series of evidence sets, $e_1, e_2, e_3, \ldots$, such that for each e_i in E and $e_0 = p$, each sentence in e_{i-1} is justified relative to e_i (or, in brief, e_{i-1} is justified relative to e_i).

In other words, any such chain of justifiers, from e_1 to some first justifier or *ad infinitum*, is an E-series for p. And we can use this notion of an E-series to define two other terms that we shall need later. The first one is:

D9. x is an evidential parent (E-parent) of y in E-series E for $p =_{df}$. y is either p or is in some evidence set e_i in E; x is in set e_{i+1}; and y would not be justified relative to e_{i+1}, if e_{i+1} were not to contain x either as a member or as a conjunct of a statement that is logically equivalent to a member of e_{i+1}.

And the second is:

D10. x is an evidential ancestor (E-ancestor) of y in E-series, E, for $p =_{df}$. y is either p or is in a set e_i in E; and there is an E-series, E', for y that is a subseries of E (that is, in E', e'_1 is a subset of e_{i+1}, e'_2 is a subset of e_{i+2}, and so on), such that in B', each member of an e'_j is an E-parent either of p or of a member of e'_{j-1}, and x is in some set in E'.

That is, roughly, y is either p or is in E-series, E, for p, and y would not be justified in E if x was not contained in some later evidence set in E. We can now amend F2 to give us the following replacement:

F3.   Any empirical statement, p, would be acceptable for s at time t, *if and only if* it would be true that: either p is initially acceptable for s at t; or (i) there is an E-series for p that justifies p for s at t, and (ii) each E-series that justifies p for s at t contains some empirical E-ancestor of p that is initially acceptable for s at t.

I believe that F3, which is entailed by F2, but which entails neither F1 nor F2 is minimal, that is, all and only theories that satisfy it are foundational. Of course F3 is not sufficient for many species of foundational theory. As we have seen, both the Cartesian and Lewisean forms of traditional foundationalism require that, of empirical statements, at most basic-reports and memory reports are initially acceptable. These theories, and also Chisholm's critical cognitivism, imply but are not implied by F3. It should be noted, however, that F3 is not sufficient for the minimal *plausible* form of foundationalism, because it allows implausible sorts of justification. Once these are ruled out, then, as will be shown in Chapter 7, we shall need to conjoin F3 with principles FP1 and FP2 to arrive at the minimal plausible theory.

THE MINIMAL NONFOUNDATIONAL THEORY

The basic opponent of foundational theories is often called the coherence theory of justification. But I think it better to view the coherence theory as just one of many nonfoundational theories, rather than its minimal version. We can, however, use what Firth calls "the heart of the coherence theory of justification" to help uncover an adequate characterization of the minimal thesis. Firth construes its 'heart' as follows:

C1. *Ultimately* every sentence that has some degree of warrant for me has that particular degree of warrant because, and only because, it is related by valid principles of inference to (that is to say "coheres with") certain other statements.[3]

Compare C1 with what Lehrer proposes as a "schema for a coherence theory of justification":

C2. S is completely justified in believing that p if and only if the belief that p coheres with other beliefs belonging to a system of beliefs of kind k.[4]

Schema C2 is considerably weaker than C1, because C2 allows some degree of warrant to result from initially acceptable beliefs (statements). In this respect, C2 is to be preferred to C1 as a candidate for the minimal non-foundational theory which should require no more than that no initially acceptable statements (beliefs) are *needed* for justification, so that it does not matter whether there are any initially acceptable statements (beliefs). However, C2 is too weak, because by not restricting kind k in any way, C2 allows its values to be systems that include initially acceptable beliefs. Let us, then, amend C2 so it excludes all initially acceptable beliefs from the system of beliefs of kind k. I shall call the result C2a. A theory that instantiates it is a coherence theory, but some nonfoundational thesis need not instantiate it, as we shall see.

The minimal thesis should agree with C1 and C2a at least to the extent that it applies to every statement that is not initially acceptable (that is, let us say, an 'initially nonacceptable' statement). And this thesis should imply that no justified, nonacceptable statements require justification by an initially acceptable statement. Let us try then:

N. Any empirical statement, p, that is not initially acceptable for s at t would be acceptable for s at t, *if and only if* it would be true that there is an E-series for p that: (1) justifies p for *s* at *t*; and (2) contains no empirical statement that is initially acceptable for *s* at *t*.

Thesis N differs from C1 in two important ways. It allows there to be initially acceptable statements, and it allows them to justify other statements. It only requires that none of them are needed to justify initially nonacceptable statements. N differs from C2a in considering statements rather than beliefs, and in partly specifying coherence in terms of E-series.

I believe that, as accords with N, the minimal thesis should allow there to be initially acceptable statements, but it may be objected that it should not allow them to justify other statements. It might seem, then, that we should add to the right-hand side of N that *none* of *s*'s E-series contain any empirical statement that is initially acceptable for *s* and that justifies *p* in part for *s*. Nevertheless, I propose N as the minimal theory, because any theory stating that every justified empirical statement is justifiable without any initially acceptable statements (so it does not matter whether there are any initially acceptable statements) would be a nonfoundational theory. If so, then the minimal thesis should be no stronger than N. But it surely should be no weaker than N. And N, the minimal thesis, conflicts with the minimal foundational thesis, F3, in the sense that either N or F3 is false if some initially nonacceptable empirical statement is justified.

OBJECTIONS TO NONFOUNDATIONAL THEORIES

With it settled that N is the basic alternative to F3, we can turn to objections to nonfoundational theories. The best place to begin, I find, is with Chisholm's attempt to show that the main nonfoundational alternatives to his thesis A should be rejected. I shall reconstruct his procedure as an attack on the chief varieties of N. There are two species of N: first, each acceptable, initially nonacceptable statement is justified by an E-series containing only acceptable E-ancestors but no initially acceptable statement; and, second, each of these is justified by some series containing an E-ancestor that is not acceptable, and, perhaps, even unacceptable in the sense that its denial is acceptable. But we can ignore E-series with such unacceptable statements, because no series requiring an unacceptable statement justifies anything.

The first species allows two important varieties. According to Chisholm, one would not permit any statement in the relevant E-series for *p* to be partly justified by *p*, and the other would allow some of these statements to be partly justified by p. The first is supposed to lead to an infinite regress and the second to a circularity.[5] As stated, however, the first does not guarantee an infinite regress. According to it, each acceptable, initially nonacceptable statement, p, requires a series, E, of acceptable, initially nonacceptable statements, excluding p. Thus each statement in any set in series E must in turn be justified by a set of acceptable, initially nonacceptable statements that does not contain p. But this does not generate an infinite regress. Assume that p is justified by e_1, containing statements, q_1, q_2, q_3, which are initially nonacceptable statements that are different from p. Assume also that q_1 justifies q_2, q_2 justifies q_3, and q_3 justifies q_1. So let e_2 also contain q_1, q_2, and q_3. We can imagine a theory that allows such an E-series to justify p for s at t, on the grounds that p and each statement in the E-series is justified relative to some statement other than itself. Here is a case that satisfies the first thesis without an infinite regress. Of course, it is bothersome that q_1, q_2, and q_3 each help justify themselves, but that is allowed by this statement of the first variety of the first species. In other words, this version allows a certain sort of circularity which might better be included in the second variety. Consequently, to rule out any sort of circularity and to guarantee an infinite regress, the first variety should be stated so that it requires of any statement in the relevant E-series for p that it have an E-ancestor in that series. Then the second would not require this.

THREE VARIETIES OF NONFOUNDATIONALISM

We have three main varieties of N. First:

N1.   Any empirical statement, p, that is not initially acceptable for s at t would be acceptable for s at t, *if and only if* it would be true that there is an E-series, E, that: (1) justifies p for s at t; (2) contains no empirical statement that is initially acceptable for s at t; (3) contains only E-ancestors of p that are acceptable for s at t; and (4) contains an empirical statement only if it contains an E-ancestor of the statement that is not analytically equivalent to the statement.

Second:

N2.   Any empirical statement, p, that is not initially acceptable for s at t would be acceptable for s at t, *if and only if* it would be true that there is an E-series, E, that: (1) justifies p for s at t;

(2) contains no empirical statement that is initially acceptable for *s* at *t*; (3) contains only E-ancestors of *p* that are acceptable for *s* at *t*; and (4) contains some empirical statement without containing any E-ancestor of the statement that is not analytically equivalent to the statement.

Third:

N3.   Any empirical statement, *p*, that is not initially acceptable for *s* at *t* would be acceptable for *s* at *t*, *if and only if* it would be true that there is an E-series, *E*, that: (1) justifies *p* for *s* at *t*; (2) contains no empirical statement that is initially acceptable for *s* at *t*; and (3) contains some E-ancestor of *p* that is not acceptable for *s* at *t*.

We can reconstruct Chisholm's reasons for rejecting the main alternative to his A as reasons to reject the three preceding theses. That is, he would reject N1 because it leads to an unacceptable infinite regress of justification. He notes that this can be avioded by making 'blind posits' or guesses. But to do this is to desert N1 for N3, which he would reject because it fails to distinguish "between knowledge, on the one hand, and a lucky guess, on the other".[6] Finally, it seems he would reject N2 because it requires circular justification.[7]

An Objection to the First Variety: Justification and Infinitely Long E-*Series*

It is clear that N1 requires an infinitely long series of E-ancestors for every acceptable, initially nonacceptable empirical statement. It also seems at first that, as Chisholm would claim, the regress is vicious in the sense that whatever requires such a regress is unacceptable. Recently, however, Aune has argued that the required regress is not vicious, because only an unreasonable thesis about justification would make it vicious. As applied to N1, this thesis would be:

A series of E-ancestors of *p* justifies *p* for *s* at *t only if s* actually justifies, individually, every statement in the series that is not initially acceptable for *s* at *t*.[8]

Contrast this with the thesis that requires only that *s* be *able* to justify, individually, any such statement in the series. The first thesis, conjoined with N1, leads to a vicious regress, because it assigns an impossible task to *s*. But the second thesis requires of *s* neither an impossible nor even an

implausible task. He must merely be able to justify any particular statement in the series. He need not, then, either be able to justify or actually justify individually the whole set of statements in the series. Thus, according to Aune, the regress is not vicious, if, as he maintains, the first
thesis about justification can be rejected for one no stronger than the
second.

I agree with Aune in rejecting the first thesis. No more should be required of s than what the second thesis states. Furthermore, assuming induction, it seems plausible that if s actually justifies a significant sample
of E-ancestors of p by other statements, and he does so in a way that
gives reason to conclude he is able to justify noncircularly any one in the
series by another, then it is reasonable to conclude that each statement in
the series is justified relative to another, and that s is able to show this for
any particular one of them. However, finding the infinite series of N1
innocent of viciousness does not solve the main problem confronting N1,
namely, it seems either that it allows infinite E-series to justify some
statements which should not be justified, or it provides no way to justify
some statements that should be justified by some E-series.

For any statement, we can generate in infinite E-series in which each
statement is justified relative to another, and which meets requirements (2)
and (4) of N1. For any set, e_i, in the series we can easily formulate another
set, e_{i+1}, such that e_i is justified *relative to* e_{i+1}. Consider any singular
statement 'Pa', where a is not a number. This statement is justified for
s at t relative to $e_1 = \{Q_1a, (x)(Q_1x \supset Px)\}$. Then the statements in e_1 are
justified relative to $e_2 = \{Q_2a, (x)(Q_2x \supset Q_1x), (x)[(Q_2a \cdot Q_1x) \supset Px]\}$.
And those in e_2 are justified relative to $e_3 = \{Q_3a, (x)(Q_3x \supset Q_2x),
(x)[(Q_3a \cdot Q_2x) \supset Q_1x], (x)[(Q_3a \cdot Q_2a \cdot Q_1x) \supset Px]\}$. This series, E_1, goes
on to infinity, because we have an infinite number of predicates of the form
Q_ix. For example, we can let $Q_ix =$ 'x is either not a number or is greater
than the number i'. This series contains no statement that is its own E-
ancestor, and, we can assume, it contains no initially acceptable statements. Thus three claims are true of E_1: first, it meets requirement (2) of
N1; second, it meets requirement (4); and, third, p, and each statement in
E_1, is justified relative to something else. Consequently, if N1 were to allow
the second and third of these three claims to be sufficient for its conditions
(3) and, as a result, (1), then, by N1, Pa is justified for s at t. But should
Pa be justified in this way? To see the problem E_1 raises for N1, consider
the requirement:

R1.   A theory of justification is acceptable only if it does not yield that some sentence and its denial are acceptable for the same person at the same time.

If a theory violates what R1 requires of acceptable theories, then it yields that some sentence and its denial are both acceptable. Thus each would be more reasonable than its denial. But this implies that each of these is also less reasonable than its denial, because each is the denial of the other. So a theory that violates R1 should be rejected.

The main problem for N1 is that if it allows the two preceding claims to be sufficient for its conditions (1) and (3), then N1 violates R1. Consider Pa and its denial, $\sim Pa$. We can construct an infinite E-series, E_2, for Pa just by substituting $\sim Px$ for Px throughout E_1. Thus, contrary to what R1 requires, both Pa and $\sim Pa$ would be more reasonable than their denials for s at t, if the two preceding claims are sufficient for the justification of p. Of course, the problem would be avoided if we could find some third claim to conjoin with the first two to form a sufficient condition for the justification of p. What might it be? Might it restrict s to the use of just one of each pair of E-series like E_1 and E_2? But it should not merely allow s to choose whichever E-series he wants. This would permit him to justify any contingent, empirical statement merely by substituting appropriately in the sentences in the evidence sets of E_1. This would be clearly unacceptable, because it violates a second restriction:

R2.   A theory of empirical justification is acceptable only if it does not provide a way to justify any contingent, empirical statement for any person at any time.

Because of requirement R2, any plausible version of N1 must require that the two preceding claims are sufficient for the justification of p, only when they are conjoined with some third clause. But what might this clause be? Obviously, an N1-theorist cannot rely either on uncovering the presence of initially acceptable statements in justifying E-series, or on making blind posits of statements in the E-series he desires to justify some statements. And there seems to be no plausible coherence feature that would be found only in certain of the infinite E-series that meet conditions (2) and (4), and contain only statements that are justified relative to something else. However, someone might require, in accordance with R2, that an E-series does not justify a statement, p, if there is no reason to pick that series instead of its analogue that would justify the denial of p. That is, he might propose N1.1, a version of N1 that conjoins the following sufficient condition for justification with the four clauses of N1:

(5) E justifies p and each E-ancestor of p in E, for s at t, if (a) E contains no empirical statement that is p or its own E-ancestors in E, (b) p and each E-ancestor of p in E are justified relative to some other statement in E, and (c) there is some reason to choose series E rather than its analogue that justifies the denial of p.

But then, I suggest, we shall find that, according to theory N1.1, few, if any, statements have justifying E-series, because few E-series meet all five requirements of theory N1.1.

Because of these problems for N1 and its various versions, I conclude that N1 allows either too many or too few statements to be justified – depending on what it requires as sufficient for an E-series to justify p for s at t. As a result, we should reject the sort of justification N1 requires – at least until someone proposes a viable emendation.

Objection to a Second Variety: Blind Posits and Justification

With N1 in doubt, two sorts of theses that avoid foundationalism remain to be considered. If Chisholm is right, that sort which allows some justifying statements not to be acceptable, that is, N3, should be rejected because it involves 'blind posits' and so fails to distinguish between knowledge and lucky guesses. It is not clear, however, that this criticism is accurate when directed at N3. It is true that if N3 is correct, then each statement, p, that is justified for someone, s, rests in part on at least one statement that is a 'mere guess', in the sense that it is no more reasonable for s than its denial. But this does not show that s has no evidence at all for p, as would be true if s were merely guessing about the truth of p. Thesis N3 allows some evidence and reasoning for and against p. It merely requires that some E-ancestor of p be not acceptable. Of course, if circular justification and infinite E-series are prohibited, then, sooner or later, some E-series for p ends with a final set of statements, none of which are acceptable. But N3 by itself does not require this.

The crucial question for N3 is not whether some statement that is acceptable according to N3 is a mere guess or blind posit, but whether any statement, q, that is not acceptable for s is an E-parent of a statement, r, that is an E-ancestor of p in an E-series that justifies p for s. When the question is put this way, it seems that the answer is negative, and N3 should be rejected. When we consider q merely as one of many remote E-ancestors of p, it is not clear that q's not being acceptable has any ill effects on the acceptability of p. But this impression changes once we realize that to be one of many remote E-ancestors of p is to be, probably, one of only a few E-parents of r. And that raises the question of whether any statement can be justified by a set of statements containing and requiring a statement such as q.

Consider the following argument about such a q and r, which are remote ancestors of p. For r, in a set e_i of E-series E for p, to be justified for a person, s, by a set, e_{i+1}, of its E-parents, the relationship of r to the members of e_{i+1} is, as we have seen, one of two kinds: either that of conclusion to premises, or that of a statement that is acceptable, given the evidence. If the relationship is the first sort, then r is a conclusion that is inferred, either deductively or inductively, from several premises, one of which, q, is required but is not acceptable for s. But a minimum requirement for an argument to justify its conclusion is that each of its premises is acceptable, and so no set of premises that requires q justifies r for s. Therefore, nothing in series E justifies r, set e_i does not justify set e_{i-1}, and, finally set e_1 does not justify p. Consequently, no series of arguments which contains such a q as a remote ancestor of p is an E-series that justifies p.

On the other hand, if such a q is considered to be contained in a set, e_{i+1}, of s's evidence, given which this r is acceptable – that is, $Cr_{s,t}(r/e_{i+1}) > 0.5$, the question arises about what else, if anything, is needed for r to be justified for s by the set e_{i+1}. Some people require that the probability of the conjunction, c, of the members of the set e_{i+1} be 1, but I think that, although this is sufficient, it is not necessary. Yet, surely, at minimum this conjunction must be acceptable for s at t – that is, $Cr_{s,t}(c) > 0.5$. Nothing is justified for someone by evidence, even if its credibility for him, given that evidence, is very high, if the evidence itself is not acceptable for him. But an evidence set is acceptable for s at t only if the conjunction of the members of the set is. And no conjunction of statements is acceptable if one of its conjuncts is not acceptable. So, since e_{i+1} contains q, which is not acceptable for s at t, then e_{i+1} is not acceptable for s at t and does not justify r for s at t. This can be established more precisely if we assume, as I propose we should, that credibility functions obey the axioms of the probability calculus. Let c be the conjunction of statements, $f_1, f_2, ..., f_m$, that are the members of e_{i+1}. Then $\mathrm{Cr}_{s,\,t}(c) = \mathrm{Cr}_{s,\,t}(f_1 \cdot f_2 \cdots f_m)$. And the following is true of any credibility function that obeys the probability axioms:

$$\mathrm{Cr}(c) = \mathrm{Cr}(f_1) \times \mathrm{Cr}(f_2/f_1) \times \mathrm{Cr}(f_3/f_1 \cdot f_2) \times \ldots$$
$$\times \mathrm{Cr}(f_m/f_1 \cdot f_2 \ldots f_{m-1}).$$

But, letting $q = f_1$, it follows that $\mathrm{Cr}_{s,\,t}(c) \leqslant 0.5$, because q is not acceptable for s at t. Thus, again, e_{i+1} does not justify r for s at t, and r is not acceptable for s at t. But then e_i, which requires r, does not justify e_{i-1} in either of the two preceding ways. Consequently, for each relationship that a statement has to a set of its E-parents that justify it, every member of that parental set is acceptable for s. But if every E-parent of each set of E-ancestors of a justified statement must be acceptable, then, contrary to N3, no E-series for any statement contains one of its E-ancestors that is not acceptable. Thus, N3, like N1, should be rejected.

Reply to Objection: A Subjectivist Theory of Justification. Although the preceding objection to N3 may seem convincing, there is a reply to it that should be considered. It states that there is a subjectivist theory of justification that is a species of N3 and also avoids this objection. Let us consider the theory proposed by Lehrer as a prime example of such a theory. It is subjectivistic because it states that what justifies a statement p for s at t is its relationship to a certain set of statements, each of which concerns only what s believes at t, but none of which are acceptable for s at t. In effect, it is s's having certain sentences of the form 's believes that x' (that is, belief-statements) true of him, rather than acceptable for him, that justifies p for him. According to Lehrer, the set of all belief-statements that are true of s is what he calls the 'doxastic system' of s. However, often "a man may believe things because of the comfort it gives him, because of greed, because of hate, and so forth".[9] This leads Lehrer to say it is not a person's doxastic system that is relevant to justification, but rather his "corrected" doxastic system, that is, "that subset of the doxastic system resulting when every statement is deleted which describes s as believing something he would cease to believe as an impartial and disinterested truth-seeker".[10] Given these definitions, we can put Lehrer's theory as follows:

S1 p is completely justified for s *if and only if B*, the corrected doxastic system of s, justifies p for s, that is:

(1) B and the set of statements believed by s, according to B, are each consistent;

(2) B contains the statement that s believes that p is more likely to be true than its denial; and

(3) for any statement, r, such that r competes with p within B (that is, such that B contains the statement that s believes r has 'strong negative relevance' to p), B also contains the statement that s believes that p is more likely to be true than r.[11]

S1 contains only one phrase that needs elucidation, namely, 'strong negative relevance'. But because its definition is so complex and because we need only an intuitive grasp of it for our purposes here, I shall say only that Lehrer unpacks it primarily in terms of negative relevance, where p has negative relevance to q just in case q "has a lower chance of being true on the assumption that p is true than otherwise".[12]

Lehrer claims his theory is a coherence theory because it satisfies what I have labeled C2. But we have found C2 to be too weak for the minimal nonfoundational view, and, *a fortiori*, too weak for the minimal coherence theory. Indeed, we can see that S1 is a species of N3, rather than N2, and so, as we shall see, it is not a coherence theory by my classification. S1 is a species of N3, because S1 permits a statement to be justified for someone by a certain set of belief-statements, even if they are not acceptable for him. Only N3 allows this. Of course, it might be suggested that this raises no problem for S1 because it is easy to show when a belief-statement about s is acceptable for s. It is acceptable for s if he believes that it is true. But as stated, S1 does not allow such grounds for acceptability, and if it is amended to allow belief-statements this unique status, they would be initially acceptable, and the resulting theory would be foundational. This can be avoided, however, by amending S1 so that any of s's belief-statements of the form 's believes that p' is justified by being in s's corrected doxastic system. This would make S1 a species of N2, and, furthermore, a coherence theory.

Lehrer could also make his theory a coherence theory by taking S1's conjunction of (1), (2), and (3) to be in disjunction with the thesis that the statement 's believes that p' is acceptable if it is a redundant member of a subset of B relative to which some statement is justified for s. Thus if q is justified for s, then so also would be statements of the form: 's believes that q is more likely to be true than r'. But it might be objected that no

statement is justified merely by being a nonredundant part of a set
that has a justificatory relationship to another statement. It might be replied, however, that if the thesis that some statements are justified relative
to such sets can be made plausible, then it may also be acceptable to claim
that this fact also justifies the justifying statements. Let us not debate this,
however, because the crucial point is whether it is reasonable to suppose
that J, the appropriate justifying subset of B according to S1, does justify
p for s, even assuming that the statements in J are justified in some way or
other. Indeed, let us assume for the moment that, contrary to subjectivism,
the statements of J are justified independently of their relationship to p.
Then, let us use this helpful assumption to uncover whether S1 provides
either a necessary or sufficient condition for the justification of p.

Problems for Lehrer's Subjectivist Theory. One objection to S1 as providing
a necessary condition for justification concerns clause (3). Assume that
$p = $ 'I see a red chair', and $r = $ 'I sometimes, but very rarely, hallucinate'.
Then r has negative relevance to p, because p is slightly less likely to be
true, given r, than otherwise. And it also seems that r has strong negative
relevance to p. Regardless of that, however, we can suppose that s believes
that r has strong negative relevance to p, because he believes that r makes
p slightly less likely than otherwise. Furthermore, s believes that r is more
likely to be true than p. According to S1, p is not completely justified for
s. But, given s's evidence other than r, p might be so very likely to be true,
that the little its chances of being true are decreased relative to r would not
stop p from being completely justified for s. And this seems true especially
if s realizes all this, and even if r is certain for s. A subjectivist might try to
avoid this objection by redefining 'negative relevance' so it requires p to
have a *significantly* lower chance of being true, relative to r, than otherwise.
However, this might destroy S1 as a sufficient condition for justification.
In some cases it might be that, as s believes, r_1 through r_n each lower p's
chance of being true only slightly. But, contrary to what s believes, p is
very unlikely given their conjunction. Thus the revised S1 would be met,
but it seems that p should not be completely justified for s. Of course,
there may be a better way to avoid this objection, and so, although I have
found none, I do not wish to take this objection to be conclusive.

There are, however, two decisive objections to the subjectivist view that
S1 provides a sufficient condition for justification. One concerns how the
set of statements that s believes to have strong negative relevance to p
might be limited so that p is an easy winner over its competitors. The sec-

ond concerns a person who is so strongly attached to p that no matter what he believes competes with p, he never believes that it is as likely to be true as p. In many cases of both sorts, it seems clear that p is not justified for the person when S1 is met for him, even if all his relevant belief-statements are justified for him.

Lehrer considers the first objection when he asks us to "imagine a man seeking to have a completely justified belief that God exists, bringing himself to a state of mind in which he believes that God exists, believes that this statement has a better chance of being true than its denial, and believes nothing else".[13] Lehrer denies that belief in God is justified for this person, because "a person who seeks after truth in a disinterested and impartial manner would not arbitrarily restrict his beliefs in this way."[14] But why would such a truth-seeker not do this? There need be nothing biased or partial about such a restriction. It might be that the person sincerely believes that God is the source of all truth and wisdom, and he wishes to restrict his beliefs to those about God before expanding them so that he is guided by God toward truth. Is this partial or biased? It seems not. But even if it is, how is a subjectivist to show this? A thesis like S1 surely will not help. Furthermore, the example does not require that the person actively strives to limit his beliefs. He may just find they are limited in spite of himself. In such a case, it seems that his doxastic system might well also be his corrected doxastic system. But, again, contrary to S1, this hardly is sufficient to justify his belief in God.

Lehrer does not consider the second problem. A fanatical believer in some deity, no matter how bizarre, can believe there is a wide variety of competitors for his belief, yet by S1 still be clearly justified in his belief merely because he is so firmly convinced that none of these competitors is as likely to be true as his belief that this god exists. Again, there seems to be no way for a subjectivist to show that in every such case the person is partial or biased. Thus, sometimes, a strong enough belief in a deity would, by S1, guarantee the person justification for his belief. But that is surely mistaken. Consequently, for two reasons, S1 is too weak as a sufficient condition for justification for a person, even if all his relevant belief-statements are justified for him. So S1 fails whether it remains a species of N3, or whether it is amended so it becomes foundational, or requires infinitely long E-series, or is a coherence theory.

Conclusion About Subjectivist Theories. I believe that S1's problems are typical for subjectivist theories, because all of them take certain unjustified beliefs or personal preferences and certain relationships among strengths or relative strengths of these beliefs or preferences to be sufficient for justification. But, for reasons like those given above, all such theories – even those that require 'strict coherence' among someone's beliefs – are too weak. Many of them are also too strong because they require relationships among beliefs – such as 'strict coherence' – that, as I previously argued, are not needed for some particular statement or belief to be justified for someone. We should, then, reject subjectivist theories of justification.

I can find just one reply for a subjectivist, namely, that, as Lehrer has tried to show, the two prime rivals of subjectivism – a foundational theory and an explanatory coherence theory – are even less plausible, and so we should adopt a subjectivist theory. I would argue, however, that if some subjectivist theory is more plausible than these two opponents, then, because it is so implausible, we should choose skepticism regarding the justification of empirical statements. But before embracing skepticism, we should consider whether or not either of these rivals provides a plausible alternative to it.

Objections to the Third Variety: Coherence and Justification

I think that few nonfoundationalists would mourn the demise of N1 and N3, because most of them probably subscribe to some sort of coherence theory of justification, and this requires N2. Indeed, I think any appeal N3 might have for a nonfoundationalist would disappear once three points are realized. First, a nonfoundationalist need not turn to N3 to avoid the claim that the justification for s of a statement, p, at t by a set of statements requires that each statement in the set be acceptable for s *before t*. This can also be avoided by N2 for coherence theories of justification that allow p and the posited set to become acceptable for s as a group at the same time. Second, N2 does not require, as N3 does, that every acceptable statement, p, must have some E-series containing a 'blind posit' that is not justified by anything – not even indirectly by its effectiveness in explanation. Third, as noted in Chapter 4 when discussing hypothetical induction, there is some reason to think that there is such indirect justification, and so there seems to be no reason to require blind posits that are never justified. It may be that, as coherence theories allow, they become justified by certain of their relationships to other statements.

Theories which are varieties of N2 are often associated with coherence theories of truth, and often rejected because they require a circularity of justification.[15] But it would be a mistake to think that a coherence theory of justification has important implications for theories of truth, or conversely, and it is clearly debatable whether the required circularity is vicious, that is, whether any theory implying it should be rejected. Consider, for example, what I take to be the minimal coherence theory of justification:

N2.1.   Any empirical statement, p, that is not initially acceptable for s at t would be acceptable for s at t, *if and only if* it would be true that there is an E-series E, such that: (a) clauses (1) (2), (3), and (4) of N2 are true of E; and (b) for p and every statement in E-series, E, either they are justified for s at t by being in a justifying set of statements, J, for s at t, or they are justified by the set J, for s at t.

Like N1 and N3, N2.1 allows foundational sorts of justification, but it requires there to be a coherence justification for every acceptable, initially nonacceptable statement. It is also compatible with a variety of theories of truth, including what is rather vaguely dubbed the 'correspondence' theory. Our concern with N2.1 however, is to discover whether to reject it. If it should be rejected, then we have reason for dismissing N2, because, I find, N2.1 is its most plausible variety.

An Explanatory Coherence Theory of Justification. One way to approach the problem of evaluating N2.1 is to find a clear example of a coherence theory, and use it as a paradigm case. Although there have been few attempts to formulate such theories clearly, it is fortunate that Lehrer has recently provided a statement of such a theory, which he later rejects for his own subjectivist theory which we have already dismissed. It is an explanatory coherence theory (EC-theory), which he and many others attribute to Sellars and Quine. For our present purposes, we can use a version that is simpler than the one Lehrer considers. It uses the following principle to determine whether or not a set is a justifying set (that is, set of statements that justifies other statements) for N2.1:

EC.   The set J is a justifying set for s at t, *if and only if* the members of J are:
       (1) the nonredundant explaining members of some system of statements, C, that has maximum explanatory coherence among those systems understood by s at t (that is, let us say here, C, is a 'maximal' system for s at t); and
       (2) the statements explained by C.[16]

Crucial to EC is the notion of maximum explanatory coherence which, for our present purposes, we can define in much the way Lehrer does:[17]

D11.   System C has maximum explanatory coherence among the set of systems, $B =_{df}$. (1) C is in set B; (2) C is consistent; and (3) for any system, x, in B, if x is consistent but conflicts with C, then (a) C explains at least as much as x, and (b) it is false that x explains at least as much as C and also explains more things better than C does.

Even with definition D11, much remains unclear about maximum explanatory coherence. One problem is to determine conditions for when one system explains better than another, but let us ignore that problem except for noting two points. First, as used here, 'x explains y' does not imply that either x or y is true, and truth is not a test for deciding which of two systems explains better. Second, what can be called 'nonevidential' or 'systemic' tests are relevant to how well a system explains. Following Quine, we can list some candidates for such tests as refutability, simplicity, familiarity of principle, scope ("implies a wider array of testable consequences"), and fecundity ("successful further extensions of theory are expedited").[18]

A different unclarity in D11 is, however, too important to ignore. It concerns what it is for x to explain at least as much as y. I find three construals that have some plausibility:

(a) x explains at least as many statements as y does;
(b) x explains at least the statements y explains;
(c) x explains at least as many statements that are to be explained as y does, and at most as many that are not to be explained as y does.

Interpretation (a) should be rejected. On some plausible theories of explanation, if a system explains p, then it explains infinitely many other statements, because it also explains ($p \lor q_1$), and ($p \lor q_1 \lor q_2$), and so on. Thus on such a view, any system that explains at least one statement explains as many as any other system.

Interpretaion (b) seems to be the view that many scientifically oriented coherence theorists would accept, but it makes EC too strong even if the explanatory systems for someone are, implausibly, limited to scientific theories. At present there is no one scientific theory that explains at least what every other one explains, not even if we consider only those theories currently in vogue. If it be replied that we should conjoin all these theories to get the maximal system, one problem is that the result may well be inconsistent, at least in its theoretical implications. But more importantly, there are many individually consistent scientific theories, such as Newtonian mechanics, which, although not in vogue, are not eliminated by D11 using (b), and clearly no consistent system explains what Newton's theory explains and also what Einstein's theory explains. Thus, if nothing of what each of these two theories explains is eliminated, then no statements are justified for anyone who understands both theories, because no system is maximal for him. This is surely too strong. The only reply is to say that one of these theories can be ignored, and so no maximal system is required to explain all that it explains. But then the problem for an EC-theorist is to find a way to determine which theory is to be rejected, and that seems to require that he show that one of the theories explains something that is not to be explained. It seems clear, then, that (b) should be amended so it considers only those statements explained by theory y that are to be explained.

As stated, (c) does not require such an amendment, but it does require that there be some way to determine which statements are to be explained. A person should not be allowed to decide this arbitrarily, because, as Lehrer notes, he can limit the statements that require explanation to exactly those that his favorite system explains very well.[19] Thus for both (c), (b), and, I find, for any plausible construal of D11, one serious problem for an EC-theorist is to find a nonarbitrary way to restrict the statements that are to be explained.

One Problem for EC-*Theories: How to Find What Is to Be Explained.* To see how difficult it is for an EC-theorist to restrict what is to be explained in a nonarbitrary way, consider one plausible way he might proceed. He might begin by limiting the statements to be explained to singular, categorical observation statements. He can do this either by identifying observation predicates and singular referring terms and then, as I did when characterizing observation-reports, define observation statements in terms of the predicates they contain. Or he could proceed as Quine does, that is, by considering a sentence to be "observational insofar as its truth value, on any occasion, would be agreed to by just about any member of the speech community witnessing the occasion".[20] The latter technique allows many statements that seem very theoretical to be observational. But, no matter which way he proceeds, the resulting set is still too large. He might next divide this set into maximally consistent subsets, but this leaves him with many inconsistent sets, not all of which are to be explained. The natural way to eliminate further is not available to an EC-theorist. That is, he cannot limit the set to those statements that are confirmed by observation, individually and independently of any explaining theory. Such statements would be initially acceptable, contrary to what N2 requires.

He might propose, instead, that the desired set include all and only *true* observation statements. But then the following objection arises. Let us assume that either Newton's theory or Einstein's theory (but not both) explains only true observation statements. If this present version of EC-theory is correct, then for all we can determine, the Newtonian theory and what it explains might be justified for us, because it explains only what is true. Most of us, following what scientists tell us, would believe – mistakenly and with no available means for discovering our mistakes – that Einstein's theory is justified. And anyone who has doggedly maintained the Newtonian theory would be justified in his belief even though he has no way to support his view except to say that what his theory explains is true. This is surely an objectionable feature of a theory of empirical justification, and it should be avoided. It seems, then, that an EC-theorist needs something more than the mere (lucky) truth of observation statements in order to limit the set of statements to be explained. He needs some nonarbitrary means that is more reliable than a mere guess or dogmatic assertion for choosing which of such conflicting theories is more reasonable.

There is another way an EC-theorist might proceed. He might try to base his elimination on agreement rather than truth. For example, he might propose the following Quine-like principle:

OE.   An empirical statement, e_i, of language L is to be explained on occasion, O_i, if and only if it is a singular observation statement and almost all members of speech community M (e.g., scientists who speak L) would assent to the truth of e_i on witnessing occasion O_1.

But is the right-hand side of OE more accessible than mere truth for an EC-theorist? Consider a person, s, who uses OE to justify the acceptance of an observation statement, e_1, that is explained by Einstein's theory but denied by Newton's. To succeed, he must verify an observational generalization, such as:

OG1.   Many members of community M would assent to e_1 on witnessing occasion O_1.

Since OG1 is empirical but not a singular observation statement, it would be justified for s, according to this EC-theory, if and only if either it is a nonredundant explanatory part of a system that is maximal for s, or it is justified by set J. But how is an EC-theorist to justify that OG1 has either status?

I have found only one procedure available for an EC-theorist who relies solely on agreement by means of OE to justify what is to be explained on each occasion. He can first assume OG1 and some of its kin, then use the set of observation sentences which they and OE pick out to determine which explanatory systems are maximal, and, finally, discover whether OG1 either is in a maximal system, or is justified by a justifying set, J, or is neither in nor justified by J. If OG1 is in or justified by J, then it is justified and so is the claim that e_1 is to be explained. If OG1 is neither in nor justified by J, then neither OG1 nor the claim that e_1 is to be explained is justified. However, our EC-theorist can always supply OG1 an explanatory role, and thus justification, by using OG1, on occasion O_1, to help explain e_2 = 'Scientist, a, assents to e_1'. Of course, it must be justified that e_2 is to be explained on occasion O_1, but this can be achieved by assuming OG2 which is like OG1, except that OG2 contains 'e_2' instead of 'e_1'. And then OG2 can be justified by having it explain e_3 = 'Scientist, b, assents to e_2'. And this goes on *ad infinitum*.

The preceding procedure for justifying OG1 requires infinitely many explaining sentences and sentences to be explained. But that is not its problem. Like the problem for N1, its problem is that it is unjustifiably arbitrary. We need only substitute '$\sim e_1$' for 'e_1' in OG1 and in e_2, and, keeping all else the same, $\sim e_1$ is justified for s at t, instead of e_1. But as we noted previously, any procedure should be rejected, if it violates restriction R2, that is, if it allows someone to justify whichever one of a statement and its denial he desires to justify. Consequently, like the problem he faces if he relies on mere truth, an EC-theorist who proposes principles like OE that rely solely on agreement has no nonarbitrary way to justify that some set from among the many conflicting maximally consistent sets of observation statements is to be explained. Thus he does not escape the preceding objection to his theory by substituting agreement for truth.

Conclusion About Explanatory Coherence Theories and What Is to Be Ex-

plained. I believe that the problem facing an EC-theorist who relies on truth or on agreement is serious enough to cast serious doubt on an EC-theory. It is clear, however, that I have not established this more general claim. Instead, let me offer a challenge to any EC-theorist: refute the following dilemma or reject your theory. An EC-theorist must find a procedure for selecting a set of statements that are to be explained. He has but two alternatives: allow a person to restrict the set arbitrarily, or provide nonarbitrary but accessible particular restrictions. But the first alternative is objectionable, because by violating requirement R2, it allows a person to pick just those statements that his favorite theory explains. And, as just indicated for two particular procedures, it seems an EC-theorist has no way to realize the second alternative.[21] Consequently, all EC-theories should be rejected, either for a less objectionable theory or for skepticism.

A Second Problem for EC-*Theories: Justification Without Explanation.* I conclude that we should reject all EC-theories until, if ever, the preceding challenge is met. And, although in Chapter 7 I shall indicate one way a nonfoundationalist might overcome this problem, there is another objection from Lehrer that I see no way for a nonfoundationalist to counter.[22] Even if being a nonredundant explanatory member of a system that is maximal for *s* is sufficient for being acceptable for *s*, it is quite implausible that if *s* has no such explanatory system, then no empirical statements are acceptable for him. As argued in Chapters 3 and 5, it is clearly reasonable that sometimes some of *s*'s basic-reports and observation-reports are acceptable for him, whether or not they are ever explained for him. That is, justification of these statements need not await explanation. Therefore EC-theories are mistaken and should be rejected. Furthermore, as far as I have found, EC-theories are the most plausible versions of N2. So I conclude that nonfoundational variety N2, like varieties N1 and N3, should be rejected because of debilitating objections to their leading examples. But there are no other varieties of nonfoundationalism that are even remotely plausible, and so I further conclude that no nonfoundational theory is acceptable. Thus we are forced either to skepticism or, hopefully, to some variety of foundationalism that has not yet been found wanting.

Postscript on Coherence Theories of Justification and Coherence Theories of Truth. I have claimed that we should keep coherence theories of justification distinct from coherence theories of truth, because conflating the two leads to confusion. At this point, however, I would like to consider them at the same time by examining an objection that supposedly refutes both of them. Lehrer aims the objection at the theory of justification.[23] As stated above, D11 allows several incompatible systems to be maximal, and so, Lehrer would claim, when this occurs an EC-theory results in incompatible statements being justified for one person at one time. But that is wrong. Furthermore, if Quine is (or at least used to be) right in claiming that scientific theory is underdetermined, then there always are two conflicting, maximal systems, even when each explains exactly what is to be explained.[24] Thus if Lehrer and Quine are both right, there is another objection sufficient to refute EC-theories. And, of course, this objection is the analogue of the crucial objection that supposedly defeats the coherence theory of truth. I think however, that neither of these objections is decisive.

The defect in N2.1, as spelled out by EC and D11, that gives rise to the preceding objection can be easily corrected by adding a clause to N2.1 to the effect that a person may use at most one of his justifying sets at any one time. It may be objected that this gives a person too much leeway. But, since each set includes only one maximal system and what it explains, it seems reasonable to allow s to choose whichever one he wants, because no such choice would ever result in s rejecting one justificatory system for another that is less reasonable. But, although this reply helps EC-theories, it is of no use to coherence theories of truth. Not only is it most implausible to allow someone's desires to decide what is true, but also, because different people have different maximal systems and different desires, determining truth in this way would very probably result in some statements *and* their denials being true, unless truth is relativized to persons. But although justification should be so relativized, truth surely should not.

TOWARD A COHERENCE THEORY OF TRUTH WITH A FOUNDATIONAL THEORY OF JUSTIFICATION

It might seem that we have found a place where coherence theories of justification are superior to such theories of truth. However, I believe a 'truth-coherence' theorist can begin a solution of this problem in a way that also allows him to avoid the two crucial objections to 'justification-coherence' theories, namely, that they have no way to justify any particular restriction on what is to be explained, and that explanation is not a necessary condition of justification. Thus his thesis may turn out to be the more plausible of the two. Once it is realized that explanation is one, but only one, important means of justification, it is quite natural and very tempting to adopt a theory of justification that goes, very roughly, as follows. The empirical statements that are initially acceptable for s at t, and the statements that are justified, for s at t, relative to the statements that are initially acceptable for s at t are to be explained for s at t. Then the empirical statements that are acceptable for s at t are, first, those that are to be explained for s at t; second, any universal and statistical observational generalizations justified by the first set of statements using enumerative induction; third, the sentences of one explanatory system that is maximal in sense (c) for s regarding these first two sets; and, fourth, what these three sets jointly justify. Of course, what results is not a coherence theory. It is instead foundational, but that by itself is no cause for alarm, not even for a 'truth-coherence' theorist.

A truth-coherence theorist can adopt the preceding foundational theory of justification and combine it with a coherence theory of truth. In this way he avoids the two objections to EC-theories. And he has a very simple way to avoid the preceding objection to coherence theories of truth that they have no way to guarantee that exactly one maximally consistent set of empirical statements is true. He need only claim that this is the set of empirical statements that any all-perfect being would believe to be true. It might be objected, however, that this should not be called a coherence theory, although it is clearly neither a correspondence theory nor a pragmatic theory. Perhaps it is more appropriate to call it a subjectivist theory of truth, because it states that a statement is true if and only if it would be believed by an entity of a certain sort. But I think we need not debate this point here. Of course, it must be admitted that this thesis is of no value for helping us determine what is true. That is, it provides no criterion that human beings can use to justify that certain statements are true. But it is not the function of such theories of truth to provide such a criterion. That is the function of theories of justification, like the one so briefly and roughly outlined above.

Quine and Sellars as Foundationalists

I find the preceding sketch of a theory of justification that supplements a foundational thesis with explanatory coherence to be quite attractive. I shall try to elaborate and defend one version of it in the next chapter. Furthermore, I believe that, contrary to most opinions, it is somewhat plausible to interpret both Quine and Sellars as holding some form of this combined thesis, in spite of some things they say, which at first glance seem to imply a rejection of foundationalism. For example, Quine says:

Any statement can be held true come what may, if we make drastic enough adjustments elsewhere in the system. Even a statement very close to the periphery can be held true in the face of recalcitrant experience by pleading hallucination or by amending certain statements of the kind called logical laws. Conversely, by the same token, no statement is immune to revision.[25]

And Sellars states:

Our aim [is] to manipulate the three basic components of a world picture: (a) observed objects and events, (b) unobserved objects and events, and (c) nomological connections, so as to achieve a world picture with a maximum of 'explanatory coherence'. In this reshuffle, no item is sacred.[26]

In spite of these quotations, however, Quine and Sellars can be foundationalists if, as is plausible, we take their main thesis to be that no particular set of statements is immune to refutation and so none is irrevocably at the foundation of empirical justification. That is, empirical justification does not have '*the* given' at its foundation. Sellars is opposed to observation statements being given and thus unalterably at the foundation, because he claims that, in the scientific millennium, singular theoretical statements will provide the most accurate and comprehensive picture of what there is. Thus he wants to be able to justify the ultimate rejection of all nontheoretical, observation statements. But none of this requires that he reject foundationalism. Indeed, his rejection of 'the' given is not a rejection of foundationalism:

To reject the myth of the given is to not commit oneself to the idea that empirical knowledge as it is now constituted has no rock bottom level of observation predicates proper. It is to commit oneself rather to the idea where even if it does have a rock bottom level, it is *still* in principle replaceable by another conceptual framework in which these predicates do not, *strictly speaking*, occur. It is in this sense, and in this sense *only*, that I have rejected the dogma of given-ness with respect to observational predicates.[27]

Quine's views are amazingly similar. He seems to hold that observation statements are individually verifiable and are the tests of explanatory systems. He says that his view of the relationship of observation sentences

to our knowledge of what is true, is very much the traditional one:
Observation sentences are the repository of evidence for scientific hypotheses. . . .
Sentences higher up in theories have no empirical consequences they can call their own; they confront the tribunal of sensory evidence only in more or less inclusive aggregates. The observation sentence, situated at the sensory periphery of the body scientific, is the minimal verifiable aggregate: it has an empirical content all its own and wears it on its sleeve.[28]

This surely seems to be a foundational thesis, indeed, one quite similar to the sort it is plausible to ascribe to Sellars. That is, both men seem to hold a foundational theory of justification that utilizes explanatory coherence but avoids 'the' given. Yet, it might be objected, Quine and Sellars differ importantly, because Quine keeps observation statements at the foundation, but Sellars wants to depose them. But there is no disagreement here, because, we have seen, Quine's characterization of observation sentences allows them to be the very singular, categorical 'theoretical' statements that Sellars wishes to place finally at the foundation.

CONCLUSION: TOWARD A FOUNDATIONAL THEORY
WITH EXPLANATORY COHERENCE

Is it reasonable to attribute some form of 'explanatory-coherence' foundational theory of empirical justification to Quine and Sellars? And is some form of this theory reasonable? I shall leave the first question for others to answer, preferably Quine and Sellars. Regarding the second, I shall make only two points in this chapter. First, there is some reason to think that such a theory avoids the objections to foundational theories which we examined previously, because it does not require only certainty at the foundation, does not restrict the statements at the foundation to basic-reports, and does not limit inferential justification to deduction and induction by enumeration or analogy. Indeed, by using maximal explanatory systems to extend acceptability from restricted bases, it clearly provides the means to derive acceptability where previous foundational theories have failed. Second, by providing a way to restrict bases plausibly and independently of explanation, it avoids both of the serious objections to nonfoundational coherence theories. This is because it puts at the foundation statements that are either initially certain, or are inferentially acceptable independently of explanation because justified by statements that are initially certain. The former statements are, of course, basic-reports that satisfy principle H3, and the latter are appropriate observation-reports, observation-entailed reports, and 'subjective' memory reports.

Because of the two preceding points, I propose to proceed as follows in the next chapter. I shall first try to elaborate and clarify an 'explanatory foundational' theory that limits what is to be explained to the four sorts of acceptable empirical statements mentioned above, and proposes to use maximum explanatory coherence to help extend justification significantly from this restricted base. I shall critically evaluate the resulting theory and its consequences. The results of that evaluation will help determine whether or not we are justified in rejecting skeptical thesis M_1S_3 and its near relatives. If the results indicate that this foundational theory should be discarded, then I would argue that no foundational theory is acceptable. And because, as we have just seen, it is unlikely that any nonfoundational theory is acceptable, that would justify the rejection of all theories of empirical justification. Only some form of skepticism would remain viable. But, of course, if this particular theory of justification proves to be plausible, then we will have found, at last, the basis for a refutation of epistemological skepticism.[29]

NOTES

[1] R. Chisholm, 'Theory of Knowledge', in R. Chisholm et al., Philosophy, Englewood Cliffs, N.J.: Prentice-Hall, 1964, p. 263.
[2] Ibid., p. 273, for Chisholm's different definition.
[3] R. Firth, 'Coherence, Certainty, and Epistemic Priority', in R. Chisholm and R. Swartz (eds.), Empirical Knowledge, Englewood Cliffs, N.J.: Prentice-Hall, 1973, p. 463.
[4] K. Lehrer, Knowledge, Oxford: Oxford University Press, 1974, p. 162.
[5] Chisholm, op. cit., p. 264.
[6] Ibid., p. 268.
[7] Ibid., p. 264.
[8] See B. Aune, 'Remarks on an Argument by Chisholm', Philosophical Studies 23 (1972), 329.
[9] Lehrer, op. cit., p. 189.
[10] Ibid., p. 190.
[11] Ibid., p. 198.
[12] Ibid., pp. 192–193; for 'strong negative relevance', see pp. 193–196.
[13] Ibid., pp. 208–209.
[14] Ibid., p. 209.
[15] See Chisholm, op. cit., p. 264.
[16] See Lehrer, op. cit., p. 165. I shall provide a different and more detailed definition of 'maximal' in Chapter 7.
[17] Ibid., for Lehrer's definition. However, a much more detailed definition will be given in Chapter 7.
[18] W. Quine, The Ways of Paradox and Other Essays, New York: Randon House, 1966, p. 234. An extensive examination of nonevidential tests will be found in chapters 8 and 9.
[19] Lehrer, op. cit., p. 170.
[20] W. Quine, The Roots of Reference, La Salle, Ill.: Open Court, 1974, p. 39.
[21] N. Rescher argues for a coherence theory of truth in The Coherence Theory of Truth, London: Oxford University Press, 1973, and it might be thought that he provides a coherence theory of justification. What is relevant is his attempt to eliminate all but one of the maximally consistent subsets of what he calls "truth-candidates" or "data" (pp.

53–70), so that the remaining one is justified as the set of true propositions. However, in chapter 5, where he suggests five ways to eliminate competing sets, the most plausible ways depend on independently establishing claims about probabilities, or plausibilities, or specially designated theses. But it is quite unclear how to establish such claims without relying on some sort of foundational theory.

22 See Lehrer, *op. cit.*, pp. 178–180.
23 *Ibid.*, pp. 181–182.
24 See W. Quine, *Word and Object*, Cambridge, Mass.: MIT Press, 1960, pp. 21–22. I discuss this in 'Reference and Ontology: Inscrutable but Not Relative', *Monist* **59** (1975), 353–372. For Quine's later views where he expresses doubts about underdetermination, see his 'On Empirically Equivalent Systems of the World', *Erkenntnis* **9** (1975), 313–328.
25 W. Quine, *From a Logical Point of View*, New York: Harper and Row, 1961, p. 43.
26 W. Sellars, *Science, Perception and Reality*, New York: Humanities Press, 1963, p. 356.
27 W. Sellars, *Philosophical Perspectives*, Springfield, Ill.: Charles C. Thomas, 1967, p. 353.
28 W. Quine, *Ontological Relativity and Other Essays*, New York: Columbia University Press, 1969, pp. 88–89.
29 I wish to thank Jaegwon Kim and Ernest Sosa for their very helpful comments on much of the material in this chapter.

CHAPTER 7

A FOUNDATIONAL THEORY WITH EXPLANATORY COHERENCE

The minimal foundational theory of the justification of empirical statements is F3, namely:

F3.   Any empirical statement, p, would be acceptable for person s at time t, *if and only if* it would be true that: either p is initially acceptable for s at t; or (i) there is an E-series for p that justifies p for s at t, and (ii) each E-series that justifies p for s at t contains some empirical statement that is initially acceptable for s at t.

We have seen that the three most discussed species of F3 – that is, the Cartesian, Lewisean, and Chisholmian versions – are implausible. I also mentioned, when introducing F3 in Chapter 6, that F3 is not the minimal *plausible* foundational thesis. To arrive at that, I claimed, we need to conjoin F3 with principles FPI and FP2, which, unfortunately, have turned out to be helpful for skepticism. These two principles, which concern inferential certainty and acceptability, can be stated conjointly as follows:

FP(1, 2). If all initially (certain, acceptable) empirical statements are of kind K, and some empirical statement of kind L is inferentially (certain, acceptable) for s at t_1, then some empirical statement which is of kind L is (certain, probable) for s at t_2, relative to a set of statements of kind K, each of which is (certain, acceptable) for s at t_2.

We are now in a position to understand why F3 needs FP(1, 2) to be plausible. One reason that F3 is not plausible is that it does not exclude two sorts of justifying E-series that are clearly inadequate. First, it does not preclude justification of p by an E-series for p that contains some initially acceptable statements but also some that are unjustified and thus unacceptable. But we have already seen in Chapter 6 that no E-series for p that contains an unjustified statement justifies p. Second, in Chapter 6 we also found reason to reject infinitely long E-series that are constituted of statements that are not initially acceptable, are not their own E-ancestor, but are justified relative to some set of statements in the series. The problem for both of these sorts of justification is that, without some additional restriction, they allow E-series to be constructed that violate requirement R1 and thus R2, because they permit an E-series for any arbitrarily chosen p and another for its denial. Because of this problem, we rejected nonfoundational theories that permitted such E-series. For a similar reason, we should also reject all foundational E-series that differ from the preceding sorts of nonfoundational infinite series only by containing some initially acceptable statement. We can easily amend an infinite series from Chapter 6 in order to construct a foundational series that violates R2. Again consider any statement, Pa, where a is not a number, and let $b =$ 'I now believe that a is p', which we can assume is initially certain for me now. Then we can construct the following infinite E-series, E_2: $e_1 = \{b, Q_1a, (x)[(Q_1x \cdot b) \supset Px]\}$, $e_2 = \{Q_2a, (x)(Q_2 x \supset Q_1x), (x)[(Q_1x \cdot Q_2a \cdot b) \supset Px]\}$, and so on. And, it is easy to see that this foundational E-series is to be rejected as was the previous one.

THE MINIMAL PLAUSIBLE FOUNDATIONAL THEORY

We can explicitly exclude both sorts of foundational series that are inadequate for the preceding reasons by amending F3 to produce a more plausible species:

F3.1.   Any empirical statement, p, would be acceptable for s at t, *if and only if* it would be true that: either p is initially acceptable for s at t; or (i) there is an E-series for p that justifies p for s at t, and (ii) each E-series that justifies p for s at t is such that: (a) it is finite, (b) it contains some empirical statement that is initially acceptable for s at t, and (c) it contains only statements that are acceptable for s at t.

Although better than F3, F3.1 also does not state the minimal plausible foundational thesis. This is because it allows finite foundational E-series composed of a few initially acceptable statements, and many that are their own E-ancestors. The first member of such a series might well contain an initially acceptable statement and, in addition, only statements that are not initially acceptable, but that are E-ancestors of themselves when they appear in some set later in the series. In Chapter 6, 1 claimed that two objections cast doubt on theories of type N2, which is the one type that allows a statement to be its own E-ancestor, because these objections raise problems for the most plausible theories of this type, namely, explanatory coherence theories. One of these problems for EC-theories is meeting the challenge to provide a nonarbitrary way to restrict the class of statements that are to be explained. More generally, it seems that this problem for type N2 theories is that they violate requirement R2 unless explicitly required to conform to it. And it is clear that this flaw is not avoided merely by the use of some initially acceptable statements at appropriate places in an E-series.

A very simple example will illustrate the problem. Let b_1 and b_2 be initially acceptable statements for s at t, and assume a theory stating that a statement, p, is acceptable for s at t if it has a finite E-series that contains a statement, q, only if q is initially acceptable for s at t, or q is justified relative to a set of statements which is in the E-series but does not contain q. Consider, then, the following E-series, E_3, for any arbitrary p_i (say p_1): $e_1 = \{\sim b_1, b_1 \lor p_1\}$, $e_2 = \{b_2, (\sim b_1 \cdot b_2) \supset p_1\}$, and $e_3 = \{b_1 \lor p_1\}$. On the preceding assumption, $\sim b_1$, b_2 and $(b_1 \lor p_1)$ are acceptable for s at t. This is achieved for $(b_1 \lor p_1)$ by having it be one of its own E-ancestors in the series. This is because: first, $(b_1 \lor p_1)$ is justified relative to e_2; second, e_2 consists of b_2, which is initially acceptable for s at t, and $[(\sim b_1 \cdot b_2) \supset p_1]$, which is justified relative to e_3; and, third, the statement of e_3 is justified relative to set e_2 which does not contain $(b_1 \lor p_1)$. So, by this foundational theory, which satisfies F3.1, this E-series justifies p_1 for s at t. But any such justification violates requirement R2, because we can substitute any arbitrarily chosen p_i for p_1. Thus F3.1 is not plausible.

One sure way to eliminate the preceding sort of E-series is to require that neither p nor any statement in a justifying E-series for p is one of its own E-ancestors in that series, and that any E-ancestor of p that is not initially acceptable, is justified relative to some of its E-ancestors. Let us then form foundational thesis F3.2 by replacing clause (ii) in F3.1 by:

(ii)   each E-series, E, that justifies p for s at t is such that: (a) it is finite; (b) it contains some empirical statement that is initially acceptable for s at t; (c) it contains only statements that are acceptable for s at t; (d) it contains a statement, q, that is not initially acceptable for s at t, only if it contains some of q's E-ancestors relative to which q is justified for s at t; and (e) it contains no empirical statement that is (or is analytically equivalent to) either p or one of its own E-ancestors in series E.

A Derivation of Plausible FP(1, 2) *from the Minimal Plausible Foundational Theory*

I claim that F3.2 is the minimally plausible foundational thesis, and that it also implies principle FP(1, 2), which I said is needed to be conjoined with F3 to produce a plausible foundational thesis. Of course, just as we needed to supplement N2.1, the minimum coherence theory, so it became detailed enough to have testable consequences, so also we shall have to flesh out F3.2 in order to evaluate it. But before I propose how this is to be done, let me show that F3.2, and so any plausible foundational theory, requires principle FP(1, 2).

Deriving Principle FP2. To make the examination less abstract and also directly relevant to the discussion throughout this book, let us assume that statements of kind K are basic-reports, and those of kind L are nonbasic statements (empirical statements that are neither basic-reports nor eternalized basic-reports). To begin, it can be shown that, with F3.2 as the basic axiom for foundational theories of empirical justification, the following is a theorem:

FT1.   All E-series for p that justify p for s at t are finite and end with a set of E-ancestors of p, each of which is initially acceptable for s at t.

It should be noted that FT1 does not imply that this last set contains all the initially acceptable statements that are required for the series to justify p. Consider again series E_3 and assume that $[(\sim b_1 \cdot b_2) \supset p_1]$ is initially acceptable for s at t. Then, the series could end with set e_2 instead of e_3, because e_2 would contain only initially acceptable statements. But e_2 does not contain $\sim b_1$, which is needed if series E_3 is to justify p for s at t. Although $\sim b_1$ occurs in e_1, neither it nor anything relative to which $\sim b_1$ is justified needs to occur in e_2, according to definition D8 for E-series, because $\sim b_1$ is initially acceptable for s at t.

To show FT1 is a theorem, given F3.2 as an axiom, assume the denial of FT1. Then some justifying E-series, E_i, has a last member, e_j, which contains a statement, q, that is an E-ancestor of p, and is not initially acceptable. Therefore, by clause (ii.d) of F3.2, q is justified relative to some of its own E-ancestors in series E_1. Thus, there is a set e_{j+1} relative to which q is justified. But that is impossible because, by hypothesis, e_j is the last set in E_i. Thus FT1 is a theorem of axiom F3.2.

We can now use FT1 to show FP2, which concerns acceptability, is also a theorem (call it FT2), given F3.2 as an axiom. Assuming that all statements that are initially acceptable for someone are basic-reports and that p is a nonbasic statement, it follows from FT1 that any E-series, E_i, that justifies p for someone ends with a set containing only acceptable basic-reports. And so either p or some other acceptable nonbasic statement that is an E-ancestor of p in E_i is justified relative to some set of acceptable basic-reports. For suppose this is false. Then neither p nor any other acceptable nonbasic statement, q, in E_i is justified relative to a set containing only acceptable basic-reports. But p and q are inferentially acceptable, and all statements in E_i are acceptable. Consequently, given our supposition, each is justified relative to some set, e_j, in E_i that contains at least one inferentially acceptable nonbasic statement, r_1. Thus F3.2 requires there be another set in E_i relative to which r_1 is justified. But, given the supposition, this set must also contain some inferentially acceptable nonbasic statement, r_2, and so on. So E_i is infinite, contrary to hypothesis, because for each inferentially acceptable nonbasic r_k in E_i, there is an inferentially acceptable nonbasic r_{k+1} that is an E-ancestor of r_k. So far we have proved the following lemma:

L1.   If all initially acceptable empirical statements are of kind K, and some empirical statement of kind L is inferentially acceptable for s at t, then some empirical statement which is of kind L is justified relative to a set of statements of kind K, each of which is acceptable for s at t.

To prove FT2 we need only conjoin L1 with one more claim, namely: 'If p is justified relative to q, then p is probable relative to q'. But as we have been using 'p is justified relative to q', it entails 'p is acceptable relative to q', and the latter means that the credibility of p relative to q is greater than 0.5. So if p is justified relative to q, then the credibility of p relative to q is high. One more step is needed, namely, the inference from high credibility of p relative to q to the high probability of p relative to q. This is guaranteed for the sense of 'relative to' which unpacks as 'if q then $Cr_{s,t}(p) > 0.5$', by what seems clearly true, namely, that $Cr_{s,t}(p) \leqslant Pr_{s,t}(p)$. That is, however high the credibility of p is for s at t, it surely is no greater than the probability or, in other words, the degree of confirmation of p for s at t. Similarly, it is also true that when 'p has high credibility relative to q' is unpacked as '$Cr_{s,t}(p/q) > 0.5$', it implies 'p has high probability relative to q'. Because of this, we get FT2 (FP2) as a theorem, for F3.2 as the foundational axiom.

Deriving Principle FP1. With FP2 derived, it is easy to see how to derive FP1, once an implication that clearly seems to be analytic is made explicit. That is, *if* each E-series for p that justifies p for s at t, (1) contains only statements that are acceptable for s at t, and (2) contains some q that is not initially acceptable for s at t, only if it contains some E-ancestors of q relative to which q is justified for s at t, *then* each E-series for p that justifies p as certain for s at t (1) contains only statements that are certain for s at t, and (2) contains a q that is not initially certain for s at t, only if it contains some E-ancestor of q relative to which q is justified as certain for s at t. That is, clause (ii.d) of F3.2, which concerns acceptability and justification, entails the corresponding claims about certainty and the justification of something as certain. Then, by means that parallel those for FT1, we can use the consequent of this implication, instead of clause (ii.d), to derive:

FT3.   All E-series for p that justify p as certain for s at t are finite and end with a set of E-ancestors of p, all of which are initially certain for s at t.

Finally, by steps like those used to derive lemma L1, we can derive FP1 (call it theorem FT4) directly:

FT4   If all initially certain empirical statements are of kind K, and some empirical statement of kind L is inferentially certain for s at t, then some empirical statement which is of kind L is justified as certain relative to a set of statements of kind K each of which is certain for s at t.

The only difference in the two sets of proofs is that in the second 'justify as certain' and 'certain' are substituends throughout for 'justify' and 'acceptable', respectively.

There is an important consequence of having FT3 required of any plausible foundational theory that is relevant to our ongoing consideration of skepticism. It concerns skeptical argument V for skeptical thesis M_1S_3, which states, roughly, that it is never reasonable for any human to believe that there are presently existing unperceived objects, nonsubjective past events, future events, or mental phenomena of others. At the end of Chapter 5, we were faced with the prospect of accepting the hypothesis that either M_1S_3 is true, or FP2 is false and some nonfoundational theory is correct, unless we could find some way to refute premise V.2 ('No nonbasic statement that is not entailed by a set of basic-reports, observation-reports, and basic memory-reports is probable, for s at t, relative to any set of basic-reports, observation-reports, and basic memory-reports about s at t that are acceptable for s at t.)' However, by the end of Chapter 6, we concluded we should reject all nonfoundational theories, and it has just been shown that FP2 (FT2) is true if some foundational theory is plausible. Thus we should accept M_1S_3, if premise V.2 turns out to be plausible. That is, with the demise of nonfoundational theories, the requirement of FP2 for plausible foundational theories, and the rejection of Cartesian, Lewisean, and Chisholmian foundational theories, the one remaining hope for avoiding thesis M_1S_3 is to devise some foundational theory which avoids the flaws of its predecessors. This is what I shall attempt next when I develop the minimal version of what I shall call the 'explanatory foundational theory' of the justification of empirical statements.

AN EXPLANATORY FOUNDATIONAL THEORY

We can begin our search for a viable foundational theory by recalling two points. First, one serious challenge facing explanatory coherence theories is the difficult task of finding some way to restrict what is to be explained that is nonarbitrary and reasonable. The crucial problem facing those foundational theories we have already dismissed is their inability to extend justification beyond their narrow base. Second, the strength of these foundational theories is their nonarbitrary and reasonable specification of a restricted foundation of statements that are justified even if not explained, while the quite different value of explanatory theories is their ability to extend justification well beyond whatever is to be explained. Consequently, where each of these theories is seriously flawed, the other is strong, and so a theory that combines these strengths in a way that avoids the flaws looks quite promising. Such a theory would further delineate thesis F3.2, by specifying the sorts of E-series which would justify empirical statements for s at t. In brief, the explanatory foundational theory specifies at least three different sorts of E-series as justifying such a p for s at t, namely: those in which p is either in or justified by the set, F, of statements that are foundational for s at t; those in which p is a member of an explanatory system, C, that is maximal for s at t, because, roughly, it best explains the statements that are foundational for s at t; and those in which p is justified by the union of sets F and C. That is, we can begin our search for an adequate characterization of the minimal

version of this sort of foundational theory by conjoining a third condition
to the second disjunctive clause on the right side of F3.2 to form F3.21:

> (iii)   there is an E-series, E, for p that justifies p for s at t, *if* either
> (a) p is a member of F, the set of foundational statements for
> s at t, or (b) p is an explanatory system, C, which is maximal
> for s at t, or (c) p is an empirical statement that is a logical con-
> sequence of the union of F and C.

Even with the addition of (iii), however, the thesis is not detailed enough
either to be of help epistemically or to be critically evaluated. To achieve
the requisite level of specification, we must give more details about how to
uncover foundational statements and about when an explanatory system
is justified relative to some set of statements. The theory I propose takes
the foundational statements to be sentences that are to be explained, and
uses the notion of a maximal system, discussed in Chapter 6 and soon to
be explicated, to help provide a thesis about the justification of explanatory systems.

On Foundational Statements

Consider first the foundational statements. There are various ways we
might identify them, depending on what we specify as being at the foundation. Given our previous conclusions about what is initially certain,
initially acceptable, and inferentially acceptable, there are two different
groups of statements we take as foundational: just those that are initially
certain or acceptable, or that group together with some that are inferentially acceptable, because, by assumption A10, they are probable, given
what is initially certain. I propose we use the broader class, because
whatever is acceptable, independent of being explained, should be considered datum to be explained. Later in Chapter 10, however, when I apply
this theory to specific situations, I shall use examples in which only basic-
reports are foundational. This will show that the explanatory-founda-
tional theory remains able to extend justification enough to refute M_1S_3,
even when we are conservative in what we allow to be foundational.

There are two more preliminary decisions to be made. Based on our
past conclusions and decisions, principles H3, BR3, and BR4 are to be
used to identify foundational statements. The question is whether we
should say that a statement is foundational for s at t, if it is either initially
certain or it is probable, via BR3 or BR4, given what is certain. Or should
we merely require that it satisfy the antecedent of H3 or the antecedent of

BR3 or BR4 for some evidence that satisfies the antecedent of H3? I propose the latter for the following reason. The second proposal is more conservative epistemically and thus accords better with our policy of being conservative when combating skepticism. It is more conservative in the sense that it does not require basic-reports to be certain if they meet the antecedent of H3, and so it does not require that any logically contingent statement ever has a probability of 1 for anyone. It is, then, compatible with Carnap's requirement of strict coherence, for example, which has *some* plausibility, in spite of my arguments in chapters 2 and 3 against it. For example, we could argue that if basic-report b_i meets the antecdent of H3 (perhaps with '1' replaced by '$1-\varepsilon$') then it is to be explained for s at t, because, as a result, $\mathrm{Pr}_{s,t}(Tb_1st) > 1-\varepsilon$, for any ε, greater than zero, no matter how small. This allows b_i not to be certain for s at t, but this makes it no less reasonable to propose that b_i is to be explained for s at t.

I know of only one objection to the preceding reasoning, namely, that with no guarantee of $\mathrm{Pr}_{s,t}(Test) = 1$, for any set, e, of basic-reports, b_1, b_2, b_3, b_4, there is no way to use assumption A10, BR3, and BR4 to show that some nonbasic statement is acceptable for s at t. And if we cannot do that, then we have no way to justify the choice of some nonbasic statement to be explained for s at t, because at minimum any such statement must be acceptable for s at t.

I begin my reply to this by proposing the adoption of one assumption I tentatively approved in Chapter 3. It is one from which A10 follows, given a modification of definition D1 for acceptability to accommodate noneternalized reports. The modified definition is:

D1a.   Statement, p, is acceptable for s at $t =_{\mathrm{df}}$. The credib lity of $Tpst$, for s at t, is high.

And the assumption is:

A5.   If e is s's evidence for p at t, then $\mathrm{Cr}_{s,t}(p) = \mathrm{Pr}_{s,t}(p/e) \times \mathrm{Pr}_{s,t}(e)$, where p and the statements in e are eternal.

In other words, I propose that the degree of credibility of an eternal p for s at t be equal to the degree of confirmation of p for s at t given e, times the degree of confirmation, for s at t, of s's evidence regarding p. As a result, if $\mathrm{Pr}_{s,t}(Tp/Te) \times \mathrm{Pr}_{s,t}(Te) > 0.5$, then, by D1a, p is acceptable for s at t, regardless of whether the evidence, e, is certain for s at t. Furthermore, unlike the probability for s at t, acceptability and degree of credibility do not depend on $\mathrm{Pr}_{s,t}(T\bar{e})$ and $\mathrm{Pr}_{s,t}(Tp/T\bar{e})$. And, although I said in Chapter

3 that I could not justify A5 by itself, I believe I can give its acceptance as an epistemic axiom some plausibility by arguing that, where e is s's evidence for p at t, its epistemic status and the epistemic status of p for s at t, given this evidence, should completely determine the acceptability of p for s at t. Any more substantial reason for accepting A5 will come, as noted previously, only from an overall justification of some epistemic theory which includes it as axiom or theorem. This, of course, is, in part, what I shall be attempting to do in what follows.

Now given A5, I shall argue that for any exceedingly small ε, if p meets the antecedent of BR3 or BR4 then $Pr_{s,t}(Tpst/Test) \geqslant 0.5 + n\varepsilon$, where n is the number of basic-reports in e. That is, for such a very small ε, this probability is not so very little greater than 0.5 that it is not also equal to or greater than $0.5 + n\varepsilon$. But if for each of n b's in e, $Pr_{s,t}(Tb_ist) \geqslant 1-\varepsilon$, then $Pr_{s,t}(Test) > 1 - n\varepsilon$.[1] As a result, by theorem T1, $Pr_{s,t}(Tpst/Test) \times Pr_{s,t}(Test) \geqslant 0.5 + 0.5n\varepsilon - (n\varepsilon)^2$. But because $0.5n\varepsilon > (n\varepsilon)^2$, we can use A5 to derive that $Cr_{s,t}(Tpst) > 0.5$ and so, by D1a, p is acceptable for s at t. Thus the objection is refuted, our conservative use of H3, BR3, and BR4 is justified, and our justification for counting p as one thing to be explained remains plausible. That is, p is acceptable for s at t, independently of any explanation whatsoever, and based on reasonable, nonarbitrary principles.

The Foundational Thesis of the Minimal Theory. We are ready to state the foundational thesis of the explanatory foundational theory. It is:

FF.   A statement, p, is foundational for s at t *if and only if* either (1) p satisfies the antecedent of H3 for s at t; or (2) p satisfies the antecedent of BR3 or BR4 for some set of evidence, e, that satisfies the antecedent of H3 for s at t.

Before moving on, it is worth noting one consequence of our conservative use of H3, BR3, and BR4 in stating FF that assists nonfoundational coherence theories. By not having the thesis require 'foundational' statements to have any epistemic status, such as being initially acceptable or certain, a theory that includes FF can easily be made a nonfoundational coherence theory. This can be done by specifying a statement is 'foundational' only in the sense that it is to be explained, and then claiming that these statements become justified when, but only when, explained. Of course, we would like to know why a statement that meets H3, BR3, and BR4 appropriately is to be explained, if it is not to be construed as acceptable unless it is explained. And it is clear that this does not solve the second objection to the explanatory coherence theory about justification without explanation. But it would seem to go a long way toward meeting that challenge which the theory has previously failed to meet. Indeed, I would hope that this ability of the explanatory foundation theory, which includes FF, to come so close to accommodating all that a coherence theorist requires, might well increase the attractiveness of the theory as a 'higher synthesis' of foundational and nonfoundational theories.

On Explanations That Are Maximal

Our next task is to specify what it is for an explanation to be maximal for a person at a time. We can begin with a definition derived from the way the term was used in Chapter 6, except for one change. We should relativize being maximal to sets of statements, because we are interested here only in systems that are maximal regarding those sentences that are to be explained. Consider as a first attempt:

> D12. System C is a maximal system, for s at t, relative to the set of statements, $F =_{df}$. C has maximum explanatory coherence, for set F, among the systems in set B_1: those understood by s at t.

And we can also consider how this was unpacked in Chapter 6 by means of the definition of maximum explanatory coherence given by D11. We shall also have to revise this definition, because we are to understand one of the key phrases of the definiens, namely, 'C explains at least as much as x does', in terms of the statements that are to be explained for s at t. Thus maximum explanatory coherence must also be relativized to sets of sentences. Let us, therefore, begin with:

> D13. System C has maximum explanatory coherence for set F, among the systems in set $B =_{df}$. (1) C is in B; (2) C is consistent; and (3) for any system, x, in B, if x is consistent but conflicts with C, then (a) C explains at least as many statements in set F as x does, and (b) it is false that x explains as many statements in F as C does and x also better explains more statements in F than C does.

On Defining Maximum Explanatory Coherence

Although both D12 and D13 are good first approximations, neither is ultimately satisfactory for our purposes because of the implication of the

minimal explanatory foundational theory that a statement is justified for
s at t, if it is a nonredundant member of a system that is maximal for s at t
relative to the set of statements that are to be explained for s at t. I shall
call this set 'F_1'. (Note: in the future whenever I speak of maximal system
or maximum explanatory coherence without relativizing it to a set, I shall
always be speaking elliptically about reference to set F_1.) Let us consider
D13 before D12, because the adequacy of the definition of 'maximal'
depends on that of 'maximum explanatory coherence'. To facilitate our
examination, however, we must first explicate three key phrases of D13:
'better explain', 'explain', and 'conflict with'. As briefly mentioned in
Chapter 6, which of two systems better explains is to be explicated in terms
of which more nearly satisfies what I have called the 'nonevidential' tests
for explanations. That is, I propose, initially, to replace the phrase 'x
explains y better than z does' by 'x and z explain y, and x is a better explanatory system than z is'. This will not allow us to capture exactly what
seems to be meant by the phrase in D13, 'x better explains more statements
than C', because that phrase seems to allow cases where x and C explain
the same number of sentences, but, although C explains some sentences
better than x does, x is a better explanation of more statements than C is.
Nevertheless, I shall argue that the replacement is justified.

On Explanation by Explanatory Systems. Hempel has helpfully delineated
two concepts of explanation: a pragmatic and a nonpragmatic concept.[2]
Regarding the former, Hempel says, "to explain something to a person is
to make it plain and intelligible to him, to make him understand it".[3]
Consequently, this pragmatic concept must be relativized to persons and
circumstances. I claim that whatever there is about 'x explains y better
than z does' that fails to be captured by 'x and z explain y, and x is a better
explanatory system than z' is to be explicated as 'x makes y plainer and
more intelligible to person s in circumstances c than z does'. Like Hempel,
however, I am interested here only in a nonpragmatic concept of explanation, and, therefore, the failure of my replacement to capture this
pragmatic feature is no objection to it. But this is not to say that nothing
pragmatic is relevant to a system being maximal for someone at some
time. It is rather that it enters the analysis of what it is to be a maximal
system not by being essential for maximum explanatory coherence, but
by requiring any system that is maximal for a person to be understood by
him and to be helpful to him in understanding what it explains and in
devising new explanations.

It should also be noted that often what would be considered a very good explanation for someone in a particular situation in this pragmatic sense would not even qualify as any sort of explanation in the nonpragmatic sense I propose we adopt. Consider Hempel's example of a man for whom the puzzling fact that his house became cold in winter whenever his television set was operating was explained to him by the observation that the thermostat for the furnace was located just above the set and the heat from the set caused the thermostat to shut off the furnace.[4] This explanation, which made what was to be explained quite clear and understandable to this man, is not an explanation by what I am calling a 'system' and so it does not meet one necessary condition for the sort of explanation I am requiring for maximal explanatory coherence. To see why not, let us turn to Hempel's conception of *potential* explanation which I shall revise in line with a proposal made by Kaplan in order to avoid a serious objection to Hempel's original definition. Kaplan offers the following:

E is *directly S-explainable* by *T* if and only if there is a sentence *C* such that the following conditions are satisfied:

(1)   *T* is a theory,
(2)   *C* is a conjunction of true basic [either atomic or denial of atomic] sentences,
(3)   *E* is a disjunction of basic sentences,
(4)   *E* is logically derivable from the set {*T, C*}, and
(5)   *E* is not logically derivable from {*C*}.

E is *S-explainable* by *T* if and only if *E* is a singular sentence which is logically derivable from the set of sentences which are directly S-explainable by *T*.[5]

Two points should be noted about Kaplan's definition. The first is that 'theory' is a technical term when defined as Hempel has done. This definition requires that a theory be true.[6] In this it differs from what I am calling a 'system' which need not be true nor even have a truth-value. But, like certain theories, it must be what Hempel calls "essentially generalized", that is, a generalized formula that is not logically equivalent to a singular formula. And a formula is generalized if it consists of at least one quantifier followed by an expression without quantifiers.[7] It is clear, however, that we should also call certain probabilistic and statistical laws essentially generalized, even though they lack quantifiers. We can achieve this by saying that a formula is generalized if and only if it begins with a quantifier, or it is a probabilistic or statistical formula that applies to at least one class of entities without specifying of any particular entity either that it is in the class or that it is not.[8] Thus $(x)(Fx \supset Gx)$, $(x)(Fa \supset Gx)$,

$Pr_{s,t}(Fx/Gx) > 0.5$, and $Pr_{s,t}(Fa/Gx) > 0.5$ are all essentially general. The second point is that the explanandum, E, is a disjunction of 'basic' statements. This might seem too restrictive, but not when we grant Kaplan's assumption that any singular sentence to be explained is first put in conjunctive normal form. Then any sentence that is logically derivable from a conjunction of explained disjunctions of 'basic' sentences is explained, according to this definition.

On P-Explanation by Explanation Sets. We can now use Kaplan's definition to revise Hempel's definition of 'potential explanation' whose crucial difference from 'explanation' is that truth is not required of any explanans. Furthermore, I shall follow Hempel rather than Kaplan, in taking any set which contains an explanatory system and a conjunction of what I shall dub 'nonmolecular' sentences as a statement of initial conditions to be what explains. And I shall call any such set an "explanation set". I shall also make additional changes to accommodate our present interests, and our need to have probabilistic explanation sets. I propose:

D14.   Explanation set $\{C, I\}$ is a P-explanation of (P-explains) $x =_{df.}$
    (1) C is an explanatory system;
    (2) $\{C, I\}$ is consistent;
    (3) I is a conjunction of either 'nonmolecular' (either atomic or denials of atomic) sentences, or absolute probability sentences whose values for 'y' in '$Pr(y)$' are conjunctions of nonmolecular sentences;
    (4) at least some of the conjuncts in I and in any probability sentence in I are observation-sentences or basic-sentences; and
    (5) x is a singular sentence that is entailed by a set, z, of disjunctions of nonmolecular sentences, such that (a) either z or '$Pr(z) > 0.5$' is derivable from $\{C, I\}$; and (b) neither z nor '$Pr(z) > 0.5$' is derivable from $\{I\}$.

I have used 'nonmolecular' where Kaplan used 'basic' to describe the statements of initial conditions, because we have already stipulated a different use for 'basic', and so, as in clause (4), I continue to use it as before. And I have allowed certain 'conjunctive' probability statements to be included among statements of initial conditions, because, as we shall see in Chapter 10, they are clearly needed for some probabilistic explanations.

Three other changes should also be noted. First, I have required that I, the statement of 'initial conditions', contain either observation-sentences (sentences whose nonlogical constants are or are definable by observation terms) or basic-sentences (either basic-reports or eternalized basic-reports or generalizations of basic-reports).[9] I do this for our purposes, because if basic-reports, observation-reports, and subjective memory-reports are to be explained, then, I believe, at least some of the conjuncts in the statement of initial conditions should be 'directly' verifiable (that is, verifiable by observation or 'inner' experience), For example, it is not clear that some $\{C, I\}$ would explain the report 'I am now seeing something yellow', if all the conjuncts of x were 'purely' theoretical and not 'directly' verifiable.[10] And because of this doubt, I again employ a principle of conservatism and put this additional restriction on the statement of initial conditions.

A second change concerns the nature of what is derivable from $\{C, I\}$. Again, because of probabilistic explanations, we cannot require that nonprobabilistic disjunctions of statements be derived. Often, as will become clear later, the only sentences that are relevant to what is being explained are probability sentences. I propose, therefore, that whatever z entails is P-explained by $\{C, I\}$, if the claim that z is probable is derivable from $\{C, I\}$, and the other conditions in D14 are met. It should be noted that, according to D14, there is no probabilistic P-explanation of something improbable. This, I maintain, is as it should be, especially for our attempt to refute skepticism by linking justification and explanation. This is not to say, however, that there is no sort of explanation of what is improbable, but only that if there is such an explanation, as has been claimed, it is of no help to us.[11]

The last change worth noting is the replacement of 'logically derivable' by 'derivable' in clauses (5) and (6). I do this because I want to allow three sorts of explanations which can be distinguished in terms of three sorts of derivability, which I shall call 'logical derivability', 'probabilistic derivability', and 'inductive derivability'. There are two ways to represent these three sorts of derivability. One is to keep the rules of inference the same as for logical derivability and to add axioms for probability and for induction to the logical axioms. The other is to increase the set of rules of inference to include some inductive rules. It might seem I should use the second approach, because in Chapter 4 I have stated three forms of inductive inference: enumerative, analogical, and hypothetical, and so each would seem to require a unique inductive rule of inference. However, since each of these forms can be transformed into a universal conditional, and it is easier to display the difference among the three sorts of derivability using only '⊢' for logical derivability, I shall assume any such inductive rules are not rules of inference but theorems of induction. So I shall isolate two sets of theorems. Let P = the set of theorems of the probability calculus,[12] and I = the set of inductive theorems. Then we have:

D15.   (a) y is *logically* derivable (deducible) from $x =_{df.} x \vdash y$;
         (b) y is *probabilistically* derivable from $x =_{df.} x \not\vdash y$ and $x \cup P \vdash y$;
         (c) y is *inductively* derivable from $x =_{df.} x \not\vdash y$ and $x \cup P \cup I \vdash y$;
         (d) y is *derivable* from $x =_{df.} y$ is logically or inductively derivable from x.

Given D15, we are permitted by D14 to include the three sorts of explanation which Hempel calls respectively, "deductive-nomological" (D15a), "deductive-statistical" (D15b), and "inductive-statistical" (D15c).[13] The systems of the first sort require no statistical ['m/n P's are Q's'] or probabilistic ['$\Pr(Qx/Px) = m/n$'] statements in order to explain; those of the second require such statements but what they explain is deducible when the probability theorems are included; and those of the third sort require, in addition, inductive theorems (or rules of inference).

We can now easily see why the previously mentioned explanation of the drop in temperature when the television was turned on is not an explanation by a system. This is because the explanans, not being generalized, is not essentially generalized and so is not a system. *A fortiori*, the explanation is not a P-explanation, and, because I shall require P-explanation for maximum explanatory coherence, this explanation, although pragmatically excellent, does not even meet the minimum requirements for the sort of explanation I am proposing.

On Conflicting Explanatory Systems. Let us turn now to explicating the relevant sort of conflict between systems. It is clear that logical incompatibility is too weak, because two explanatory systems rarely entail a contradiction when conjoined. At least some statement of initial conditions must also be added if any conflicting consequences of the systems are to arise. Furthermore, I would maintain that the conflict between consequences need not be logical. Perhaps, then, we should say that if the consequences are causally or metaphysically (in Kripke's sense) or logically incompatible, then the systems conflict. However, this would create a problem for quantitative theories, that is, those expressed in mathematical terminology. There are cases where one theory has mathematically formulated consequences that are mathematically incompatible with those of another, but the differences are so small that they fall well within the realm of allowable experimental error. For example, the consequences of classical physics when it is restricted to relatively slow speeds and 'middle-sized' objects closely approximate but differ from those of relativistic quantum physics. Should we conclude that the theory of 'restricted classical physics' and relativistic quantum theory conflict, just because of this? I think not, and so I propose that we say that two systems conflict if some consequence of one theory is '*discernibly* incompatible' with a consequence of the other, either causally, metaphysically, or logically. That is, I shall require that where two systems conflict, there is, at least in principle, an experimental way to determine which, if either has the correct consequence. I propose then:

D16.   Systems C_1 and C_2 conflict $=_{df}$. There is some set of statements of initial conditions, I, such that: (1) I is causally (and so metaphysically and logically) compatible with C_1 and C_2 individually, but (2) two sentences, which are *discernibly* incompatible, either causally, metaphysically, or logically, are derivable from $\{C_1 \cdot C_2 \cdot I\}$.

Final Definition of Maximal Explanatory Coherence. Finally, with its three key phrases explicated by definitions D14, D15, and D16, we can replace D13 by an acceptable one concerning explanation sets:

D17.   Explanation set $\{C, I\}$ has *maximum explanatory coherence* for set F among the sets in set $B =_{df}$.
(1) $\{C, I\}$ is in B; and
(2) $\{C, I\}$ is consistent, and for any system, C_i, that is in B, if C_i is consistent but C and C_i conflict, then for any y:
(a) $\{C, I\}$ P-explains at least as many statements in F as $\{C_i, y\}$ P-explains, and
(b) it is false that $\{C_i, y\}$ P-explains as many statements in F as $\{C, I\}$ does, and C_i is also a better explanatory system than C is.

On Defining Maximal Explanation Sets

Let us turn now to consider D12, which concerns maximal systems. In doing this, we should keep in mind how its key phrase is unpacked in D17, and that being maximal is to be proposed as central to a condition that is sufficient for justification. Of course, one change in D12 is immediately required by D17, namely, that explanation sets containing explanatory systems, rather than the systems alone, are what are maximal. But other changes are also needed. For example, assume that today a person, s_1, understands only one explanation set for three of his foundational statements at t, namely, p = 'I am now hearing (something that is) thunder', b_1 = 'I now believe with certainty that I am now hearing thunder'; b_2 = 'I am now having an auditory experience of thunder'. Further, assume that the one explanation set that s_1 understands is {'Whenever thundering results from Zeus's throwing thunderbolts, the noise causes me to have an experience of thunder, believe I hear thunder, and actually hear thunder' (C_1); 'It is thundering now, and it is caused by Zeus' (I_1)}. If we assume D12 and the explanatory foundational theory, F3.21, then it follows that C_1 and I_1 are justified for s_1 at t. But this is surely mistaken. It is not enough for justification that, by default, {C_1, I_1} has maximum explanatory coherence among the explanation sets that s_1 understands. There clearly are better explanations of these three statements that are generally quite well understood, and s_1's inferior explanation does not deserve to be justified for him because he fails to grasp what most of us quite easily understand. For example, a better explanation system, C_2, which replaces Zeus and his thunderbolts by discharges of static electricity, is readily available and understandable.

We avoid the preceding objection to D12 by enlarging the set of explanatory systems from which a maximal one is to be picked by including in the set all those explanation sets, such as {C_1, I_2}, that are generally understood at t. Then because C_2 is better than C_1, the set {C_1, I_1} is not maximal for s_1 at t, and the objection is avoided. Of course, system C_2 should not be justified for s_1 at t, even if it is the best explanation in the relevant set, because s_1 does not understand it. So we must require that a person understand any explanation set that is maximal for him. Let us, then, replace D12 by:

D18.   Explanation set {C, I} is maximal for s at t, relative to set $F =_{df}$ (1) s understands {C, I} at t, and (2) {C, I} has maximum explanatory coherence for set F among the explanation sets in set B_2: those either understood by s at t or generally understood at t.

Notice that D18 also accommodates a quite different person, s_2, perhaps like Einstein, who at one time is the only person to understand the best available explanation set. By D18 and the explanatory foundational theory, he and he alone is justified in believing that set at that time. For many of the rest of us at that time, some inferior explanation set that is generally understood would probably turn out to be justified. This, I believe, is as it should be.

Definition D18 is not free of objections, however. Consider s_3 who has an explanation set $\{C_3, I_3\}$ which only he understands, but which, contrary to what s_3 believes, is clearly inferior to some other set, $\{C_4, I_4\}$, that s_3 understands but believes does not explain what is foundational for him at t. In this case, $\{C_3, I_3\}$ is not justified for s_3 at t, because, according to D18, it is not maximal for s_3 at t. But suppose $\{C_4, I_4\}$ is the best explanation available at t. Then, by D18 and F3.21, system C_4 would be justified for s_3 at t, even though he falsely believes that it does not explain what is to be explained for him at t. This is quite implausible, so we should reject D18. I propose we require that a person have a true belief about which of his foundational statements are explained by any system that is to be maximal for him. And I also think it is necessary for him to believe that system. We need not also require, however, that he believe the system is maximal for him. Let us consider, then:

D19. Explanation set $\{C, I\}$ is maximal for s at t, relative to set $F =_{\text{df}}$. (1) s understands and believes $\{C, I\}$ at t; (2) for any statement in set F, if it is explained by $\{C, I\}$, then s believes that $\{C, I\}$ explains it; and (3) $\{C, I\}$ has maximum explanatory coherence for set F among the explanation sets in set B_2: those either understood by s at t or generally understood at t.

An Objection to Definition D19: It Is Too Restrictive a View of Justification. Definition D19 is not free of objections, however. Someone might object that D19 places too strong a requirement on justification. Imagine a person in a very primitive society at present whose explanations, like the one in terms of Zeus, are far from the best. Is such a person never to be justified in any of his explanatory beliefs? Surely not, according to this objection. Fortunately, we need not doubt whether the 'inferior' explanations given in primitive societies are ever justified for the members of that society. This objection fails because it construes an explanation set's being maximal as a necessary condition for its justification. But our minimal version of an explanatory foundation theory states it only as crucial to a sufficient condition. Thus it leaves open the question of when such 'primitive' systems are justified. That question is to be answered by an extension of the minimal thesis, and such an extension goes well beyond what is required for our immediate concern: the refutation of skeptical thesis M_1S_3.

A Second Objection to D19: *What Is Generally Understood and Believed May Not Be Justifiable.* Another objection to D19 is clearly relevant to our purpose in devising a definition of 'maximal explanation set'. It states that being maximal, as defined by D19, is too weak to be a sufficient condition for a system being justified, because at some time the general level of understanding might be so low compared to what is required to understand the best extant explanatory system that no system generally understood should be justified for anyone at that time. And, more importantly for our purposes, none of these inferior systems that are generally understood should be used to 'refute' a skeptical thesis. This is especially true given my announced policy of being epistemically conservative when confronting skepticism. Although I have enunciated this principle of conservatism and thus agree we should use it here, I am far from clear that we would violate the principle if we allowed justification of a generally understood system which is greatly inferior to the best system that is understood by only a few experts. And the claim that no such inferior system is ever justified for anyone is even more debatable. Surely, we need not be so epistemically conservative to allow justification only for experts. Nevertheless, let me make two points that, without rebutting this objection directly, will, I believe, considerably weaken its force.

The first point is that, although in Chapter 10, I shall use certain generally understood systems in my attempt to derive consequences incompatible with skeptical thesis M_1S_3, I shall also briefly indicate how much more difficult and less widely understood scientific theories count equally well against M_1S_3. Thus anyone who thinks that D19 is too liberal to use when rebutting skepticism, could use D19a instead. Their difference is that clause (3) of D19 is replaced by:

(3a) $\{C, I\}$ has maximum explanatory coherence for set F among the explanation sets in B_3: those understood by someone at t.

Of course, if we use D19a, we may only be able to show that certain complex explanatory systems are justified for only a small number of people. But that would be enough for our aim of refuting skepticism. And, should that be achieved, it would seem to be reasonable to liberalize the sufficient condition for justification of systems to allow most of the rest of us to be justified in accepting inferior systems. So it seems that using D19a instead of D19 would ultimately have the same results regarding skepticism.

The second point is that, because of objections like the present one, when I propose the final version of our explanatory foundational theory, I shall not take a set's being maximal for s at t, relative to set F_1 (the set of statements to be explained for s at t) as sufficient for its being acceptable. This will be conjoined with other conditions including one to the effect that if there are explanations sets for F_1 accepted by those who are experts at t concerning what explains the members of F_1, then at least one of the 'best' of these has a system that does not conflict with the system of the set that is maximal for s at t relative to set F_1. Here one of the 'best' sets accepted by certain experts at t for set F is one of those that has maximum explanatory coherence for set F_1 among the sets that are accepted by those experts at t. In many cases, the 'best' sets held by experts will include the foremost scientific theories. And, although I maintain that a person need not always understand and believe such theories in order to have an acceptable explanation set, we should at least require, for our conservative sufficient condition for the acceptability of such sets, that his maximal set not conflict with every one of them.

A Final Objection and a Final Definition: Explaining All Foundational Statements. Even D19 and D19a are not without a flaw. Each definition allows a system to be justified for someone at a time when that system is the best in set B_2 or B_3, but it explains only a small percentage of those statements that are to be explained for that person at that time. But an explanatory system must do better than that if it is to be justified. Indeed, invoking our principle of epistemic conservatism again, I propose that we require that any maximal explanation set explains all the statements that are to be explained for s at t. After all, at any one time there will be at most a few statements that are to be explained for any one person. Furthermore, it is clear that there should be some statements to be explained for s at t, if some explanation set is to be maximal for s at t. So let us make two changes in D19 to accommodate these two latest requirements, and one final change to accommodate that 'pragmatic' element in being maximal for someone, which we noted previously. What results is:

D20.   Explanation set $\{C, I\}$ is *maximal* for s at t, relative to set $F =_{\mathrm{df}}$.

(1) s understands and believes $\{C, I\}$ at t;
(2) there are sentences in F, all of which are P-explained by $\{C, I\}$;
(3) at t, s believes that $\{C, I\}$ explains each member of F;
(4) $\{C, I\}$ has maximum explanatory coherence for set F among the explanation sets in B_2: those that are understood by s at t or are generally understood at t; *and*
(5) $\{C, I\}$ is as helpful to s at t, for understanding the members of F and for devising other explanations of other data, as any set that satisfies clause (4).

And, as before, we construct D20a from D20 by replacing set B_2 by B_3. Here at last, I claim, we have a definition of 'maximal explanation set' – either D20 or D20a – that we can adopt. Each of these is more restrictive than D19. In this respect, each may help dissipate the force of the preceding objection to D19. This is not to say that no problems remain, but rather that any which remain unexamined will be kept in abeyance until the final version of our minimal explanatory foundation theory is devised.

Toward a Minimal Explanatory Foundational Theory

Now that we have replaced D12 by D20 and D13 by D17, and have defined the three crucial terms of D17 in D14, D15, and D16, we are almost ready to give a final characterization of the minimal version of the explanatory foundational theory. But, first, five amendments will be proposed for clause (iii) of F3.21, which embodies our first attempt to add to the minimal plausible foundational thesis, F3.2, what is needed to produce the minimal explanatory foundational theory.

Five Amendments to Foundational Thesis F3.21. The first amendment concerns a problem for clause (b) of F3.21. When 'maximal system' is explicated by means of definitions D17 and D20, it is possible that two or more conflicting explanation sets will be maximal for one person at one time, unless the 'nonevidential' tests for explanatory systems combine to produce exactly one maximal system for each person at any one time. But, as will become clearer after we consider these tests in chapters 8 and 9, it is implausible to expect that there never will be any 'underdetermination of theory' in this sense.[14] So we must rephrase (iii) in F3.21 to accommodate any underdetermination, by providing a provision for singling out one from many maximal systems. I propose to do this in terms of the 'Jamesian' principle that if more than one conflicting system is maximal for s at t, then s has the epistemic right to use whichever one he wants at t to explain whatever is foundational for him at t. As noted in Chapter 6, this principle seems quite plausible, because no choice that such a person makes would result in his rejecting one system for another that is less credible for him at that time.

The second amendment is to counter one problem for conditions (b) and (c) of clause (iii). Once F3.21 is changed so it accommodates explanation sets, these conditions allow any logical consequence of $F \cup \{C, I\}$ to be justified for s at t. But it may be that C contains some clause or I conjunct that is irrelevant to the P-explanation of what is foundational for s at t. Sentences that are deducible from $F \cup \{C, I\}$ with essential dependence on these irrelevant clauses or conjuncts should not be justified for s at t. Consequently, no C or I which has such clauses or conjuncts should be justified for s at t, because certain sentences are deducible from these irrelevant clauses or conjuncts alone and so would be justified for s at t if what deductively yields them is justified for s at t.

On the Minimal Version of an Explanation Set. I propose to eliminate irrelevant clauses and conjuncts by using the notion of a 'minimal version' of $\{C, I\}$. To unpack this phrase, we need some auxiliary concepts. Let I_m be a shortest conjunction of the conjuncts of I such that $\{C, I_m\}$ P-explains exactly those members of set F that $\{C, I\}$ P-explains. Then let C_p be C rewriten in prenex normal form with its matrix in conjunctive normal form, and let there be n nonequivalent C_p^i's, each of which has at least one conjunctive clause of C_p, and is either C_p itself or C_p without one or more of its n conjunctive clauses. Thus we get a set of unique formulas, including one that is logically equivalent to C. For example, if $C = (x)[(y)(Fy \lor Gy) \supset Hx]$, then $C_p = (x)(\exists y)[(\sim Fy \lor Hx) \cdot (\sim Gy \lor Hx)]$. And one C_p^i is $(x)(\exists y)(\sim Fy \lor Hx)$. Our definition is:

> D21. $\{C_m, I_m\}$ is a *minimal version* of explanation set $\{C, I\}$ for set $F =_{\mathrm{df.}} \{C_m, I_m\}$ P-explains exactly those members of F that $\{C, I\}$ P-explains; and C_m is some C_p^i such that no $\{C_p^i, I_m\}$ P-explains exactly the members of F that $\{C, I\}$ explains, and also has fewer conjuncts of C_p than C_m has.

I shall require that a justifying set, $\{C, I\}$, be its own minimal version for the relevant foundational set. That is, I shall say, $\{C, I\}$ is $\{C, I\}_m$ for set F, which means that every $I_m = I$, and every $C_m = C$, for set F. As a result, there will be no justification of irrelevant statements because $\{C, I\}$ will contain none when it is $\{C, I\}_m$.

An Objection to Clause (iii) *of* F3.21: *Some Probabilities Are Too Low for Acceptability.* Even with the first two amendments, a third problem for (iii) remains untouched, and so requires a third amendment. In chapter 3, when we were considering arguments to show that acceptability requires certainty, I indicated a tentative and provisional approval of three assumptions, namely, A3, A5, and also A8 which is equivalent to A3. And, earlier in this chapter I proposed we adopt A5, which entails both A3 and A8. But any of these three assumptions gives rise to a problem for clause (c) of (iii), and so I shall state the objection using the weaker A3 rather than A5. That is, I shall use:

A3.   If e is s's evidence for p at t, then $\mathrm{Cr}_{s,\,t}(p) \leqslant \mathrm{Pr}_{s,\,t}(p/e) \times \mathrm{Pr}_{s,\,t}(e)$.

The objection is this. Let p be a statement deducible from $F_1 \cup \{C, I\}_m$. Then, according to amended clause (c), p is acceptable for s at t. So, because by definition D1, p is acceptable for s at t only if $\mathrm{Cr}_{s,\,t}(p) > 0.5$, it follows that p is acceptable for s at t, given A3, only if $\mathrm{Pr}_{s,\,t}(p/F_1 \cup \{C, I\}_m > 0.5$. But, according to this objection, the product of these two probabilities is sometimes less than 0.5, and so clause (c) is not sufficient for acceptability. What supposedly makes this product too low is, of course, not the first probability – it equals 1, because p is deducible from $F_1 \cup \{C, I\}_m$. It is the second probability which is the probability of the union of three sets. Assume these are: set $S_1 =$ the set of sentences that satisfy the antecedent of H3 for s at t; set $S_2 =$ the set of sentences that satisfy BR3 or BR4 for evidence $e = S_1$; and set $\{C, I\}_m$ for set F_1. Thus $\mathrm{Pr}_{s,\,t}(F_1 \cup \{C, I\}_m) = \mathrm{Pr}_{s,\,t}(S_1/S_2 \cup \{C, I\}_m) \times \mathrm{Pr}_{s,\,t}(\{C, I\}_m/S_2) \times \mathrm{Pr}_{s,\,t}(S_2)$.[15] And, because $\mathrm{Pr}_{s,\,t}(S_1) = 1$, it follows that $\mathrm{Pr}_{s,\,t}(S_2) = \mathrm{Pr}_{s,\,t}(S_2/S_1)$. But it seems that sometimes $\mathrm{Pr}_{s,\,t}(S_2/S_1)$ is not very high – assume it is less than 0.7. And it seems reasonable that at the same time $\mathrm{Pr}_{s,\,t}(\{C, I\}_m/S_2$ is low, surely no greater than 0.7. Thus sometimes $\mathrm{Pr}_{s,\,t}(F_1 \cup \{C, I\}_m) > 0.49$, and so is $\mathrm{Cr}_{s,\,t}(p)$, assuming A3, even though p meets what clause (c) requires.

This objection is difficult to evaluate because we have no means available for determining any maximum values for specific probabilities that are less than 1. Nevertheless, in our present conservative mood we should find a way to guarantee that the sort of case which generates this objection never arises. Someone might propose to do this by lowering the minimum degree of credibility required for acceptability or by allowing $Cr_{s,t}(p)$ to exceed $Pr_{s,t}(p/e) \times Pr_{s,t}(e)$. But I think neither approach is remotely plausible. I immediately dismiss the first proposal, which requires the rejection of definition D1. I introduced the epistemic concept of credibility in this discussion in order to give a quantitative understanding of acceptability which requires a statement to be more reasonable, that is, more credible, than its denial. But this first proposal, coupled with D1, would allow a statement to be acceptable when less credible than its denial.

The second proposal requires the rejection of assumptions A3, A5, and A8. One way to do this is to identify $Cr_{s,t}(p)$ with $Pr_{s,t}(p)$ which, unless $Pr_{s,t}(e) = 1$ or $Pr_{s,t}(p/\bar{e}) = 0$, is greater than $Pr_{s,t}(p/e) \times Pr_{s,t}(e)$. But, as I argued in Chapter 3, I find this quite implausible, because, where e is s's total evidence for p at t, it seems unreasonable that the credibility of p for s at t should in any way be positively affected by evidence that is unavailable to s at t or by probabilities involving the denial of the evidence that is available to s at t. Thus I hold that $Pr_{s,t}(p/\bar{e}) \times Pr_{s,t}(\bar{e})$ should never increase the credibility of p for s at t, as it would if, as is usual, it is greater than zero, and also $Cr_{s,t}(p) = Pr_{s,t}(p)$. So I reject the second proposal as I did the first. Furthermore, the second, like the first, is also unsatisfactory, because, with D1, it would sometimes yield that a sentence is acceptable for someone when it is improbable relative to his evidence and his evidence is improbable.

I believe that, without rules for putting maximums on probabilities, the best we can do is to amend clause (c) so that when p is a consequence of a q, such as $F_1 \cup \{C, I\}_m$, p is acceptable for s at t only if q is also. This third amendment would seem to exclude some of these consequences, but many would be included, given one additional assumption that seems quite unexceptional:

All.   If $Cr_{s,t}(p) = n$, p entails q, and q is contingent, then $Cr_{s,t}(q) > n$.

This is, of course, true for probabilities and I find credibilities should agree with probabilities at least in this regard. For example, any logical consequences of either $S_1 \cup S_2$ or $S_1 \cup \{C, I\}_m$, would be acceptable for s at t, if S_2 or $\{C, I\}_m$ is, respectively. This is easily shown. Given F3.21 we have the following: $Pr_{s,t}(S_1) = 1$, and $Cr_{s,t}(\{C, I\}_m) > 0.5$. Thus, by A5, $Pr_{s,t}(S_2/e_1) \times Pr_{s,t}(e_1) > 0.5$, and $Pr_{s,t}(\{C, I\}_m/e_2) > 0.5$, where $e_1 = S_1$ and $e_2 = S_1 \cup S_2$, because, at t, those two sets are s's evidence for S_2 and $\{C, I\}_m$, respectively. Also, by A5, $Cr_{s,t}(S_1 \cup S_2) = Pr_{s,t}(S_1 \cup S_2/e_3) \times$

$\text{Pr}_{s,t}(e_3)$, and $\text{Cr}_{s,t}(S_1 \cup \{C, I\}_m) = \text{Pr}_{s,t}(S_1 \cup \{C, I\}_m/e_4) \times \text{Pr}_{s,t}(e_4)$. Here $e_3 = e_1$ and $e_4 = e_2$, because s's evidence for $S_1 \cup S_2$ is $S_1 = e_1$, and his evidence for $S_1 \cup \{C, I\}_m$ is $S_1 \cup S_2 = e_2$. Also $\text{Pr}_{s,t}(S_1 \cup S_2/e_1) = \text{Pr}_{s,t}(S_1/e_1 \cup S_2) \times \text{Pr}_{s,t}(S_2/e_1) = \text{Pr}_{s,t}(S_2/e_1)$. Therefore, $\text{Cr}_{s,t}(S_1 \cup S_2) = \text{Pr}_{s,t}(S_2/e_1) \times \text{Pr}_{s,t}(e_1) = \text{Cr}_{s,t}(S_2)$. Thus $S_1 \cup S_2$ and, by All, what it entails are acceptable for s at t, if S_2 is. Similarly, $\text{Pr}_{s,t}(S_1 \cup \{C, I\}_m/e_2) = \text{Pr}_{s,t}(\{C, I\}_m/e_2)$. Therefore, $\text{Cr}_{s,t}(S_1 \cup \{C, I\}_m) = \text{Pr}_{s,t}(\{C, I\}_m/e_2) \times \text{Pr}_{s,t}(e_2) = \text{Cr}_{s,t}(\{C, I\}_m)$. So $S_1 \cup \{C, I\}_m$ and what it entails are acceptable for s at t, if $\{C, I\}_m$ is.

It may seem that I could also conclude that $S_1 \cup S_2$ is always acceptable for s, because S_2 is always acceptable for s. But that would be a mistake. Although each member of S_2 is acceptable for s at t, according to BR3, BR4, and H3, that does not guarantee that the set or conjunction of those members is acceptable. It is easy to see how problems like those created by the lottery paradox would often arise if we allowed the acceptability of a conjunction to be inferred from the acceptability of its conjuncts. For example, we can imagine a case where $\text{Pr}_{s,t}(p_1/S_1) > 0.5$ and $\text{Pr}_{s,t}(p_2/S_1) > 0.5$ by BR3, but $\text{Pr}_{s,t}(p_2) < 0.7$, and $\text{Pr}_{s,t}(p_1/p_2) < 0.7$. Then $\text{Pr}_{s,t}(p_1 \cdot p_2) < 0.5$, and $(p_1 \cdot p_2)$ would not be acceptable for s at t, even though, individually, p_1 and p_2 would be. So there may well be cases where $\text{Pr}_{s,t}(S_2) < 0.5$.

The problem that the lottery paradox raises for the acceptability of set S_2 should make us cautious about how we identify set F_1, the set of statements that are to be explained. It is tempting to identify F_1 with $S_1 \cup S_2$ under all conditions, but there are two reasons to reject that claim. The first stems from the preceding problem about S_2. If $\text{Pr}_{s,t}(S_2) < 0.5$, then $\text{Pr}_{s,t}(S_1 \cup S_2) < 0.5$. Surely, then, we would not want to require an explanation set to explain an unacceptable set of statements. For example, in the preceding case let $p_1 = $ 'I am now seeing something that is black', and $p_2 = $ 'I am now seeing something that is a swan'. It is easy to imagine a case where $0.5 < \text{Pr}_{s,t}(p_1/S_1) \simeq \text{Pr}_{s,t}(p_2/S_1) < 0.7$, and $\text{Pr}_{s,t}(S_1) = 1$ because S_1 satisfies H3. And if, as is at least somewhat plausible, $\text{Pr}_{s,t}(p_1/p_2) < 0.7$, then $\text{Pr}_{s,t}(p_1 \cdot p_2) < 0.5$. Consequently, we must require that $F_1 = S_1 \cup S_2$ only when $\text{Pr}_{s,t}(S_2) > 0.5$.

The second reason for caution is that, generally, explanation sets explain eternal sentences rather than those whose truth-values vary according to persons, places, or times. So we should not require an explanation set to explain $S_1 \cup S_2$ which contains only reports and thus no eternal sentences. We can easily solve this problem, however, by requiring any explanation set that is justified for s at t to explain F_1 whose members are the members of $S_1 \cup S_2$ eternalized to s at t. It should be remembered, incidentally, that there are two ways to eternalize a report, r, to s at t, both of which I symbolize by *Trst*. One of these is to take a 'semantic ascent' and read *Trst* as 'r is true of s at t'; the other is to replace 'I' and 'now' in r by 's' and 'at t' respectively. I shall allow explanation sets to explain either sort of eternal sentence when they explain F_1. Usually, of course, they will explain the second, nonsemantic sentences. It might be objected that I should be more liberal and allow the explanation of the members of $S_1 \cup S_2$, or the members of F_1. Indeed, many of our own informal explanations do explain reports that have not been eternalized, as I shall indicate in Chapter 10. Nevertheless, I again suggest we remain conservative at present, while our goal is to refute epistemological skepticism.

The Final Version of the Minimal Explanatory Foundational Theory

I am almost ready to propose a revised version of F3.21, but first I wish to make two more changes so that the theory is more usable as a criterion. Let us replace reference to foundational statements in clause (iii.b) of F3.21 by an explicit mention of those conditions which, according to thesis FF, make a statement foundational. Thus no questions are begged about the epistemic status of the statements that meet these conditions when they are not explained. Thus a nonfoundationalist could take these statements to be foundational for explanation but not epistemically foundational. We need not, however, unpack the phrases 'maximal explanation set', and 'maximum explanatory system'. Finally, as previously noted, we want nó explanation set that is justified according to the minimal theory to conflict with all the best explanation sets for F_1 that are accepted by experts on F_1 at t. So we have the following quite complicated statement of the minimal explanatory foundational theory:

F3.22.   Any empirical statement, p, would be acceptable for s at t *if and only if* it would be true that:
   A. either p is a member of set T_1 = the set of sentences that are initially acceptable for s at t, or there is an E-series for p that justifies p for s at t;
   and:
   B. each E-series for p that justifies p for s at t is such that:
      (1) it is finite, and
      (2) it contains some empirical statement that is initially

acceptable for s at t, and

(3) it contains only statements that are acceptable for s at t, and

(4) it contains a statement, q, that is not initially acceptable for s at t, only if it contains an E-ancestor of q, and

(5) it contains no empirical statement that is itself (or is analytically equivalent to) one of its own E-ancestors;

and:

C. there is an E-series that justifies p for s at t, *if and only if p* is a member of *either*:

(1) T_2 = the set of empirical sentences such that for each one, q, q is justified for s at t relative to set T_1, and $\mathrm{Pr}_{s,t}(q/T_1) \times \mathrm{Pr}_{s,t}(T_1) > 0.5$; *or*

(2) T_3 = the set of empirical sentences such that for each one, r, s's evidence for r at t is S_i which is a subset of the set $T_1 \cup T_2$, and $\mathrm{Pr}_{s,t}(r/S_i) \times \mathrm{Pr}_{s,t}(S_i) > 0.5$; *or*

(3) T_4 = the set of conjunctions of the members of the explanation set, u, such that s's evidence for u at t is S_j which is a subset of $T_1 \cup T_2 \cup T_3$, and $\mathrm{Pr}_{s,t}(u/S_j) \times \mathrm{Pr}_{s,t}(S_j) > 0.5$; *or*

(4) T_5 = the set of empirical sentences such that for each one, v, s's evidence for v at t is S_k which is a subset of $T_1 \cup T_2 \cup T_4$ but not of $T_1 \cup T_2$, and $\mathrm{Pr}_{s,t}(v/S_k) \times \mathrm{Pr}_{s,t}(S_k) > 0.5$;

and:

D. p is a member of:

(1) T_1, if p is in set S_1 = the set of empirical sentences that satisfy H3 for s at t;

(2) T_2, if p is in set S_2 = the set of empirical sentences that satisfy BR3 or BR4, for evidence $e = S_1$;

(3) T_3, if p is in set S_3 = the set of empirical sentences that are entailed by some S_i that is a subset of $S_1 \cup S_2$, and $\mathrm{Cr}_{s,t}(S_i) > 0.5$;

(4) T_4, if (a) p is the conjunction of the members of the set $S_4 = \{C, I\}$, (b) $\{C, I\}$ is its own minimal version for foundational set F_1 whose members are the members of $S_1 \cup S_2$ eternalized to s at t, (c) $\mathrm{Pr}_{s,t}(F_1) > 0.5$, (d) $\{C, I\}$ is maximal for s at t relative to F_1, (e) if

some experts about F_1 at t accept explanation sets for F_1, then at least one of the best of these does not conflict with S_4, and (f) at t, s chooses $\{C, I\}$ to explain the members of F_1;

(5) T_5, if p is in set $S_5 =$ the set of empirical statements that are entailed by some S_j that is a subset of $S_1 \cup S_2 \cup S_4$ but not of $S_1 \cup S_2$, and $Cr_{s,t}(S_j) > 0.5$.

Three More Differences Between F3.21 and F3.22. Three points should be noted about differences between F3.21 and F3.22 that have not been covered in the preceding discussion. First, because of its clause (iii), F3.21 implies that a statement, p, is acceptable if p is foundational for explanation, that is, p is in S_1 or S_2, and there is a justifying E-series for p. But p being in S_1 is, as F3.22 implies, sufficient for p being initially acceptable, whether or not there is such an E-series. And this is as it should be. Not only is no E-series needed to justify p when it is initially acceptable, there is no guarantee that there always is one for such a statement. This is because no evidence and thus no E-series is needed to justify p when it is initially acceptable, and it may be that for some p, p would be justified relative to a set of its E-ancestors in an E-series only if p is one of them. But such an E-series is prohibited by clause (e) of (ii) in F3.21 and by clause B(5) of F3.22.

The second point is that I have divided the replacement for clause (iii) of F3.21 into clauses C and D. I did this because I wanted to have each of the four sorts of inferentially acceptable statements delineated without reliance on the one sufficient condition for statements being of that sort that is provided by the *minimum* explanatory foundational theory in clause D. That is, C delineates these four sets, and D provides just one sufficient condition for membership in each of those four sets plus a fifth condition that is sufficient for being initially acceptable. This allows additional clauses to be conjoined with C and D in order to provide additional sufficient conditions for each set in C, when the theory is expanded beyond its minimal version.

The third point concerns the reason I considered sets T_3 and T_5 separately, especially since clauses D(3) and D(5) can be so easily conjoined into one sufficient condition for membership in $T_3 \cup T_5$. I keep T_3 and T_5 separate, because when the minimal theory is expanded, there might be some new sufficient conditions for membership in T_3 or T_5 that should be kept distinct from those for membership in the other set, and so I do not want to foreclose this possibility. For our present purposes, however, we need not keep the sets distinct, and so, as we shall soon see, I shall not.

A Criterion for Acceptability That Is Derivable from F3.22. As stated, F3.22 may well be too complicated to use or test. We can, however, derive a much simpler sufficient condition for acceptability from F3.22 once we realize two points. First, according to F3.22, if an empirical sentence, p, satisfies one of the five conditions of clause D, then clause A is also true, because of clause C. But clause A is, by itself, sufficient for p being acceptable for s at t. So, if a sentence meets one condition of clause D, it is acceptable for s at t. That is, we have available the following simpler thesis, which is true if F3.22 is, and which we shall use instead of F3.22 in much of the following discussion:

F3.221. Any empirical statement, p, is acceptable for s at t, if *either*:
   (1) p is in S_1 = the set of sentences that satisfy the antecedent of H3 for s at t; *or*
   (2) p is in S_2 = the set of sentences that satisfy the antecedent of BR3 or BR4, for $e = S_1$; *or*
   (3) (a) p is the conjunction of the members of the set $S_4 = \{C, I\}$, (b) $\{C, I\}$ is its own minimal version for set F_1 whose members are the members of $S_1 \cup S_2$ eternalized to s at t, (c) $\text{Pr}_{s,t}(F_1) > 0.5$, (d) $\{C, I\}$ is maximal for s at t relative to F_1, (e) if some experts about F_1 at t accept explanation sets for F_1, then at least one of the best of these sets does not conflict with S_4, and (f) at t, s chooses $\{C, I\}$ to explain the members of F_1 (that is, let us say, p is S_4 which is the *best* explanation set for s at t, relative to F_1); *or*
   (4) p is in set $S_6 = S_3 \cup S_5$ = the set of sentences that are entailed by some S_i that is a subset of $S_1 \cup S_2 \cup S_4$ and $\text{Cr}_{s,t}(S_i) > 0.5$.

An Objection to Theory F.322. Our future discussion will generally center on the relatively simple F3.221. However, there is an objection to F3.22 that would be missed if we ignored F3.22 completely. It arises because clause B of F3.22 provides five individually necessary conditions for acceptability, and it is not obvious that anything that meets one of the last four sufficient conditions stated in clause D of F3.22 also satisfies each of these five necessary conditions, and also is acceptable, as is required if F3.22 is correct. In particular, if F3.22 is correct, then for any sentence, p, that is in set T_2, T_3, T_4, or T_5 because it satisfies a clause of D, there is an E-series that meets at least four conditions: it is finite, it justifies p for s at t, it contains only acceptable statements, and it contains no empirical statement that is its own E-ancestor. But, according to the present objection, it is unreasonable to think that these four conjointly necessary conditions are always satisfied when some clause of D is satisfied, and so it is not reasonable to accept F3.22. The way to rebut this objection, of course, is to indicate that there is always at least one justifying E-series for any sentence in set S_2, S_3, S_4, or S_5, which meets all of these necessary conditions for being a justifying E-series.

It is clear that there is always a justifying finite E-series for p if p meets clause $D(2)$ that is, p is in S_2. Any such p has an E-series with just one member, $e_1 = S_1$. So by H3, $\mathrm{Pr}_{s,t}(S_1) = 1$, and by either BR3 or BR4, $\mathrm{Pr}_{s,t}(p/S_1) > 0.5$. Consequently, by A5, $\mathrm{Cr}_{s,t}(p) > 0.5$. Thus not only is p justified relative to e_1, this E-series meets all requirements of clause B and also justifies p for s at t, because the evidence in e_1 is initially certain for s at t. It is also clear that if p is in S_3 or S_5, because of meeting $D(3)$ or $D(5)$ then there is a justifying E-series for p that satisfies clause B, *if* there is a justifying E-series for set S_i (the relevant subset of $S_1 \cup S_2 \cup S_4$) that satisfies clause B. This is because if there is such an E-series for S_i, then there is also a series for p when it meets $D(3)$ or $D(5)$. In this series for p, evidence set $e_1 = S_i$, and any set e_j in the series for S_i is e_{j+1} in the series for p. Thus this series meets what clause B requires, and also justifies p for s at t, *if* the first series justifies S_i for s at t and satisfies clause B. This is true, because, by meeting $D(3)$ or $D(5)$, p is entailed by S_i, and $\mathrm{Cr}_{s,t}(S_i) > 0.5$. So by A5, p is highly credible for s at t, and, by definition D1a, p is acceptable for s at t.

Furthermore, it is easy to find an E-series that satisfies clause B for such an S_i for any p that meets conditions $D(3)$ or $D(5)$. Consider $D(3)$ first. In this case, S_i is a subset of $S_1 \cup S_2$, and if S_i contains statements that are not initially acceptable, then s's evidence for S_i is S_1. Therefore, because by $D(3)$, $\mathrm{Cr}_{s,t}(S_i) > 0.5$, and $\mathrm{Pr}_{s,t}(S_1) = 1$, it follows, with A5, that $\mathrm{Pr}_{s,t}(S_i/S_1) > 0.5$. So there is an E-series for S_i with just one member, $e_1 = S_1$ and this E-series meets all requirements of clause B. Similarly, for any p meeting $D(5)$, there is also an E-series that satisfies clause B. In this case, S_i is a subset of $S_1 \cup S_2 \cup S_4$, but not of $S_1 \cup S_2$. So s's evidence for S_i would be some S_j that is a subset of $S_1 \cup S_2$. Thus, because by D(5), $Cr_{s,t}(S_i) > 0.5$, we get by A5, $Pr_{s,t}(S_i/S_j) \times Pr_{s,t}(S_j) > 0.5$. And since, as previously, s's evidence for this S_j is S_1, we get a two-membered E-series for this S_i with $e_1 = S_j$ and $e_2 = S_1$, both of which are acceptable for s at t, as required by B(3). For S_j this is true, because $Pr_{s,t}(S_j) > 0.5$, and so $Pr_{s,t}(S_j/S_1) \times Pr_{s,t}(S_1) > 0.5$. That is, by A5, $Cr_{s,t}(S_j) > 0.5$.

Finally, we can also construct an E-series for a p that satisfies clause D(4). Such a p is a conjunction of the members of the explanation set, S_4, that is the best for s at t relative to foundational set F_1. In such a case, I would claim that the evidence for set S_4 is F_1, and, as above, the evidence for F_1 is S_1. So we have a two-membered E-series for p, namely, one with $p_1 = F_1$, and $e_2 = S_1$. Again, there is an E-series that meets all that clause B requires, including B(3), because by D(4), $Pr_{s,t}(F_1) > 0.5$, and so $Pr_{s,t}(F_1/S_1) \times Pr_{s,t}(S_1) > 0.5$. That is, $Cr_{s,t}(F_1) > 0.5$. We can conclude, then, that whatever satisfies clauses D(2) through D(5) also meets what clause B requires. Unfortunately, it is not as easy to show that a statement that meets any one of these four clauses of D is also acceptable for s at t because, as F3.22 implies, it is justified for s at t by some E-series.

The Objection Elaborated: Some Explanation Sets Are Not Probable Relative to Foundational Evidence. It is clear that any statement, p, satisfying either D(2), D(3), or D(5) is justified for s at t by the E-series for them described above. In these cases $Cr_{s,t}(p) > 0.5$, because, for D(2), $Pr_{s,t}(p/S_1) \times Pr_{s,t}(S_1) > 0.5$, and, for D(3) and D(5), p is entailed by an S_i such that $Cr_{s,t}(S_i) > 0.5$. The problematic case, of course, is a sentence that satisfies clause D(4), and so is the conjunction of the members of S_4, which is an explanation set meeting certain conditions. The objection to the claim that such a p is acceptable for s at t is as follows. If S_4 is acceptable for s at t, because justified by the E-series mentioned above, then, by A5, $Pr_{s,t}(S_4/F_1) \times Pr_{s,t}(F_1) > 0.5$, because $S_1 \cup S_2$ is s's evidence for p at t. But surely $Pr_{s,t}(S_4/F_1) < 0.5$, because F_1 often consists of only a few basic-reports and observation-reports eternalized to s at t and no large, complex set of theoretical statements is probable relative to such a meager set. So, contrary to F3.22, this E-series does not justify p for s at t, because an E-series for p justifies p at t, only if set e_1 in the series is s's evidence for p at t, and p is probable relative to e_1 eternalized to s at t. But in this case $e_1 = S_1 \cup S_2$. So we should reject F3.22 because of D(4), and also, of course, F3.221 because of its clause (3).

The crux of the issue raised by the preceding claim can be most clearly stated as concerning whether or not it is unreasonable to accept the conditional:

C.   If $\{C, I\}$ is 'the best' explanation set for s at t, relative to set F_1 – that is, $\{C, I\}$ is its own minimal version for set F_1; $\mathrm{Pr}_{s,t}(F_1) > 0.5$; $\{C, I\}$ is maximal for s at t, relative to set F_1; at least one of the best explanation sets for F_1 at t does not conflict with $\{C, I\}$ and, at t, s chooses $\{C, I\}$ to explain F_1 – then $\mathrm{Pr}_{s,t}(\{C, I\}/F_1) \times \mathrm{Pr}_{s,t}(F_1) > 0.5$.

According to the objection, this conditional is clearly unreasonable, because the probability of an explanation set, given merely the set of foundational sentences it explains is often quite low. A second objection we should also consider is that even if each of these two probabilities in the consequent of C is high, their product is less than 0.5.

The crucial question for both objections concerns the plausibility of conditional C. The way to establish its implausibility is to find some statement to conjoin with its antecedent so that the resulting conditional is clearly false. But what might serve as such a conjunct? Consider all the various amendments I made when I defined 'minimal version of $\{C, I\}$', 'maximal explanation set', and 'maximum explanatory coherence', and when I devised clauses C and D of F3.22 to replace clause (iii) of F3.21. The point of all the work was, of course, to restrict the sorts of explanation sets that are found to have high credibility for a person at a time. So only certain very special explanation sets are awarded this high credibility by F3.22. And, since what I did also serves as my attempt to rule out such a falsifying conjunct, I conclude that there are no such conjuncts, and so we are justified in rejecting these objections. This, of course, is not to say that I have made it reasonable to accept the preceding conditional, but only that what I have done makes it not unreasonable to accept it. But might I do better than that?

On Justifying Hypothetical Induction. I know of just two ways to increase the reasonableness of the preceding conditional, only the second of which would be successful. The first is based on two claims. First, the form of induction that in Chapter 4 was called 'hypothetical induction' and 'inference to the best hypothesis' is a reasonable form of inference. Second, in the statement of that form of inference the phrase, 'Hypothesis T explains basic-reports, $b_1, b_2, ..., b_n$, better at t than any hypothesis that conflicts with T' is to be relativized to persons as well as times and explicated as 'system C is a member of the explanation set that is the best for s at t, relative to F_1'. From the second claim we can derive that conditional C is equivalent to the universally quantified conditional constructed by using the conjunction of the two premise-forms for hypothetical induction as antecedent, and its conclusion-form as consequent, when 'probable' is replaced by 'credible' and A5 is assumed. So because, as the first claim states, this form of inference is reasonable, so is its corresponding conditional and what is equivalent to it.

Unfortunately for this first way to justify C, no one seems to have justified the use of hypothetical induction, although many are strongly inclined to accept it because of its success in reconstructing the actual procedures often used to justify scientific theories. Nevertheless, I hope to correct this defect. The master argument of this book, which is an attempt to refute skeptical theses, such as M_1S_3, can also be understood, in brief, as an attempt to justify an epistemological theory which consists of F3.22 plus certain other axioms, such as A5, and then to use them to refute the skeptical theses. But once this theory is justified, so also is the preceding conditional and, thereby, hypothetical induction which corresponds to it. This, which is what I called the 'beneficial side effect' of the master argument in Chapter 1, is the second way to justify the conditional. But in this case its justification rests upon the justification of theory F3.22 by the master argument of this book. Consequently, I cannot rely on the reasonableness of hypothetical induction to show the reasonableness of the conditional, as the first approach requires. The order of justification is just reversed, as the second approach proposes.

Three Last Objections to Theory F3.22. I believe that, although I cannot yet show conditional C to be reasonable, the preceding discussion is sufficient to show C is not unreasonable. We can, then, reject the objection to F3.22 that it is unreasonable to think that every sentence that is acceptable according to F3.22 has an E-series which both justifies the sentence and meets what clause B requires of justifying E-series. Of course, there may be other objections I have failed to consider, but I believe that there are no others with any force. Nevertheless, I would like to try to dispel three more objections that might seem convincing to someone.

First Objection: Doubts About a Foundationalist Use of Hypothetical Induction. The first objection arises from some lingering doubts about hypothetical induction left unsolved in Chapter 4. The problem raised there was that one premise required by the use of hypothetical induction did not seem to be suitable for inferences from foundational sentences to non-foundational empirical statements, because this premise seemed not to be justifiable relative to evidence that consists only of foundational statements, analytic statements, and nonempirical epistemic principles. This premise stated, in effect, that hypothesis T explains the relevant foundational statements better than any conflicting hypothesis. This problem led us to draw the tentative conclusion that hypothetical induction does not provide the sort of inferences needed to extend justification beyond what is foundational and so refute skeptical thesis M_1S_3. If all this is true, then the question arises whether this problem also plagues F3.22, because, as I have just noted, a conditional that corresponds to a hypothetical inductive inference is implied by F3.22.

To see that F3.22 escapes this problem, let us first recall what we were attempting in Chapter 4 and how it differs from what F3.22 requires of us. In Chapter 4 we were trying to find a way to justify nonbasic statements relative to basic-reports, and, following philosophers, such as Descartes and Chisholm, we conducted our search by looking for premises consisting of basic-reports and analytic sentences from which to infer that some nonbasic statement is probable or acceptable. In Chapter 5, however, we unpacked the ambiguity of 'p is probable relative to e' and began to search for a sufficient condition for $\mathrm{Pr}_{s,\,t}(p/e)$ being high, just as in Chapter 3 we had looked for a sufficient condition for a basic-report being certain and found, I argued, H3. Furthermore, once H3, BR3, and BR4 were justified, we found a way to combine their antecedents to provide two sufficient conditions for the high probability of certain nonbasic statements. These two sufficient conditions are reproduced in clause D(2) of F3.22 and clause (2) of F3.221. It should be clear now that the epistemic role of the antecedents of H3, BR3, and BR4 and D(2) is quite different from the role of the antecedents of the conditionals corresponding to the various sorts of inferences discussed in Chapter 4. In the present four cases, none of the sufficient conditions are statements of evidence relative to which nonbasic statements are probable or acceptable for s at t. But all the examples in Chapter 4 are cases where the sufficient conditions do express evidence. Thus the restrictions placed on the sufficient conditions in Chapter 4 do not apply to any of the four antecedents mentioned above. That is, they need not be restricted to what is justifiable by foundational and analytic sentences, and epistemic principles.

The preceding discussion shows why the problem for the use of hy-

pothetical induction posed in Chapter 4 does not also arise for theory
F3.22. That theory does not require that a certain explanation set be
justified or acceptable relative to the antecedent of clause D(4). Rather it
states that if the antecedent of D(4) is met by set p, then p is justified relative to a certain foundational set, F_1. In this respect, D(4) resembles BR3
and BR4 which provide sufficient conditions for certain reports being
probable, given (and so, relative to) foundational evidence composed of
basic-reports. In none of these cases does the antecedent function to state
the evidence relative to which something is probable, justified, or acceptable. So no foundational restrictions apply to these antecedents, and
the problem that surfaced in Chapter 4 for hypothetical induction does not
affect F3.22 and F3.221.

*Second Objection: A Sentence Is Acceptable for Someone Only If He Justi-
fies that It Is.* I have concluded that a person need not concern himself
with the antecedent of D(4) in order for a certain explanation set to be
acceptable for him. Yet someone might complain that it surely is not
enough for a set being acceptable for s that, completely unknown to him,
it satisfies the antecedent of D(4). Surely, in addition, s must at least justify
that the set is acceptable for him. And, given F3.22, this requires that he
justify the antecedent of D(4). So s's justification of the antecedent of D(4)
is required after all. But this complaint is doubly dubious. First, it is quite
dubious that a person needs to have any understanding of what it is to
justify something in order that something be acceptable for him. The
ability to go through some procedure that succeeds in justifying something is not widely found among human beings, but the deficiency should
not require that nothing is inferentially acceptable for someone. So the
fact that a person has not succeeded in justifying a statement seems clearly
not to be sufficient for the statement not being inferentially acceptable for
that person. Second, even if actual justification were required, it is false
that F3.22 requires that each person proceed to justify the acceptability of
any particular explanation set by justifying the antecedent of D(4). That
clause states only one sufficient condition for acceptability of such sets,
and so F3.22 allows there to be many other ways that someone might justify that a certain set is acceptable for him.

   Despite the mistakes in the preceding complaint, it is worth noting that
we have not eliminated all concern about justification of instantiations of
the antecedents of the four conditionals in clause D. In particular, freeing
our friend s from being concerned about such justification is of no help to

those of us who will want to use D(4) to rebut skeptical thesis M_1S_3 by showing that certain explanation sets are sometimes acceptable for someone. Might not we, at least, be required to rely only on foundational evidence for the antecedent of D(4), if we are to succeed in our attack on skepticism? Let me sidestep this question here by postponing an answer to it until we have seen, by the end of Chapter 10, just how we actually proceed in using F3.22 to refute thesis M_1S_3.

The Third Objection: The Master Argument of the Book, and Begging the Question Against Skepticism. The last objection to F3.22 might well issue from a skeptic whose thesis we are preparing to attack. He might argue that even if he is quite conciliatory and grants conditions D(1) and D(2) as well as the consequences of accepting them, D(4) is much too weak a reed upon which to rest any such attack. After all, there are plausible skeptical reasons against the use of enumerative induction, and hypothetical induction, which corresponds to clause D(4), is certainly dubious if enumerative induction is. At the very least, he might insist, use of clause D(4) is question-begging aginst skepticism, and so its use will not provide a refutation.

The trouble with this objection, however, is that it misconstrues the form of the attack on skepticism that is being followed in this book. The preceding discussion and rejection of objections to the minimal version of the explanatory foundational theory, F3.22, are aimed only at showing that the theory is not unreasonable. It would clearly be wrong to proclaim that the results of the present discussion justify F3.22 and then proceed to refute M_1S_3 merely by applying F3.22 to various nonbasic statements about presently existing but unperceived external objects, nonsubjective past occurrences, future events, or mental phenomena of someone else. But that, of course, is not the way we are proceeding. It is true that our last major task, in Chapter 10, will be to apply thesis F3.221, as indicated, in order to show that if the minimal explanatory foundational theory is correct, then M_1S_3 is false because some statements about the unperceived present, the nonsubjective past, the future, or other minds are sometimes acceptable for some of us. Nevertheless, as a quick glance back at Chapter 1 and its master argument will verify, what we will have done in part II of this book concerns only four of the eleven premises in the master argument, each of which must be justified if we are to justify the rejection of epistemological skepticism by that argument. Thus many other premises are needed in order to justify, finally, thesis F3.22 and its consequences.

CONCLUSION AND REVIEW OF THE MASTER ARGUMENT

Our results at the end of Part II are relevant to premise V.2 ('No nonbasic statement that is not entailed by a set of basic-reports, observation-reports, and basic memory-reports is probable, for s at t relative to any set of basic-reports, observation-reports, and basic memory-reports about s at t that are acceptable for s at t') of the most plausible skeptical argument we have found. Thus it is relevant to premise II of the master argument ('It is reasonable today for human beings to believe that the most plausible attempts to justify each skeptical thesis, M_1S_1 through M_1S_3, fail). This is because we will have cast enough doubt on V.2 to preclude using it to justify some conclusion. We will have done this showing, first in this chapter, that there are no damaging objections to the explanatory foundational theory, and then in Chapter 10, that the theory yields results that contradict premise V.2. The latter is, of course, also directly relevant to premise XIX ('The explanatory foundational theory has consequences that contradict all forms of moderate skepticism about physical objects, the past, the future, and other minds').

Two other premises of the master argument to which our present conclusions are clearly relevant are the following. First, X ('It is at least as reasonable, today, for human beings to adopt the explanatory foundational theory as any other theory of empirical justification that is adequate for human decisions'). Second, XI ('For any theory of empirical justification, T, that is adequate for human decisions, either the explanatory foundational theory is consistent with appreciably more pretheoretical, commonly and firmly accepted beliefs of mankind than T is, or it is more reasonable, in 1977, for human beings to adopt the explanatory foundational theory rather than T').

It is clear that the work we have just completed and the results to be reached at the end of Chapter 10 comprise a significant part of our central task. Nevertheless, it should be equally clear that much else must be done in order to use the master argument to refute skeptical thesis M_1S_3. Once that whole task has been completed, I maintain that it will be easy to see that the charge of question-begging is unfounded. Let us, then, move to the next task before us. It is not, unfortunately, the attempt to show that the explanatory foundational theory yields that M_1S_3 is false. This is because to show that, we must have available all that is needed to justify that some explanation set is maximal for someone at some time. But this requires that we be able to compare certain of the explanatory systems in the competing sets in order to determine which set is best for that person at that time. And this can be done only if we have a plausible list of the nonevidential tests that are used to evaluate systems. It is the complex and difficult task of the next two chapters to devise, explicate, and justify such a list.

NOTES

[1] For an informative discussion of related issues, see P. Suppes, 'Probabilistic Inference and the Concept of Total Evidence', in J. Hintikka and P. Suppes (eds.), *Aspects of Inductive Logic*, Amsterdam: North-Holland Publishing, 1966, pp. 49–65.

[2] See C. Hempel, *Aspects of Scientific Explanation*, New York: Free Press, 1965, p. 426.

[3] *Ibid.*, p. 425.

[4] *Ibid.*, p. 427.

[5] D. Kaplan, 'Explanation Revisited', *Philosophy of Science* **28** (1961), 435.

[6] Hempel, *op. cit.*, p. 272.

[7] *Ibid.*, p. 271.

[8] Cf. Hempel, *op. cit.*, p. 377.

[9] For my previous attempt to define 'observation term', see my *Materialism and Sensations*, New Haven. Conn.: Yale University Press, 1971, pp. 64–71.

[10] *Ibid.*, pp. 72–78 and p. 102, for my definition of 'pure theoretical term'.

[11] For a view that an inductive explanation of a statement, p, does not require an inference from the explanans of p to the conclusion that p is probable, see W. Salmon, *Statistical Explanation and Statistical Relevance*, Pittsburgh: University of Pittsburgh Press, 1971; and 'A Third Dogma of Empiricism', in R. Butts and J. Hintikka (eds.), *Logic, Methodology, and Philosophy of Science: Proceedings of the Fifth International Congress*, Dordrecht: Reidel, 1977, pp. 253–270.

[12] For a set of axioms for the probability calculus, see note 3 of Chapter 2.

[13] See Hempel, *op. cit.*, pp. 373–393.

[14] I have discussed underdetermination of theory, in 'Reference and Ontology: Inscrutable but Not Relative', *Monist* **59** (1976), 353–372.

[15] It is important to note that for ease of reading, I shall no longer eternalize noneternal sentences before embedding them in probability formulas. Instead, I shall assume it has been done, as, for example, I have done here in the case of sets S_1 and S_2.

CHAPTER 8

EXPLANATORY SYSTEMS: CONDITIONS OF
ADEQUACY AND SYSTEMIC TESTS

Our last major task is to try to establish the claim that if the minimal explanatory foundational theory of justification is correct, then the epistemological skeptical thesis M_1S_3 is false. In order to accomplish the task we need to find some instantiations of some of the antecedents either in clause D(4) of F3.22 or clause (3) of the simpler F3.22, so that, with either principle, they imply what M_1S_3 denies, namely, that some statements about the unperceived present, the nonsubjective past, the future, or other minds are sometimes acceptable for some people. It is clear from our discussions through Chapter 5, however, that we shall have to find instantiations of the clauses of F3.22 or F3.221 that concern explanation sets. This is because in Chapter 5 we found that merely depending on principles H3, BR3, and BR4 yields nothing that conflicts with M_1S_3. Consequently, we shall not only have to find an explanation set, $\{C_i, I_i\}$, that is maximal for someone at some time, but we must also be able to justify the claim that it is maximal. And this will require that, among other things, we be able to justify that $\{C_i, I_i\}$ meets the minimum conditions of adequacy for explanation sets, and that no conflicting explanation set that explains as many members of the chosen foundational set as $\{C_i, I_i\}$ does is a better explanation set than $\{C_i, I_i\}$ is. But, as noted previously, uncovering which of two explanation sets is better depends on evaluating each with respect to the 'nonevidential' tests that apply to explanatory systems. And all this requires, of course, that we have a somewhat detailed understanding of the two sorts of nonevidential tests: those providing minimum conditions of adequacy and the systemic tests which apply to minimally adequate systems.

Let me begin the search for nonevidential tests by listing all the proposals I have found which there is some reason to think are relevant to the evaluation of explanatory systems and explanation sets. By gleaning the works of Hempel, Quine, and Ullian, we can arrive at the following initial group of tests: explanatory relevance, testability, refutability, fecundity, scope, simplicity, economy, conservatism, familiarity of principle, lawlikeness, essential generality, pure generality, essential universality, pure universality, consistency, and truth. Others will be added as we proceed. Most of these sixteen proposed tests require considerable elucidation before we shall be able to decide whether they are tests for minimum adequacy, or systemic tests, or neither. We can however, quickly show that five of them are neither sort of test and, after some explication, we shall be able to reduce the number of independent tests to seven by combining several tests as one. I shall consider all these tests here, except for economy and simplicity which I shall reserve for special treatment in Chapter 9.

FIVE TESTS TO BE EXCLUDED

I shall begin by noting that truth is no test of a system, but rather what many of us hope accrues to those systems that meet the various relevant tests. Once we have subjected a system to all the 'other' tests, there is nothing we can do, in addition, to see if it meets the 'test' of truth. This is why I have considered what I call 'systems' rather than Hempelian 'theories', which succeed in explaining only if true. I want to maintain that if one explanation set is clearly the best ever developed by human beings because it excels in all the other 'tests', it would still explain adequately and be very reasonable even if, unluckily for us, it is not true. Two other proposals I exclude are essential generality and consistency of either explanatory systems or explanation sets. This is because, although both tests are clearly necessary conditions of adequacy, they are also, by definition, necessary conditions of P-explanation by explanation sets. By definition of 'explanatory system', such a system must be essentially generalized; and by definition D14, an explanation set P-explains something only if the set and, thereby, its systems are consistent.

The fourth test to be excluded is explanatory relevance because, like consistency, it is primarily a requirement for a set being a P-explanation rather than being adequate. According to Hempel, an explanation meets the requirement of explanatory relevance when "the explanatory information adduced affords good grounds for believing that the phenomenon to be explained did, or does, indeed occur".[1] Hempel also says, "Deductive nomological explanations satisfy the requirement of explanatory relevance in the strongest sense possible: the explanatory information they provide implies the explanandum sentence deductively and thus offers logically conclusive grounds why the explanandum phenomenon is to be expected'.[2] In our terms, this requirement seems to amount to the condition on P-explanations by explanation sets that what they P-explain is 'derivable' from the sets. Here, it should be remembered that, by definition D15, derivability includes deducibility, which is required for deductive-nomological explanations; probabilistic derivability, which is used with deductive-statistical explanations; and inductive derivability, which inductive-statistical explanation involves. But since, by definition D14, all P-explanations require such derivability, the requirement of explanatory relevance need not be added as a condition of adequacy.[3]

The last test I wish to exclude is fecundity, about which Quine says so tersely, "successful further extensions of theory are expedited".[4] This one I exclude not because it is already included in the characterization of P-explanation, but rather because it does not constitute a nonevidential test for explanation sets. That is, it is not relevant to deciding whether a set provides minimally adequate explanations or is a better explanation set than some other set. It is, instead, a means for helping someone decide whether to accept one explanation set at a certain time t from among a group of these sets that are equally good, according to the nonevidential tests. It is a pragmatic factor relevant to his decision, because it can be determined for any person or group of people at any time only by uncovering the specific situation in which the person or group is considering the alternative explanation sets. In one particular situation, it may be that set $\{C_1, I_1\}$ is more helpful than $\{C_2, I_2\}$ to scientists who are working on related projects, even though there is no other reason to prefer $\{C_1, I_1\}$. This might be because accepting $\{C_1, I_1\}$ rather than $\{C_2, I_2\}$ in this situation is more likely to free these scientists from certain current dogmas which have impeded development of new theories. In other situations, however, accepting $\{C_2, I_2\}$ might be more fruitful, such as just after a period that is turbulent with new ideas when a time of stability is needed to evaluate what has occurred. In short, fecundity affects what makes an explanation set, $\{C, I\}$, maximal for s at t without affecting how good a system C is. It does not, then, provide a nonevidential test for systems. But, although we must include it somewhere, we need not add it as a new test. Fecundity is already covered in clause (5) of definition D20 in which 'maximal' is defined. This clause is, roughly, that $\{C, I\}$ is as helpful to s at t for understanding F and devising explanations, as any set that has maximum explanatory coherence for set F among those either understood by s or generally understood.

TESTABILITY AND REFUTABILITY

I now wish to examine certain groups of the proposed tests to discover

whether some in each group might be collapsible into others. I shall begin
by considering testability in principle and refutability. Turning to Hempel
again, we find him saying that a scientific theory, T, is testable in principle
just in case it is "possible to derive from T, in the broad sense we have
considered, certain test implications of the form 'if test conditions C are
realized, then outcome E will occur', but the test conditions need not be
realized or technically realizable at the time when T is propounded or con-
templated".[5] Contrast this with the test of refutability which requires, according to Quine and Ullian, that "some imaginable event, recognizable
if it occurs, must suffice to refute the hypothesis".[6] As stated here, it is
clear that these two tests are related. Furthermore, according to Hempel,
whatever meets the requirement of explanatory relevance is also testable.
So, if he is right, we can exclude testability as we did explanatory relevance.
Hempel's reason for this claim is that if T explains P and has explanatory
relevance to P, then P is derivable from T, and T has "at least one consequence of empirical character, and this fact confers upon it testability and
empirical content".[7]

On Testability in Principle

We can grant that an explanation set has empirical content if it P-explains
an empirical statement, and that an explanatory system, C, has empirical
content, if there is an I such that $\{C, I\}$ P-explains an empirical statement,
p.[8] When this is true, $(I \supset p)$ is contingent and derivable from C alone, that
is, as I shall say, $(I \supset p)$ is a *conditional consequence* of C and p is a *conditional P-explanandum* of C. We can also grant that all explananda of the
explanation sets that we are considering are empirical statements. But it is
far from clear that every empirical sentence that is a conditional consequence of an explanatory system is, in an important sense, a *testable* consequence, as I would insist is required for an explanatory system to be testable in principle. By a *consequence of a system*, I mean a contingent sentence, whether conditional or not, that is derivable from the system. And,
I shall insist, a testable consequence of a system must consist only of basic-
sentences or observation-sentences, that is, as I shall say, 'experiential
sentences'.[9] I suggest, then the following definition.

D22. $(I \supset p)$ is a *testable consequence* of system $C =_{\text{df}}$. (1) $\{C, I\}$
         P-explains p, (2) I and p consist of experiential sentences
         (basic-sentences or observation-sentences); and (3) there are
         two consistent sets of eternalized basic-reports or observation-

reports, e_i and e_j, such $(I \cdot p)$ is very probable relative to e_i and $(I \cdot {\sim}p)$ is very probable relative to e_j.

In short, a testable consequence of a system is a conditional consequence of the system that is both verifiable and falsifiable by eternalized reports.·

On the assumption that being testable requires having testable consequences, it is far from clear that each system with empirical relevance has a testable consequence. Nevertheless, it might be replied at this point that for science, at least, part of what a hypothesis is designed to explain consists always of singular observation-sentences derivable from the hypothesis, and so if an explanation set succeeds in P-explaining these explananda, it has at least one testable consequence and is both testable and refutable.

I find two reasons to reject this reply. First, although it is a widely accepted dogma that at least the ultimate explananda of science are either the observable behavior of living and nonliving things, or else the observation-sentences that describe this behavior, there are two reasons to doubt this behavioristic thesis. First, as I have argued in previous chapters, some of the things to be explained for a person at certain times are particular basic-reports. But, second, even if the thesis were amended to include some basic-sentences as explananda, because each is testable by at least one person, there remains the objection that some hypotheses are designed to explain statements about the unobservable behavior of microentities, and do so very well. For example, in neurophysiology someone might devise a hypothesis to explain a set of statements to the effect that nerve impulses are transmitted from neuron to neuron along certain paths in particular brains at precise times. These statements would surely be empirical consequences of any explanation set that succeeded in P-explaining them, but none are basic-sentences and, on many views, none of these sentences is an observation-sentence. Thus none occur in what I have called 'testable consequences' of the set. Consequently, because I find that a test of testability should be able to accommodate such explanation sets and such views about observation-sentences, we should not accept the reply that each scientific explanation set which P-explains at least one empirical sentence explains an observation-sentence. Nor, of course, should we accept the claim that a scientific explanation set has testable consequences because it explains an empirical statement.

My second objection to the preceding reply is that an explanation set is testable only if it has at least one testable consequence whose consequent is not derivable from just those sentences it is designed to explain. My point is that no hypothesis that is carefully crafted so it P-explains some one statement that, it turns out, is a testable, observation-sentence should, thereby, be considered to meet the condition of testability. So I conclude that we should maintain a test of testability that is not met by an explanation set just because it has explanatory relevance. We should, then, keep these two tests distinct.

On Refutability and a Definition of Testability

Although Quine has given us but the briefest description of refutability, I believe that the preceding discussion of testability applies equally well to refutability, with one exception. As defined above, a testable consequence is, roughly, a statement that is highly probable relative to one set of eternalized reports and improbable relative to another. But, as I interpret it, a refutable consequence is merely such a statement that is refutable, that is, clearly improbable relative to some set of eternalized observation-reports and basic-reports. Thus, on my construal, any explanation set that meets the test of testability also meets that for refutability, but not conversely. We need, then, just a single test concerning testability in principle, where 'testability in principle' is defined as follows:

D23.   The explanatory system, C, is *testable in principle* $=_{df.}$ C has a testable consequence whose consequent is not derivable from those sentences that C is constructed to explain.

There is an objection to D23, however. It is possible that a scientific hypothesis is constructed to explain certainly purely theoretical statements and succeeds in this quite well without having any consequences of its own that are testable in the sense given by D22. Indeed, it might be that the only way to derive such a testable consequence would be to embed the hypothesis in a broader theory or conjoin it with a group of auxiliary hypotheses, such as certain methodological principles relating theoretical characteristics to observable measurements.

The obvious reply to this objection is to be holistic about explanatory systems. That is, such a system C should include certain hypotheses, whether methodological or some other sort, which allow C to be testable in the way that D23 requires. Of course, any hypothesis can be conjoined with some auxiliary principles to form a system that is testable. So it might be objected anew that although the test of testability may be different from that of explanatory relevance, it is of no worth for evaluating explanatory systems because each one can be easily adjusted to become testable. For example, we can always replace a system C_i that seems to lack testability by C_j, which is just C_i conjoined with an observation-report, p. Then there is always an I, such that $(I \supset p)$ satisfies definition D22. However, all this second objection shows is that the test of testability is of no consequence when taken alone, because it can always be met. But that clearly does not show it is of no value when it functions, as it clearly does, in conjunction with the other nonevidential tests. For example, it is likely that C_j with its one observation-report would not fare well by the test of scope, because it is likely that a competitor of C_j would have the experiential consequences of C_j and more, because of some of its generalizations.

An advocate of C_j can counter the preceding response, however, by adding as many observation-reports and basic-reports as are needed to obtain a system that has the experiential consequences of its competitors with the greatest scope. However, as we shall see, this is not enough for a system to meet either the test of scope, or a related one, cumulativity, which will be discussed later. Furthermore, neither this new system nor C_j meets another of the proposed tests we shall examine next, that is, neither is purely universal because of its *ad hoc* addition of reports. Consequently, it is a mistake to reject the test of testability either for the reason that it is redundant or for the reason that any system can be adjusted to meet it without any ill effects.

A MINIMUM NONEVIDENTIAL TEST FOR EXPLANATORY SYSTEMS

It is reasonable that a test of testability is relevant to how good an explanatory system is. I do not, however, wish to speculate at this point about whether it should be a test for minimum adequacy or a systemic test. Nevertheless, let me state one general principle for use of both sorts of test which I believe is noncontroversial because it states the minimum effect that any nonevidential test can have on the comparative worth of a pair of explanatory systems. I shall call it the 'minimum nonevidential test' for the comparative evaluation of two explanation sets. The crux of the test is that set $\{C_1, I_1\}$ is better than set $\{C_2, I_2\}$ if system C_1 is minimally adequate but system C_2 is not, or C_1 does better than C_2 on some systemic tests, and at least as well as C_2 on all others. I believe, however, that, if $\{C_1, I_1\}$ and $\{C_2, I_2\}$ have no common explananda, then they should be incomparable regarding systemic tests. For example, it is unusually easy to find a simpler, more economical system if no restrictions are put on what comparable systems must have in common. Further, it is clearly not enough that they have just one common explanandum and what it entails, because, again, a simpler, more economical system is often available that explains that one sentence but much less overall than its more complex competitor. It is, however, too much to require that comparable explanation sets agree at the theoretical level, because it is here, as we shall see in Chapter 9, that tests of simplicity and economy should be determining factors. Consequently, it seems reasonable to require for this minimal test that the better set P-explain at least all the sentences that the defeated set P-explains at the level of observation-sentences and basic-sentences, that is, experiential sentences. More precisely, I propose that if C_2 is minimally adequate, then $\{C_1, I_1\}$ is better than $\{C_1, I_2\}$ only if $\{C_1, I_1\}$ 'indiscernibly approximates' (or, in short, 'approximates') these 'experiential' sentences that are P-explained by $\{C_2, I_2\}$. This change is needed because, as noted when discussing conflict among systems in Chapter 7, there are cases where $\{C_1, I_1\}$ has mathematically formulated consequences that differ from those of $\{C_2, I_2\}$, but the differences are so small that they fall within the realm of allowed experimental error. Consequently, no experimental conclusion that agrees with one set would count against the other. That is, although, strictly speaking, $\{C_1, I_1\}$ would not have the exact experiential consequences of $\{C_2, I_2\}$, $\{C_1, I_1\}$ would approximate those of $\{C_2, I_2\}$ so closely that there is no experiment which would decide between them. No more than this should be required of $\{C_1, I_1\}$ in its competition with $\{C_2, I_2\}$.

Finally, with the preliminaries completed, we can state the minimum nonevidential test for explanation sets as follows:

> MN. For any two explanation sets, $\{C_1, I_1\}$ and $\{C_2, I_2\}$, that P-explain some experiential sentences, *if* either (a) $\{C_1, I_1\}$ is minimally adequate and $\{C_2, I_2\}$ is not; or (b) each experiential sentence that is P-explained by $\{C_2, I_2\}$ is 'approximated' by a sentence P-explained by $\{C_1, I_1\}$, and C_1 does at least as well as C_2 on some of the systemic tests for explanatory systems and better than C_2 on the rest of the tests, *then* $\{C_1, I_1\}$ is a better explanation set than $\{C_2, I_2\}$.

So, for example, if the only relevant difference between $\{C_1, I_1\}$ and $\{C_2, I_2\}$ is that C_1 is testable in principle but C_2 is not, then C_1 would be a better system than C_2. Unfortunately, test MN will not help in all situa-

tions because often some systemic tests will favor one system while others
will select another conflicting one. And not only is any proposal about
how to handle all such situations controversial, it is also unclear how to
justify the choice of a particular proposal. Consequently, I shall at this
point restrict myself to clarifying and proposing tests to use in the application of MN. However, at the end of Chapter 9, after discussing the
tests of economy and simplicity, I shall speculate a little by offering, with
some slight justification, a preference ranking among systemic tests. Anything more than that, I believe, would require a major work in itself, and
that is well beyond the scope or need of this book.

UNIVERSALITY AND LAWLIKENESS

The next group of tests from our original list that I wish to consider
together are essential universality, pure universality, and lawlikeness.
Let us say, modifying Hempel slightly, that a system is *essentially* universal
if it is logically equivalent to one that "is of universal form and not equivalent to a singular sentence", and it is *purely* universal if it is logically
equivalent to one "of universal form and contains no individual constants". Hempel also claims that a sentence is of universal form if "it
consists of one or more quantifiers . . . and all the quantifiers occurring
in it are universal".[10] Here, however, as I did in Chapter 7, concerning
generality, I shall supplement Hempel's sufficient condition by adding
another one concerning probabilistic and statistical statements, and I
shall also claim that the disjunction of these two conditions is necessary.
That is, a formula (which need not be a sentence) is universal just in case
it is a formula that is logically equivalent to one that includes one or
more quantifiers, all of which are universal, or to one that is a probabilistic
or statistical formula that applies to at least one class of entities without
specifying of any particular entity either that it is in the class or that it is
not.

On Lawlikeness

When we turn to a clarification of lawlikeness, the task becomes considerably more difficult. At one point in his discussion of laws, that is,
true lawlike sentences, Hempel divides laws into those that are fundamental and those that are derivative, and then says that a sentence, which
contains only "purely qualitative" predicates is "fundamental lawlike"

if it is purely universal.[11] A crucial phrase here, of course, is 'purely qualitative' which, unfortunately, neither he nor I is able to explicate fully. I can agree with him that in a formalized language with a fixed set of primitives, a purely qualitative *defined* predicate is one that can be defined without explicit "reference to any one particular object or spatio-temporal location".[12] And I also agree with him that it is extremely difficult to characterize a purely qualitative *primitive* predicate. Indeed, I know of no fully adequate characterization. This is one reason why the clarification of lawlikeness is so frustratingly complex.

Hempel later admits that his first candidate for a sufficient condition for lawlikeness is mistaken, and he proposed two new requirements: first, that any lawlike sentence be essentially universal, and, second, that it support or "sustain counterfactual and subjunctive conditional statements".[13] The first amendment is needed in order to deny lawlikeness to statements such as 'Anyone who is identical with Hempel is a philosopher', and 'Everyone who admires everyone admired by Smith admires Smith'.[14] The first is not a lawlike sentence because, given a logic with identity, it is logically equivalent to 'Hempel is a philosopher'. And the second is not lawlike, because it is logically equivalent to 'Smith admires Smith'. The second change is made because many essentially and purely universal sentences are merely accidental generalizations, and so are not lawlike. Consider the essential and purely universal generalization: 'All persons who become presidents of the third largest country are males'. Being a male is, presumably, an accidental feature of presidents of the United States, because no sort of law denies women the presidency. Such a sentence is denied lawlikeness by requiring of a lawlike sentence that it would be true only should its subjunctive version be true. But for the preceding example, its subjunctive version is: 'For any person at all, if that person should become president of the third largest country, then that person would be male'. And it would seem that this conditional is false.

Unfortunately, as Hempel would agree, uncovering truth conditions for subjunctive conditionals is no less perplexing than clarifying what it is for a primitive predicate to be purely qualitative. So, for a second reason, the concept of lawlikeness remains quite unclear. Nevertheless, although it is far from satisfactory, I propose we adopt the following Hempelian definition of lawlikeness.

D24.   An explanatory system, *C* is *lawlike* $=_{df.}$ (1) All the predicates of C are purely qualitative, (2) C is essentially and purely universal, and (3) if C should be true, then its corresponding subjunctive version would also be true.

On Probabilistic and Statistical Lawlikeness. At first glance it might seem that D24 does not allow any probabilistic or statistical universal statements to be lawlike, because none imply any relevant subjunctive conditional, as clause (3) seems to require of all lawlike statements. But Hempel and some others disagree with this. Consider Hempel's example about a tetrahedron which we can construe as concerned with following probability statement: '$\Pr(Lt/Ht) = \frac{1}{4}$', where 'Lx' = 'x has the outcome of landing on side III', and 'Hx' = 'x is a homogeneous, regular tetrahedron with "I", "II", "III", and "IV" marked on its four sides, and x is tossed a large number of times'. According to Hempel, this probability statement implies something like the following subjunctive conditional: 'If the tetrahedron, t, should be tossed a large number of times, t would have the outcome of landing on its side III on about $\frac{1}{4}$ of the tosses'.[15] It would seem, then, that Hempel would agree to interpreting the essentially and purely universal probability statement, '$\Pr(Lx/Hx) = \frac{1}{4}$', as follows: 'For any x, if x should be a homogeneous, regular tetrahedron that is tossed a large number of times, then the relative frequency of the outcomes in which x lands on side III among the tosses of x would be approximately $\frac{1}{4}$. And generalizing to cover all relative probability statements of the form '$\Pr(Ox/Ex) = r$', we could get:

> For any x, if an experiment of kind E should be performed on x many times, then the relative frequency of the outcomes of the experiments in which x is O among the number of experiments is approximately r.[16]

It becomes quite clear that relative probability statements do not imply their 'corresponding' subjunctive versions if, as Hempel and others maintain, these versions are conditionals of the above form. The problem is the one that always arises when a statement of the form 'The probability of Q, given P, is r' is interpreted as being or implying a conditional. As we have previously noted, if P implies that the probability of Q is r, then $(P \cdot S)$ implies that the probability of Q is r. But '$\Pr(Q/P) = r$' does not imply '$\Pr(Q/P \cdot S) = r$'. Indeed, often these conditional probabilities are quite different. This destroys the implication Hempel requires, as is easily shown by letting Ix = 'A malicious demon causes x to land on III after each toss'. Then we have $\Pr(Ox/Ex) = \frac{1}{4}$ and $\Pr(Ox/Ex \cdot Ix) = 1$. But $(Et \cdot It)$ conjoined with the two subjunctive conditionals supposedly implied by these two relative probability statements yields that the relative frequency of the outcomes of the experiments of kind E – which includes those of kind $(E \cdot I)$ – performed on t among the number of experiments is approximately $\frac{1}{4}$ and also approximately 1. But the conjunction of $(Et \cdot It)$ with the two conditional probability statements does not yield that contradiction. Therefore the conjunction of the two probability statements does not imply the conjunction of the two subjunctive conditionals. But this conclusion in turn implies that at least one of the two probability statements does not imply its 'corresponding' conditional. And since it seems clear that one of the two implies 'its' conditional only if the other one does, we can conclude that no probability statements or statistical statements are lawlike, if clause (3) requires that, as Hempel assumes, the corresponding subjunctive formula be a conditional statement.

It might be suggested that the required subjunctive is not a conditional statement, but rather a 'formula' like: 'The degree of confirmation that something would be O, *given* that it should be E, is r'. But I am even less able to fathom the logical features of this sort of subjunctive than to uncover the truth conditions for the Hempelian conditionals. As a result, I am far from prepared to say that a probabilistic and statistical statement, which is essentially and purely universal and contains only purely qualitative predicates, is lawlike only if what it contains implies some sort of nonconditional subjunctive formula.

Conclusion About Lawlikeness and Universality

I have tried to explicate lawlikeness so it might serve as a test for explanatory systems, but, unfortunately, it remains quite vague because of the unclarity enshrouding the concepts of pure qualitative predicate and subjunctive statement. Because of this, lawlikeness does not provide a clear and precise test for systems, and I propose three others instead, two of which capture two precise features of statements that are clearly lawlike. The first conjoins two tests from our original list, and becomes the test of being essentially and purely universal. However, since by definition, any system is essentially generalized, and any statement that is universal in form and essentially generalized is also essentially universal, we need only consider the test of pure universality as a separate test of systems. The second test I shall call the 'test of nonprobabilistic universality', where a formula is nonprobabilistically universal just in case it is universal and contains no probability or statistical formulas. I propose this additional test, because, at the very least, if all other relevant considerations are roughly equal, then a nonprobabilistic system is to be preferred to one that is probabilistic. The third test concerns whether a system is 'fully quantitative', that is, whether all its nonlogical predicates are 'quantitative', that is, whether all its nonlogical predicates are quantitative terms, where a quantitative term is one that, like 'weight', 'volume', 'temperature' and 'pressure', takes numerical modifiers. Because such terms make for more accurate and more precisely testable explanations and predictions, it is clear that, all else being equal, a fully quantitative system is preferable to one that is, at least in part, merely 'qualitative'.

FOUR MINIMAL NONEVIDENTIAL TESTS FOR EXPLANATION SETS

So far, I have considered twelve different tests, have rejected eight for various reasons, and have proposed the adoption of four: testability, pure universality, nonprobabilistic universality, and, let us say, 'quantitation'. But, so far, I have not suggested which are tests for minimum adequacy, and which are systemic tests. I have, however, proposed a principle, MN, that provides one way to use the tests. Indeed, we can devise species of MN for each of these four tests. What results will be minimum nonevidential tests for testability (MN.1), pure universality (MN.2), nonprobabilistic universality (MN.3), and quantitation (MN.4). The four tests, stated as one, go as follows:

> MN.1–4. For any two explanation sets, $\{C_1, I_1\}$ and $\{C_2, I_2\}$, *if* either (a) C_1 is minimally adequate but C_2 is not; or (b) each experiential sentence that is P-explained by $\{C_2, I_2\}$ is approximated by a sentence P-explained by $\{C_1, I_1\}$, and all else is equal regarding nonevidential tests *except that*: C_1 is [(1) testable in principle but C_2 is not, (2) purely universal but C_2 is not, (3) nonprobabilistically universal but C_2 is not, (4) fully quantitative but C_2 is not], *then* $\{C_1, I_1\}$ is a better explanation set than $\{C_2, I_2\}$.

SCOPE AND GENERALITY

The next two tests I wish to consider are scope and generality. Generality is mentioned by Quine and Ullian but about it they say little more than,

"The most celebrated triumph on this score was Newton's, when he showed how the elliptical paths of heavenly bodies and the parabolic paths of earthly projectiles could be accounted for by identical, general laws of motion".[17] Their idea seems to be something like the notion of cumulativity which we will examine next and also something like what Nagel says when he discusses the "scope of predication". He requires that lawlike statements be "unrestricted universal" in the sense that they are universal statements whose predicates have "unrestricted scope of predication". And, following Nagel, we might say that a predicate, 'Px', has restricted scope if 'Px' entails that x is located in "a fixed spatial region or a particular period of time".[18] So, for example, 'x is traveling in Europe' has restricted scope, but 'x is traveling' does not.

Hempel seems to have a conception of scope much like Nagel's, but he argues that, as understood by Nagel, a test of scope is of no value because any restricted universal, such as 'All apples in this basket are red' is logically equivalent to an unrestricted universal, such as 'Any thing that is not red is not an apple in this basket'.[19] Nagel might reply to this that the consequent predicate of the second universal is 'an apple in this basket', and that has restricted scope. Rather than debate this point, however, it is more important to note that Nagel's characterization of restricted scope does not warrant the conclusion that 'All apples in this basket are red' is restricted because 'x is an apple in this basket' does not entail that x has some particular, fixed, spatial or temporal location. But since we want to be able to infer that this universal is limited in scope, we need to find additional conditions regarding what restricts scope. Hempel's solution to this problem seems to be to understand a sentence's having 'nonlimited scope' as its being essentially universal and having only purely qualitative predicates.[20] But we have agreed with Hempel that there seems to be no usable test for when a predicate is purely qualitative, and so Hempel's solution is of no practical help.

It might seem that we could make more progress by turning to the notion of scope provided by Quine and Ullian, which, I have noted, concerns how wide an 'array of testable consequences' a hypothesis (explanatory system) has. I assume by width of this array Quine and Ullian do not mean the number of different 'test sentences' explained by a hypothesis, because by the principle of addition, there will be infinitely many if there is one. Rather, I believe, Quine and Ullian are more likely to be concerned with something more like the number of different kinds of test sentences that are explained by an hypothesis. But if so, I am afraid there is little

hope of devising a test concerning these kinds, because I despair of finding
a plausible and useful way to delineate such kinds.

Newton on Scope

It might be argued at this point that it would be best to ignore scope except
for that feature of it already captured in our conceptions of essential and
pure universality, but I think that would be a mistake. As Quine and Ullian point out, scope or generality has been, historically, an important
test of scientific theories. Indeed, Newton emphasized it when he stated
his rules to guide scientists in choosing scientific theories. His rule III is:

*The qualities of bodies, which admit neither intensification nor remission of degrees, and
which are found to belong to all bodies within the reach of our experiments, are to be es-
teemed the universal qualities of all bodies whatsoever.*

   For since the qualities of bodies are only known to us by experiments, we are to hold
for universal all such as universally agree with experiments; and such as are not liable
to diminution can never be quite taken away.[21]

Newton can be viewed, somewhat loosely, as saying that at any time we
should explain the results of experiments by the most general theories that
are not disconfirmed by any available evidence. But how are we to understand what it is for hypothesis H_1 to be more general, that is, have greater
scope, than H_2?

   I believe that the best way to explicate Newton's point is to concentrate on simple cases where it seems intuitively clear that one universal
statement has greater scope than certain others. Consider H_1 = 'All apples are red', and its contrapositive 'Anything that is not red is not an
apple', both of which I take to have greater scope than H_2 = 'All
McIntosh apples are red', and H_3 = 'All apples are red or green', and
their contrapositives. According to Newton, if no available evidence conflicts with the first of these, then we should incorporate it into our theory
instead of either H_2 or H_3. In what relevant ways does the first differ from
the latter pair? It is not that, unlike H_1, predicates in H_2 and H_3 require
some fixed limit of their extensions. None of the three has that sort of
predicate. Nor is it that the predicates of H_1 have either more or less
members in their extensions than do the predicates of the other two. They
might have the same number of members. For example, the antecedent-
predicates of 'Each natural number is followed by a number' and 'Each
rational number is followed by a number' have the same number of entities in their extensions as, of course, does their common consequent-

predicate. But, I would claim, the latter sentence has greater scope because something being a natural number entails that it is a rational number, but the converse implication is false. Indeed, it is plausible to argue that it is necessary that the set of natural numbers is the same size as the set of rational numbers. And, of course, it is necessary that the set of things that are followed by numbers is the same size as itself. So it may well be that some universal statements have greater scope than others even when the extensions of the predicates of the former are, necessarily, the same size as the extensions of the corresponding predicates of the latter.

On Defining Scope

I suggest that what makes $H_1 = $ '$(x)(Ax \supset Rx)$' have greater scope than $H_2 = $ '$(x)(Mx \supset Rx)$', and also $H_3 = $ '$(x)[Ax \supset (Rx \vee Gx)]$' are certain analytic relationships between their antecedent-predicates and between their consequent-predicates. That is, H_1 has greater scope than H_2 because the antecedent-predicate of H_2, 'Mx' entails 'Ax', while the converse entailment claim is false, and 'Rx' mutually entails itself. And H_1 has greater scope than H_3 because, while 'Ax' mutually entails itself, the consequent-predicate of H_1, 'Rx', entails '$(Rx \vee Gx)$', but not conversely. And one of these two reasons is also true regarding the contrapositives of H_1, H_2, and H_3. For example, '$(x)(\sim Rx \supset \sim Ax)$' has greater scope than '$(x)[(\sim Rx \cdot \sim Gx) \supset \sim Ax]$' for the first of the two reasons, because '$(\sim Rx \cdot \sim Gx)$' entails '$\sim Rx$' but not conversely, and '$\sim Ax$' mutually entails itself.

The preceding discussion might seem to suggest that we need only disjoin the two reasons given above in order to form a condition that is both necessary and sufficient for one hypothesis to have greater scope than another. But that would be mistaken on two counts. The first is that we should allow H_1 to have greater scope than $H_4 = $ 'All McIntosh apples are red or green', but in this case neither the antecedent-predicates nor the consequent-predicates mutually entail each other. What seems to be required is the relevant sort of asymmetry in the entailment relationships between either of the antecedent-predicates without this being counterbalanced by the wrong sort of asymmetry for the other pair of predicates. For example, I would claim that H_1 does not have greater scope than $H_5 = $ 'All McIntosh apples are red and hard', because whatever greater scope H_1 has over H_5 by virtue of the more general antecedent-predicate of H_1, is lost because of the more specific consequent-predicate of H_5.

The second mistake of the preceding suggestion is that H_1 should count as having greater scope than $H_6 = $ '$(x)(\sim Rx \supset \sim Mx)$' which is the contrapositive of H_2. But in this case, there are no entailment relationships either between antecedent-predicates or between consequent-predicates. Nevertheless, there is one relationship that H_1 and its contrapositive have to H_2 and H_3 and their contrapositives, but not to H_5, namely, each of the first pair entails each of the second four, but not conversely, but neither of the first two entails H_5. Thus we might suppose, H_1 has greater scope than H_2 and H_3, because H_1 entails each of them; and H_1 does not have greater scope than H_5, because H_1 does not entail H_5.

It would be a mistake, however, to take system C_1's entailing C_2 without being entailed by C_2, to be sufficient for C_1 having greater scope than C_2, even granting of course, that C_1 is essentially generalized. Let C_1 be C_2 conjoined with just one basic-report. Then, by the preceding suggestion, C_1 would have greater scope than C_2. But that is surely wrong, because, as in the case of H_1 and H_2, greater scope should be somehow related to greater generality. It might be proposed, then, that we require C_1 to be purely universal in order to have greater scope than C_2. This eliminates the preceding problem, but, unfortunately, it is too strong a necessary condition for C_1's having greater scope than C_2. Many essentially universal systems will not be purely universal because they contain individual constants such as 'the sun', or 'North America'. Some of these should be allowed to have greater scope than others. I suggest that such a system, C_1, need do no more than entail a purely universal statement that entails C_2; C_1 need not be purely universal itself. But even this is too strong for a necessary condition. We must allow for cases where C_1 does not entail C_2, but merely 'indiscernibly approximates' C_2. What results, finally, is:

D25.   Explanatory system C_1 has *greater scope (is more general) than* explanatory system $C_2 =_{\text{df}}$. System C_1 entails some essentially and purely universal conditional, U, which entails an approximation of C_2; but C_2 does not entail any approximation of C_1.[22]

It is easy to use D25 to show that H_1 has greater scope than H_2, H_3, H_4, and H_6, but not H_5. Since H_1 is itself essentially and purely universal and logically implies H_2, H_3, H_4, and H_6, but not conversely, H_1 has greater scope than each of these systems, according to definition D25. But because H_1 does not entail any approximation of H_5, H_1 does not have greater scope than H_5. I propose that we adopt definition D25 and also add a test of scope to the three we have already accepted.

Three Objections to the Definition of Scope. Definition D25 may not satisfy everyone. Indeed, I can think of three objections to it that someone might raise. The first is that hypothesis H_1 should have greater scope than $H_7 =$ 'All McIntosh apples are hard' because the antecedent-predicate of H_1 is 'more general' than that of H_7, and the consequent-predicate of H_1 is not 'less general' than that of H_7. But D25 does not allow this, because H_1 entails nothing that entails H_7. My reply to this is that the purpose of a test of scope is, following Newton, to force continued generalization of particular hypotheses that are supported by particular evidence until just before one arrives at hypotheses that are falsified by that evidence. In this respect, H_7 should be generalized to $H_8 =$ 'All apples are hard', if the latter is not disconfirmed. And if this succeeds, then both H_1 and H_8 should be generalized to $H_9 =$ 'All apples are red and hard' because, by D25, H_9 has greater scope than both H_1 and H_8. But if H_7 is not to be generalized to H_8 at a particular time, and H_7 is the most general hypothesis available then regarding apples and hardness, H_7 should not be rejected for H_8. And where H_7 is not to be rejected for H_8, it surely should not be replaced by H_1, especially where, as in our case, the purpose of a test of scope is to force the continued generalizing of a particular explanatory system until one is falsified by available evidence. Consequently, it would be a mistake to allow H_1 to have a greater scope than H_7.

The second objection to D25 is that H_1 should be construed as having greater scope than $H_{10} =$ 'All McIntosh apples are the color of stop lights', because the antecedent of H_1 satisfies D25 relative to H_{10} and their consequent-predicates ascribe the same property. So even if it is mistaken to consider H_1 to have greater scope than H_9, because their consequent-predicates are quite unrelated, there is no need to require that H_1 entail a hypothesis in order to have greater scope. Surely, it is enough that the antecedent-predicate of H_1 entails that of H_{10}, but not conversely, and their consequent-predicates ascribe the same property. I find, however, that like the previous objection, this one also fails to accommodate the point of a test of scope. This is, once again, to require the use of the most general hypothesis that is supported but unviolated by some particular evidence. And, like any nonevidential test, a test of scope should yield results in all cases, given only the evidence available at the time. That is, we should be able to use the test and achieve results in all cases, regardless of what empirical evidence is available. But this would not be true if comparison of scope depended on whether predicates ascribe the same or different properties or, similarly, whether or not they are coextensive. This is because it is likely that in many cases the evidence available will provide no way to justify whether or not two of the relevant predicates are coextensive or coascriptive or neither. But D25 allows us to use the test in all cases, regardless of the empirical evidence available for the hypotheses being compared. It is for this reason that I reject the second objection.

The last objection is that D25 does not accommodate comparisons of scope for probabilistic hypotheses, because it is defined only for systems that entail universal conditionals, and so there is no way for a probabilistic system to achieve the entailment relationship that D25 requires. Although this point is correct, it casts doubt on D25 only if there should be a test of scope for probabilistic systems. And, although I believe we could devise a definition of scope for probability statements that is similar to the one for conditionals, there is no reason to do so for our purposes because I shall argue, there should be no test of scope for systems that are probabilistic.

Consider probabilistic analogues of H_1 and H_2, namely, H_{11} = '$\Pr(Rx/Ax) = n$,' and H_{12} = '$\Pr(Rx/Mx) = m$'. A definition of scope should give H_{11} greater scope than H_{12}, but even granting that, it is false that, all else being equal, we should abandon H_{12} for H_{11} for Newtonian reasons. If we can generalize without refutation to H_1, there is never a reason to adopt H_1 and also H_2, because H_1 entails H_2 and whatever can be explained by H_2 is also explained by H_1. But H_{11} does not entail H_{12} for $0 < m, n < 1$, and H_{11} does not automatically explain all that H_{12} explains. Consider, for example, that we want to explain why it is probable that McIntosh apples are red and hard, that is H_{13} = '$\Pr(Rx \cdot Hx/Mx) > 0.5$'. Since $\Pr(Rx \cdot Hx/Mx) = \Pr(Rx/Mx) \times \Pr(Hx/Rx \cdot Mx)$, we could explain H_{13} by H_{12} and H_{14} = '$\Pr(Hx/Rx \cdot Mx) = r$', if $mr > 0.5$. But whenever only H_{11}, H_{12} and H_{14} are available for explaining H_{13}, there is no way to use H_{11} instead of H_{12} in an explanation of H_{13}. Consequently, there are times when we might well need H_{11} and also H_{12} to explain different statements, and so, in general, their differences in scope should not be taken as indicating that, if all else is equal regarding nonevidential tests, H_{11} is a better explanatory system that H_{12}. Therefore, I shall restrict tests of scope to systems that entail conditional statements, as in the following minimal version of a nonevidential test of scope:

MN.5   For any two explanation sets $\{C_1, I_1\}$ and $\{C_2, I_2\}$, if either (a) C_1 is minimally adequate but C_2 is not; or (b) each experiential sentence that is P-explained by $\{C_2, I_2\}$ is approximated by a sentence P-explained by $\{C_1, I_1\}$, and all is equal regarding nonevidential tests *except that*: C_1 has greater scope than C_2, *then* $\{C_1, I_1\}$ is a better explanation set than $\{C_2, I_2\}$.

CUMULATIVITY

It might be felt at this point that by ignoring Quine's view of scope which concerns the width of array of testable consequences, I have overlooked a quite different and legitimate conception and test of scope. Indeed, in Chapter 6 when discussing the explanatory coherence theory, I discussed the phrase, 'x explains at least as much as y does', when interpreted as 'x explains at least the statements that y explains'. Perhaps, for x to have a wider array of testable consequences than y has is for x to explain all the testable sentences that y explains and also some others. I agree that something very much like this has often been thought to be required for scientific progress, that is, I assume, for x to be a better explanatory system than y. Recently, Lauden has examined two versions of such a test which he calls "the cumulativity postulate". The strong version is "that the replacement of one theory by another is progressive – or represents cognitive growth – if and only if the successor can explain everything explained by the predecessor *and something else as well*". The weaker test merely "*requires that T_2 is progressive with respect to T_1 if and only if all the facts thus far explained . . . by T_1 can be explained . . . by T_2, and T_2 can also be shown to explain some fact . . . not explained by T_1*".[23]

As stated, the tests provide necessary and sufficient conditions for one theory being better than another, but this is wrong on both counts. Neither test provides a sufficient condition, because T_2 would then be better than T_1 if it were merely T_1 conjoined with $(T_1 \supset p)$, where p is one statement not explained by T_1. Further, as Laudan points out with several examples taken from the history of science, explanatory progress does not occur only if there is cumulativity.[24] Nevertheless, as Laudan notes, cumulativity "is unquestionably a worthwhile desideratum".[25] That is, although cumulativity is not a test for minimal adequacy, some version of such a test is a systemic test. But which version?

Although it seems that Laudan would disagree, I suggest that the minimal version of a systemic test of cumulativity be adapted, with two important changes, from the strong version, once we define cumulativity in a way that corresponds to the definition of scope:

D26.   Explanatory system C_1 is *cumulative relative to* explanatory system $C_2 =_{df}$. System C_1 entails an essentially and purely universal conditional, U, which entails an approximation of each experiential sentence that is entailed by C_1; but there is an experiential sentence entailed by C_1 which is not approximated by any sentence entailed by C_2.

Then the minimal test of cumulativity is:

MN.6 For any two explanation sets, $\{C_1, I_1\}$ and $\{C_2, I_2\}$, *if* either (a) C_1 is minimally adequate but C_2 is not; or (b) each experiential sentence that is P-explained by $\{C_2, I_2\}$ is approximated by a sentence P-explained by $\{C_1, I_1\}$, and all else is equal regarding nonevidential tests *except that*: C_1 is cumulative relative to C_2, *then* $\{C_1, I_1\}$ is a better explanation set than $\{C_2, I_2\}$.

Both of the ways the preceding view of cumulativity differs fom the one stated by Laudan concern our notion of 'approximation'. The first concerns the mention of approximation in the definition of cumulativity. The reason for this, of course, is the same as was given for the inclusion of a similar clause in the definition of scope. It is worth noting here, incidentally, that if C_1 has greater scope than C_2, then C_1 is cumulative relative to C_2. But, of course, being cumulative does not imply having greater scope. The second difference is the requirement in MN.6, as in all the preceding minimal tests, that $\{C_1, I_1\}$ P-explains approximations of all the experiential sentences P-explained by $\{C_2, I_2\}$. Here again the reason for including this is the same as it was for the other minimal tests. It might be thought, however, that this general requirement for minimal tests is not needed for the test of cumulativity, because of what the definition of cumulativity requires of C_1 regarding approximation. But this would be a mistake, because each requirement regarding approximation can be satisfied without satisfying the other. Consider three fully experiential systems, $S_1 = \{(x)(Px \supset Qx), Pa\}$, $S_2 = \{(x)[(Px \cdot Rx) \supset Qx], (Pb \cdot Rb)\}$, and $S_3 = \{(x)[(Px \cdot Tx) \supset Qx], (Pb \cdot Tb)\}$. And assume that just '$Px$' and '$Qx$' are experiential. Then system C_1 of S_1 is cumulative relative to C_2 of S_2, but S_2 P-explains Qb and S_1 does not. Further, S_3 P-explains everything experiential that S_2 does, namely, Qb and what it entails, but C_3 of S_3 is not cumulative relative to C_2. So these two requirements are independent.

An Objection to the Minimal Test of Cumulativity

I believe that MN.6 is acceptable. However, Laudan might raise an objection to it that is similar to the one he raised against the strong cumulative postulate, namely, that "the chief difficulty with it, of course, is that we cannot enumerate the entire class of true consequences of any two universal theories, T_1 and T_2, and so any *direct* comparison of their true consequences is out of the question".[26] But a case-by-case comparison of consequences – whether or not true – is not required, and even if it were, induction from observed cases might well be adequate.

Consider again the current status of classical Newtonian physics. It has been rejected as a theory with universal application, because it conflicts with test results concerning objects whose sizes and speeds made them untestable when the theory was first proposed and confirmed by observing 'ordinary-sized' objects at 'ordinary' speeds. That is, while classical physics continues to explain the behavior of such objects at such speeds adequately, it fails for smaller objects and greater speeds. The theory I have called 'restricted classical physics' is Newtonian physics when its application is limited to what it explains adequately. As one physics textbook states:

Classical physics is the physics of ordinary-sized objects moving at ordinary speeds; it embraces Newtonian mechanics and electromagnetism. . . . For object speeds approaching that of light classical physics must be supplanted by relativity physics; for object sizes of about 10^{-10}m, approximately the size of an atom, classical physics must be supplanted by quantum physics. For subatomic dimensions and speeds approaching that of light only relativistic quantum physics is adequate. . . . Relativistic quantum physics is the most comprehensive and complete theoretical structure in contemporary physics.[27]

That is, according to this quotation, relativistic quantum physics is cumulative relative to 'restricted' classical physics. Further, this claim can be justified without a case-by-case examination of consequences. So Laudan's objection is mistaken. I propose, then, that we accept minimal nonevidential test MN.6.

CONSERVATISM AND FAMILIARITY

The next pair of tests that are obviously quite similar are conservatism and familiarity of principle. Once again Quine and Ullian give but little guidance when they say about conservatism that "the less rejection of prior beliefs required, the more plausible the hypotheses – other things being equal. The plausibility of a hypothesis varies inversely with the plausibility of the prior beliefs that it disallows".[28] Quine is about as helpful when he says that one benefit of molecular theory is "familiarity of principle: the already familiar laws of motion are made to serve where independent laws would otherwise have been needed".[29] Although one of these tests concerns principles and the other beliefs, the main difference between them seems to be that conservatism gives some epistemic weight to what is believed, while familiarity ascribes it to that with which we are familiar, whether believed or not. Yet I would think that what is important about familiar principles is whether or not they are believed. There are surely many familiar principles that are justifiably disbelieved, such as, 'The more times a fair coin has come up heads in a row, the more likely it will come up tails the next time'. It is mistaken to give such principles some degree of plausibility just because they are familiar. The usual view is that 'prior' belief, but not familiarity alone, is what adds to plausibility. And whether this view is correct about prior belief, it is surely right about familiarity without belief. So let us concentrate on conservatism alone.

Quine and Ullian are not alone in considering a test of conservatism. Fortunately, some of the others have presented us with more detailed statements. For example, Sklar considers, among others:

P1.   If you believe some proposition, on the basis of whatever positive warrant may accrue to it from the evidence, a priori plausibility, and so forth, it is unreasonable to cease to believe the proposition to be true merely because of the existence of, or knowledge of the existence of, alternative incompatible hypotheses whose positive warrant is no greater than that of the proposition already believed.[30]

Chisholm's latest revision of his principle B might be partially unpacked and reformulated in our terms as follows:

P2.   If a person, s, believes that he perceives that something is F, and no set of statements that are not unreasonable for s tend to confirm that s is not perceiving that something is F, then it is reasonable for s that he is perceiving that something is F.[31]

And, in Chapter 1, I proposed a species of the following principle that concerns theories of justification. It was there listed as CP:

P3.   If (1) it is at least as reasonable at t, for human beings to believe a theory, T_1, of kind K, as to believe T_2 of kind K, and (2) T_1 is consistent with appreciably more pretheoretical, commonly and firmly accepted beliefs of mankind than T_2, then T_1 is more reasonable than T_2.

These three principles of conservatism are interestingly different. The first makes a claim about what is a bad reason for ceasing to believe something; the second, in effect, gives conditions for when a hypothesis is more credible for someone that its denial; and the third merely proposes a way to discern when one theory is more credible than another. Thus while the second proposes what is sufficient for being reasonable, the third merely orders the credibility of pairs of statements without determining their level of credibility, except where the pair is a hypothesis and its denial. We have already, in Chapter 4, seen problems for Chisholm's original principle and a variety of amended vesions, including one like P2. Indeed, I concluded that it is reasonable to believe that no epistemic principles meeting what Chisholm requires of such principles are satisfactory. Similarly, I conclude that no version of a systemic test of conservatism modeled on Chisholm's epistemic rules is satisfactory.

AN EXAMINATION OF PRINCIPLE OF CONSERVATISM P1

I find it very difficult to explicate P1 so it is both plausible and a principle of conservatism. Consider the following three different explications that utilize some of our terminology and the assumption that it is unreasonable not to believe H just in case it is reasonable to believe H. First, consider one that is close to a literal interpretation of P1:

P1a.   If, at t, a person, s believes H_1, then even if, at t, s knows that there is a hypothesis, H_2, that conflicts with H_1 such that $Cr_{s,t}(H_2) \leqslant Cr_{s,t}(H_1)$, it is still reasonable (acceptable) for s to believe H_1 at t.

Second, a conditional that is more plausible than P1a:

P1b.   If, at t, s believes H_1, then it is false that if s should know that there is a hypothesis, H_2, that conflicts with H_1, such that $Cr_{s,t}(H_2) \leqslant Cr_{s,t}(H_1)$, then, at t, it would not be reasonable for s to believe H_1.

Finally, there is an explication in terms of a conditional credibility statement:

P1c. $Cr_{s,t}(H_1/e) > 0.5$, for $e = \{$'At t, s believes H_1', 'At t, s knows that there is a hypothesis H_2, that conflicts with H_1, such that $Cr_{s,t}(H_2) \leqslant Cr_{s,t}(H_1)'\}$.

It is clear that P1a is mistaken, because if it is true then so is a conditional which conjoins '$Cr_{s,t}(H_1) < 0.5$' with the antecedent of P1a. But clearly the second conditional is false. Explicans P1c, however, avoids this problem because it replaces the hypothetical of P1a by a conditional credibility statement. Nevertheless, it is most implausible that H_1 is acceptable for s at t, given just evidence e. At best, it might be argued that H_1 is not unacceptable for s at t given evidence e – that is, $Cr_{s,t}(H_1/e) > 0.5$ – but that is not because of any epistemic effect of s's belief. It would rather be because the claim about H_2 does not count against H_1, and so the denial of H_1 is no more credible for s at t than H_1 is, given the fact about H_2. This takes us to P1b which I find plausible, but not because of s's belief about H_1. It is plausible because its consequent, which denies a conditional, is quite reasonable. That is, just as s's belief is not sufficient for the reasonableness of H_1 for s at t, neither is the claim about H_2 in P1b sufficient for H_1 not being reasonable for s at t. It is clear that this claim conjoined with '$Cr_{s,t}(H_1) > 0.5$' does not imply that it is not reasonable for s to believe H_1 at t. So P1b is plausible, but it is not a principle of conservatism. It does not provide some way for s's belief to affect the epistemis status of H_1 for s, because its consequent is true regardless of what is used as antecedent.

A Fourth Principle That Is a Relative of P1

I believe that no explication of P1 will provide a plausible principle of conservatism. It might be thought, however, that we can construct a reasonable principle that is like P1 in its antecedent, but is more like P3, with its mere ordering of the reasonableness of two hypotheses, in its consequent. Consider, for example:

P4. If e_1 and e_2 are s's total evidence at t for H_1 and H_2 respectively, and $Cr_{s,t}(H_1/e_1) \geqslant Cr_{s,t}(H_2/e_2)$, and H_1 and H_2 conflict, then if s believes H_1 at t, $Cr_{s,t}(H_1) > Cr_{s,t}(H_2)$.

This is clearly a principle of conservatism and not one that is implausible for any of the previous reasons, because P4 does not imply anything about the level of $Cr_{s,t}(H_1)$, except that it is greater than $Cr_{s,t}(H_2)$ and, thus, greater than zero. Nevertheless, there is some reason to doubt P4. As Sklar has an opponent of conservatism say, "There is nothing in the way of 'rationality' which makes the first hypothesis to come along preferable to one of the others".[32] This seems a plausible objection. Consider a case where s has acquired his belief in H_1 irrationally at a previous time when the available evidence strongly favored H_2. Assume also that s's evidence shifted over time until at t it finally makes H_1, which s had held dogmatically in the face of evidence, as credible for s as H_2. It seems clear that s's dogmatic belief in H_1 should not increase the credibility of H_1 at t or at any other time. Furthermore, if we assume that H_1 and H_2 are conflicting explanation sets, then it seems equally clear that s's belief in H_1 at t does not make it a better explanation set. So P4 is no more helpful for our purposes than P1 or P2.

An Examination of Principle P3

Principle P3 avoids all the previous objections because it merely orders a pair of theories regarding reasonableness and ascribes some epistemic significance to the commonsense beliefs of mankind rather than to those held by only one person. But is this second difference helpful – in particular, with regard to whether one explanation set is better than another? To answer this question adequately for our present purposes, we must revise P3 so it becomes a test for explanation sets. Again, let us use the form previously proposed as the minimum version of a test that is somehow relevant to the comparative worth of two explanation sets. That is:

P5.   For any two explanation sets $\{C_1, I_1\}$ and $\{C_2, I_2\}$, *if* either (a) C_1 is minimally adequate but C_2 is not; or (b) each experiential sentence that is P-explained by $\{C_2, I_2\}$ is approximated by a sentence P-explained by $\{C_1, I_1\}$, and all is equal regarding nonevidential tests *except that*: C_1 is consistent with appreciably more commonly and firmly accepted beliefs of mankind than C_2 is, *then* $\{C_1, I_1\}$ is a better explanation set than $\{C_2, I_2\}$.

Is P5 a plausible nonevidential test for explanatory systems? Two points are relevant here. First, although my original version of principle P3 has no restrictions on its application, I have so far applied it primarily to metaphysical theories about what there is and theories of justification. As I argued in Chapter 1, principle P3 seems plausible when restricted to those sorts of theories. But granting the plausibility of a version restricted to these two domains, the question arises whether it would still be reasonable when extended to include explanation sets. Second, P3 is truly

what Sklar calls a principle of "last resort", because it requires that there
be *no* reason of any sort to prefer T_1 to T_2, rather than that, as P5 states,
everything regarding other nonevidential tests be equal.[33] This raises the
question of whether we should consider a test of conservatism to be a
nonevidential test for explanation sets, even granting its applicability to
them. I shall argue that conservatism is not to be used as a nonepistemic
test to help uncover which of a pair of sets is better. Rather it is to be
taken as one factor affecting the fecundity, that is, the utility for particular
people in particular situations, of using one explanation set instead of
another. Consequently, it would be one factor affecting which set is maximal for s at t, because of clause (5) of definition D20, but it would not
affect which is the best explanation set.

Conclusion: No Nonevidential Test of Conservatism for Explanatory Sys-
tems

To see why I exclude conservatism from nonevidential tests, consider an
example where, at t, a scientist is stymied in his attempt to explain phenomenon, p_1. Assume that this is because, unconsciously perhaps, he is
looking for an explanatory system that, unlike C_2, does not conflict with
C_1, because $\{C_1, I_1\}$ provides at least as good an explanation of a phenomenon, p_2, which is similar to p_1, as set $\{C_2, I_2\}$ does. Assume also that C_1
conflicts with fewer commonly held beliefs that the scientist also accepts
than C_2 does. It is often true in such a case that explanatory progress for
the scientist is more likely to be achieved by his rejecting $\{C_1, I_1\}$ for $\{C_2,$
$I_2\}$ and then rethinking the data regarding p_2. And whenever this is true,
and it helps him uncover an explanation of p_2, then, I maintain, it is false
that $\{C_1, I_1\}$ is more credible for him than $\{C_2, I_2\}$. Indeed, in some of
these cases $\{C_2, I_2\}$ might turn out to be the acceptable set for s at t. But if
we were to adopt P5, then set $\{C_1, I_1\}$ would be better, and so $\{C_2, I_2\}$
should be rejected for $\{C_1, I_1\}$. This is mistaken. We should rather conclude, first, that the two sets are equally good explanation sets, if they do
equally well by all nonevidential tests, excluding conservatism. And,
second, that in spite of being favored by conservatism, the scientist in this
case should cease using $\{C_1, I_1\}$ to explain p_1, for pragmatic reasons, that
is, reasons that depend as much on particular people in particular situations as upon characteristics of explanation sets.

We should, then, reject test P5, because it mistakes the relevance of
conservatism to the acceptability of explanatory sets. But this reason for
rejecting P5 does not affect P3 which allows us to retain conservatism as a
test that is truly of last resort for explanation sets, because it applies only

to those sets that are best according to all other considerations. But should we construe conservatism this way, or would it be better to keep it as merely one factor affecting the fecundity of explanation sets for people at times? We should use P3 as a test of last resort for explanation sets if, whenever *nothing* else at all favors $\{C_2, I_2\}$ over $\{C_1, I_1\}$ but conservatism favors $\{C_1, I_1\}$ for s at t, then the result is that $\{C_1, I_1\}$ is minimally more credible for s at t, than $\{C_2, I_2\}$ I tend to accept this result. After all, should we not believe that the vast majority of people are innocent in the correctness of their common beliefs, at least until there is some reason of some sort to think that they are mistaken? Nevertheless, I am far from sure about this in the case of explanation sets, and so at this point I conclude only that P5 should be rejected because conservatism is not relevant to how good an explanation set is. It is, instead, one factor to consider when evaluating how helpful it would be for fostering explanatory progress to accept one explanation set rather than another, or even none at all.

INTERIM CONCLUSION ABOUT NONEVIDENTIAL TESTS

In this chapter, we have examined seventeen proposed nonevidential tests for explanation sets. After definitions of key terms, we settled on six minimal nonevidential tests, namely, those concerning testability in principle, pure universality, nonprobabilistic universality, quantitation, scope, and cumulativity. The others have been rejected either because of being unnecessary, or too vague, or irrelevant to how good an explanation set is. I have not, however, proposed which of the six surviving tests are tests for minimal adequacy and which are merely systemic tests. And, obviously, I have not suggested a preference ranking for systemic tests. Both of these tasks must await the detailed and complex investigation of tests for economy and simplicity that comprises Chapter 9.

NOTES

[1] C. Hempel, *Philosophy of Natural Science*, Englewood Cliffs, N.J.: Prentice-Hall, 1966, p. 48.

[2] *Ibid.*, p. 52; and also Hempel, *Aspects of Scientific Explanation*, New York: Free Press, 1965, p. 247.

[3] For one who rejects the requirement of explanatory relevance, see W. Salmon, *Statistical Explanation and Statistical Relevance*, Pittsburgh: University of Pittsburgh Press, 1971; and "A Third Dogma of Empiricism", in R. Butts and J. Hintikka (eds.), *Logic, Methodology, and Philosophy of Science: Proceeding of the Fifth International Congress*, Dordrecht: Reidel, 1977, pp. 257–270.

[4] W. Quine, *The Ways of Paradox and Other Essays*, New York: Random House, 1966, p. 234.

[5] Hempel, *Philosophy of Natural Science*, p. 30. See also *Aspects of Scientific Explanation*, p. 248.

[6] W. Quine and J. Ullian, *The Web of Belief*, New York: Random House, 1970, p. 50.

[7] Hempel, *Aspects of Scientific Explanation*, p. 248.

[8] By 'empirical sentence', I mean, roughly, a sentence whose nonlogical terms are 'empirical terms'. By 'empirical term' I mean, roughly, a term whose true or false application to an entity is justified by *s* at *t*, only if, at *t*, *s* has some experiential evidence or theoretical scientific reason to support the claim. This is not how I defined the phrase in *Materialism and Sensations*, New Haven, Conn.: Yale University Press, 1971, pp. 71–72. I now find the previous definition confusing to readers.

[9] By 'observation sentence', I mean, roughly, a sentence whose nonlogical terms are 'observation-terms'. For my previous definition of 'observation-term', see *Materialism and Sensations*, p. 69.

[10] Hempel, *Aspects of Scientific Explanation*, p. 271.

[11] *Ibid.*, p. 272.

[12] *Ibid.*, p. 268

[13] *Ibid.*, pp. 281–293, for problems facing Hempel's first condition; and pp. 339–340 for his amendments to it.

[14] I heard of the example about Smith from Peter Geach.

[15] Hempel, *Aspects of Scientific Explanation*, pp. 377–378.

[16] *Cf.* J. Fetzer, 'A Single Case Propensity Theory of Explanation', *Synthese* **28** (1974), 171–198, for similar unpackings of conditional probability sentences.

[17] Quine and Ullian, *op. cit.*, p. 44.

[18] E. Nagel, *The Structure of Science*, New York: Harcourt, Brace, and World, 1961, p. 59.

[19] See Hempel, *Aspects of Scientific Explanation*, p. 292.

[20] *Ibid.*, pp. 272–292.

[21] I. Newton (A. Motte, trans.), *Mathematical Principles of Natural Philosophy*, Berkeley: University of California Press, 1971, vol. 2, p. 398.

[22] *Cf.* K. Popper on *p* having "greater universality than" *q*, in his *The Logic of Scientific Discovery*, New York: Harper and Row, 1968, pp. 121–123.

[23] L. Laudan, 'Two Dogmas of Methodology', *Philosophy of Science* **43** (1976), 588.

[24] *Ibid.*, pp. 589–591.

[25] *Ibid.*, p. 593.

[26] *Ibid.*, p. 587.

[27] R. Weidner and R. Sells, *Elementary Modern Physics*, 2nd ed., Boston: Allyn and Bacon, 1968, p. 4.

[28] Quine and Ullian, *op. cit.*, p 44.

[29] Quine, *op. cit.*, p. 234.

[30] L. Sklar, "Methodological Conservatism", *Philosophical Review* **84** (1975), 378.

[31] R. Chisholm, *Theory of Knowledge*, 2nd ed., Englewood Cliffs, N.J.: Prentice-Hall, p. 76.

[32] Sklar, *op. cit.*, p. 395.

[33] See Sklar, *op. cit.*, p. 392.

CHAPTER 9

THE SYSTEMIC TESTS OF ECONOMY
AND SIMPLICITY

The last pair of nonevidential tests for explanation sets that I shall consider come under the headings of simplicity and economy, the latter being, I suppose, what Quine and Ullian call "modesty", that is, the test that "other things being equal, the less story the better".[1] One translation of this slogan is that if everything is equal, the more economical a system is in its ontology, the better it is. Unfortunately, however, economy and especially simplicity cover a bewilderingly large variety of proposed tests, unlike the sorts of tests previously considered. Furthermore, because of this superabundance of competitors, a comprehensive and detailed examination of the available alternatives coupled with a well-reasoned defense of one or more tests is beyond the scope of this chapter. I shall try, however, to describe the leading candidates of each sort briefly, indicate quickly my reasons for rejecting or accepting them, and propose, with a modicum of defense, a new test of each sort which avoids the problems of its predecessors.

ON CLASSIFYING TESTS OF SIMPLICITY AND ECONOMY

There is a helpful way to begin to find our way through the maze of proposals. We can follow points made by Rudner in order to eliminate many sorts of proposed tests for simplicity or economy.[2] And we can then decide which of the remaining classifications are relevant to simplicity, and which concern economy. It will help us in this task to remember two points. First, we are interested only in conceptions of simplicity and economy that affect how good an explanation set is because of its explanatory system. Thus the tests are not to depend on the psychological, sociological, or historical conditions of any person or group of persons who wish to use the system. Second, the principle known as Occam's Razor seems relevant to economy but not simplicity. The latter seems to concern the degree of structural complexity and the amount of systematization of systems, rather than whether systems 'multiply entities beyond necessity'.

Given the two preceding points, we can quickly eliminate any tests that are subjective or nonlinguistic. The first sort are rejected because subjective considerations, such as the psychological state of a particular scientist, are pragmatic considerations affecting the fecundity of an explanation set instead of systemic tests of systems. The second sort is exlcuded because, as we have construed explanatory systems, they are linguistic entities. Yet to require the tests to be linguistic is not to restrict them to purely notational or syntactical features of systems. There are also semantical characteristics, such as those whose descriptions require semantic concepts like reference, extension, meaning, and intension of terms, or values of variables, or truth and falsity of sentences. For example, the economy of a system might be characterized in terms of its ontic commitments, and the latter, following Quine, as determined by what must be the values of the bound variables of the system if it is to be true. But not all semantic features of a system relate its terms, variables or sentences to nonlinguistic entities. That is, not all semantic features are what I have called 'nonformal'; some are 'formal', such as any relating only linguistic entities.[3] Consider one relating only mentioned terms ('p' has the same extension as 'q'), or relating only mentioned sentences ('P' is true in L_1 just in case 'Q' is true in L_2), or relating bound variables and their substituends that result in true sentences. So we need two main varieties of linguistic tests: formal and nonformal. Under the second we have just one classification: nonsyntactical (including semantic) tests of simplicity or economy. Under the first we have three: notational, syntactic, and nonsyntactic tests.

We can easily exclude all notational tests, such as any depending on the number or order of letters in the sentences of the system. Surely no features of a system that depend on the spelling of words in some language or on other accidental notational features is relevant to which of two systems is better. I also wish to reject all nonformal views of simplicity and economy. This cannot be justified so easily or quickly, but let me begin a justification as follows. As Goodman notes, simplicity of a system is related to the amount of systematization and integration found in the system. And this latter pair seems to depend in some way on what Goodman calls "the basis for a system", that is, some relatively small group of statements from which all the statements of the theory are derivable.[4] So, it is plausible at this point to assume that simplicity is some structural feature of bases of systems because systematization and integration seem to be structural characteristics. Consequently, if we should find a desired basis for a system, then what would be needed would be merely some syntactical features of that basis. But such features are clearly formal. It would, however, be a mistake to conclude from this that we can ignore not only nonformal tests but also all nonsyntactic tests. This is because it is far from clear that all bases of one system would be equally simple, and so various bases with different terms as primitive might have to be examined. But this would require a consideration of different sets of definitions, and definitions, in requiring at least coextensivity, are semantic. So, although the most plausible tests of simplicity are formal, we should not conclude in advance that they are syntactic.

ON TESTS OF ECONOMY

I have claimed that we can reject all nonformal tests of economy, and, let me add, all notational or syntactic tests. We can begin to see why this is so by beginning our search for a viable test with an examination of one test that is nonformal and semantic. Consider one version of Occam's Razor that applies to what we might call nonobservational or 'pure' theoretical entities. In short, it prescribes that no one should postulate more pure theoretical entities than are needed for explanation. More fully and clearly, if system C_1 explains all that system C_2 explains, and the explanations of C_2 imply the existence of entities of more pure theoretical kinds than those of C_1, then C_1 should be used rather than C_2 (that is, C_1 is a better explanatory system than C_2). Note that the relevant asymmetry is not that C_2 requires more pure theoretical entities than C_1 does, but rather that it requires the existence of entities of more pure theoretical kinds. This is as it should be. If C_1 is cumulative relative to C_2, it might well imply the existence of more pure theoretical entities, but, nevertheless, require far fewer kinds of pure theoretical entities. Surely, this increase that cumulativity often brings should not count against a system.

A Nonformal, Semantic Test of Economy

To clarify the preceding statement of Occam's Razor and turn it into a minimum version of a nonevidential test for explanation sets, we need to realize that, in general, conditional P-explananda, rather than categorical existence claims, are derivable from systems alone. Thus we must rephrase the preceding approximation so it concerns the conditional P-explananda of systems. We can begin to do this by considering the following first attempt at a definition of economy:

> Explanatory system C_1 is *more economical than* explanatory system $C_2 =_{df.}$ (1) System C_1 has all the conditional experien-

tial P-explananda that C_2 has; (2) there are at most n pure theoretical kinds, T_1^1 through T_1^n, such that for each i, where $1 \leqslant i \leqslant n$, the existence of a T_1^i is conditionally P-explained by C_1; (3) there are at least m pure theoretical kinds, T_2^1 through T_2^m, such that for each j, where $1 \leqslant j \leqslant m$, the existence of a T_2^j is conditionally P-explained by C_2; and (4) $m > n$.

According to the preceding definition, economy is clearly nonsyntactical because it involves the concept of a pure theoretical kind. It might also seem initially to be nonformal because it relates a system to nonlinguistic entities. However, Carnap might say, this definition is in the 'material mode' of speech. It would be more perspicuous if put in the 'formal mode', because, literally, statements are conditional P-explananda of systems. And once we switch to talk of such statements we should also switch to talk of pure theoretical terms in these conditional P-explananda. Then what results would clearly seem to be a formal notion of economy. Nevertheless, it would still be nonsyntactic, because the concept of a pure theoretical term is not a syntactic one. As I have argued elsewhere, it is to be unpacked in part by means of the concept of an observation-term, and the latter is defined in terms of what is observable by a standard observer in standard conditions.[5] So the definition becomes formal but remains nonsyntactic, as is clear once we replace clauses (2) and (3) of the preceding attempt by:

(2)   there are at most n pure theoretical terms, 'T_1^1' through 'T_1^n', such that for each i, where $1 \leqslant i \leqslant n$, the sentence 'Something is a T_1^i' is a conditional P-explanandum of C_1;

and by:

(3)   there are at least m pure theoretical terms, 'T_2^1' through 'T_2^m', such that for each j, where $1 \leqslant j \leqslant m$, the sentence 'Something is a T_2^j' is a conditional P-explanandum of C_2.

A Formal Version of the Test of Economy, and an Objection: Ramseyized Systems. The second version of the definition is clearly a proposal that captures the intuition regarding economy that is expressed in the test by Occam's Razor. Nevertheless, a nonevidential test of economy based on the preceding definition faces two objections which require further revisions of the definition. To see this, let me first state the minimal version of the test of economy for explanation sets:

MN.7   For any two explanation sets, $\{C_1, I_1\}$ and $\{C_2, I_2\}$, set $\{C_1, I_1\}$ is a better explanation set than $\{C_2, I_2\}$, *if* either (a) C_1 is minimally adequate but C_2 is not; or (b) each experiential sentence that is P-explained by $\{C_2, I_2\}$ is approximated by a sentence P-explained by $\{C_1, I_1\}$, and all is equal regarding nonevidential tests, *except that*: C_1 is more economical than C_2, *then* $\{C_1, I_1\}$ is a better explanation set than $\{C_2, I_2\}$.

The first objection is that test MN.7 coupled with the preceding definition gives an unfair advantage to Ramseyized versions of systems, because no sentences containing pure theoretical terms are derivable from them. Such systems contain no pure theoretical terms, but, instead, only predicate variables.[6] Consequently, if the preceding proposal were correct, then any Ramseyized version of a system is better than the system, because all else is equal between a system and its Ramseyized replacement. But, according to this objection, a scientific instrumentalism which argues for the use of Ramsey-sentences should not automatically be given such an advantage by a systemic test. Thus the preceding candidate should be rejected.

There is a reply to this objection, however. While it is true that a Ramseyized version of a system would fare as well as its un-Ramseyized system by tests of testability, nonprobability, cumulativity, and structural simplicity, no Ramsey-sentence is universal in form, because it contains existential quantifiers essentially. Thus no Ramsey-sentence passes the test of pure universality; it is false that everything is equal regarding all systemic tests except for economy; and no Ramseyized system is automatically better than its un-Ramseyized original.

There are two problems for this reply. First, as argued previously, truth is not necessary for the best explanation set, and so an advocate of Ramseyizing could restrict his systems to Ramsey-clauses, that is, Ramsey-sentences less the existential quantifiers for the 'Ramsey-variables' (that is, the predicate variables that replace the pure theoretical predicate of un-Ramseyized systems). A Ramsey-clause is purely universal just in case its un-Ramseyized versions are. But, second, even if the first problem can be avoided by insisting that having some truth value is better than having none, there are certain situations in which the preceding test would still give an unfair advantage to Ramseyized systems with quantifiers. One would occur if the test of economy should take preference over the test of pure universality. This is not totally unreasonable. The other is the quite common situation where the un-Ramseyized system either is not a sentence because, for example, it contains a probability formula such as 'Pr $(Px/Qx) = n$', or is not universal, because it contains an existential quantifier or singular term essentially. Such situations occur when a system requires some existentially quantified sentence or a singular, categorical sentence that is purely theoretical to explain something observable.[7] But even in such a situation, it seems that the Ramseyized version should not automatically become the better of the two systems. So some change should be made in the preceding version of the test.

The required amendment is easily made. We need merely require that economy be defined solely in terms of Ramseyized versions of systems, and conditional P-explananda of systems that have the form 'Something is ϕ_i' where each 'ϕ_i' is a unique Ramsey-variable corresponding to exactly one pure theoretical term in the un-Ramseyized system. As a result, we have two new replacements for clauses (2) and (3). First:

(2)   there are at most n Ramsey-variables, 'ϕ_1^1' through 'ϕ_1^n', such that for each i, where $1 \leqslant i \leqslant n$, 'Something is ϕ_1^i' is a conditional P-explanandum of $R\text{-}C_1$ (the Ramseyized version of C_1).

Second:

(3)   there are at least m Ramsey-variables, 'ϕ_2^1' through 'ϕ_2^m', such that for each j, where $1 \leqslant j \leqslant m$, 'Something is ϕ_2^j' is a conditional P-explanandum of $R\text{-}C_2$.

A Second Objection: On Quarks Affecting Economy. Even after the second change in the definition of economy, an objection to test MN.7 remains. Take two systems, C_1 and C_2, that have exactly the same testable conditional consequences, and differ regarding systemic tests only in that 'Something is Q' is a pure theoretical conditional consequence of C_2 but not of C_1. Then C_1 would, by the preceding test, be better than C_2. But suppose that 'Qx' = 'x is a quark', where quarks are, let us assume, the ultimate constituents of certain of the pure theoretical entities, such as protons and neutrons, that are assumed in C_1. System C_1 has no implications about quarks nor any about a Ramsey-variable corresponding to 'Qx'. But, surely, because of the order brought by the postulation of quarks, with their 'colorful' and 'flavorful' properties, system C_2 should be counted as at least as good a system as C_1, contrary to the preceding version.[8] In this respect, the 'addition' of quarks to physics is quite different from the postulation of the ether, phlogiston, of effluvia, even though it may be that quarks, like the others, are not needed to explain any experiential data.

I see no way to avoid this objection from the value of postulating quarks, and so another amendment is required. The only systemic tests that might seem to counterbalance this effect of the preceding test is some sort of simplicity test, because of the organization brought about by quarks. But, as we shall see, the only tests of simplicity which will survive our scrutiny will not consider such a factor. Furthermore, we should not rely on some other systemic test to counteract a test of economy, because economy may take precedence in some, perhaps all, cases. We can avoid this problem by adapting definition D21 in Chapter 7, which concerns minimal versions of explanation sets, to apply to minimal versions of explanatory systems for the experiential conditional P-explananda of systems. The idea would be to compare for economy only those systems that have no clauses that are irrelevant to these experiential explananda. For any two systems of this sort, the system with less theoretical baggage would be more economical. First, then, we need a definition of the relevant sort of minimal version of a system. To do this we should recall that for a system C, C_p is C rewritten in prenex normal form with its matrix in conjunctive normal form with n conjuncts, and there are n nonequivalent C_p^i's, each of which has at least one conjunct of C_p and has only conjuncts of C_p. The definition is:

D27. mC is a *minimal experiential version* of $C =_{df}$. (1) mC has exactly the experiential conditional P-explananda of C, and (2) mC is a C_p^i such that no C_p^j has exactly the experiential conditional P-explananda of C, and has fewer conjuncts than mC has.

Finally, I now claim, we have a satisfactory definition of economy that produces no problems for test MN.7. We want to compare for economy only those systems that are their own minimal versions. So we have:

D28. Explanatory system C_1 is *more economical than* explanatory system $C_2 =_{df}$.
   (1) C_1 and C_2 are their own minimal experiential versions;
   (2) C_1 has all the experiential conditional P-explananda of C_2;
   (3) there are at most n Ramsey-variables, 'ϕ_1^1' through 'ϕ_1^n', such that for each i, where $1 \leqslant i \leqslant n$, 'Something is ϕ_1^i' is a conditional P-explanandum of mC_1;
   (4) there are at least m Ramsey-variables, 'ϕ_2^1' through 'ϕ_2^m',

such that for each j, where $1 \leqslant j \leqslant m$, 'Something is a ϕ_2^i' is a conditional P-explanandum of mC_2; and
(5) $m > n$.

Test MN.7, when taken with definition D28, would not provide a comparison of systems *cum* quarks or the ether, *if* neither of these is needed to derive any conditional consequences of the systems whose consequents are experiential P-explananda of the systems. This is not to say that a system with such quarks or the ether might be better than some other system because its minimal experiential version is. A system with these entities is not to be compared for economy, because it is not its own minimal experiential version. This should cause no alarm because MN.7, like all the other minimal nonevidential tests we shall consider, provides only one sufficient condition for one set being better than another. If more is wanted, then we could relegate D28 to a definition of economy for only those systems that are their own minimal versions. But for our needs, D28 with MN.7 is adequate.

Conclusion About Tests of Economy: Plausible Tests Are Formal and Nonsyntactical

Test MN.7 is clearly a formal test of economy. Furthermore, the problems that Ramseyized systems raise for nonformal tests show, finally, why I concluded that any plausible test of economy is a formal test. Thus, because, as previously argued, all plausible tests of simplicity are formal also, we can ignore all nonformal tests of each sort. Test MN.7 is also nonsyntactical. Must we also conclude that no plausible tests of economy are syntactical? It surely seems so, because, in the material mode, economy seems to concern postulated, theoretical entities, and, even when put in the formal mode, nonsyntactical notions are needed to pick out pure theoretical terms. But it might be objected that some test of economy might merely concern 'superfluous' conditional P-explananda of the form 'Something is P', where 'p' is *any* nonlogical constant or predicate variable. Such a test might seem to be syntactic, but I claim it is not because there is no syntactical criterion for when such a consequence is superfluous. If it is an experiential conditional P-explanandum then it is clearly not superfluous. But being experiential cannot be decided on purely syntactical grounds. Thus, I believe it reasonable to conclude that all plausible concepts of economy, and so all plausible tests of economy, are formal and nonsyntactical. But what can we say about concepts and tests of simplicity?

ON TESTS OF SIMPLICITY

When we turn to an examination of tests of simplicity, as distinct from economy, we are faced with a stupefying superabundance of candidates that are wildly different in content and in plausibility. In fact, I find the complexity of the topic of simplicity and its attendant problems to be so great that I shall attempt to do only two things. First, I shall try to eliminate certain proposed tests on either of two grounds: irremedial flaws in the formulation of the test, or irrelevance to how good an explanatory system is. Second, I shall propose a minimal version of *one* test of simplicity which I shall argue is relevant to comparative evaluations of explanatory systems. I shall not claim, however, that this is the only plausible test of simplicity, but I will argue that its plausibility exceeds that of all the extant proposals of which I am aware.

Let me begin by giving three categories for sorting concepts of simplicity: those concerned only with syntactical features of 'bases' of systems, those also concerned with their semantic features, and those that consider at least some of their features that are neither syntactical nor semantic. There are examples of all three sorts. The first category includes all those for which simplicity depends only on the number of primitive extralogical predicates of a system, the number of places in the primitive predicates, and the number of postulates of the system. It also includes certain of those that determine simplicity by means of the content of, or information contained in a system. Goodman's 'calculus of simplicity' belongs either in the first or second category, depending on how features of predicates, such as reflexivity and symmetry are understood. If whether a predicate is irreflexive depends upon its interpretation, then Goodman's test belongs in the second category. But, if the irreflexivity of, say, 'Rxy', is decided by including '$(x)Rxx$' among the postulates of systems, then reflexivity, and similarly, the other properties of predicates on which the calculus relies would be syntactical. One example of the third sort of test is that proposed by Friedman, because, as we shall see, he holds that simplicity depends in part on the tests a person is able to perform.[9] Finally, although the test I shall propose considers only certain syntactical features of systems, it is, like all the preceding minimal nonevidential tests, semantic, because it requires that we isolate experiential P-explananda of systems. Nevertheless, unlike the concept of economy, which is semantic, this concept of simplicity is itself syntactical. Semantic considerations enter only when the concept is embedded in a nonevidential test.

On Simplicity as Content or Information

Let me begin our examination of proposed tests of simplicity by considering three that equate it with content, or information, or informativeness.
There have been diametrically opposed views about the relationship between simplicity and content. This alone should raise doubts about the
relevance of content to simplicity. Quine and Ullian claim that "the
simpler a hypothesis is, the fewer ways there are for it to go wrong".[10]
That is, C_1 is simpler than C_2, if there are fewer possible situations in
which C_1 is false than in which C_2 is false, that is, if C_1 has less content
than C_2. Barker, who follows Kemeny's lead, explicates the notion of the
number of possible situations in which a system is false in terms of
Carnapian state descriptions which, given a relevant vocabulary, provide
descriptions of all possible states of affairs. Using this approach, we need
only count how many state descriptions make C_1 and C_2 false individually.
Then the simpler system is the one with the smaller number, according to
Quine and Ullian. But not according to Barker, or Popper either! Barker
claims that C_1 is simpler than C_2, if C_2 can come out true in fewer ways
than C_2 can, that is, if there are more possible states of affairs in which C_1
is false than in which C_2 is false.[11] And Popper argues that C_1 is simpler
than C_2, if C_1 has greater content that C_2, that is, if C_1 is more easily falsifiable than C_2, or, it surely seems, if there are more possible states of affairs
in which C_1 is false than in which C_2 is false.[12]

There is good reason to reject both of these opposed views, as Goodman
has clearly shown.[13] He considers three sentences: (1) 'All maples not in
Eagleville are deciduous' – $(x)[(Mx \cdot Ex) \supset Dx]$; (2) 'All maples are deciduous' – $(x)(Mx \supset Dx)$; and (3) 'All maples, and all sassafras trees in
Eagleville, are deciduous' – $(x)\{[Mx \lor (Sx \cdot Ex)] \supset Dx\}$. It seems clear
that (2) is structurally simpler than either (1) or (3). But (1) has less content than (2), because (1) is false in fewer possible situations than (2) is.
Consequently, greater simplicity differs from less content. And (3) has
more content than (2), because (3) is false in more possible states of
affairs than (2) is. So greater simplicity differs from greater content. That
is, content seems clearly unrelated to simplicity. It might seem, nevertheless, that content is important for evaluating systems, and so an additional
systemic test of content should be devised. But should it agree with
Quine?

I suggest that Popper is right in proposing that one "methodological
rule" is "a rule favoring theories with the highest possible empirical content".[14] But if we accept Popper's notion of empirical content, which dif-

fers in one important respect from Barker's, then we need no new test, because I have already urged, with help from Newton, the adoption of a test that basically agrees with Popper's rule, namely, the test of scope. This is because, for Popper, x has greater empirical content than y just in case "the class of potential falsifiers of x includes the class of potential falsifiers of y as a *proper subclass*".[15] And this class inclusion is determined by derivability relationships like those for scope or cumulativity. So no new test is required to accommodate Popper. But what about Barker, who does not even demand overlap of potential falsifiers to determine differences in content of x and y? All Barker requires is that for a sufficiently large but finite universe, the number of potential falsifiers of x differs from that for y. Thus (4), 'All apples are red and hard' – $(x)[Ax \supset (Rx \cdot Hx)]$, would have greater content than (2) for Barker. But Popper claims that these two are incomparable regarding content. Again, whom should we follow? Again I propose that we rest content with the test of scope which agrees with Popper. We are concerned with systemic tests for deciding which of two explanatory systems is better, and I see no reason to hold that, all else being equal, (4) is a better system than (2), given a vocabulary containing 'Ax', 'Dx', 'Hx', and 'Rx', because (4) is falsified by more possible states of affairs than (2) is. But this is not the only reason to avoid Barker's approach. Someone who is unhappy with the preceding result could avoid it by replacing 'Rx' and 'Hx' in his vocabulary by 'Qx' = '$Rx \cdot Hx$', and, relative to that vocabulary, (2) and (4) have equal content. The test of scope avoids this relativity because it requires logical relationships among the predicates of systems in order to determine comparative scope.

On Simplicity as Informativeness

A different notion of content, namely, 'informativeness', has recently been proposed as the clue to determining comparative simplicity. Sober says that "the simplicity of a hypothesis can be measured by attending to how well it answers certain kinds of questions. I claim that the more informative a hypothesis is in answering these questions, the simpler it is. The informativeness of hypotheses relative to questions is characterized by the amount of extra information they need to yield answers".[16] In short, Sober's precise principle can be stated as follows:

> System C_1 is simpler than C_2 relative to question Q if and only if the set of minimum extra information (MEI set) that is sufficient for C_1 to answer Q has less content than the MEI set that is sufficient for C_2 to answer Q.[17]

Sober goes into considerable detail in showing how to determine when one MEI set has less content than another. For our purpose, it is enough to note that when a system is 'self-sufficient' with respect to a question, that is, it needs no other information to answer the question, then its MEI set for that question contains only a tautology and so it has the minimum content relative to that question. So any system that is self-sufficient with respect to a question is simplest (that is, none is simpler) relative to that question.

Consider now the question, Q_1: 'Is an (arbitrarily chosen) individual, a, an F or not an F?" Consider also three different systems: $C_1 =$ '$(x)Fx$'; $C_2 =$ '$(x)(Gx \equiv Fx)$'; and $C_3 =$ '$(x)[Gx \cdot (Gx \supset Hx) \cdot (Hx \supset Fx)]$'. Relative to Q_1, systems C_1 and C_3 are self-sufficient, but C_2 needs either Ga or $\sim Ga$. Indeed, in Sober's view, C_3 is maximally simple relative to Q_1, and any other system, no matter how incredibly complex, is maximally simple relative to Q_1 if it yields an answer to Q_1. But surely this is a grossly implausible result regarding structural simplicity and the relative worth of systems. Clearly, C_1 is simpler than C_3 relative to Q_1, and so, I should think, is C_2, and also $C_4 =$ '$(x)[Ga \cdot (Gx \supset Fx)]$'.

Sober's thesis also faces another problem, at least given our interest in simplicity. It is quite unclear how to use a notion of simplicity that is always relative to questions in order to evaluate systems, because, in general, systems are relevant to more than one question and what is simpler relative to one is less simple or even irrelevant relative to another. Consider question Q_2: 'Is a being G equivalent to a being F?' System C_1 needs at least to be supplemented by $(Fa \supset Ga)$ to answer Q_2. But, in Sober's view, C_2 and C_3 are self-sufficient with respect to Q_2. Thus they are maximally simple relative to Q_2, and consequently, simpler than C_1 relative to Q_2. As a result, for Sober's proposal to provide a systemic test of comparative simplicity, we need to find a way to isolate one question or set of questions as what is relevant to deciding which of two systems is better, all else being equal.

I find only four alternatives that are even remotely plausible, even making the dubious assumption that Sober can, as he claims, limit questions to those with 'natural' predicates such as 'green', rather than 'artificial' predicates such as 'grue'.[18] One is to take the required set to be the set of questions (with natural predicates) to which either system is relevant, for some arbitrarily chosen set of individuals. We might then claim that the simpler system is the one that is simpler relative to more questions in this set. But this makes the test useless, because if a hypothesis is relevant to one question, then, by the principle of addition, it is relevant to infinitely many. So all contingent systems would be equally simple. A second alternative, which Sober notes, is to take the required set of questions to be those to which both systems are relevant. But this does not help if we again take the simpler to be the one that is simpler relative to more questions in the set. In this case, there are infinitely many whenever there is one to which both are relevant. And Sober's own proposal about what to do in this case is not helpful. He says that when some questions in the required set favor one system as simpler, but others favor the other, then we must weigh the value of the different questions somehow. But he admits he can offer no criterion for this.[19] The same problem arises for the third alternative, which takes the simpler to be that system with the greater number of questions for which it is either simpler than the other or relevant when the other is not. Consequently, I see no hope of using any of these three alternatives.

The last alternative I have found is to make nonrelativistic simplicity be determined by simplicity relative to the set of questions each of whose pairs of answers consist in one of the foundational sentences for person s at time t, and its denial. Then, although simplicity would not test explanatory systems, it would still be relevant to determining which explanation set is maximal for s at t. But this is no help either. Assume that 'Fa' is the one sentence to be explained for s at t. Then the relevant question is Q_1 again, and so C_3, and its much more complex relatives that entail 'Fa', would be as simple as C_1. But that is implausible, and so this last alternative fails as did the other three. I conclude that Sober's attempt to relate simplicity to what he calls 'informativeness' fails.

On The Simpler as Being More Testable

Simplicity seems clearly different from content, information, and informativeness. What other candidates are there? One is the nonsyntactical, nonsemantic thesis of Friedman that the simplicity of predicates or, alternatively, classes, is determined by certain facts about the tests for that predicate or class that a person can perform, at – I add – a certain time. It is because of this reference to a person's ability that the test is neither syntactical nor semantic. We can state Friedman's principle by partially unpacking it as follows:

> Class C is simpler than class D for person s (at time t) if and
> only if, of the tests that s can conduct (at t), the set of tests for

class D that are *independent* of all information *parasitic* on class C is a proper subset of the set of tests for class C that are *independent* of all information *parasitic* on class D.[20]

We also need to unpack two of Friedman's technical terms. First:

A test for class C is independent of information I if all its results are compatible with I being true of the test object and also compatible with I being false of the test object.[21]

Concerning the second, I shall simplify Friedman's definition somewhat because that will help us see where the crucial problem arises:

Information I for class C is parasitic on class D if and only if *either*

(1) $(x)[x \in C \supset (Ix \equiv x \in D)$, and
(2) $(K)(x)\{[x \in K \supset (Ix \equiv x \in D)] \supset (x \in K \equiv x \in C)\}$;
or
(3) $(\exists I^*)(x)(I^*x \supset Ix)$, and I^* satisfies (1) and (2).[22]

Friedman gives several examples to illustrate his principle, including one where C is the class of square things, and D is the class of things that are green and square. About this example, he says,

Suppose I stands for 'is green'. Condition 1 is met, for anything that is square and that is green is green and square. Condition 2 is met, for given the meanings of I and $[D]$, no . . . [class] other than . . . $[C]$ satisfies the first condition. Thus I is information for . . . $[D]$ parasitic on . . . $[C]$.[23]

Friedman goes on to argue that, by his principle, class C is simpler than D. Unfortunately, his argument fails because there are classes that falsify condition (2), and so, contrary to what he says, condition (2) is not met. Consider class K_1 which is the class of square things whose sides are longer than ten inches. Class K_1 satisfies the antecedent of condition (2), but $\sim(x \in C \supset x \in K_1)$, which falsifies the consequent of (2). So condition (2) is not met for I in the preceding example. Indeed, for any C, D, and I that meet condition (1), there is a K, similar to K_1, that falsifies condition (2). So, by Friedman's definitions, no information for a class is ever parasitic on any other class.

It might be objected that I have ignored condition (3), and, although in this example (1) and (2) do not show I to be parasitic because of K_1, this can be shown by using some I^* that meets condition (3). But, because there is something that is square with sides less than ten inches long, (2) is falsified. Such an object instantiates the antecedent of (2) and also the denial of its consequent. Consequently, I see no hope for Friedman's stated principle. But perhaps amendments would help. However, the most obvious one which avoids the problem K_1 creates, faces its own objection. Change the consequent of condition (2) to $(x \in K \supset x \in C)$. Then, because $(x \in K_1 \supset x \in C)$, class K_1 does not violate the new (2). But consider instead K_2, that is, the class of things that are green just in case they are square. Class K_2 meets the antecedent of the new (2), but not its consequent, because some things in K_2, namely, those not green, are not square. But might there be an I^* that meets condition (1) and the new (2)? There is always one that meets (1), and implies I, namely, $I^* = $ 'is a member of D'. But then let K_3 be the class of things that are green and square just in case they are green. Class K_3 fails to meet condition (2) for I^*, because some things in $K_3 -$ again nongreen things – are not square. I think, therefore, that we should either abandon Friedman's term "parasitic on", or allow that no information for one class is parasitic on another. Then all tests for one class would be independent of all information parasitic on another class. Whichever alternative we take, Friedman's principle becomes:

> Class C is simpler than class D for person s (at time t) if and only if, of the tests that s can conduct (at t), the set of tests for D is a proper subset of the set of tests for C.

And if, for ease of examination, we assume that s is a person who is able to conduct each test for C or D, then, for s, C is simpler than D if and only if each of the tests for D is a test for C, but not conversely. And, since "a test is a procedure which either falsifies or corroborates a hypothesis",[24] it is easy to see that the revised principle yields that no class is simpler than another, and so it is valueless. Take again classes C and D above. One of the tests that falsifies $(a \in D)$, namely, one that establishes that a is not green, does not falsify $(a \in C)$. And one of the tests that corroborates $(a \in C)$, namely, one that establishes that a is square, does not corroborate $(a \in D)$. So neither set of tests is a subset of the other and, by the revised principle, neither class C nor class D is simpler than the other. And since class D is a subclass of C, it is easy to see that no set of tests for one class is a proper subset of the set for another class, unless the first set is empty. Consequently, the revised principle is of no help. Something like the notion of being parasitic is needed to exclude enough tests so that one set becomes a subset of the other. But that notion seems irremediable, and I am aware of no other. Consequently, Friedman's approach seems doomed, just like all others we have examined.

The Rejection of Three More Tests

What candidates remain? There is Goodman's calculus which, like one version of Friedman's, concerns predicates, and also three others that Goodman convincingly dispatches. The latter are tests based either on the number of extralogical primitive predicates of a system, or on the number of places in these predicates, or on the number of postulates of a system. Intuitively, each of these tests seems somewhat relevant to structural simplicity, but unfortunately none are viable. As both Goodman and Barker note, it is always easy to reduce the number of primitive predicates to one. For example, assume that a system, S_1, has three primitive one-place predicates, 'Fx', 'Gx', and 'Hx', and let us assume that each is true of something. Then we can replace all three predicates by just one three-place predicate. As Barker says,

We could let '$Kxyz$' be this predicate; it would be so explained as to be true of a sequence of three things x, y, and z if and only if x is an F, y is a G, and z is an H. By using this new three-place predicate 'K', the statements that belong to the earlier system all can be reformulated in accord with these rules:

> For 'Fx' read '$(\exists y)(\exists z)Kxyz$';
> For 'Gx' read '$(\exists y)(\exists z)Kyxz$';
> For 'Hx' read '$(\exists y)(\exists z)Kyzx$'.

The new system S_2 is to contain all and only those statements which can be got from statements of S_1 by means of these rules.[25]

In such a way, all systems can be replaced by equivalent ones with only one primitive, and so, by the first test, for each system there is another one that is at least as simple as it is. The first test is useless.

Goodman has pointed out that the preceding vitiating problem is avoided by a test that concerns only the number of predicate places, because each place must be preserved, as it was in the preceding example, even where primitive predicates are not. But Goodman is correct in arguing that mere number of places is no measure of complexity, because, as he says, "Replacement of [a set of predicates] by single predicate is always possible, but not replacement of single predicate by set. For example, the one-place predicates '. . . . is a parent' and '. . . . has a parent' will not serve instead of the two-place predicate '. . . . is a parent of——' ".[26] That is, a basis with just these two one-place predicates does not seem to be equal in simplicity to a base with just the one two-place predicate. Yet if the number of predicate places determined the degree of simplicity, then the two bases would be equally simple. So this second test is also mistaken. The third test is no better, even if it does seem to capture something like our intuitive notion of simplicity. It is obvious that the number of extralogical postulates of a system can be reduced to one by conjoining them. Indeed, Goodman and Quine have even shown how, by using a certain sort of definition of the primitive predicates of a system, all of its postulates can be made deducible from certain truths of elementary number theory.[27] So, in one sense, no 'extralogical' postulate is needed. Nothing can be simpler, by the third test, than that.

On Goodman's Calculus of Simplicity

Are we left then only with Goodman's calculus? Of those tests proposed thus far, it is the only one of which I am aware that is plausible enough to consider. It is clearly the most complex and detailed test available, but it is by no means clear that what it tests is relevant to the structural simplicity of explanatory systems. According to Goodman, the simplicity of a system is a function of certain structural properties of its extralogical primitive predicates, that is, the predicates in its basis. He says, "The relevant structural kinds of basis are those defined by giving the number of predicates and the number of places in each, together with any or no information concerning three further properties".[28] These three properties are reflexivity – $(x)Rxx$; symmetry – $(x)(y)(Rxy \supset Ryx)$; and what Goodman calls "self-completeness" – $(x)(y)(z)(w)[(Rxy \cdot Rwz \cdot x \neq y \cdot w \neq z \cdot x \neq z) \supset Rxz]$.[29] As he develops his calculus, "Reflexivity tends to *increase* complexity. . . . On the other hand, both symmetry and self-completeness tend to *reduce* complexity."[30] Further, all one-place predicates have the same complexity-value, namely, the minimum value set at 1. So all bases composed of the same number of one-place predicates and nothing else have the same complexity-value. This, as we shall see, is the source of a variation on an objection raised to Goodman's calculus by Barker.

Barker claims that in Goodman's theory, *no* interrelations among predicates of a system are relevant to the complexity of the system, because the only relevant factors are predicate places, and the reflexivity, symmetry, self-completeness, and number of the individual predicates of the bases of systems. But, says Barker, this overlooks relationships crucial to that simplicity which is relevant to the "problem of choosing among competing systems of empirical hypotheses".[31] As stated, this objection is mistaken, because Goodman has a way to deal with *some* interrelationships among primitive predicates, namely, his proposal about how to deal with what he calls the "secondary complexity of a basis". What the calculus, briefly discussed above, determines are 'primary' complexity-values. The 'over-all' structural complexity is determined by a rule to the effect that whenever two bases, b_1 and b_2, are equal in primary complexity, the overall structural complexity of b_1 is greater than that of b_2, if the secondary complexity of b_1 exceeds that of b_2. And this secondary complexity is determined by finding the maximum value each basis has relative to some true description of its predicates.[32] For example, if b_1 consists of one three-place predicate, and b_2 consists of three one-place predicates, then both might well have a primary complexity-value of 3. But the maximum for one three-place predicate is 15, while the maximum for three one-place predicates is 3.[33] So, by Goodman's rule, b_1 has more overall complexity than b_2, that is, b_2 is structurally simpler than b_1. Consequently, *some* relationships among predicates are important in Goodman's calculus, and so Barker's objection, as stated, fails.

Objection to Goodman's Calculus: Fails to Accommodate All Relevant Relationships Among Predicates. Barker's objection can be revived by reformulating it to claim that Goodman's calculus fails to consider *some* – indeed, many – of the relationships among predicates that are crucial for determining comparative structural simplicity. This point can be made by pointing out that there are systems with the same overall 'Goodman-simplicity' that differ in the structural simplicity that is relevant to evaluating systems, that is, I shall say, they differ in 'relevant simplicity'. As a result, Goodman's theory does not provide a sufficient condition for sameness of 'relevant' simplicity, and so we should reject it for our purposes. Consider three systems each of whose predicate bases consist of three one-place predicates: 'Fx', 'Gx', and 'Hx'. Then, by Goodman's calculus, they are equally simple. But let $C_1 =$ '$(x)(Fx \lor Gx \lor Hx)$', and $C_2 =$ '$(x)(\exists y)[Fx \supset (Gx \equiv Hy)]$', and $C_3 =$ '$(x)(\exists y)(x)[Fx \supset (Gy \cdot Hz)]$'. I believe it to be clear that these do not have equal 'relevant' structural simplicity. That is, the structures of these three systems with the same predicates differ widely in complexity, both in their prefixes, which contain their quantifiers, and in their matrices. So, even if sameness of overall Goodman-simplicity is a necessary condition of sameness of 'relevant' simplicity, it is not sufficient.

I also believe that sameness of Goodman-simplicity is not necessary for sameness of 'relevant' simplicity, because difference in Goodman-simplicity does not seem sufficient for difference in relevant simplicity. To see why I doubt this, consider three predicates: 'Ixy' $=$ 'x's speed is faster than

y's which is 55 m.p.h.', 'Fxy' = 'x's speed is faster than y's which is faster than 55 m.p.h.', and 'Ex' = 'x's speed exceeds the U.S. speed limit'. Then we let C_4 = '$(x)(y)(Ixy \supset Ex)$' and C_5 = '$(x)(y)(Fxy \supset Ex)$'. These two systems have the same number of primitive predicates with the same number of predicate places distributed in the same way, and the same logical form – all that seems sufficient for sameness of that structural simplicity which is relevant to nonevidential tests of explanatory systems. But C_4 and C_5 differ in primary Goodman-simplicity. Predicate 'Ixy' is irreflexive and self-complete, and so, by Goodman's calculus, its complexity-value equals 2 (that is, V[Ixy] = 2).[34] But 'Fxy', while irreflexive, is neither self-complete nor symmetrical, and so V[Fxy] = 3. Consequently, V[C_5] = 4 > V[C_4] = 3, because the value of each one-place predicate is 1. So, C_4 is Goodman-simpler than C_5. Thus, intuitively at least, Goodman's calculus seems to provide neither a necessary nor a sufficient condition of sameness of 'relevant' structural simplicity. Consequently, it seems we should reject it as irrelevant to evaluating explanatory systems. It might be objected, however, that I have shown at most that Goodman-simplicity is not 'relevant' simplicity, and this does not preclude it from being one, additional, desideratum for evaluating systems. I admit the point of the objection but let me add another reason to reinforce my case against including a systemic test of Goodman-simplicity. It seems quite unreasonable to me that on the assumption that all is equal regarding systemic tests except that C_4 is Goodman-simpler than C_5, it would result that, with a relevant I_i, $\{C_4, I_i\}$ would be better than $\{C_5, I_i\}$. But this would be true by a minimal nonevidential test for simplicity that uses Goodman-simplicity, because C_4 entails C_5 and so $\{C_4, I_i\}$ P-explains whatever $\{C_5, I_i\}$ P-explains.

Toward a Viable Test of Structural Simplicity

It is beginning to seem that we shall find no plausible test of structural simplicity. Perhaps we should agree with what Quine and Ullian suggest, namely, there is no such test, because our intuitions of simplicity have no objective grounds.[35] Instead of ending with that discouraging result, let me try instead to set the search for an objective test on a somewhat different path from those previously taken. One point that systems C_1 through C_5 in the preceding section illustrate, I think, is that differences in the relationships among predicates *in different systems* are relevant to differences in the structural simplicity of those systems. Another, I maintain, which is especially well highlighted by C_1 and C_2, is that differences in quantifier complexity are also relevant. Indeed, I feel certain that for 'relevant' complexity, $V[C_3] > V[C_2] > V[C_1]$, because, in each case, the complexity of the prefix structure and the matrix structure of C_3 is greater than that of C_2, which, in turn, is greater than that of C_1. But the difficulty is how to turn this intuition into a test.

The crucial step for finding a test of structural simplicity is to find some way to put all systems to be compared into forms which make the comparisons fair to all. The obvious way to do this is to proceed as we did in uncovering minimal versions of explanation sets, that is, rewrite each system in prenex normal form and then put its matrix in conjunctive normal form. In the present case, however, complete fairness to all seems to require we go one step farther and put the matrices in conjunctive Boolean normal form. Then all quantifiers in a system are to be in the prefix, while its matrix is to consist of conjuncts, each of which contains exactly one occurrence of each primitive predicate or its denial as a disjunct, and no conjunct occurs more than once in the matrix. This procedure not only gives a common general form for all systems, but it also provides a way to accommodate the intuition that the fewer extralogical postulates a system has, the simpler it is. That is, although all systems to be compared are to have just one extralogical postulate, they will differ in the number of conjuncts that occur in their matrices. In some respects, each of these conjuncts can be viewed as something like a postulate. This might prompt someone to propose a test whereby one system is simpler than another if the matrix of the first contains fewer conjuncts than the matrix of the second. By such a test, $V[C_3] > V[C_2] > V[C_1]$, because the conjunctive Boolean normal form of C_3 contains four conjuncts, that of C_2 contains two conjuncts, and that of C_1 contains one conjunct. Should we adopt such a test?

One thing that should make us resist the suggested test is seeing the results it yields when comparing C_3 with $C_6 = \text{'}(x)[Fx \supset (Gx \cdot Hx)]\text{'}$. By the preceding proposed test, $V[C_3] = V[C_6] = 3$, because the matrices of C_3 and C_6 have the same form. But notice the considerably greater quantifier complexity of C_3. Its prefix has two alternations of quantifiers (that is, two sets of adjacent quantifiers one of which is universal and the other, existential), but C_6 has none. And it is well known that computational complexity increases greatly as the number of quantifier alternatives increases.[36] Surely, then, this feature of C_3 shows C_6 to be structurally simpler than C_3 despite being equal in matrix-simplicity. That is, overall structural simplicity depends on both matrix-simplicity and prefix-simplicity, and so we must aim at devising a test that accommodates both. But to achieve this goal, we must first do some preparatory tasks.

A Tentative Proposal for a Test of Structural Simplicity. For any system, there are versions in prenex normal form with the least number of quantifier alternations, but there is no guarantee that one of those with the fewest alternations will also have the fewest conjuncts in the conjunctive Boolean normal form of its matrix. Consequently, we must decide which sort of simplicity is to have preference. I suggest that we require the basic consideration to be prefix-simplicity because of the seriousness of the effect of quantifier alternations on ease of computability. Then once we have found those versions with the fewest alternations, we determine matrix-complexity by finding which among those versions have the fewest conjuncts. To help us clarify this point, let me propose three definitions. The first two are:

D29. C_1^p is a *prefix-simplest* version of $C_1 =_{df}$. C_1^p is logically equivalent to C_1, is in prenex normal form, and has as few quantifier alternations in its prefix as any sentence that is definitionally equivalent to C_1 and is in prenex normal form;

And:

D30. C_1 is *prefix-simpler* than $C_2 =_{df}$. All prefix-simplest versions of C_1 have fewer quantifier alternations than all prefix-simplest versions of C_2.

It might be thought that matrix-simplicity could be defined merely in terms of the number of conjuncts in matrices of certain prefix-simplest versions of systems. There is, however, a problem for such a definition. Consider sets $\{C_1, I_1\}$ and $\{C_2, I_1\}$, where $C_1 = $ '$(x)[(Fa \supset Gx) \cdot (Gx \supset Ha)]$', and $C_2 = $ '$(x)[(Fa \supset Ga) \cdot (Gx \supset Hx)]$', and $I_1 = $ 'Fa'. Also assume that only 'Fx' and 'Hx' are experiential formulas. Consequently, the two sets P-explain the same experiential sentences. But while C_1 has four conjuncts in the conjunctive Boolean normal form of its matrix, C_2 has eight conjuncts because it contains four terms, including 'Ga' and 'Gx'. I believe that C_1 should not turn out to be matrix-simpler than C_2 because of containing 'Gx' but not 'Ga'. Consequently, I suggest that we allow each occurrence of 'Ga' and 'Gx' to count as an occurrence of the same formula. The third definition, then, goes as follows:

D31. C_1 is *matrix-simpler* than $C_2 =_{df}$. Some prefix-simplest version of C_1 has fewer conjuncts in the conjunctive Boolean normal form of its matrix than any of the prefix-simplest versions of C_2, where each occurrence in a matrix of an atomic formula which is or instantiates the same formula is an occurrence of the same formula.

We are, at last, in position to state my suggestion for the minimal version of a nonevidential test of structural simplicity:

MN.8   For any two explanation sets, $\{C_1, I_1\}$ and $\{C_2, I_2\}$, *if* either (a) C_1 is minimally adequate but C_2 is not; or (b) each experiential sentence that is P-explained by $\{C_2, I_2\}$ is approximated by a sentence P-explained by $\{C_1, I_1\}$, and all is equal regarding nonevidential tests *except that*: C_1 is prefix-simpler than C_2, or C_1 is as prefix-simple as C_2 and C_1 is matrix-simpler than C_2, *then* $\{C_1, I_1\}$ is a better explanation set than $\{C_2, I_2\}$.

Have we finally found a test of structural simplicity that is both relevant to the comparative worth of explanatory systems and also has no vitiating deficiencies? I have some hope that we have, but I wish to do no more here than suggest the test and wish that it survives the scrutiny of others. Before leaving the complex topic of simplicity, however, let me add one last note. Test MN.8 will generally not allow the use of that technique described by Barker for reducing the number of extralogical predicates to one, because often that will increase the number of quantifier-alternations beyond necessity. As a result, the number of primitive predicates in the prefix-simplest versions of systems will, of course, vary considerably.

A PROPOSAL FOR THE TESTS OF MINIMUM ADEQUACY AND THE SYSTEMIC TESTS

Two last tasks confront us in this chapter. The first is to divide the surviving nonevidential tests into two sets: tests for minimum adequacy, and systemic tests. The other is to suggest a ranking among the systemic tests. In the second case, I shall primarily propose and let others evaluate. Here, however, my hope is not so much that my suggestion will endure, but rather that if there is a viable rank ordering, it will emerge from the criticisms of this one.

The first task is quite easily accomplished. Of the eight surviving tests, I find only one that is clearly a test for minimum adequacy, namely, testability in principle. Four of the others – scope, cumulativity, economy, and simplicity – are clearly unsuitable because they are tests for comparing pairs of systems, and it is unreasonable to think that any system bettered by another according to one of these tests is not minimally adequate. This leaves only the tests of pure universality, nonprobabilistic universality, and quantitation. But each of these is clearly only a systemic test. There are satisfactory explanations that lack quantitative predicates, and many probabilistic explanations are adequate, even if not ideal. Similarly, there are adequate explanatory systems that are not purely universal because they include some individual constant or existential quantifier which is needed to explain the observable behavior of some individual. It might be objected that essential universality should be a test of minimum adequacy, because no explanatory system should be equivalent to a singular sentence. But we have already precluded that possibility by making essential *generality* a necessary condition of being an explanatory system. Furthermore, it is false that a system is minimally adequate only if all its quantifiers are universal.

With this first task completed we can now say that an explanatory system, C, is minimally adequate, only if it is testable in principle, and, therefore, only if, with some appropriate I, it forms an explanation set {C, I} that P-explains some testable sentence. Consequently, because of the requirements for being an explanation set that P-explains something, we can say that an explanatory system is minimally adequate, only if it is (1) consistent, (2) essentially generalized, (3) has explanatory relevance, and (4) is testable in principle. And, on the assumption that I have examined all nonevidential tests for explanatory systems and found all but these four to be merely systemic tests, I propose that we take the conjunction of these four tests as sufficient as well as necessary for minimum adequacy. Further, since being an explanatory system that is testable in principle is sufficient for being an explanatory system that has all four of these characteristics, I propose, tentatively, the following principle of minimum adequacy:

> MA.   An explanatory system, C, is minimally adequate *if and only if* C is testable in principle.

The second task is much more difficult, and I shall only contribute a little toward its completion. On the assumption, which is surely debatable and I hope debated, that I have isolated the seven correct systemic tests, I suggest, with only minimal attempt at justification, the following hierarchy of tests: (1) scope, (2) cumulativity, (3) quantitation, (4) pure universality, (5) nonprobabilistic universality, (6) economy, and (7) structural simplicity. Then if we were to use this hierarchy, we could replace the minimum test, MN, and its various species, MN.2 through MN.8, by the following general schema for systemic tests, when $n = 7$:

ST. For any two explanation sets, $\{C_1, I_1\}$ and $\{C_2, I_2\}$, that are minimally adequate, *if* C_1 does as well as C_2 on systemic tests up through i in the hierarchy of systemic tests, for $0 \leqslant i \leqslant n$, and C_1 does better on test $i + 1$ than C_2, *then* $\{C_1, I_1\}$ is a better explanation set than $\{C_2, I_2\}$.

Why did I suggest the preceding hierarchy? Regarding all but quantitation, I chose this ordering because it seemed to me that those six systemic tests divide naturally into three sorts that can themselves be ranked, namely, those involving the range of systems – (1) and (2), those concerning universality of systems – (3) and (4), and those aimed at some sort of simplicity – (5) and (6). And, taking my lead from Newton, I put those involving range at the top, and next those aimed at universality which is somewhat related to range. This left economy and simplicity at the bottom. But how did I decide the ordering within each group? My reason for placing scope before cumulativity is that if C_1 has greater scope than C_2, then C_1 has all consequences of C_2. In such a case, C_1 is, I take it, to be preferred to a system that merely has all experiential consequences of C_2, and so is cumulative relative to C_2 but not greater in scope than C_2. But for the other orderings I fell back almost entirely on intuition.

My 'reasons' for the placement of quantitation are almost as weak. It should go below scope, for if C_1 has greater scope than C_2 and C_2 is quantitative, then C_1 is quantitative wherever C_2 is. So if C_1 exceeds C_2 in scope, all of the quantitative advantages of C_2 are also found in C_1. Surely, if C_1 has all those advantages of C_2 and also has greater scope than C_2, then C_1 is to be preferred to C_2 even if C_2 is fully quantitative but C_1 is not. My reason for preferring cumulativity is less forceful. In this case, if C_1 is cumulative relative to C_2, and C_2 is quantitative, then C_1 entails approximations of all the experiential sentences that C_2 entails, and so C_1 is quantitative wherever C_2 is at the experiential level. This is what inclines me to prefer cumulativity. If C_1 is cumulative relative to C_2, then C_1 has the most important quantitative advantage of C_2, namely, the quantitative precision that is crucial for testing by measurement. However, I believe that quantitative precision should not be sacrificed for economy or simplicity, and so

I find quantitation belongs above those two. But its worth relative to universality is unclear to me. Nevertheless, because the insistence, since Galileo, that mathematical language is the language that is needed to understand the universe has aided in so many scientific successes, I propose that quantitation never be sacrificed for universality.

So much for how I chose the hierarchy. I hope for better reasons – mine or others' – in the future. For now, then, I leave the hierarchy largely undefended. However, to avoid finishing on such an unsatisfying note, let me end instead by replacing general minimal nonevidential principle MN by a more specific one that is reasonable if and only if, as I dare to hope, it is reasonable to claim that the seven systemic tests, MN.2 through MN.8, are *the* correct minimal versions of systemic tests for explanatory systems. It is:

MN*. For any two explanation sets $\{C_1, I_1\}$, $\{C_2, I_2\}$, set $\{C_1, I_1\}$ is a better explanation set than $\{C_2, I_2\}$, *if either* (a) C_1 is minimally adequate but C_2 is not, *or* (b) each experiential sentence that is P-explained by $\{C_2, I_2\}$ is approximated by a sentence P-explained by $\{C_1, I_1\}$, and the following disjunction is true when 'C_1' replaces 'x' and 'C_2' replaces 'y', but false for the converse substitution: (1) x has greater scope than y, or (2) x is cumulative relative to y, or (3) x is fully quantitative but y is not, or (4) x is purely universal but y is not, or (5) x is nonprobabilistically universal but y is not, or (6) x is more economical than y, or (7) x is structurally simpler than y.

CONCLUSION: THE BEST EXPLANATIONS AND SKEPTICISM

We have finally reached the end of our long, but all too brief discussion of nonevidential tests for minimum adequacy and systemic tests. This was the final preliminary task before we attempt to show that the explanatory foundational theory implies the falsity of skeptical thesis M_1S_3 (that is, it is never reasonable for any human being, s, to believe a sentence if it entails the existence of a particular physical object that s is not perceiving, or the occurrence of a nonsubjective event in the past, or the occurrence of a future event, or the existence of a mental phenomenon of another being). We had to complete the present task first, because throughout the previous discussion it had become clear that the only hope for justifying claims about the unperceived present, the nonsubjective past, the future, and the minds of others depends on justification through explanation. That is, such justification depends on the clauses of the epistemic principles F3.22 and F3.221 that concern explanation sets. But those clauses can be satisfied only by explanation sets that contain explanatory systems that are best among one particular group of systems. Now, with our tentative, but I believe somewhat plausible, selection of seven systemic tests for explanation sets, we can begin to determine the implications of the explanatory foundational theory for epistemological skepticism.

NOTES

[1] W. Quine and J. Ullian, *The Web of Belief*, New York: Random House, 1970, p. 51.

[2] See R. Rudner, 'An Introduction to Simplicity', *Philosophy of Science* 2 (1961), 109–115.

[3] I have discussed formal rules briefly in 'Reference and Ontology: Inscrutable but Not Relative', *Monist* 59 (1976), 362–64.

[4] See N. Goodman, *Problems and Projects*, Indianapolis: Bobbs-Merrill, 1972, p. 338.

[5] For my previous definition of 'observation-term', see my *Materialism and Sensations*, New Haven, Conn.: Yale University Press, 1971, p. 69.

[6] I have discussed Ramsey-sentences in *Perception, Common Sence, and Science*, New Haven, Conn: Yale University Press, 1975, pp. 164–167.

[7] *Ibid.*, pp. 176–177, for an example of an explanation that uses a singular sentence with a pure theoretical term.

[8] For a philosophically interesting article on quarks, see S. Glashow, 'Quarks with Color and Flavor', *Scientific American* 233 (Oct. 1975), 38–50.

[9] See K. Friedman, 'Son of Grue: Simplicity *vs.* Entrenchment', *Nous* 7 (1973), 370.

[10] *Op. cit.*, p. 46.

[11] See S. Barker, *Induction and Hypothesis: A Study in the Logic of Confirmation*, Ithaca, N.Y.: Cornell University Press, 1957, pp. 176–182.

[12] See K. Popper, *The Logic of Scientific Discovery*, New York: Harper and Row, 1968, sections 42 and 43.

[13] *Op. cit.*, p. 335.

[14] See Popper, *op. cit.*, p. 121.

[15] *Ibid.*, p. 123.

[16] E. Sober, *Simplicity*, London: Oxford University Press, 1975, p. vii.

[17] *Ibid.*, pp. 15–19 for Sober's discussion of the relationship of "extra information" to simplicity.

[18] *Ibid.*, pp. 19–23.

[19] *Ibid.*, p. 25.

[20] Friedman, *op. cit.*, p. 370.

[21] *Ibid.* I have rephrased Friedman's formulation by replacing 'is applicable to' by 'is true of'.

[22] *Ibid.* Note the differences in the quantifiers of clause (2). Friedman's are equivalent to '$(K)(\exists x)$'. I doubt that he wants that pair.

[23] See Friedman, 'Empirical Simplicity as Testability', *British Journal for the Philosophy*

of Science **23** (1972), 29. I have also made changes here from talk of predicates to talk of classes, so that this passage agrees with Friedman's other article.

[24] *Ibid.*, p. 27.

[25] Barker, *op. cit.*, p. 173.

[26] Goodman, *op. cit.*, p. 341.

[27] *Ibid.*, pp. 325–333.

[28] See Goodman, *The Structure of Appearance*, 2nd ed., Indianapolis: Bobbs-Merrill, 1966, pp. 104–107.

[29] *Idid.*, p. 83, for self-completeness.

[30] Goodman, *Problems and Projects*, pp. 342–343.

[31] Barker, *op. cit.*, p. 175.

[32] See Goodman, *The Structure of Appearance*, pp. 104–107.

[33] *Ibid.*, p. 104.

[34] *Ibid.*, p. 102.

[35] See Quine and Ullian, *op. cit.*, pp. 45–47.

[36] I am greatly indebted to my colleague, Scott Weinstein for bringing this point to my attention.

CHAPTER 10

THE EXPLANATORY FOUNDATIONAL THEORY AND SKEPTICISM

We are ready to begin our attempt to discover whether correct use of the explanatory foundation theory yields something that contradicts skeptical thesis M_1S_3, that is, yields that at some time, t, it is acceptable for someone that there are physical objects he does not perceive at t, that nonsubjective events have occurred before t and will occur after t, and that other beings have mental phenomena. The way to proceed, of course, is to use the explanatory foundational principle F3.22 or, as I shall do, the simpler principle, F3.221, which it entails, and to search for those instantiations of clauses in the principle which yield what is desired. To do this, we obviously need the principle before us, and so I shall repeat it here:

F3.221 Any empirical statement, p, is acceptable for s at t, if *either*:
(1) p is in $S_1 =$ the set of sentences that satisfy the antecedent of H3 for s at t; *or*
(2) p is in $S_2 =$ the set of sentences that satisfy the antecedent of BR3 or BR4, for $e = S_1$; *or*
(3) (a) p is the conjunction of the members of the set $S_4 = \{C, I\}$, (b) $\{C, I\}$ is minimally adequate and is its own minimal version for set F_1 whose members are the members of $S_1 \cup S_2$ eternalized to s at t, (c) $\text{Pr}_{s,t}(F_1) > 0.5$, (d) $\{C, I\}$ is maximal for s at t relative to F_1, (e) if some experts about F_1 at t accept explanation sets for F_1, then at least one of the best of these sets does not conflict with S_4, and (f) at t, s chooses $\{C, I\}$ to explain the members of F_1 (that is, let us say, p is S_4 which is the *best* explanation set for s at t, relative to F_1); *or*
(4) p is in set $S_6 =$ the set of sentences that are entailed by some S_i that is a subset of $S_1 \cup S_2 \cup S_4$, and $\text{Cr}_{s,t}(S_i) > 0.5$.

As we found in Chapter 5, nothing in sets S_1 or S_2 will provide what we want to falsify skeptical thesis M_1S_3, because applying principles H3, BR3, and BR4 yields nothing that conflicts with M_1S_3. So the crucial clause of

F3.221 is the third. That is, we need to uncover some explanation sets that instantiate clause (3) of F3.221.

The crucial phrase in clause (3) is 'maximal', and because its definition is quite complicated, let me also reproduce it here:

D20.   Explanation set $\{C, I\}$ is *maximal* for s at t, relative to set $F =_{df}$.

(1) s understands and believes $\{C, I\}$ at t;

(2) there are sentences in F, all of which are P-explained by $\{C, I\}$;

(3) at t, s believes that $\{C, I\}$ explains each member of F;

(4) $\{C, I\}$ has maximum explanatory coherence for set F among the explanation sets in B_2: those that are understood by s at t, or are generally understood at t;

(5) $\{C, I\}$ is as helpful to s at t for understanding the members of F and for devising other explanations of other data as any set that also has maximum explanatory coherence for F among the sets in B_2.

Unfortunately, I must repeat one more definition, namely, that for 'maximum explanatory coherence', which is the crucial notion nested in the definiens of D20. It is:

D17.   Explanation set $\{C, I\}$ has *maximum explanatory coherence* for set F among the sets in set $B =_{df}$.

(1) $\{C, I\}$ is in B; and

(2) $\{C, I\}$ is consistent, and for any set, $\{C_i, I_i\}$, that is in B, if C_i is consistent but C and C_i conflict, then:

(a) $\{C, I\}$ P-explains at least as many statements in F as $\{C_i, I_i\}$ P-explains, and

(b) it is false that $\{C_i, I_i\}$ P-explains as many statements in F as $\{C, I\}$ does, and $\{C_i, I_i\}$ is also a better explanation set than $\{C, I\}$ is.

SOME ASSUMPTIONS THAT SIMPLIFY THE USE OF F3.221

It is easy to see how difficult it is to show that some situation instantiates clause (3) of principle F3.221. To show that condition (d) of the clause is satisfied, we have to show that the five defining clauses in D20 are met, and to show that the fourth of these is correct, we must establish that both defining conditions of D17 are met. And the second clause of D17 requires consideration of the systemic tests for explanatory systems. Nevertheless, I believe we are justified in making some simplifying assumptions which will ease our burden considerably. I am going to use explanation sets which it is reasonable to assume are understood and believed by me and provide me with as much explanatory help right now as any others that I understand or are generally understood. The reasonableness of both parts of this assumption will be seen by noting my examination and the use of the sets, and also their various features that I shall discuss. I shall also assume that I believe that the sets explain the members of the relevant F_1, which in each case is, as we shall see, nonempty. As a result, it is plausible to assume that for each explanation set I shall propose, $\{C, I\}$, it is maximal for me now, if $\{C, I\}$ P-explains the members of F_1, and $\{C, I\}$ has maximum explanatory coherence for set F_1 among those sets that are in B_2.

We can simplify even more. As we shall soon see, each $\{C, I\}$ that I shall use in my examples explains all sentences in F_1 and is chosen by me now to explain these sentences. Finally, there is one last assumption that I hope the reader will grant, namely, that I now understand all the relevant explanation sets that are generally understood now. Granting this and unpacking a bit, we can say that for each of the sets I shall choose, $\{C, I\}$, it is maximal for me now, if, first, for any set, $\{C_i, I_i\}$, that I understand now, that P-explains the members of F_1, and whose system, C_i, conflicts with C, it is false that $\{C_i, I_i\}$ is a better explanation set than $\{C, I\}$ is. Then, given all the preceding assumptions and predictions, we can derive the following thesis about what is acceptable for me now from F3.221 with the aid of D17 and D20:

CA.   Empirical sentence, p, is acceptable for Cornman at t_n, if:
            (1) p is either entailed or P-explained by my chosen set $\{C, I\}$ for F_1;
            (2) $\mathrm{Pr}_{s,t}(F_1) > 0.5$;
            (3) $\{C, I\}$ is its own minimal version;
            (4) C is minimally adequate;
            (5) for any set $\{C_i, I_i\}$, that is understood by Cornman at t_n, that P-explains the members of F_1, and whose system conflicts with C, it is false that $\{C_i, I_i\}$ is a better explanation set than $\{C, I\}$; and
            (6) if some experts about F_1 at t accept explanation sets for F_1,

then at least one of the best of these sets does not conflict with $\{C, I\}$.

The preceding simplification makes it much easier to see how to proceed to accomplish the main task of this chapter. We want examples which give me a foundational set for which the explanation sets that meet statement CA entail or P-explain statements about the unperceived present, the non-subjective past, the future, or other minds that contradict skeptical thesis M_1S_3. Thus in each example, we must first find basic-reports that satisfy the antecedent of H3 for me now, then find which observation-reports or subjective memory reports, if any, satisfy BR3 or BR4 respectively for evidence that consists of the basic-reports that meet H3. When the members of these two sets of statements are eternalized to me now, the resulting sentences are the members of the foundational set that is to be explained for me now, if it is probable for me now. Third, we must uncover which explanation set instantiates the antecedent of CA for this foundational set, and, fourth, we need to see whether what results contradicts M_1S_3. Of course, it is not enough for our purposes to find just one sentence that contradicts M_1S_3 by contradicting just one of its four species. For example, it is not enough to derive the denial of the claim that it is never reasonable for any human being to believe that there is a presently existing unperceived physical object, because we also want to be able to refute the other three species of M_1S_3, that is, epistemological skepticism about the nonsubjective past, the future, and other minds. We want, then, one or more examples that will produce a denial of each of the four species of M_1S_3 about what is never reasonable for any human being. I shall offer two examples: one to contradict the species of M_1S_3 about physical objects I am not perceiving now, nonsubjective past events, and future events; and one to contradict its species about mental phenomena of other beings.

ON USING THE EXPLANATORY FOUNDATIONAL THEORY TO COUNTER SKEPTICISM

There is a variety of examples which will allow us to use CA to prove that relevant claims about the unperceived present, the nonsubjective past, or the future are acceptable for me now. These range from mundane, prosaic explanations of common events to very complex scientific explanations of esoteric occurrences. For example, a common explanation of why I have a visual experience of mail in my box, and, indeed, see this mail, is that a postman puts mail in my box in the morning whenever he has mail for my address, and this morning a postman had mail for my address. So mail was put in my box this morning. But because it has remained there until now when I am looking in the box, I have now a visual experience of mail in my box, and, furthermore, I see the mail and believe that I see it. Consequently, in a quite rough way, we often postulate the existence of a mailman and the event of his delivering mail to us in the past to explain what we now experience and see. Thus, if a more precise version of this explanation meets CA, as is likely in some situations for me, and, I would suppose for some others also, it would then be acceptable for us that some event occurred in the past, if CA, and its kin for these others, is correct.

A similar, equally mundane situation that often occurs to me illustrates one way to justify that some claim about something existing at that time but unperceived by me then is acceptable for me then. It often happens that when I am home in the morning I have an auditory experience of loud barking coming from out front, and I believe I am hearing barking in front of my house. My usual explanation of this is that my dog, Kim, is outside, and whenever that is true and a postman is delivering mail to my house, Kim barks loudly at him. And, once I postulate the event of a postman who, unperceived by me, is delivering mail now, I not only explain the loud barking but prepare the way for the explanation of why I have an experience of barking, hear barking, and believe I hear barking. And, whenever such an explanation is explicated to become an explanation set that meets CA, then, granting CA, it would be acceptable for me that a postman, whom I am not perceiving, is delivering mail. Of course, more precise scientific explanations would also help refute M_1S_3, such as one that might be used to explain why I am having an auditory experience of clicks, and hear and believe I hear certain clicks. Such an explanation might include the statement that I am listening to a Geiger counter that is recording the natural radioactivity of some uranium-238 which began its radioactive decay over one billion years ago and will continue for well over another one billion years until the substance becomes lead. This explanation, if refined to meet CA, would yield, with CA, that certain events have occurred in the remote past and other similar ones will occur in the distant future.

The three preceding examples give, of course, mere hints of how CA, and so F3.22, can be used to combat skepticism regarding the unperceived present, the nonsubjective past, and the future. Now I wish to turn to an example which I shall develop in detail so that we can see clearly how one particular explanation set for certain basic-reports that I fully believe at the present time yields, with CA, the acceptability for me now of a set of sentences which together imply the present existence of something I do not perceive now, the occurrence of a nonsubjective past event, and the occurrence of a future event. The example is interesting, then, because it provides what we need to combat three of the four species of M_1S_3. It is also interesting because its foundational set includes just two eternalized reports, both of which are basic-reports. This example, therefore, should mollify anyone who was displeased with my decision in Chapter 7 to expand foundational sets to include observation-reports and basic memory-reports. That is, the example should satisfy those who wish to be extremely conservative in our attempt to refute skepticism, and so urge that we limit foundational sets to basic-reports.

The example is this. Assume that I firmly believe that I am not now having any perceptual experience of the sun, and also believe that I had a visual experience of the sun setting over a lake earlier in the day. Assume further that what I now firmly believe about my present lack of perceptual experience and my present belief about the past compose what is to be explained for me now. I shall offer the following rough explanation which when explicated becomes, I claim, the explanation set that satisfies CA for this foundational set. The earth rotates on its axis about once every day as it goes around the sun about once every year in such a way that if the sun was dropping below the horizon about six hours ago, then at that time whoever saw the sun at that time from where I am now had a visual experience of the sun setting over a lake. But because the sun is facing the other side of the earth now, it is not perceivable from where I am now. Thus I am not having any experience of the sun now. Nevertheless, about six hours ago I was here and saw the sun dropping below the horizon. So, it follows that about six hours ago, I had a visual experience of the sun setting over a lake, and because, when I have that sort of experience I remember it for quite some time, I believe right now that I had such an experience in the past. This explanation, which I shall refine considerably, implies, among other things, the past, future, and presently unperceived existence of the sun. Of course, it also implies something about the past and future of the earth, and something about my own past. And it does all this, even though it is used to explain just two basic-reports. But does its refined version meet what CA requires, which it must if the statements it entails are to be acceptable for me now, given the correctness of F3.22?

On Explicating and Evaluating an Explanation That Counters Skepticism

Let me show how the preceding example fares by CA, by carefully proceeding though eight successive steps. First, I list the only two relevant basic-reports that, let us assume, I understand and believe with certainty at the present time, namely, time t_n. They are: $b_1^1 = $ 'I am now believing that several hours ago I had an experience of the sun setting over a lake', and $b_2^1 = $ 'I am not now having any experience of the sun'. It is plausible that these are the only two relevant basic-reports that I believe with certainty now, at t_n, because, as I stand by the edge of the water, I am thinking only of my previous experience of the sun setting and my present lack of any experience of the sun. It is also reasonable that I understand both of these rather simple reports now. And because these are the only two basic-reports that I firmly believe now, only they are capable of satisfying the antecedent of H3 for me now. It is plausible that only they are in my foundational subset S_1^1.

This leads to the second step which is to show that b_1^1 and b_2^1 do meet H3. This can be done by showing that for any basic-report, n, that I understand and believe with certainty at t_n, $Pr_{c,n}(Tb_1^1 ct_n / Trct_n) = Pr_{c,n}(Tb_2^1 ct_n / Trct_n) = 1$. But at t_n, the only values for 'r' are b_1^1 and b_2^1. Because of this, the crucial conditional probabilities are $Pr_{c,n}(Tb_1^1 / Tb_2^1) = x$, and $Pr_{c,n}(Tb_2^1 / Tb_1^1) = y$. That is, both of these basic-reports satisfy the antecedent of H3, if and only if $x = y = 1$, and one of them does only if the other does. Consequently, if it is plausible that, in my situation at t_n, $x = y = 1$, then, because b_1^1 and b_2^1 meet the rest of the antecedent of H3, we can conclude that they and they alone are in foundational subset S_1^1, and have the probability of 1 for s at t.

As mentioned when discussing a somewhat similar example in Chapter 2, I have no way to determine precisely whether or not $x = y = 1$. But I urge that we proceed as follows. When there is no *prima facie* reason to reject the joint certainty of two basic reports, p and q, being true of s at t, and there is a *prima facie* plausible explanation for s at t of both of the reports, and each one satisfies the rest of the antecedent of H3, then it is reasonable that $Pr_{s,t}(Tp/Tq) = Pr_{s,t}(Tq/Tp) = 1$. In the present example, b_2^1 is a given report above the present and b_1^1 expresses a present belief about something occurring several hours ago. Because of this time gap, I contend that there is no *prima facie* reason to reject the joint certainty of b_1^1 and b_2^1. Consequently, because the explanation that I offered of these two basic-reports has, I maintain, *prima facie* plausibility, then it is reasonable that

$\text{Pr}_{c,\,n}(Tb_1^1/Tb_2^1) = \text{Pr}_{c,\,n}(Tb_2^1/Tb_1^1) = 1$, and, as a result, b_1^1 and b_2^1 satisfy H3.

The third step is to determine what nonbasic-reports belong in foundational subset, S_1^1. In the present case, the task is easy. At the current, conservative stage of our confrontation with skepticism, we should take a nonbasic-sentence not to be foundational for me if it fails to satisfy BR3 and BR4. And the two reports in S_1^1 are not the right sort to allow some observation-report or basic memory-report to satisfy BR3 or BR4. So the foundational set for me now is just the eternalized members of S_1^1. That is, we are to consider explanation sets for F_1^1 which consist of '$Tb_1^1ct_n$,' and '$Tb_2^1ct_n$,' which are b_1^1 and b_2^1 eternalized to Cornman now, at t_n. In particular, we want an explicated version of the somewhat rough explanation that, in the example, I chose to explain the two members of S_1^1.

The fourth step is to lay out this precise version of my explanation in this first example, and show how the 'eternalized' sentences, '$Tb_1^1ct_n$,' and '$Tb_2^1ct_n$,', are derivable from the explanation. So we want a consistent set, $\{C^1, I^1\}$ whose I^1 is a conjunction of nonmolecular sentences, and from which is derivable, deductively or inductively, either these two eternalized sentences, or, at least, statements ascribing high probability to them. I propose the following explication. First, system C^1 is what results when the conjunction of the following six sentences is restructured with all its quantifiers properly prefixed:

C_1^1:   The earth rotates on its axis about once every 24 hours as it revolves around the sun about once a year.

C_2^1:   If C_1^1 is true, and, at time t, the sun is at the horizon in the west relative to location, L, on the earth, then several hours after t, the sun is facing the side of the earth opposite L.

C_3^1:   If, at t, the sun is facing the side of the earth opposite a place L on the earth and someone is at L, then, at t, he is not perceiving the sun.

C_4^1:   If, at t, Cornman is not perceiving the sun, then the report b_2^1 is true of Cornman at t.

C_5^1:   If, at t, someone sees the sun at the horizon in the west over a lake, then, at t, he has a visual experience of the sun setting over a lake.

C_6^1:   If, at t, Cornman has a visual experience of the sun setting over a lake, then report b_1^1 is true of Cornman for many hours after t.

Finally, I^1 is the conjunction of the following nonmolecular sentences:

I_1^1:   At t_n, Cornman is where he was several hours before t_n.

I_2^1:   Several hours before t_n, the sun was at the horizon in the west over Raquette Lake, and Cornman saw it there.

It is clear that $\{C^1, I^1\}$ is consistent, and C^1 essentially generalized, because essentially, but not purely, universal. It is also obvious that this explanation set, but not I^1, yields (deductively) the two nomolecular statements: 'b_1^1 is true of Cornman at t_n' (from C_5^1 and C_6^1, with I_2^1), and 'b_2^1 is true of Cornman at t_n' (from C_1^1 through C_4^1, with I_1^1 and I_2^1). So, by definition D14, $\{C^1, I^1\}$ P-explains those two eternalized versions of my two basic-reports that are the members of my foundational set, F_1^1. This completes the fourth step and leads to the fifth which is to show that $\{C^1, I^1\}$ is its own minimal version, and then derive from it some sentences which, if acceptable for me now, would refute the species of M_1S_3 concerning the unperceived present, the past, and the future.

To see whether $\{C^1, I^1\}$ is its own minimal version, we must do two things. First, we are to decide whether both conjuncts of I^1 are needed with C^1 to derive the two eternalized sentences. It is clear that they are. So $I = I_m$. Second, we put C^1 in prenex normal form with its matrix in conjunctive normal form, and then see whether all the resulting conjuncts are needed with I_m to derive the same two sentences. Again it is easy to see that $C^1 = C_m^1$, because in the present case, each subsystem, except C_1^1 is a universal conditional statement, and so once their quantifiers – all universal – are placed in the prefix and the matrix is made to consist in the conjunction of the matrices of the six subsystems, we achieve the conjunctive normal form merely by transforming each conditional conjunct into its equivalent disjunction and using De Morgan's theorem on all conjunctive antecedents. But since each C_i^1 is needed with I_m for the derivation, then each conjunct in the matrix is also needed, and $C^1 = C_m^1$. Consequently whatever is logically derivable from $\{C^1, I^1\}$ is acceptable for me now, if $\{C^1, I^1\}$ is. Again the derivations we want are simple, because it is clear that $\{C^1, I^1\}$ yields at least the following:

q_1^1:   The sun exists at t_n, but is not perceived by Cornman at t_n (from $C_1^1, C_2^1, C_3^1, I_1^1, I_2^1$).

q_2^1:   The sun and Cornman existed several hours before t_n (from I_2^1),

q_3^1:   The earth and the sun existed at least 24 hours before t_n and will exist at least 24 hours after t_n (from C_1^1).

And, if acceptable, q_1^1 refutes skepticism about physical objects that exist unperceived at t_n; q_2^1 refutes skepticism about the nonsubjective past before t_n; and q_3^1 refutes skepticism about the past and about the future.

With the first five steps completed, we have, in effect, shown that the three q_i^1's meet clause (1) of CA. And since both members of F_1^1 have a probability of 1 for s at t, and, as just seen, $\{C^1, I^1\}$ is its own minimal version, clauses (2) and (3) of CA are also met. This leaves three more steps, one each for clauses (4), (5), and (6) of CA. The sixth step requires us to justify that system C^1 is minimally adequate. Following our discussion at the end of Chapter 9, we can say that a system is minimally adequate, if it is testable in principle, because, as I proposed, an explanatory system is minimally adequate if and only if it is consistent, has explanatory relevance, is essentially generalized, and is testable in principle. And being a testable explanatory system is sufficient for all four, because any system in a set that P-explains something meets the first three conditions, and, by definition D23, a system must P-explain something experiential with some I, if it is to be testable. It is also clear that this system is testable in principle. System C^1, with some experiential statement of initial conditions, P-explains experiential sentences that are not derivable from the two it is designed to explain with I^1. One of these is $r =$ 'At t_1, Jones has a visual experience of the sun setting over a lake'. This is P-explained by C^1 (more precisely, C_5^1) and $I^1 =$ 'At t_1, Jones sees the sun at the horizon in the west over Lake Winnipesaukee'. Furthermore, because I_3^1 is an eternalized observation-report, and r is an eternalized given-report, we need only those two sentences to show C^1 is testable in principle. Thus because $\mathrm{Pr}_{j,1}(I_3^1 \cdot r / I_3^1 \cdot r) = 1$, and $\mathrm{Pr}_{j,1}(I_3^1 \cdot \bar{r} / I_3^1 \cdot \bar{r}) = 1$, system C^1 is testable in principle, according to definition D23.

Explanation Set $\{C^1, I^1\}$, *and Systemic Tests.* We turn now to the seventh step which is the most difficult task of discovering whether $\{C^1, I^1\}$ fares at least as well by the systemic tests as any set that has a minimally adequate system which conflicts with C_1, that is understood by me, and that P-explains the members of F_1^1. One problem, of course, is that there are so many systems that conflict with C^1, such as one that merely replaces C_1^1 by $C_7^1 =$ 'The earth revolves on its axis about once every 20 hours as it revolves around the sun about once every 200 days'. But it is obvious that the new system is no better than C^1 by any of the seven systemic tests I have urged, and so it is no threat to replace C^1. And, although C^1 is no better than it, the new theory would, nevertheless, not show anything is acceptable for me if I adopt it now, since it is clear that it conflicts with all the best explanation sets for S_1^1 that experts accept now. Therefore, it fails to satisfy clause (6) of CA. Unfortunately, the demise of this system is scant help to us in solving our present problem.

We can simplify our task somewhat, however, by noting three facts about system C^1, namely, that C^1 is nonprobabilistically universal, maximally economical, because containing no pure theoretical terms, and prefix-simplest, because containing no quantifier alternatives. Consequently we can ignore tests MN.3 (nonprobabilistic universality), MN.7 (economy), and one of the 'subtests' of MN.8 (prefix-simplicity), because nothing exceeds C^1 by these tests. Another quite plausible assumption will also help. No explanation set, which today someone understandingly accepts and also believes explains the members of F_1^1, contains a system that is purely quantitative. This is obviously true of those of us who are not experts about visual experiences and believings. Furthermore, there is no quantitative psychophysical theory today that explains visual experiences and believings. So we can ignore the test of quantitation, MN.4, both when comparing my system, C^1, with others in B_2, and also when searching for the best explanation sets that today's experts accept as explanations of the members of F_1^1. Consequently, this assumption simplifies both of our last two tasks.

An even more helpful discovery is that no system from which (an approximation of) C^1 is derivable conflicts with C^1. By definition D16 for conflict, if some C^i conflicts with C^1, then there is an I that is compatible with C^i and C^1 individually, but yields (discernibly) incompatible sentences when conjoined with both C^1 and C^i. But if C^1 (or some approximation of C^1) is derivable from C^i, then no I^i compatible with C^i yields (discernibly) incompatible results when conjoined with both C^i and C^1. So such a C^i and C^1 do not conflict. This conclusion helps us considerably in two different ways. First, it shows that no system that has greater scope than C^1 conflicts with C^1, because, by definition D25, C^1 (or an approximation of C^1) is entailed by any system with greater scope than C^1. So no conflicting system betters C^1 by MN.5, the test of scope. Second, the conclusion also allows us to ignore all the minimal nonevidential tests, including the three we have not yet examined – cumulativity, pure universality, and matrix-simplicity, *if* all the subsystems of C^1, namely C_1^1 through C_6^1, are experiential. This is because a set $\{C^i, I^i\}$ betters $\{C^1, I^1\}$ by any of the eight minimal nonevidential tests, only if each experiential consequence of C^1, that is, each experiential sentence derivable from C^1 is (approximated by) a consequence of C^i. So if C^1 is experiential, it must be derivable from C^i, if $\{C^i, I^i\}$ is to better $\{C^1, I^1\}$ by one of these tests. But no such C^i conflicts with C^1, and thus no set containing a system that conflicts with C^1 is a better explanation set than $\{C^1, I^1\}$ by any of these eight systemic tests. Thus our present task eases enormously, if system C^1 is experiential.

Happily, C_1^1 through C_6^1 are experiential, which requires that they be constructed from observation-formulas or perception-formulas. Subsystem C_1^1 is a perception-sentence, because each of its nonlogical (and nonmathematical) terms is an observation-term or definable by observation-terms. This is also true of C_2^1. However, each of the other four subsystems contains either 'perceive x' or 'visual experience of x' which are neither observation-terms nor definable by observation-terms. Nevertheless, each of these four subsystems is constructed by quantifying over combinations of basic-formulas or perception-formulas. Subsystem C_3^1 has an antecedent constructed from two observation-formulas, and a consequent that is appropriately constructed from the observation-report, 'I am now perceiving the sun'. Subsystems C_4^1 and C_5^1 have formulas made from observation-reports in their antecedents. And the consequent of C_5^1, like the antecedent of C_6^1, comes from a given-formula. Finally, the consequents of C_4^1 and C_6^1 are made from eternalized versions of basic-reports. Consequently, all subsystems of C^1, and so C^1, are constructed from basic-formulas or perception-formulas. Thus system C^1 is an experiential sentence, which, as argued above, is P-explained by $\{C^1, I^1\}$.

We have now seen that no system that conflicts with C^1 surpasses C^1 by any of the seven minimal nonevidential tests that are systemic tests, because C^1 is an experiential sentence P-explained by $\{C^1, I^1\}$. And even if that were not true, nothing betters C^1 by the tests of nonprobabilistic universality, economy, or prefix-simplicity, and nothing that conflicts with any system has greater scope than that system. Furthermore, we have seen that C^1 is minimally adequate because testable in principle, and, at present, is not bettered by any purely quantitative system. Consequently, we can conclude that no explanation set whose system conflicts with C^1 is a better explanation set than $\{C^1, I^1\}$. A fortiori, no set that Cornman understands at any time, that explains the two members of F_1^1, and whose system conflicts with C^1 is better than $\{C^1, I^1\}$. Of course, this does not show that no system is better than C^1, but it does complete the seventh step on our way to showing that set $\{C^1, I^1\}$ satisfies the antecedent of CA.

Explanation Set $\{C^1, I^1\}$ and the Best Explanations by Today's Experts

The eighth and last step is to discover whether or not any explanation sets for foundational set F_1^1 that are best for today's experts fail to conflict with $\{C^1, I^1\}$. If we find reason to think some of these do not conflict with this set of mine, then we will be able to conclude, by CA, that whatever is entailed by explanation set $\{C^1, I^1\}$ is reasonable for me now. How might an explanation set explain b_1^1 and b_2^1 when eternalized to me now, yet also conflict with $\{C^1, I^1\}$? Given the definition of conflict between explanation sets that was given in Chapter 7, one easy way to construct a set that conflicts with $\{C^1, I^1\}$ is to change the times of revolution stated in C_1^1 and C_2^1 in a discernible way. But although, as already noted regarding C_7^1, this would produce conflict, it is surely reasonable for us to deny that the new set is one of the best of those accepted by experts now. A more bothersome set is constructed by making two changes in $\{C^1, I^1\}$. The first is to replace C_5^1 by C_8^1: 'If, at t, someone is not seeing the sun but is having a visual hallucination of the sun setting over a lake, then, at t, he has a visual experience of the sun setting over a lake'. The second is to replace I_2^1 by I_4^1: 'Several hours before t_n the sun was at the horizon in the west over Raquette Lake, and Cornman was at that lake then but did not see the sun'. And then add I_5^1: 'Several hours before t_n, Cornman had a visual hallucination of the sun setting over a lake'. Now the new set conflicts with $\{C^1, I^1\}$, because I_4^1 is incompatible with I_2^1, but both sets explain the members of F_1^1.

Although I hope that no expert would explain my present belief about a past visual experience in terms of my hallucinating, I am willing to stipulate for our present purposes that some would explain it in this way. Furthermore, let us also assume that this new explanation set, or some refinement of it that also conflicts with $\{C^1, I^1\}$, is among the best that experts accept. Still, all is not lost, because we only need to find reason to think that at least one of these best does not conflict with $\{C^1, I^1\}$. Indeed, it seems quite plausible that many experts would accept sets that are basically refinements upon $\{C^1, I^1\}$. For example, some might well replace C_4^1 and C_5^1 by purely universal subsystems, although it is dubious they would merely universally generalize those two. It is reasonable, however, that some experts about explanations of sensory experiences and believings would replace C_4^1 and C_6^1 by something like the following purely universal pair:

C_9^1:   If, at t, a perceptually normal human being in normal perceptual conditions is not perceiving an object, x, then, at t he does not have a perceptual experience of x.

And:

C_{10}^1:   If, at t, a human being has a perceptual experience of something, he is aware of the experience, and he has a normal memory from t until many hours after t, then, many hours after t, he believes that he had the experience several hours ago.

The two newest subsystems are purely universal, unlike what they replace, and it is likely that, because of this, some experts would prefer this replacement to $\{C^1, I^1\}$. And, clearly, other experts might arrive at a more refined set whose subsystems have greater scope – perhaps subsystems applying to all sentient beings. Of course, the set with C_9^1 and C_{10}^1 requires different statements of initial conditions, including statements to the effect that, at present, Cornman is a perceptually normal human being, and is in perceptually normal conditions. It would also include a sentence concerning my visual experience several hours ago, and the normalcy of my memory. But, none of these changes in C^1 and I^1 results in a set that conflicts with $\{C^1, I^1\}$. Indeed, I can derive a statement equivalent to C_4^1 from C_9^1, and one equivalent to C_6^1 from C_{10}^1 with the proper sort of statement of initial conditions. For example, a statement which includes that at t, Cornman is a perceptually normal perceiver in perceptually normal conditions will, with C_9^1, yield a sentence equivalent to C_4^1.

The preceding point is important for our present task, because it makes it reasonable that some of the explanations for F_1^1 that experts accept now do not conflict with $\{C^1, I^1\}$. Of course, this is not enough to show that one of the best that these experts accept does not conflict with my relatively inexpert attempt. Nevertheless, if that last explanation set with C_9^1, C_{10}^1, and a new statement of initial conditions is either not now accepted by any experts or not among the best they accept, it is surely plausible to assume that some of these experts' best explanations are merely refinements of this refinement of my unskilled explanation set and do not conflict with my set. So I conclude that we are justified, after all, in concluding that at present some of the best explanations of F_1^1 by today's experts about such perceptual experiencings and believings do not conflict with $\{C^1, I^1\}$. That is, we have reason to maintain that $\{C^1, I^1\}$ meets the sixth and last conjunct of the antecedent of CA. So, assuming CA, we can infer that whatever is entailed by $\{C^1, I^1\}$ is acceptable for me now. And, as we have seen, this includes those three sentences, q_1^1, q_2^1, and q_3^1, which, if acceptable, refute epistemological skepticism about the unperceived present, the nonsubjective past, and the future. So, we can finally conclude that each of these three species of skeptical thesis M_1S_3 is refuted now, *if* F3.22, and thus CA, are acceptable epistemic principles. Furthermore, the preceding discussion of what experts accept should also satisfy that critic of my definition of 'maximal set' in Chapter 7 who demanded that only the 'best' explanation sets available should be used to refute skepticism. But, unfortunately, nothing from the preceding example affects the species of M_1S_3 about the mental phenomena of others.

ON SKEPTICISM ABOUT OTHER MINDS

The venerable problem of other minds has been widely discussed, but, like most skeptical problems, never solved. The litany of failed attempts is too well known for me to spend time discussing all of them individually and in detail. But it is worth noting that the failures can be grouped into four separate groups. Three of these groups include the attempts to justify claims about mental phenomena of others by inferring them from premises primarily about observable bodily behavior of others. They differ regarding whether their argument forms are deductive, analogical-inductive, or enumerative-inductive. The fourth set can be grouped under the heading of those that propose some sort of 'criteriological' relationship between certain observable bodily behavior and 'inner' psychological phenomena. By now, after extensive criticism by Plantinga and others, I find it quite clear that these last attempts have failed to find something less than a logical relationship but more than a causal relationship between behavior and the mental.[1] And with that failure goes the failure to establish 'outward criteria' for 'inner' states. I shall, then, consider these attempts no more.

It is somewhat disheartening that all four sorts of attempts have failed even while assuming something we shall not, namely, that all statements about observable behavior of others which are thought to be epistemically relevant to claims about the minds of these others, are uncritically accepted as justified. That is, these attempts fail in spite of the fact that they ignore the difficult skeptical problems about justifying claims about currently observed physical bodies, currently existing but unobserved physical bodies, and the existence of bodies in the past. As a result, these attempts involve the unjustified use of a whole stock of statements about what is unobserved now or occurred in the past. This should surely help bring success, especially for attempts that rely on enumerative or analogical induction. In addition, subjunctive conditionals concerning physical objects are often uncritically used, especially in attempts that use deduction. But even these gratuitous assumptions fail to produce success. Fortunately, as we shall see, the minimal explanatory foundational theory provides the means for success even when none of these debatable assumptions are made.

The Failure of Justification by Deduction, or Analogical or Enumerative Induction

Although in Chapter 4, I only considered the failures of deduction and enumerative and analogical induction to provide justifying inferences from basic-reports and analytic sentences to physical-object sentences, these failures are easily transformable into reasons that show why none of these argument forms warrant inferences from behavioral statements and analytic sentences to sentences about mental phenomena of others. Deduction's failure becomes clear with the justified demise of analytical behaviorism.[2] Just as we saw in Chapter 4 that the proven failure of analytical phenomenalism warrants the rejection of the claim that certain basic-sentences entail physical-object statements, so also the established inability of attempts to analyze psychological sentences, such as belief-sentences, by behavioral sentences, justifies rejecting all attempts to deduce sentences about the minds of others from premises about their bodily behavior.

The historically important attempts to use analogical reasoning fail for a different reason, which is easy to uncover by using the argument form laid out in Chapter 4.[3] For each of us, there is at most one person, o_2, whom he can justify noninductively to have psychological property P_{m+1}, namely, himself. Consequently, there is at most one person who is like another person, o_1, in having behavioral properties, P_1, P_2, $\ldots$, P_m, and whom o_2 is noninductively justified in claiming has P_{m+1}. But an analogy with one person is not strong enough to warrant that o_1 has P_{m+1}. So if someone is to succeed in justifying that another person has P_{m+1} using analogical induction, he must establish inductively that still others have P_{m+1}. But he will never succeed if he restricts himself to analogical induction for each additional person, o_3 because then for o_3 he would need to show that others have P_{m+1} and for each of those still others. So a person will succeed in justifying a claim about the mind of another, o_1, by using analogical induction, only if he succeeds for still others by using some other form of induction. But if one of these forms works for these others, it is likely that it will work for o_1. So it seems that analogical induction either will not succeed or is unnecessary for success regarding the minds of others. We can, then, ignore it for our present purposes.

Enumerative induction, as we described it in Chapter 4 following Plantinga, would seem to be no more helpful, because it requires the justification of a general claim, such as 'Probably, every A is B', in something like what Plantinga calls a "direct inductive argument", by means of enumerated supporting instances. For example, one way to use enumerative induction to establish that o_2 is in pain at t_1 would be to justify two probability claims, such as: 'The probability that a person is in pain at t, given that his left arm is badly cut at t, is greater than 0.7', and 'The probability that o_2's left arm is cut at t_1, is greater than 0.8'. From these premises, with the principle that '$\Pr(Px/Qx) = n$' entails '$\Pr(Pa/Qa) = n$', for any individual constant, 'a', we can derive that it is probable that o_2 is in pain at t_1. Unfortunately, in order to establish the first, universal premise by enumeration requires justifying a sizable number of instances of particular people being in pain when their arms are badly cut. But, as previously noted, each of us can succeed in this justification noninductively only in his own case. So, as with analogical induction, it seems clear that we need some other kind of induction to supplement enumerative induction. We have seen that analogical induction will not help. This leaves only hypothetical induction, which, as I will indicate next, succeeds without the need of other forms of induction. So we can conclude that enumerative induction will not succeed unless supplemented by a form of induction that succeeds without enumerative induction. It surely seems, then, that we should ignore enumerative induction just as we have analogical induction.

On Ayer's Enumerative Inductive Argument for Other Minds. There is, however, an ingenious attempt to avoid the preceding conclusion that we should note. Ayer has proposed a revision of the standard analogical argument.[4] When it is suitably explicated, it becomes an enumerative inductive argument which, in many cases, is supported by a large number of instances. We can best see Ayer's argument by recasting it close to the way that Plantinga did when examining it. However, two important changes should be noted. The first is a reformulation of Plantinga's premise (1) to avoid his objection to the argument, and the second turns his premise (3) into a probability statement to avoid certain problems of detachment. The argument is:

(1)   Each of the many cases of a human body being badly cut such that I have determined by observation and experience whether or not it was accompanied by pain that was felt by the being whose body was badly cut, was accompanied by pain felt by the being whose body was badly cut.[5]

Therefore

(2)   The probability, for me, is close to 1 that a being that has a

human body feels pain at time t, given that the being's body is
badly cut at t.

(3)   The probability, for me is very high that, at t_1, someone else's
human body is badly cut.[6]

Therefore

(4)   It is probable, for me, that, at t_1, someone else is feeling pain.

Let us assume that I have badly cut various parts of my body many times
and each time experienced pain. So, although in each case only one person
is involved, this argument avoids objections to the preceding version, because it considers cases of physical states accompanied by mental states
instead of persons. Thus there are many supporting instances, even though
there is only one person involved.

The preceding argument avoids Plantinga's objection and the previous
objection to the use of enumerative induction to justify claims about other
minds. Nevertheless, it seems clear that it fails, because the form of the
inference from (1) to (2) allows clearly mistaken inferences and so is an
incorrect argument form. To see this, consider an example in which the
only car that I have tested for gas mileage is my own gas-guzzling green
station wagon. Then consider the following argument.

> Each of the many, many, cases of a car getting less than 10
> miles per gallon such that I have determined by observation
> whether or not it was accompanied by the car being green, was
> accompanied by the car being green.

Therefore

> The probability, for me, is close to 1 that a car gets less than
> 10 miles per gallon, given that it is green.

Surely, this inference is mistaken, because no matter how many cases I
examine, my sample class is much too narrow and biased to warrant the
inference. So some restrictions must be placed on this argument form to
forbid such inferences. But once that it is done the inference from (1) to
(2) is also forbidden, and Ayer's argument fails.

The Explanatory Foundational Theory and Other Minds

With the justified demise of the four preceding sorts of attempts to justify
claims about other minds, the way seems clear to turn to hypothetical

induction, or inference to the best explanation, or, more precisely, inference to what is P-explained or entailed by some explanation set that meets condition (3) of F3.221 for some foundational set. No other means seems both available and plausible. If it be objected that I have ignored Chisholm's critical cognitivism, I can only reply that no one has yet produced a set of epistemic rules that will warrant the inferences we want in this case. Furthermore, the prospects of finding such rules appear to be dim, given the failure of the rules Chisholm has proposed for inferences from basic-sentences to physical-object statements. On the other hand, it is easy to imagine many situations in which some claim about another's mind is justified, if the best explanation of his bodily behavior justifies what the explanation entails. Consider, for example, that one of the best P-explanations, for many of us, of Jones's moaning will also P-explain that Jones is in pain. This is because so many of us do not know enough about the science of neurophysiology to explain these facts in any way except by using subsystems that are explicated as follows: 'The probability is close to 1 that a person is in pain, given that he is badly cut', and 'The probability is very high that a person is moaning, given that he is badly cut and in pain'. These subsystems, taken with the statement of initial conditions: 'It is very probable, for me now, that Jones is badly cut now', have as consequences not only 'It is probable, for me now, that Jones is moaning now', but also, 'It is probable, for me now, that Jones is in pain now'. Thus both 'Jones is moaning now' and 'Jones is in pain now' are P-explained for me and, consequently, are acceptable for me now if the relevant explanation set satisfies clause (3) of F3.221. But it is reasonable that such explanation sets often satisfy clause (3) for many people. So for these people, F3.221 provides a solution to the problem of other minds, if, of course, F3.221 is worthy of their use.

A Problem for Justifying Statements About Other Minds by Their Explanatory Roles. The minimum explanatory foundational theory of empirical justification yields justification of some sentences about other minds for some of us at some times, because of our postulating the mental in appropriate explanation sets to help explain observable behavior. But this sort of justification is not fully satisfactory. Imagine someone who, now or perhaps much later, knows much more physiology than most of us. It might well be that the explanation set he chooses from among those best for him to explain the two sentences about Jones might not consist of anything like the two preceding subsystems. It might, instead, be some precise, quantitative successors of: 'The probability is close to 1 that a human being's c-fibers are firing, given that he has a severe laceration', and 'The probability is very high that a human being is moaning, given he has a severe laceration and his c-fibers are firing'. This knowledgeable person would not be able to use F3.221 to justify any ascription of pain to Jones. More generally and annoyingly, no one who knows enough about the central nervous system of human beings to explain all human behavior by neurophysiological theory, and chooses it because he considers it the best and most helpful theory available would be able to rely on his explanations to justify claims about the minds of others. And we have already seen that no other means of justification seem helpful for any of us.

The preceding state of affairs is unlikely to hinder most of us for quite some time, if ever. As Ziff says in discussing what he calls the "complex conceptual scheme" with which we confront the world, "The fact that there are other minds is an integral part of this scheme and at present essential to it".[7] Yet in spite of this, something like Quine's overly quick argument against the explanatory use of the mental may well be fully justified for some of us at some time in the future. That is, it is plausible that there will be a time, say t, when the following well-known quotation from Quine, with my added temporal references, will be true:

If [at t] there is a case for mental events and mental states, it must be just that the positing of them, like the positing of molecules, has some indirect sympathetic efficacy in the development of theory [at t]. But if a certain organization of theory is achieved [at t] by thus positing distinctive mental states and events behind physical behavior, surely as much organization could be achieved [at t] by positing merely correlative physiological states and events instead.[8]

It is clear that time t has not yet arrived, but if it should come, no one in the forefront of physiology, who explains behavior only physiologically, would be justified in postulating psychological properties to help explain human behavior, and so none of these experts would have a way to justify their claims about other minds. This would be a very disconcerting situation, which, without stopping our present refutation of skepticism about other minds, constitutes a weakness in any theory of justification that cannot avoid it. Fortunately, there is one sort of situation in which principle F3.221 will yield justification for one person about psychological characteristics of another, regardless of the state of neurophysiology. In these situations, what best explains foundational statements about a person's own mental states also yields a P-explanation of a sentence about the mind of another. And this is true, even if the explanation postulates nothing mental as an explanans. This brings us to the second example of justification by explanation that we shall examine in detail.

On Predicting the Pain of Another by Explaining One's Own. Let us assume that I am now in great pain, that I am having a visual experience of myself and another with badly cut arms. We can also assume that these three facts are to be explained for me now, because the basic-reports that express them satisfy H3. What is the best sort of explanation of these facts that I am likely to choose now? When not trying to be precise, I would probably explain all this by postulating that it is close to certain that a human being who is badly cut feels great pain, and, furthermore, it is evident that I am badly cut. At the same time, it is equally likely that my friend Jones who is standing next to me is also badly cut, and that I see both of our wounds. But it is most probable that a person will have a visual experience of two badly cut bodies, and also believe that he is seeing two badly cut people, given that he sees these wounds. Taken together, the preceding claims have the consequence that it is probable that I have great pain now, and have the relevant visual experience and belief now. So these postulated probability claims explain my three foundational statements.

Something that is not foundational for me is also derivable from my assumptions, namely, that it is probable that Jones is in great pain. So my assumptions also explain Jones's being in pain. Thus, if F3.221 is reasonable, and my explanation, once it is suitably explicated to become an explanation set that P-explains 'Jones is now in pain', satisfies F3.221, then, according to F3.221, it is now acceptable for me that Jones is in pain. And, as we shall see more clearly after explication, this is achieved without my postulating any mental state of Jones as part of any explanation of any bodily behavior. Therefore, because it is likely that even experts in physiology in the distant future will occasionally find themselves in similar situations, we can conclude that even those who explain only by the most advanced physiological theory will have a way to use the minimal explanatory foundational theory to counter skepticism about other minds. But to justify this conclusion adequately, I must explicate my explanation and show it satisfies F3.221.

Before I begin my explication, I shall make simplifying assumptions like those made for the first example. This will once again allow us to use principle CA which is so much easier to apply than F3.221. Let us assume, as we did for the first example, that for me, now, there are only three sentences to be explained which are explicated as: 'Tb_1^2cn', 'Tb_2^2cn', and

Tb_3^2cn'. These are the following sentences eternalized to Cornman now, at t_n: b_1^2 = 'I am now believing that I am seeing another person and myself with badly cut arms', b_2^2 = 'I am now having a visual experience of another person and myself with badly cut arms', and b_3^2 = 'I am now having an experience of great pain', respectively. Thus F_1^2 contains just these three eternalized sentences about me now at t_n. Then the explication of my explanation will be explanation set $\{C^2, I^2\}$, where C^2 is composed of:

C_1^2: $\Pr_{x,t}(Tb_3^2yt/Cyt) > 0.8$;

and:

C_2^2: $\Pr_{x,t}(Tb_1^2xt \cdot Tb_2^2xt/Syxt \cdot Sxzt \cdot y \neq z) > 0.8$.

Here Cyt = 'At t, y is badly cut'; and $Sxyt$ = 'At t, x is seeing y with a badly cut arm'. Finally, there is the statement of initial conditions, I^2, which consists of just one sentence:

I_1^2: $\Pr_{c,n}(Scjn \cdot Sccn \cdot j \neq c) > 0.8$.

Given that '$Sxyt$' entails 'y is badly cut', it is easy to see that $\Pr_{c,n}(Ccn) > 0.8$, and $\Pr_{c,n}(Cjn) > 0.8$. Then also given the principle, previously discussed, that for any individual constant, 'a', '$\Pr(Px/Qx) = n$' entails '$\Pr(Pa/Qa) = n$', it is easy to derive that $\Pr_{c,n}(Tb_1^2cn) > 0.64$, that $\Pr_{c,n}(Tb_2^2cn) > 0.64$, and that $\Pr_{c,n}(Tb_3^2cn) > 0.64$. Finally, a much more complicated derivation yields something more interesting for our purposes, namely, that $\Pr_{c,n}(Tb_3^2jn \cdot j \neq c) > 0.5$. Furthermore, each of these four probability statements is derivable from $\{C^2, I^2\}$ in a way that qualifies the eternalized sentence it contains as being P-explained by $\{C^2, I^2\}$. So $\{C^2, I^2\}$ P-explains for me now the three members of F_1^2, as desired, and also P-explains that 'I am now having an experience of great pain' is true now of Jones who differs from me. Therefore, if set $\{C^2, I^2\}$ meets all six conditions of principle CA, then, assuming CA, all four of these eternalized reports are acceptable for me now, including a sentence about a mental phenomenon of someone else.

It is clear that set $\{C^2, I^2\}$ meets clauses (1) through (4) of CA. It meets (1) and (2), because, as just noted, it P-explains the three members of F_1^2, each of which has a probability of 1 for me now. This set is its own minimal version, and so it meets condition (3). Statement I^2 consists of just one nonmolecular sentence which is needed to P-explain the members of F_1^2. Thus I^2 is I_m^2. Further, both C_1^2 and C_2^2 are also needed, with I_m^2, to explain the members of F_1^2. So C^2 is C_m^2, and thereby $\{C^2, I^2\}$ is its own minimal version. In order to justify that $\{C^2, I^2\}$ meets clause (4) of CA, we must show that C^2 is minimally adequate. It is clear that C^2 is testable in principle, and so is minimally adequate. Let $I_2^2 = \mathrm{Pr}_{c,\,n}(Scjn \cdot Scsn) > 0.8'$, where s = 'Smith'. Then $\{C^2, I^2\}$ P-explains q = 'Tb_3^2sn'. And the content of I_2^2 conjoined with q is very probable, given $(To_1^2cn \cdot q)$, where o_1^2 = 'I am now seeing Jones and Smith with badly cut arms', while the content of I_2^2 conjoined with $\sim q$ is very probable, given $(To_1^2cn \cdot \sim q)$. Consequently, by definition D23, C^2 is testable in principle.

Explanation Set $\{C^2, I^2\}$ and Systemic Tests. To see if C^2 meets the fifth condition of CA, we must discover how C^2 fares by the seven systemic tests when compared with conflicting systems. Here, as it was for C^1, the task of answering this question is somewhat eased because C^2 is experiential. Each subsystem of C^2 is experiential, because each of its nonlogical constants is constructed from a basic-formula ('Tb_1^2xt', 'Tb_2^2xt', 'Tb_3^2xt'), or from a perception-formula ('$Sxyt$', and 'Cxt'). Unfortunately, however, we cannot conclude about C^2 what we did about C^1, namely, that it is an experiential sentence that is derivable from itself. The problem is, of course, that C^2 is not a sentence because of those general probability formulas I have assigned to it. Nevertheless, we can quickly dispense with the tests of scope, cumulativity, pure universality, economy, and prefix-simplicity. System C^2 is purely universal and by definitions D25 and D26, no purely universal probabilistic system is bettered in scope or in cumulativity, because a system is bettered in either of these ways only if it has a nonuniversal probability statement that is entailed by a universal probability statement of another system. This is because no universal probability statement is entailed by another. And, being experiential, C^2 is maximally economical. Also, although we have devised no test of simplicity for probabilistic systems, surely one that has only purely universal subsystems is maximal in prefix-simplicity. But what determines matrix-simplicity is far less clear to me. Perhaps it can be understood in terms of something like Boolean normal forms of the contents of the probability statements, but I leave that for others to decide.

We are left with assessing the relative position of C^2 with respect to quantitation and nonprobabilistic universality. However, because it is once again reasonable to assume that there is no purely quantitative explanation set available for a foundational set composed of eternalized basic-reports, we can again ignore the test of quantitation. Thus, only the fact that C^2 is probabilistic bars our being ready to conclude that C^2 satisfies condition

(5) of CA. Unfortunately, it is difficult to see how to compare a nonprobabilistic system with one that is probabilistic regarding their experiential consequences and any conflict between them, because the consequences of probabilistic sets are probabilistic sentences. Nevertheless, we can compare such sets regarding what they P-explain, as definition D14 allows. So let us say that $\{C_1, I_1\}$ is better than $\{C_2, I_2\}$ by the test of nonprobabilistic universality, if C_1 is nonprobabilistically universal but C_2 is not, and each experiential sentence P-explained by $\{C_2, I_2\}$ is P-explained by $\{C_1, I_1\}$. Given this test for nonprobabilistic universality, our question becomes whether there is an explanation set with a nonprobabilistically universal system that conflicts with C^2, that I understand now, and that P-explains the experiential sentences P-explained by $\{C^2, I^2\}$. And based on definition D16 for conflict, I believe it is plausible that a nonprobabilistic system, C_1, conflicts with a probabilistic system, C_2, if, for a nonprobabilistic I, such that '$I \cdot \mathrm{Pr}_{s,t}(I) > 0.5$' is compatible with C_1 and C_2 individually, there is some set of sentences, S, derivable from $\{C_1, I \cdot \mathrm{Pr}_{s,t}(I) > 0.5\}$ such that S or '$\mathrm{Pr}_{s,t}(S) > 0.5$' is discernibly incompatible with some set of sentences derivable from $\{C_2, I \cdot \mathrm{Pr}_{s,t}(I) > 0.5\}$.

It is easy to find a nonprobabilistically universal system that conflicts with C^2, according to the preceding condition. Assume that nonprobabilistic $C^i = $ '$(x)[(Px \supset Q) \cdot (Rx \supset \sim Cjn)]$'. Here '$Q$' is the conjunction which has a sentence, p, as a conjunct just in case '$\mathrm{Pr}_{c,n}(p) > 0.5$' is derivable from $\{C^2, I^2\}$. And 'Pa' and 'Ra' are any sentences creating no incompatibilities with $\{C^2, I^2\}$ or C^i individually. Then $\{C^i, Pa\}$ P-explains all that $\{C^2, I^2\}$ does, but C^i conflicts with C^2, because for $I = $ '$Scjn \cdot Ra$', $\{C^i, I\}$ yields '$\sim Cjn$', but $\{C^2, \mathrm{Pr}_{c,n}(I) > 0.5\}$ yields $\mathrm{Pr}_{c,n}(Cjn) > 0.5$. And, obviously, '$\mathrm{Pr}_{c,n}(\sim Cjn) > 0.5$' is inductively incompatible with '$\mathrm{Pr}_{c,n}(Cjn) > 0.5$'.

Is there a monprobabilistically universal explanation set like $\{C^i, Pa\}$ that is understood by me and therefore, we are assuming, in general? Furthermore, is any such theory generally believed today? Rather than discuss these questions here, I am going to assume that if some generally understood and accepted explanations of people having certain visual experiences, certain beliefs, and pains are nonprobabilistically universal, then either one of those is available to me and believed by me, or one of the best explanations accepted by experts is nonprobabilistically universal, approximated by an experiential set understood and believed by me, and P-explains whatever $\{C^2, I^2\}$ does. Indeed, I shall indicate just such an explanation in the following discussion about clause (6) of CA and sets accepted by experts. Consequently, whether or not $\{C^2, I^2\}$ meets clause (5) of CA, it is reasonable that I have some set that improves on $\{C^2, I^2\}$ by having a nonprobabilistically universal set, or $\{C^2, I^2\}$ is not bettered by a set with a nonprobabilistically universal system.

Explanation Set $\{C^2, I^2\}$ and the Best Explanations by Today's Experts. We have found reason to think that explanatory system, C^2, is minimally adequate and that $\{C^2, I^2\}$ or some nonprobabilistic, experiential relative that I accept survives the seven systemic tests when compared with sets that have systems conflicting with C^2, that I understand now, and that P-explain the members of F_1^2. Therefore, explanation set $\{C^2, I^2\}$ or this relative meets clause (5) of CA. Thus we need only show it meets clause (6) in order to conclude that CA yields that what $\{C^2, I^2\}$ P-explains is acceptable for me now. The last question, accordingly, is whether at least one of the best sets that experts now accept for explaining the members of F_1^2 does not conflict with $\{C^2, I^2\}$. How might one of the current experts about things like pains, visual experiences, and perceptual beliefs best explain the members of F_1^2? I think they would aim at quantitative systems that are nonprobabilistically universal. However, the current rudimentary state of psychophysics, which proposes psychophysical laws for deriving statements about quantitative properties of sensations, makes it unlikely that any of today's experts have explanations that are even partly quantitative. Nevertheless, there might be some experts who would accept nonprobabilistic explanation sets. For example, I believe it likely that some expert might replace C_1^2 by something like:

C_3^2:   If a human being suffers a serious laceration and this affects nerve fibers that are 'pain receptors', and this results in certain patterns of nerve impulses being transmitted through his central nervous system to reach a 'pain center' in his brain at t, then, at t, he has an experience of intense pain.[9]

And this expert might be able to replace C_2^2 by two nonprobabilistic and purely universal subsystems. One of these might contain a sufficient condition for someone having a visual experience of certain objects in terms of electromagnetic radiation being reflected from appropriate objects in such a way that it affects the retinas of his eyes and results in nerve impulses being transmitted through his optic nerves until they suitably affect the 'sensory projection area' for sight in his brain.[10] The second might be something similar that relates neurological activity to a certain sort of perceptual belief. I believe it is plausible to assume that there are experts who accept explanations at about the level of complexity of C_3^2 and some similarly complex pair of replacements for C_2^2. However, I believe it quite unlikely that any of today's experts have explanation sets with greater scope and precision than ones such as this. Indeed, if any of these experts accept purely universal and nonprobabilistic subsystems for the members of F_1^2, I believe that some of the best are very similar to one containing C_3^2 and two replacements for C_2^2 that resemble those I have tried to indicate. This gives some reason to believe that if today's experts accept nonprobabilistic explanations of the three sentences in F_1^2, at least one of the best they accept will consist of something like the three subsystems I have roughly described, plus a very complicated statement of initial conditions that concerns things like electromagnetic radiation, nerve fibers, and nerve impulses. But, even with such complicated I, some of these sets seem quite unlikely to conflict with $\{C^2, I^2\}$. So I believe we can conclude that $\{C^2, I^2\}$ meets condition (6) of CA when compared with the best nonprobabilistic sets.

What about probabilistic explanation sets? It is easy to find some that are as good as $\{C^2, I^2\}$ and conflict with it, and that might be adopted by some experts. We can create one merely be replacing C_1^2 by C_4^2: $\mathrm{Pr}_{x,t}(Tb_3^2 yt/Cyt) = 0.7$'. But, of course, the crucial question is whether some current expert would be willing to assign a probability as high as that of C_1^2. If none of these experts would do this and some would assign the conflicting lower probabilities, then it would be reasonable that some of these conflicting sets would be among the best for experts now, and $\{C^2, I^2\}$ would fail to satisfy CA for probabilistic explanation sets. Let us assume, for the moment, that this is true. What are its consequences for the claim that $\{C^2, I^2\}$ meets clause (6) of CA? Given our previous conclusion about the best nonprobabilistic sets, it is likely that this assumption has no effect at all. That is, we have seen a rough example of the sort of nonprobabilistic explanation set that it is plausible to maintain is among the best experts' nonprobabilistic sets today, and that does not conflict with $\{C^2, I^2\}$. But because such a set is purely and nonprobabilistically universal, is maximally economical and prefix-simplest, and seems to have as great a scope as any we are likely to find today, it is very reasonable that it is at least as good as any probabilistic system proposed by current experts. Therefore, even if $\{C^2, I^2\}$ fails to meet clause (6) when compared only with the best probabilistic sets, it is, nevertheless, plausible that it does meet clause (6), because it does not conflict with nonprobabilistic sets that are at least as good as the best probabilistic sets. We can conclude, then that $\{C^2, I^2\}$ meets principle CA, and so, with CA, it yields that, contrary to skepticism about other minds, it is acceptable that someone else is in great pain now.

Another Explanation That Counters Skepticism About Other Minds. Although we have finished our examination of $\{C^2, I^2\}$, I would like to reinforce my conclusion that there is an explanation set that meets all the conditions of CA and, with CA, contradicts skepticism about other minds. Let us assume that only probabilistic sets for set F_1^2 are accepted by experts, and all the best of these conflict with $\{C^2, I^2\}$, because '$\mathrm{Pr}_{x,t}(Tb_3^2yt/Cyt) < 0.5$' is derivable from them. And let us also assume that one of the best of these replaces C_1^2 by $C_1^3 = $ '$\mathrm{Pr}_{x,t}(Tb_3^2yt/Cyt \cdot Myt) > 0.8$', where $Myt = $ 'At t, y is moaning or screaming', and adds 'Mcn' as a conjunct to the content of I^2. This new set explains the three members of F_1^2 but conflicts with $\{C^2, I^2\}$ and, what is worse for our concern, does not have the consequence that $\mathrm{Pr}_{c,n}(Tb_3^2jn \cdot j \neq c) > 0.5$.

Would this hypothetical situation stymie my attempt to find some claim about mental phenomena of others that is acceptable for me at some time? Thankfully, it would not, because there are other situations in which my foundational set, F_1^3, will include the three sentences in F_1^2 and also 'Tb_1^3cn', where $b_1^3 = $ 'I am now having an auditory experience of another person and myself moaning'. Given that a set that includes subsystem C_1^3 is one of the best for F_1^3 that is accepted by today's experts, my explanation set, $\{C^3, I^3\}$, for F_1^3, which includes C_1^3 and has the following replacement for C_2^2 and I^2, would seem not to conflict with all of the best for F_1^3. Instead of C_2^2, it has

C_2^3: $\mathrm{Pr}_{x,t}(Tb_1^2xt \cdot Tb_2^2xt \cdot Tb_1^3xt/Sxyt \cdot Sxzt \cdot Hxyt \cdot Hxzt \cdot y \neq z) > 0.8$.

And, instead of I^2, it has:

I^3: $\mathrm{Pr}_{c,n}(Scjn \cdot Sccn \cdot Hcjn \cdot Hccn \cdot j \neq c) > 0.8$.

Here $Hxyt = $ 'At t, x is hearing y moaning'. The new set P-explains all four sentences in F_1^3, and also has as a consequence '$\mathrm{Pr}_{c,n}(Tb_3^2jn \cdot j \neq c) > 0.5$', which solves my present problem about how to justify that someone else is now in great pain, given CA and assuming that $\{C^3, I^3\}$ satisfies CA. But also, given our hypothetical case, $\{C^3, I^3\}$ would seem to satisfy clause (6) of CA, and, for reasons like those for $\{C^2, I^2\}$, the other five clauses as well. So, even if set $\{C^2, I^2\}$ were not to meet clause (6) because its probabilities are too high for experts, it is reasonable that there are related sets for related situations that do meet clause (6), and also have the consequences relevant to refuting skepticism about other minds.

CONCLUSION ABOUT THE EXPLANATORY FOUNDATIONAL THEORY AND SKEPTICISM

The present stage of our attempt to refute the four species of moderate skepticism is finished. Indeed, we now have available all the material we need to justify those premises of the master argument that remained unjustified at the end of Chapter 1, namely, premises II, X, XI, and XIV. In fact, Chapter 10 has provided us with what will show the reasonableness of premise XIV ('The explanatory foundational theory has consequences that contradict all forms of moderate$_1$ skepticism about physical objects, the past, the future, and other minds'). The two primary examples we examined here showed us how the explanatory foundational theory implies that certain statements about physical objects I do not perceive now, or about something nonsubjective that happened 24 hours ago, or will happen 24 hours from now, or about someone else's pain are acceptable for me at a certain time. Each of these sentences contradicts one of the four species of skeptical thesis M_1S_3, which can be stated together as follows:

> It is not reasonable at any time, t, for any human being, s, to believe a sentence if it entails: (a) the existence of some particular physical object that s is not perceiving at t; (b) the occurrence of some particular event before t that is nonsubjective for s; (c) the occurrence of some particular event after t; (d) the existence of a mental phenomenon of a being other than s at any time.

Furthermore, I believe it is clear that in their retreat from thesis M_1S_1 to M_1S_3, skeptics have retrenched as much as they can if they are to remain moderate$_1$ skeptics of each of those four kinds. Therefore, because what the explanatory foundational theory implies contradicts thesis M_1S_3, and, of course, theses M_1S_1 and M_1S_2, it is reasonable to conclude that the consequences of this foundational theory contradict all forms of moderate skepticism about physical objects, the past, the future, and other minds. That is, premise XIV is reasonable for us now, today.

The last main task before us is to establish those last three unjustified premises by the results of our lengthy series of arguments since Chapter 1. Accordingly, in the final chapter we shall finish by summarizing our progress since Chapter 1, apply the results to the master argument, and draw final conclusions.

NOTES

[1] See A. Plantinga, *God and Other Minds*, Ithaca, N.Y.: Cornell University Press, 1967, ch. 9.

[2] For a more detailed discussion of the failure of analytical behaviorism, see my *Materialism and Sensations*, New Haven, Conn.: Yale University Press, 1971, pp. 132–140.

[3] See J. S. Mill, *An Examination of Sir William Hamilton's Philosophy*, 6th ed., London: Longmans, 1889, pp. 243–244; and for a discussion of other minds and analogy, Plantinga, *op. cit.*, ch. 8.

[4] See A. J. Ayer, *The Problem of Knowledge*, Harmondsworth: Penguin, 1956, pp. 214–222.

[5] Premise (1) avoids Plantinga's objection (in Plantinga, *op. cit.*, pp. 253–260) because, first, it is logically possible that I have determined by observation and experience that someone's being badly cut is accompanied by pain felt by the being whose body is badly cut; and, second, it is logically possible that I have determined by observation and experience that someone's being badly cut is *not* accompanied by pain felt by the being whose body is badly cut. Just imagine that in each case I am this being.

[6] For problems in 'mixing' probabilistic and nonprobabilistic premises, see P. Suppes, 'Probabilistic Inference and the Concept of Total Evidence', in J. Hintikka and P. Suppes (eds.), *Aspects of Inductive Logic*, Amsterdam: North Holland Publishing Co., 1966, pp. 49–50.

[7] P. Ziff, 'The Simplicity of Other Minds', *Journal of Philosophy* **62** (1965), 578.

[8] W. Quine, *Word and Object*, Cambridge, Mass.: MIT Press, 1960, p. 264.

[9] *Cf.* R. Melzack, *The Puzzle of Pain*, New York: Basic Books, 1973, especially pp. 75–77.

[10] See R. Hochberg, *Perception*, Englewood Cliffs, N.J.: Prentice-Hall, 1964, especially pp. 13–15.

CHAPTER 11

SUMMARY AND CONCLUDING REMARKS

With the main task of Chapter 10 complete, we have available all we need to justify the three premises of the master argument that we have not yet examined. To see that the material for this last task can be found in the previous chapters, and to help recall my overall aim and strategy in this book, let me begin this final stage of the work by presenting a general overview of the main goals and the major accomplishments that have resulted from the many, small, piecemeal arguments, objectives, proposals, and rejections that have populated the preceding chapters.

GENERAL REVIEW

Epistemological skepticism comes in many forms, all of which should be carefully distinguished from ontological nihilism. Unlike ontological nihilism, none of these epistemological theses imply the nonexistence of any entity, such as unperceived physical objects, past events, future events, or minds of others. Some of them state that it is never reasonable for someone to believe any claim about a particular entity he is not presently perceiving and has never experienced (moderate$_1$ skepticism). Others say that such claims are never known, while still others embody the stronger thesis that it is always unreasonable to believe these claims. There are also 'second-level' skeptical theses that assign various epistemic statuses to the 'first-level' views. My most general aim has been to provide an argument for the conclusion that it is unreasonable to believe what I take to be the most important first-level skeptical thesis, namely, moderate$_1$ skepticism. And, by providing these grounds, I also would have what I need to refute the Humean second-level thesis that moderate$_1$ skepticism is reasonable and the weaker view that it is not unreasonable. If, along the way, I should also convince some epistemological skeptic to change his mind, that would be a beneficial by-product of my efforts. It is, nevertheless, not one of my goals. What convinces a believer to change and what makes his belief unreasonable are all too often quite unrelated. I have concentrated solely on the latter task.

Just how is one to refute a thesis of epistemological skepticism without

begging a multitude of crucial questions? Before I began, I was particularly
worried about just what sort of reasoning should be used and how complicated the inferences it employs can be. These are, in a clear sense, meta-
problems, because they concern the implements I am permitted to use to
justify a thesis, and so it is not immediately obvious that any restrictions
should be imposed other than those required for the justification of any
sort of thesis. Yet, in the present case, the thesis is peculiar, because it
states the unreasonableness of all versions of moderate skepticism which,
in turn, asserts the unreasonableness, for a human being, of any claim
implying the existence of a particular entity he is not perceiving and has
never experienced. Many people tend to believe that any justification of
such a thesis should be limited to short, simple arguments that involve
only the most elementary forms of deduction and only premises whose
acceptability is easy to discern. This restriction would be required if the
skeptical thesis I am attempting to refute concerned all forms of human
reasoning except this very elementary sort. I am, of course, not considering
that thesis. Nevertheless, I have agreed to limit my argument against
moderate$_1$ skepticism – the master argument of the book – to a four-step
argument, each step of which has a relatively simple deductive form, and
premises whose reasonableness can be exhibited relatively easily. I did this
in part to prepare myself a defense against an onslaught from a skeptic
about human reasoning, even though I am convinced that these precau-
tions are really not required for my particular task. My more important
reason for this self-imposed restraint, however, is that I wanted to achieve
that 'beneficial side effect' of the master argument, namely, the refutation
of skepticism about induction, without reliance on inductive arguments.
Surely, an inductive justification of induction is suspect, in spite of some
attempts to prove otherwise.

Of course, a skeptic, like Hume, about all sorts of human reasoning
except the most elementary, might be unappeased by my restrictions. I
shall, however, speculate no more about such a person; I shall rather wait
to see whether someone proposes a particular objection to my 'excesses'.
But I do want to consider here the objection that I have failed to adhere
to my own guidelines for one or both of two reasons. The first is that,
although the master argument has only four steps and no step contains
more than four premises, the logical forms of steps 2 and 3 are much too
complicated to qualify as simple. I shall answer this merely by claiming
that they are quite simple, although not elementary; and by offering to
exhibit their simple forms to anyone who asks me. The second reason is

that, as demonstrated throughout the book, my justification of many of the premises of the master argument is so complex and extended that there is no way to exhibit their reasonableness in any easily comprehended way. The rest of this review constitutes my reply to this second charge. It is a major aim of this summary to bring together the various bits of evidence that have accumulated throughout the book, and make clear how they justify those premises of the master argument whose reasonableness is not easy to grasp.

I have found only one way to argue successfully for the claim that it is unreasonable for human beings to believe any version of moderate$_1$ skepticism with its denial of the reasonableness of any belief about what is not now experienced and never has been. This required me to produce a particular theory of the justification of empirical sentences, show that it is reasonable to adopt the theory, and exhibit its consequences that contradict moderate$_1$ skepticism. As noted at the end of the introduction, these were the three main problems I faced as I began the main body of the book. The task of Chapter 1 was primarily to find an appropriate procedure for justifying theories of justification, lay out the procedure in simple and clear deductive form, and justify all the premises of the argument that I could at such an early point in the book. This constituted the second and third steps of the master argument, although, as previously noted, the conclusion of the first step is relevant to premise X of step 3.

The idea behind the second and third steps, taken together, is that there are ways to justify a particular set of principles or theory of a certain kind by showing that the adoption of some theory or other of that kind is needed for human beings to achieve a goal that is worthwhile and important for them. This sort of justification, which Feigl calls 'vindication', has been more admired than discussed in detail. Indeed, the only philosophers whom I have found to use it with some care and precision are Reichenbach and Salmon in their similar attempts to vindicate the straight rule of induction. Not only have their attempts failed, but it is also true that the principle of vindication that seems to be implicit in their work, namely, VP1, is too limited in what it allows to count as vindicating facts about theories. Principle VP1 states that if one theory is *the* best way to achieve some worthwhile and important goal – perhaps because it is the most efficient and effective way – then it is reasonable to adopt that theory. The problem is that all too often there is no way to decide whether some theory is better than all the rest. I proposed, therefore, that we can also vindicate using principle VP3 (premise IV), which counts a theory, T, reasonable if some theory of a same kind as T is required to achieve a worthwhile and important goal, there is no reason to think T to be flawed, and T is more reasonable than any of its competitors. At this point, therefore, the two central questions became whether some theory of empirical justification or other is required for some appropriate goal, and whether some particular theory of that kind is more reasonable than all others, and seems to avoid all objections.

In Chapter 1, I argued, as seems clearly true, that the human goal of making and carrying out decisions that it is reasonable for human beings to think are morally correct is worthwhile and important for them (premise VI). Furthermore, because there are so many difficult and important cases that call for careful, precise decisions about what to do, two sorts of guiding principles are needed in these situations to direct human beings toward decisions there is reason to think are moral. The first sort consists in principles of moral obligation that prescribe and proscribe actions for people in particular situations by relating obligation to certain of the empirical facts of the situations. The second sort required are theories of empirical justification that provide means for uncovering which claims about these empirical facts it is reasonable to accept (premise V). These three premises – IV, V, and VI – yield the intermediate conclusion, VII, which states that if there is a particular theory of empirical justification that provides bases for human decisions that is the most reasonable of its kind, then it is reasonable for humans to adopt it. This concluded step 2, all of whose premises were, I claim, justified in Chapter 1.

The vital problems for step 3 of the master argument were, first, to find a principle that could be used to show one theory of empirical justification to be the most reasonable, and second, to show that a particular theory satisfies the principle. Only the first of these problems could be solved in Chapter 1; the resolution of the second still lies before us. What made the first problem so worrysome for me was my realization that the considerations usually invoked when comparing two hypotheses for reasonableness very often fail to identify just one as most reasonable. This, of course, echoes what plagued those earlier attempts to vindicate the straight rule. I proposed, nevertheless, the adoption of principle CP.1, which is based on one I had used previously to evaluate metaphysical theories about the external world. It is a principle of conservatism which uses comparisons of how well theories agree with commonly accepted beliefs as a means of last resort for favoring theories that conform more closely to common sense. I reasoned for theories of justification, as I did for metaphysical theories, that if there is nothing which shows either of two theories to be more reasonable than the other, except that the first requires appreciably less change in commonly and firmly accepted beliefs that arise quite naturally and independently of theories and doctrines, then it is more reasonable to accept the first theory (premise VIII). My hope, of course, was, and still is, that this additional desideratum would single out from all the theories of justification that are otherwise as reasonable as any theory just one theory which thereby becomes the most reasonable. Then if I could go on to make it reasonable that this particular theory faces no objections, I could derive, with the help of previous conclusion VII, that it is reasonable to adopt this theory.

Unfortunately, to reach the preceding, important conclusion, I had first to find and develop a theory of justification that I could successfully argue provides bases for human decisions, is as reasonable as any competitor and more conservative of human beliefs than any otherwise as reasonable as it is, and is free of objections. I now claim to have done most of this by developing and defending what I call the 'minimal explanatory foundational theory' of empirical justification. I have not, of course, fully justified my claim, but let me give a brief review of what I have done and sketch a preview of what I plan to do shortly. In part I, I considered what I would argue are the most plausible foundational opponents of my proposed theory. These included a Cartesian theory that requires a foundation of noninferential or initial certainty, and extension of justification by deduction alone; a Lewisean theory that allows some instances of what is no more than initially acceptable at the foundation plus extension by inductive inference; and a Chisholmian view that uses only the directly evident as foundational but adds nondeductive and noninductive epistemic principles. In each case, I argued that either the theory fails to extend acceptability beyond the base in any appreciable way, or it employs principles that are either unacceptable or not usable for inferences from what is purely foundational.

In Chapter 6, I considered the three principle varieties of nonfoundational theory, and argued that theories of these sorts face serious objections. Most theories, whether they require an infinite regress of justification, or a circularity of justification, or 'blind' posits of evidence that is not justified, fall prey to the charge of arbitrariness. That is, these theories allow a wide variety of sentences to be acceptable for someone, depending only on what he wants justified or what he believes. I suggested, however, that one nonfoundational theory, the explanatory coherence theory, could avoid this charge by adapting some features of the explanatory foundational theory so they pick out the sentences to be explained without identifying them as acceptable even if not explained. But I argued that this requirement of no acceptability without explanation is surely implausible and so even this amended theory is unreasonable.

On the other hand, after I amended formulations of the minimal explanatory foundational theory extensively, I claimed that it is immune to a wide variety of objections, including those that were so damaging to its chief competitors. I can give some idea of why this is so by highlighting the two crucial theses of principle F3.22, which was developed in Chapter 7 to make explicit the basic features of the explanatory foundational theory. The first is the foundational thesis which states that certain nonstanding basic-reports, observation-reports, and subjective memory-reports are acceptable for someone, even if not explained for him, whenever they satisfy principles H3, BR3, or BR4 in appropriate ways. This feature of the explanatory foundational theory captures the strength of foundational theories that counters the endemic weakness of nonfoundational theories. That is, it specifies in a nonarbitrary and reasonable way the sentences that are to be explained for a person at a time, and claims that these foundational sentences are at least acceptable without being explained.

The second crucial thesis is that whatever explanation of those sentences that are to be explained for someone at some time is 'best' for him at that time for those sentences, and whatever is a consequence of that explanation, are also acceptable for him then. Here, of course, the explanation that is 'best' in this way must meet six different conditions, including being minimally adequate, having no clauses that are not needed to explain what is to be explained, and having maximum explanatory coherence for the foundational set among explanations that are either understood by the person or are generally understood, and do not conflict with all explanations that are widely accepted by experts. And, of course, having maximum explanatory coherence for such a foundational set depends in part on excelling in some of the nine systemic tests discussed in chapters 8 and 9. Nevertheless, it is clear that some explanation does sometime satisfy all six of these requirements, and is, thereby, 'best' for someone at that time. When that is true, then what is acceptable for that person then is significantly expanded beyond the narrow foundation with which he began. This fact gives some reason to believe that the explanatory foundational theory has that strength of nonfoundational theories whose lack so often plagues foundational theories, namely, the ability to extend justification significantly in ways that, unlike Chisholm's procedures, involve no principles that are unreasonable.

I have not yet shown, of course, that the explanatory foundational theory includes no unreasonable principle, because I have not yet provided reason to think the theory faces no objections (premise XI). I shall have done that only after I have explicitly restated those objections previously rejected, and examined and refuted all others I can devise. I shall do this shortly. After that, I shall argue that the explanatory foundational theory provides bases for human decisions (premise X). At that point, not only will I have justified premises X and XI, but, as I shall argue then, I will also have justified the claim that the explanatory foundational theory is as reasonable as any theory of empirical justification that provides bases for human decisions. If I can also, as I intend, show that the theory is more conservative of human beliefs than its competitors that are otherwise as reasonable as it is (premise IX), I shall at last be able to conclude, with the aid of intermediate conclusion VII, that it is reasonable for us now to adopt this explanatory foundational theory.

One of the objections to the explanatory foundational theory, indeed, to any theory of empirical justification, is that some version of moderate$_1$ skepticism is reasonable, and so no theory of justification that conflicts with that skeptical thesis is reasonable. Of course, it is the task of the first step of the master argument to dispel this objection, because that concludes that it is not reasonable for us to believe any such skeptical theses (intermediate conclusion III). I have not, however, completed this first step, because it depends in part on premise II which states that it is reasonable for us to believe that the most plausible attempts to justify moderate$_1$ skepticism theses fail. This, as I argued in the introduction, is sufficient for none of these skeptical theses being reasonable (premise I). When I examine premise II in detail, I shall claim that I have indeed examined the most plausible skeptical arguments earlier in the book, and each one fails to justify its conclusion because it requires at least one premise that is no more reasonable than its denial.

The fourth and last step of the master argument uses the previous intermediate conclusions that it is reasonable for us to adopt the explanatory foundational theory (conclusion XIII), and that no form of moderate$_1$ skepticism is reasonable (conclusion III) to argue for the final conclusion, XVI, that all these forms of skepticism are unreasonable. Of course, these two claims are not sufficient for the final conclusion. But, as premise XV states, the conjunction of III and XIII with the statement that the explanatory foundational theory has consequences about the acceptablity of certain sentences that contradict what these skeptical theses state (premise XIV), is sufficient. It was the task of Chapter 10 to show that principle F3.22 has such consequences for each of the four sorts of situations covered by moderate$_1$ skepticism. That is, in certain situations, F3.22 yields that sentences implying the existence of an unperceived physical object, or the occurrence of a particular nonsubjective past event, or some particular future event, or a particular mental phenomenon of another are sometimes acceptable for someone. Consequently, if in what follows I am able to justify those two intermediate conclusions, III and XIII, I shall have finished the central task of this book. I shall also have justified the conclusion of the extension of the master argument which denies skepticism about induction which states that it is unreasonable to adopt any form of induction. As I argued at the end of Chapter 7, hypothetical induction, or inference to the best explanation, is reasonable, if the explanatory foundational theory is (premise XVII). But, obviously, some form of induction is reasonable, if hypothetical induction is (premise XVIII). So some form of induction is reasonable, and skepticism about induction is false (conclusion XVIII).

The extended master argument contains thirteen premises, only four of which remain to be considered. These are II from step one, and IX, X, and XI from the third step. Six of the rest (IV, V, VI, VIII, XIV, and XVII) were justified in Chapter 1; premise I was justified in the Introduction: premise XVII at the end of Chapter 7; and premise XIV throughout Chapter 10. It is time, finally, to turn to the four remaining premises. I shall begin with XI which states that it is reasonable for us now to believe that the explanatory foundational theory is free of objections. I do this first because, as we shall see, the reasonableness of II and IX depend in part on the reasonableness of XI.

ON OBJECTIONS TO THE EXPLANATORY FOUNDATIONAL THEORY

In Chapter 7 when I attempted to find an objection-free formulation of the minimal explanatory foundational theory, I began with F3.21 as a first approximation, and after proposing several definitions which themselves required numerous changes, and a series of seven amendments to F3.21, I finally arrived at principle F3.22 as the final statement of the basic epistemic principle of the minimal thesis. Let me begin my justification of premise XI by reviewing the most important objections to F3.22 that I have already dispatched.

Objections to F3.22 *Previously Rejected*

There are four places where F3.22 and its offspring, F3.221 are most susceptible to attack. In terms of the simpler F3.221, these are included in its first three clauses that state four individually sufficient conditions for acceptability. The first is the claim that what satisfies H3 is acceptable; the second and third are the implications that whatever satisfies either BR3 or BR4 is probable relative to a particular set of basic-reports; and the fourth concerns the six conditions listed in clause (3) which are supposedly conjointly sufficient for the acceptability of an explanation set. Let us consider each of the four.

Objections to Principle H3. Principle H3 was developed in Chapter 2 in response to a series of objections to H1 and then H2. Principle H1 states that a given-report is initially certain, if a person understands it and believes it with certainty. It was refuted by an objection taken from Reichenbach that someone might fully believe and understand two given-reports, where the probability of one, given the other, is less than 1. In such cases, H1 leads to inductively inconsistent results on my assumption that epistemic certainty requires a probability of 1. The second attempt, H2, avoids this problem by adding to the antecedent of H1 a conjunct which requires inductive consistency among all basic-reports that are fully and understandingly believed. But H2 must also be amended. One amendment is needed to counter Goodman's objection that some basic-reports fully believed at different times are inductively inconsistent. This objection was avoided by relativizing probability, and so epistemic certainty, to time. Thus what is certain now when fully believed by someone may not be a few moments later, when he confidently believes something that is inductively inconsistent with its being certain then.

One more change in H2 was mandated by an example concerning a well-established psychophysical law which, when conjoined with a statement about a person's brain state, entails the falsity of a pain-report that the person fully believes. Then, on the assumption that this conjunction is probable, given a set of basic-reports fully believed by an examining scientist, it follows that the pain-report is not certain, contrary to H2. This objection, and a modification of it where the person believing the pain-report is this scientist, is avoided by further relativizing probabilities to persons. Then when the person is not the scientist the pain-report could be certain for the person but not the scientist. When the person is the scientist, the report would not be certain for him.

The principle that emerged from my discussion was H3, which is designed to escape the wide variety of objections to H1 and H2 by relativizing probabilities to persons and times and by forbidding inductive inconsistencies. I claim that, because of these features of H3, it is reasonable for us to conclude that H3 is free of objections. The only other objection to H3 that I have been able to find is one based on Carnap's thesis of strict coherence, which allows no logically contingent sentence to have a probability of 1. I argued in Chapter 2, however, that this thesis is dubious, because, at the very least, statements that are clearly physically impossible, such as one stating that Elsie the cow jumps over the moon, seem clearly to have a probability of zero for some of us now. So their denials have a probability of one. I conclude, then, that H3 is not the cause of objections to F3.22.

Objections to Principles BR3 *and* BR4. Principle F3.22 can be attacked by objecting to BR3 or BR4. However, as argued in Chapter 5 where both principles were proposed, I find no objections to BR3 which evolved out of BR1 and BR2 in response to objections. Principle BR3 states a sufficient condition for an observation-report's being probable, given a set of four particular basic-reports. It thereby provides for foundational theories, a sufficient condition for that critical link between what is initially probable or certain, and what is inferentially acceptable. It is difficult to evaluate principles like BR3 by themselves, because they concern relative probabilities which yield nothing about what is 'absolutely' acceptable. I tried to solve this problem by considering situations that satisfy H3 for the basic-reports in the antecedent clause of the relative probability statements given in the principle being examined. In such a situation, a principle like BR2 or BR3 conjoined with H3 yields that a particular observation-report is 'absolutely' probable for a person at a time. Whenever this result proved to be implausible, I rejected the offending principle. I concluded from this examination that if no basic-report that a person understands and fully believes is 'negatively relevant' to the high probability of an observation-report, p, of the form, 'I am now perceiving something F' (such as, yellow), then p is probable for a person, given four things: he is having an experience of something F, he fully believes that he is perceiving something

F, he fully believes that he and the relevant conditions are normal; and he is trying hard to be rational. That is, I concluded that BR3 is correct. I further concluded that, when, in addition, the conjunction of these four basic-reports satisfies H3 for the person at the time, it is probable and also acceptable for this person at this time, that he is perceiving something with the observable characteristic, *F*. I argued for this conclusion by endorsing Carnap's epistemic understanding of probability, according to which '*p* is probable for *s* at *t*' means that the degree of confirmation of *p* for *s* at *t* is high, and then proposing that when a person fully believes that conjunction of basic-reports and no basic-report he believes is negatively relevant to *p*'s being probable, then it surely seems that *p* is highly confirmed for that person at that time. I have found no need to reject this reasoning or conclusion, and as a result, claim there is reason to think that BR3 faces no objections.

Principle BR4 closely resembles BR3. The only differences are that BR4 concerns a basic memory-report, *m*, of the form, 'I am now remembering that, a short time ago, I had an experience of something *F*' (such as, yellow), and requires a slightly different set of basic-reports given which *m* is probable for a person when no basic-report he fully believes is negatively relevant to *m*'s being probable. I did little to argue for BR4, except to claim that the epistemic status of basic memory-reports is similar to that of observation-reports. That is, the level of confirmation of a memory-report about one's own recent 'subjective' past, given an appropriate set of basic-reports is at least that of an observation-report about one's own present perception, given a set of basic-reports appropriate to it. One idea behind this claim is that a person is at least as likely to be right about one of his own recent 'subjective' experiences, given a particular psychological state, as to be right about a present observation, given a particular psychological state. I would expect, therefore, to find no objections to BR4, if I find none for BR3. And, as just noted I have reason to think I shall find none for BR3. I conclude, then, that it is reasonable to expect there to be no objections to BR4.

On the Acceptability of Explanations

It is clear, I believe, that, in spite of the six complex requirements I packed into clause (3) of F3.221 which provide a sufficient condition for the acceptability of explanations, that clause is the most vulnerable spot in F3.221. Nevertheless, I believe it is reasonable to count it as free of objections. To show why I claim this, let me, as before, review the major objections to clause (3) that I have already claimed to refute, and then consider the only one I have found that has not yet been refuted.

Theories of justification are prone to two sorts of problems: they overly restrict acceptability – the crucial problem for most foundational theories – or they spread acceptability too widely or arbitrarily – the curse of most nonfoundational theories. The first problem does not face F3.22, in spite of the fact that it is foundational. It avoids this because it extends acceptability beyond the foundation through justification by explanation, and because, being minimal, it puts no specific necessary condition on acceptability. This, of course, does not imply that some full explanatory foundational theory beyond this minimal thesis avoids this problem. But if all extensions beyond F3.22 should face irritating objections, that would count against F3.22 only if there should be some other trouble-free minimal principle that avoids objections when extended. But we already have reason to doubt the existence of such a principle, and our later discussion will further confirm this.

The minimal explanatory foundational theory has faced the second problem, however, in at least three different guises. One results from allowing at least two conflicting explanation sets to be acceptable for one person at one time; the second arises when acceptability is granted to conjunctions that create the lottery paradox; and the last occurs when acceptability is granted to sentences in explanation sets that are irrelevant to explaining what is to be explained.

In Chapter 7, I proposed ways to handle these three problems. The first which concerns uniqueness, is like the problem that has so far defeated Salmon's attempt to justify exactly the straight rule of induction, and also like the problem for probability functions that Carnap has tried to help solve by adding requirements like strict coherence to the axioms of the probability calculus. I have proceeded in much the way Carnap and Salmon did by placing several restrictions on the explanation sets found acceptable by F3.22 and F3.221. These include being minimally adequate, being its own minimal version, and having maximum explanatory coherence among a specific group of sets. It is clear, however, that these strictures do not always isolate just one set. I added, therefore, one last condition to the effect that among the sets remaining after this extensive weeding, the acceptable set is the set the person chooses to make the explanation. If he fails to choose exactly one, then F3.22 provides no way to infer that some set is acceptable. This is, of course, one of the places that F3.22 is incomplete, and must be further developed to become a complete theory. That does not, however, negate the fact that F3.22 avoids this problem of uniqueness.

Lottery-type paradoxes arise when statements, such as, 'Number one in a fair million-ticket lottery will not win', are individually probable, but, when enough of them are conjoined, the result is improbable. I have rejected conjunctive closure of acceptability, that is, I follow Kyburg and claim that the individual acceptability of a group of statements does not imply the acceptability of their conjunction. Nevertheless, I have also argued in Chapter 3 that when individually acceptable statements are used together as evidence, their conjunction must be acceptable. It is, then, where F3.22 requires the use of acceptable statements as evidence that it might face this problem.

This problem of 'conjunctive evidence' arises for F3.221 at most in clauses (3) and (5). In clause (3) the foundational set, F, that is to be explained might contain statements that are acceptable individually but not conjointly. Since F is the evidence for the explanation set that is acceptable because it explains F, the members of F should be conjointly acceptable. I guaranteed this for F3.221 by inserting in clause (3) condition (c) which states that F is probable for s at t. Then, because s's evidence for F is set S_1 which is certain for s at t, it follows, by A5a, that F is acceptable whenever clause (3) is satisfied.

The problem arises for clause (5) because it assigns acceptability to sentences entailed by some subset of sentences that have proved to be individually acceptable by one of the previous clauses of F3.221. But again there is no guarantee that the conjunction of the sentences in this subset is acceptable, and so no guarantee that what this set entails is acceptable. But I avoided this problem by requiring that any such set have a high credibility, and thus be acceptable. Once again, F3.221 remains mute about the acceptability of what other subsets entail. It might be thought, incidentally, that clause (4) falls prey to the lottery paradox, because it assigns acceptability to all consequences of explanation sets that satisfy clause (3). This allows some conjunctions of consequences of such a set to be acceptable, but this causes no problem, because these are just the conjunctions that are themselves consequences of the set, and so should be counted acceptable if the set is.

The most bothersome of the three problems concerning undeserved justification arises because of the ease with which irrelevant clauses can be smuggled into explanation sets. A prime example of the sort of smuggling that has worried me continually concerns a religious fanatic who wants

his belief in his god to be justified, and turns to the explanatory foundational theory to make the task easy. Principle F3.22 contains six features
that are aimed at prohibiting illicit justification of such sentences. Some
of these sentences will be excluded from set B_3, because they contain
clauses that would be generally rejected by those who are experts about
what is being explained. Recall a previous example from Chapter 7, where
$F = \{$'At t_n, Cornman believes he hears thundering', and set $\{C_1,\ I_1\}$,
with $C_1 = $ 'Whenever Zeus causes thundering and someone hears it, then
he believes he hears thundering', that is, '$(t)(x)[(Tzt \cdot Hxt) \supset Bxt]$', and
$I_1 = $ 'At t_n, Zeus causes thundering, and Cornman hears it', that is, '$Tzt_n \cdot$
Hct_n'. It seems quite clear that the first conjunct of I_1 is generally rejected
by experts about F. Assume for the moment, however, that no experts
about F reject 'Tzt_n'. There is still a way to prohibit the use of I_1. This is
because $\{C_1,\ I_1\}$ satisfies clause (3) of F3.221 only if it P-explains F, and it
P-explains F, only if, by definition D16, I_1 is experiential. But 'Tzt_n' is not
experiential.

The third precaution comes from definition D15 for explanatory systems
which does not allow any conjunct of pC, the prenex normal form of C,
with its matrix in conjunctive normal form, to be definitionally equivalent
to a singular sentence. This stops the use of $C_2 = $ '$Tzt_n \cdot C_1$', and $I_2 = $
'Hct_n' to circumvent the preceding stricture, because all singular sentences
are forced into the statements of initial conditions. Unhappily, none of
the three preceding features of F3.22 stop other sorts of illicit introduction
of sentences into an explanation set. Consider $\{C_3,\ I_3\}$, where $C_3 = $ 'If
someone hears thundering at t, then he believes he hears thundering at t,
and Zeus causes thundering at t', that is, '$(x)(t)[Hxt \supset (Bxt \cdot Tzt)]$', and
$I_3 = $ 'At t_n, Jones is in pain, and Cornman hears thundering', that is,
'$Pjt_n \cdot Hct_n$'. In this case, neither 'Pjt_n', about someone else's pain, nor
'Tzt_n' are excluded by anything yet mentioned. However, the requirement
of clause (3) of F3.221 that $\{C_3,\ I_3\}$ be its own minimal version for F, rids
us of both 'Pjt_n' and 'Tzt_n'. The first is prohibited, because I_3 is not minimal for F with C_3. System C_3 requires only 'Hct_n' to explain F. The second
is avoided, because C_3 is not minimal with $I_4 = $ 'Hct_n', or even with I_3.
Only one conjunct from pC_3, with its quantifiers, namely, $C_4 = $ '$(x)(t)$
$(\sim Hxt \vee Bxt)$', is needed to explain F. Consequently, $\{C_3,\ I_3\}$ must be
replaced by $\{C_4,\ I_4\}$ if clause (3) is to be satisfied, but then no illicit justification occurs.

Another loophole remains, however. Consider $\{C_5,\ I_3\}$ with $C_5 = $ '(x)
$(y)(t)[(Pxt \cdot Hyt) \supset Byt]$'. None of the five preceding restrictions exclude

this set. But this would allow the illicit justification of 'Pjt_n', if it were not for the sixth limitation. It is clear that C_4 is more general than C_5. Then, assuming that the person in question believes C_4, and, probably C_5 because it is deducible from C_4, the use of C_5 is prohibited by condition (c) of clause (3) of F3.221. That is, there must be no system more general than C_5 that is believed by the person, and P-explains F with I_3. But C_4 is more general than C_5, and so $\{C_5, I_3\}$ must be replaced by $\{C_4, I_3\}$, and the latter by $\{C_4, I_4\}$, because I_3 is not minimal for F with C_4. The result is a set with no sentence receiving undeserved acceptability. This, I find, is true for any explanation set that meets these six conditions, and so I conclude that F3.22 avoids this third way that theories of justification might be too liberal in assigning acceptability.

I believe that the restrictions built into F3.22 through definitions, subsidiary principles, and its own clauses are adequate to handle the only three ways I have been able to find that a theory of justification might assign acceptability where it should not. Consequently, the minimal explanatory foundational theory is not plagued by this sort of objection. There are, however, three others that were also considered previously. They can be grouped together as concerned with the use of clause (3) of F3.221, or, alternatively, the foundational use of hypothetical induction to justify particular explanation sets. The first objection was that F3.221 requires a justifying E-series for every sentence that it finds to be inferentially acceptable, but that is implausible for some explanation sets. The only evidence available for such a set, S_4, is F, and so $\mathrm{Pr}_{s,t}(S_4/F) > 0.5$. But often an explanation set contains a very complicated explanatory system, and it is unreasonable that such a set is probable, given only a few basic-reports and observation-reports. My reply was that clause (3) provides a very detailed and demanding sufficient condition for when an explanation set is acceptable, and thereby probable, given only foundational evidence. And I argued that by combating all the other objections to clause (3), as I just reviewed, I had therein rebutted the objection that the condition of clause (3) is not sufficient. That reply, of course, remains undaunted.

The second objection arose at this point, namely, that in using clause (3), I had, in effect, used hypothetical induction to justify nonfoundational statements, and that, to say the very least, begs the question against skepticism about induction. My retort was to deny that I had claimed or implied that either clause (3) or hypothetical induction was reasonable. I only had argued that it is plausible to believe that they faced no objections. It is to be only after every premise of the master argument has been justified, that F3.22, and thus hypothetical induction, will be justified by what I am doing. But that method of justification, which I have just reviewed, is question-begging *at most* against skepticism regarding all reasoning or regarding all but the most elementary deductive reasoning. I am not, however, concerned with those two forms of skepticism.

The third objection concerning my use of clause (3) of F3.221 to refute skepticism is a complaint that I would have to exceed my own stricture about the sort of reasoning I allow myself when I attempt to use clause (3) to show that in particular situations F3.22 has consequences that contradict all versions of moderate$_1$ skepticism. This is because the antecedent of (3) is so complicated that there is no relatively easy way to show that some situation instantiates it, and thus, contrary to what I required of myself, there is no easy way to justify premise XIV of the master argument. Indeed, it might be added that this has been clearly substantiated by the laborious and difficult discussion in Chapter 10.

The first point to note about this objection is that it is not an objection to the explanatory foundational theory, but is rather aimed at my particular justification of a different premise of the master argument, namely, XIV. Nevertheless, let me say something about it here. I certainly agree that there is no sense in which Chapter 10 can be said to be relatively easy to grasp. I claim, however, that once someone has worked his way through Chapter 10, he will find it relatively easy to see the reasonableness of the *general* hypothesis that each species of moderate$_1$ skepticism is contradicted by *some* explanation set that satisfies clause (3) of F3.221. I say this, because after reading Chapter 10, it is relatively easy for someone to construct by himself simple and testable explanation sets that explain certain of his own foundational sets, that are not generally rejected by experts, that contain no irrelevant clauses, and that have explanatory systems which are purely universal and purely experiential, are believed by him, and have consequences that if acceptable, contradict some species of moderate$_1$ skepticism. In such a situation, I maintain that it would be relatively easy for a person who has read Chapter 10 to see that the explanation set satisfies clause (3) of F3.221 and, with F3.221, has consequences that contradict moderate$_1$ skepticism. So, I would argue, the complexity encumbering the discussion in Chapter 10 prepares the way for a relatively easy grasping of the general existential claim that is sufficient for the truth of premise XIV of the master argument. And, if I am correct in this, then the admitted difficulty of Chapter 10 does not imply that I have exceeded the restrictions I placed upon myself. Indeed, we might look at the great complexity of what has preceded the present discussion as like the training of someone in a certain skill where the result is a developed ability to do certain tasks easily which otherwise would be difficult or even impossible.

It might be replied at this point that although philosophers already well-trained in related activities might well be able to assimilate the 'advanced training' in the earlier parts of this book, but surely very few others would succeed. And, although this may be enough to keep me from violating my own limits in justifying premise XIV, it surely shows that the minimal explanatory foundational theory does not provide bases for human decisions, as the master argument requires. Such bases must be usable by the many human beings who have not developed the necessary philosophical skills, according to this objection, and we have just seen that the theory is much too complex for such use. This is indeed a serious objection, but once again it is aimed at my justification of the explanatory foundational theory. In this case, however, this is not the appropriate place to pursue it, because it is aimed at premise X which states that the theory does provide bases for human decisions. Let me postpone my reply, then, until we discuss premise X.

One Last Objection to F3.22: *Green Versus Grue Emeralds.* I have been able to find only one additional objection that is aimed at the minimal explanatory foundational theory rather than at my use of it. This last objection is that no theory of justification that is otherwise reasonable solves Goodman's 'new riddle' of induction, and so none of them, including F3.22, is plausible. I argued that this is mistaken, because the explanatory foundational theory provides a solution like Goodman's, but avoids Zabludowski's crushing objection to that solution. The point is that any explanation set that includes in its system 'All emeralds are grue', or Zabludowski's more baroque concoction, contains something that would be generally rejected by experts. Thus no such set is maximal for someone and none prohibits another explanation set from being acceptable, even when their systems conflict.

I have just reviewed all the most plausible objections to the minimal explanatory foundational theory and summarized the reasons I used to reject each one of them. Because of this, we can surely conclude that it is reasonable for us now to believe that there are no objections to the explanatory foundational theory. That is, we have justified premise XI of the master argument. It might be thought, however, that this conclusion is premature, because I have not yet shown that it is not reasonable for us to believe any form of moderate$_1$ skepticism, and that is, in itself, an objection to any theory of justification. I have two replies to this remark. The first is that although a theory of justification is reasonable only if a skeptical thesis that conflicts with it is not reasonable, it is false that the reasonableness of such a theory requires that someone show that the skeptical thesis is not reasonable. At most, this last claim must be true, if someone is to establish the reasonableness of the theory of justification. But an objection to my establishing the reasonableness of a theory is not an objection to the reasonableness of the theory. My second reply is that, with premise XI justified, we are now in position to show that it is not reasonable to accept any form of moderate$_1$ skepticism. This is because we can now justify premise II of the master argument, which we shall now consider.

PREMISE II AND THE REJECTION OF SKEPTICAL ARGUMENTS

Premise II of the master argument states it is reasonable today for human beings to believe that the most plausible attempts to justify the versions of moderate$_1$ skepticism, M_1S_1 through M_1S_3, fail. One crucial task for justifying premise II is the uncovering of the most plausible skeptical arguments. My strategy for this was to begin with arguments offered by particular philosophers. Then, after refuting those, to construct arguments based on a careful understanding of what drove such philosophers to skepticism and arguments for it, until, after repeatedly refining my first attempts, I arrive at the strongest skeptical argument I am capable of formulating. Finally, if I am able to show that this last argument contains a premise that is not reasonable for us to accept, then I claim that we have reason to believe that the most plausible attempts fail.

In Chapter 2 where I began my search, I noted that most skeptical arguments are aimed to support skepticism about knowledge rather than justification, and often, as do Lehrer and Unger, they rely on extremely strong requirements for knowledge. Unger, however, also argues against the reasonableness of empirical statements, as did Oakley. But we found reason to reject Unger's claim that something is reasonable for someone only if he knows something, and Oakley failed because his argument against the adequacy of foundational theories, depends on factors that are irrelevant to the explanatory foundational theory. At this point, I was left to my own creations, and so I began my quest for the strongest argument I could devise by relying on two theses that are widely accepted and often believed to 'lead to' skepticism. One is the 'Lewisean' principle, L4, that an empirical sentence is inferentially acceptable, only if it is probable relative to evidence that includes something certain. The other is, in effect, that no empirical sentences are epistemically certain. The resulting argument was skeptical argument I, which, through a series of revisions, led me to my final attempt, argument V.

I rejected argument I, because by the extended reasoning of Chapter 2, I concluded that principle H3, which provides a sufficient condition for the certainty of basic-reports, is not unreasonable, because it avoids all the objections I could find to test it. I further claimed it to be reasonable that some basic-reports sometimes satisfy H3 for some people. Consequently, it is not unreasonable to claim that some basic-reports are certain for some of us. Because of this, a premise of argument I is not reasonable, and so this skeptical argument fails to justify its conclusion. Unfortunately, this defect was easily corrected in argument II, which retreats from the overly strong claim of I by allowing some basic-reports, but no other empirical sentences, to be initially certain. Then, while relying on the Cartesian principle, L3, that permits inferential acceptability only for sentences that are probable relative to evidence that is certain, argument II states that no other empirical sentences are certain relative only to basic-reports. The conclusion is that only basic-reports are sometimes certain for us. My discussion of this argument, which centered on principles L3 and L4, occupied Chapter 3, where I argued for the conclusion that inferential acceptability does not require certainty. Thus, a premise of argument II was found not to be reasonable, and so this second skeptical argument was discarded with the first.

One effect of the rejection of L3 and L4 was to free foundational theories from the need to put certainty at epistemic foundations. This required a change in strategy in formulating skeptical arguments, and led to argument III, which assumed no requirement of certainty. According to this argument, only basic-reports are initially acceptable, but no nonbasic sentences are probable relative to any set of basic-reports. Consequently, with the aid of a basic foundational principle, FP2, it follows that no nonbasic statements are ever acceptable, and moderate$_1$ skeptical thesis M_1S_1 is justified. My attack on this argument involved one of the two most important discussions of this book, because it is my attempt to show it is not unreasonable to claim that some nonbasic statements – in particular, observation-reports – are probable relative to a set of basic-reports. Success in this endeavor would not only show that a premise of argument III is not reasonable, but it would also provide the first extension of acceptability beyond a very restricted and frustratingly restricting foundation of basic-reports.

Argument III resisted refutation until Chapter 5, where I proposed and defended principle BR3. I began my attack with the assumption that observation-reports had the best chance of being probable relative to a set of basic-reports. Next, I tried to find a set of principles that would yield that probability, but faced no debilitating objections. In Chapter 4, I tried theories that allowed only deduction alone, then those that added enumerative or hypothetical induction, and, finally, Chisholm's critical cognitivism with its nondeductive and noninductive epistemic rules. Unhappily, none of these provided the extension of acceptability I sought and also survived close scrutiny. Nevertheless, a suggestion by Heidelberger about how Chisholm might avoid the critical objection to his theory led, in Chapter 5, to the interpretation of 'p is probable relative to e' as '$\Pr(p/e) > 0.5$', and to BR3 which states a sufficient condition for when that relative probability statement is true, for p as an observation-report and e a particular set of basic-reports. I reasoned that BR3 escapes objections, and that it is plausible to claim that some observation-reports sometimes satisfy BR3. So, at last, I was able to justify rejecting skeptical argument III, because it is not unreasonable to think that some observation-reports are probable relative to sets of basic-reports.

At this point, a second retreat was forced on those seeking to justify some form of moderate$_1$ skepticism. Because of observation-reports and BR3, thesis M_1S_1 was abandoned for M_1S_2 which granted inferential acceptability to observation-reports, but to nothing else nonbasic. This led to skeptical argument IV that primarily differed from III by stating that nothing that is both nonbasic and not an observation-report is probable relative to a set of basic-reports and observation-reports. My response to this reasoning was to propose and defend BR4 which closely resembled BR3, except that it provides a sufficient condition for when a memory-report about one's own recent 'subjective' experience is probable, given a set of basic-reports. I also argued that it is reasonable that some of these basic memory-reports satisfy BR4, and so, contrary to argument IV, some nonbasic sentences that are not observation-reports are probable, given only basic-reports.

At the end of Chapter 5, I suggested a third retrenchment for those arguing for moderate$_1$ skepticism. This time both observation-reports and basic memory-reports are allowed to be inferentially acceptable, but nothing else nonbasic is. The result is skeptical thesis M_1S_3. I then argued that any significant retreat from thesis M_1S_3 would signal the abandonment of moderate skepticism. So M_1S_3 represents the weakest moderate$_1$ skeptical thesis, and I claimed, when argument IV is revised to accommodate this change to M_1S_3, what results – argument V – is the strongest skeptical argument I have been able to find. Consequently, if after my extensive examination of this whole series of arguments, and my careful attempt to arrive at the strongest argument available, I am able to refute argument V, then it will be reasonable, at last, to claim that the most plausible arguments for the three moderate$_1$ skeptical theses fail. That is, premise II of the master argument will be justified.

As noted at the end of Chapter 5, the two crucial premises for argument V are the basic foundational principle, FP2, and the statement that only sentences entailed by a set of basic-reports, observation-reports, and basic memory-reports are probable, given a set of those three sorts of sentences. The only way to avoid FP2 is to reject foundationalism for nonfoundationalism, but, as I shall review when examining premise IX, that move does not result in a viable theory of justification. However, as shown in Chapter 10, the minimum explanatory foundational theory extends acceptability to explanation sets with their nonreductively universal systems and to what is derivable from them. And, as just reviewed, this theory does this without facing any objections. It is, therefore not unreasonable for us to adopt this theory and its consequences, for the acceptability of many sentences not entailed by any set of basic-reports, observation-reports, and basic memory-reports is probable, given a set containing only such reports. Thus, like its predecessors, argument V contains a premise that it is not unreasonable to reject, and so V also fails to justify its conclusion. And, because V is the most plausible argument for a form of moderate$_1$ skepticism that my painstaking search has uncovered, it is now reasonable for us to conclude that premise II of the master argument is true: 'It is reasonable today for human beings to believe that the most plausible attempts to justify each skeptical thesis, M_1S_1 through M_1S_3, fail'.

A last pair of premises from the master argument remains to be examined: IX and X. Let us turn to X, which states that the minimal explanatory foundational theory provides bases for human decisions. I have already noted one objection to this premise to the effect that F3.221 is too complicated for any human beings, except perhaps for a few philosophers, to use to help decide what they ought to do. That shows that the theory does not provide bases for human decisions. The only other objection I have found to premise X is that F3.22 is critically incomplete, and thus in many important cases provides no way to help determine what to do. No such theory of justification provides bases for human decisions.

Both of these objections fail because they misinterpret what it is for a theory of justification to provide bases for human decisions. As stated, the first objection rests on the premise that a theory provides bases for human decisions only if the theory, itself, is readily usable by human beings with no special abilities or training. It is clear this claim is false, because there are many specific areas, such as medicine and law, where what is used to guide decisions requires both special abilities and special training. The reply to this, of course, is to amend the falsified premise to say that a theory of justification provides bases for human decisions only if the theory itself is readily usable by someone with no special skills in epistemology. This consequent is also false for principle F3.221. But that causes no problem for F3.221, because this new premise is also mistaken. Consider the simplifying assumptions I made in Chapter 10 which allowed us to use the much simpler CA instead of F3.221. Because such simplifying assumptions are justifiable, it is false that a theory of justification *itself* must be readily usable by the epistemically unskilled if it is to provide bases for decisions.

It is easy to see what the next move will be. As already amply acknowledged, the task that CA imposes on someone is still much too complex to be readily usable by the unskilled. The discussion in Chapter 10 demonstrated that. So nothing said so far falsifies the newly amended premise that a theory of justification provides bases for human decisions only if what results from the theory once all justifiable simplifying assumptions are made is readily usable by someone who is epistemically unskilled. This third premise also yields that F3.221 does not provide bases for human decisions because of the complexity of CA.

I find the last premise to be false also, but in this case the reason is a bit more subtle. My reason for this is similar to part of John Stuart Mill's response to the criticism of the principle of utility that "there is not time, previous to action, for calculating and weighing the effects of any line of conduct on the general happiness". Mill replied,

It is a strange notion that the acknowledgment of a first principle is inconsistent with the admission of secondary ones. To inform a traveler respecting the place of his ultimate destination, is not to forbid the use of landmarks and direction-posts on the way. . . . Whatever we adopt as the fundamental principle of morality, we require subordinate principles to apply it by; the impossibility of doing without them, being common to all systems, can afford no argument against any one in particular; . . . [1]

In short, the application of the principle of utility itself requires calculations that are too complicated and time-consuming to be readily usable whenever moral decisions are to be made. Consequently, it is incumbent upon human beings to devise a wide range of 'rules of thumb', each of which covers a group of situations whose morally relevant factors quite generally dictate, with the principle of utility, the same sort of action. It is these subsidiary guiding principles which are readily applicable by either people unskilled in the calculations required for a direct application of the fundamental principle, or by those who have no time for such calculations. In these cases, the principle of utility does not provide bases for human decisions by being readily applicable itself, or after simplifying assumptions are made. Rather, it provides such bases by directing the formulation and giving the justification of these subsidiary guiding principles, which, in turn, are easy for most human beings to apply.

The explanatory foundational theory of justification provides bases for human decisions in a very similar way. Subsidiary rules of thumb about what sorts of explanations are best for most of us in similar situations that call for explanations can be devised and readily used by most of us. Both the formulation and justification of these guiding rules would be based on a careful examination of the sorts of explanation sets that actually satisfy clause (3) of F3.221 in the sort of situation covered by each rule. A very simple example of such a rule might be that it is generally true that the best explanation – in the strict sense of clause (3) – of someone's perceiving another person's writhing and screaming is that the second person is in pain, and this causes him to writhe and scream. When these rules of thumb are justified as reliable approximations by means of the 'fundamental' principle, F3.221, and they are correctly applied by someone when he attempts to explain something specific, then that person's explanation is acceptable for him at that time. In providing this justification of readily and easily usable rules, the explanatory foundational theory provides bases for human decisions.

The second objection to premise X results from a different confusion about what it is for a theory to provide bases for human decisions. The objection succeeds only if this requires that the theory provide a *complete* epistemic basis in the sense that it provides all the epistemic means for determining the reasonableness of those empirical statements that human beings need, in difficult cases, to justify which decision is morally correct. It is clear that F3.22 does not provide such a complete basis, and it might be worth noting five reasons why this is true. First, there are many cases where no basic-report satisfies the antecedent of H3 for someone, perhaps because the person is not fully convinced about any basic-report. In some of these cases, some basic-reports would seem to be acceptable, perhaps even certain, for him, yet F3.22 provides no way to determine when this is true. A similar incompleteness exists for observation-reports and basic memory-reports when a person does not fully believe all the basic-reports in the relevant evidence set. Quite often, some of these are acceptable for the person, but F3.22 remains mute about that. A third sort of case not covered by F3.22 arises when someone's foundational set, F, contains basic-reports, observation-reports, and, perhaps basic memory-reports, where each is acceptable, but their conjunction is not. Then F does not satisfy clause (3) of F3.221, and so it yields nothing about the acceptability of an explanation set. But some acceptable subset of F may deserve explanation, and its best explanation should therefore be acceptable. There is another way that F3.221 fails to assign acceptability to explanation sets, when some might well deserve it. This is when no set meets all the conditions of clause (3), such as when a person chooses more than one explanation or when some conflicting set is slightly more economical or has greater scope. It is plausible that some sets with these 'deficiencies' would sometimes be acceptable.

The fifth gap in F3.22 is somewhat different from the first four. It concerns the problem of the status of sentences found acceptable or certain in the past with respect to the set of sentences found acceptable or certain at the present time. There are basically two issues to be decided: under what conditions they attain acceptability or certainty now, and when, in addition, they should be included in what is acceptable to use as evidence. Being a theory of justification, rather than a theory of evidence, not even the complete explanatory foundational theory need settle the second issue. But, of course, it must be settled if a full basis for human decisions is to be provided. Nevertheless the theory must address the first issue, about which it is clear the minimum theory says nothing. And, although it would go well beyond the scope of this book to deal with this adequately, let me just briefly indicate the sort of approach that I find most congenial to the minimal theory.

It is often thought that once a statement is ensconced in someone's evidence set it remains there, and any later, new applicant for acceptability must appropriately accord with the old. However, the explanatory foundational theory gives epistemic priority to the present by assigning certainty or acceptability now to given-reports and observation-reports about the present. So the old must conform to the new, if it is to retain its status of acceptability or certainty. In line with this, the complete theory might include a principle like:

PP1. If (1) at t, s understands the observation-report, $p =$ 'I am now perceiving something that is F', and believes with certainty that p was true of him a short time ago, (2) it is certain, for s at t, that he is remembering that, a short time ago, he had an experience of someting that is F, and (3) the acceptability, for s at t, that p was true of him a short time ago is inductively consistent with the probabilities of the reports in s's foundational set at t, *then* it is acceptable for s at t that, a short time ago, he perceived something that was F.

Of course, PP1 also needs to be supplemented, at least regarding when statements 'from the past' are to be explained, and when they can be incorporated into present evidence. The first extension, of course, must be included in the complete theory of justification, but the second belongs to a theory of evidence.

It cannot be doubted that the minimal theory is incomplete, but, contrary to the objection before us, that does not show the theory provides no bases for human decisions. It can be seen from the examples in Chapter 10, and from the many that readers can construct for themselves, that the minimal theory provides some – indeed, quite a few – bases for human decisions. That is all premise X requires. It is clear that there is a wide variety of cases where the minimal theory provides epistemic means for determining the reasonableness of a wide variety of empirical sentences. A good number of these are epistemically relevant to difficult human decisions, such as when a doctor must decide what to do on the basis of the best explanation of certain symptoms he is observing, or a teacher must decide whether to report a student for cheating, based on the best explanation of what he observes in reading his examination. We can, then, reject this second and last objection to premise X. The minimal theory does, indeed, provide bases for human decisions, even though it clearly does not provide a full basis for them.

It might be objected at this point that it surely would be much better to have a theory that encompasses a significantly wider variety of cases than the minimal theory does, and so we are hardly justified in accepting it on the grounds that it provides *some* bases for human decisions. I agree that, all else relevant being equal, a more comprehensive theory is to be preferred. This point is not relevant to premise X, however, because it concerns matters pertaining to the comparative reasonableness of the minimal theory. It should, therefore, be used to launch an objection to premise IX, which concerns such reasonableness. I shall consider it next when evaluating IX, the only premise that remains to be justified.

PREMISE IX: THE MINIMAL THEORY VERSUS ITS MAIN COMPETITORS

We can justify premise IX, if we can show that no theory of empirical justification that provides bases for human decisions is more reasonable for us than the minimal explanatory foundational theory, and that any that is as reasonable as the minimal theory is consistent with appreciably fewer pretheoretical, commonly and firmly accepted beliefs of mankind than the minimal theory is. Luckily, for our purposes, almost every theory of justification I have found is clearly less reasonable than the minimal theory, because of serious, vitiating objections. Thus all of these can be discarded without invoking what human beings commonly believe. Indeed, as I shall review, the results of Chapter 6 show us to be justified in preferring the minimal theory to any kind of nonfoundational theory; and the examination of 'traditional' foundational theories in Part I established all of them to be inferior to the minimal theory. Because of this, the major part of the present task will be to try to uncover some yet unexamined foundational theory that avoids objections or perhaps some procedure for making decisions that eschews claims about justification and acceptability, but is, nevertheless, at least as reasonable as the minimal theory.

The Minimal Theory Versus Nonfoundational Theories

In Chapter 6, I tried to render a precise delineation of the three main varieties of nonfoundational theories of empirical justification. I did this in terms of evidential series (E-series) that supposedly justify a sentence, p, for a person, s, at a time, t. What makes all three nonfoundational is that they require there to be a justifying E-series for p that contains no empirical sentence that is initially acceptable for s at t. They differ regarding what they allow in this justifying E-series. In brief, one variety, N1, allows only acceptable statements in this E-series, and requires each empirical sentence, q, in the E-series to have an evidential ancestor (E-ancestor) in the series that is not definitionally equivalent to q. This sort of theory necessitates infinitely long E-series. The second, N2, differs from type N1 only by allowing sentences in a justifying E-series to be their own

E-ancestors. Thus N2 permits circular justification. The last variety, N3, avoids both infinite series and circular justification by allowing some members of an E-series that justifies p not to be acceptable themselves. Thus N3 allows 'blind posits' in justifying E-series.

I argued for the rejection of all theories of type N3 on the grounds that if a set e_i in an E-series for p contains q, which is not acceptable for s at t_0 then there is a sentence in e_{i-1}, and indeed in each e_j, for $j < i$, that is not acceptable. Consequently, e_2, which supposedly justifies p, contains a sentence that is not acceptable, and so p is not justified by e_1 or, as a result, by that E-series. My objections to types N1 and N2 were less decisive, however; they were basically challenged to find some way to avoid their common, most serious objection, that is, that any theory of either type allows sentences arbitrarily chosen from some large group to be acceptable. For example, a theory of justification that allows any arbitrarily chosen observation-report to be justified for s at t should be rejected. In Chapter 6, I gave an example of an infinitely long E-series that could be used for any sentence whatsoever, that satisfies all that N1 requires, and in which every sentence is justified relative to the set that immediately follows it in the series. The challenge, which I offer once again to defenders of N1-type theories, is to provide additional constraints on infinite E-series that allow such theories to avoid the charge of arbitrariness without restricting justification so much that it results in a wide-ranging skepticism. Until that challange is met, it is clear that the minimal theory is more reasonable than any nonfoundational theory of type N1.

In Chapter 6, I also launched the charge of arbitrariness against theories of type N2 with their circular justification. In this case, however, I noted a way the most plausible theory of this sort – the explanatory coherence theory – could avoid the charge. When I proposed hypothesis EF, in Chapter 7, as the foundational thesis of the minimal theory, I remarked that EF assigns no epistemic status to what is foundational. It merely states that what satisfies it is *explanatorily* foundational, that is, given certain restrictions, it is what is to be explained. Because of this, the explanatory coherence theory can adopt EF, and thereby would seem to avoid being arbitrary in just the same way that F3.22 does. It might be urged, then, that these two theories are equally reasonable, and also are in accord with the same common beliefs because they have the same consequences for acceptability.

There are, however, three important differences between the explanatory coherence theory with EF, and principle F3.22, and they strongly favor the latter. The first two were noted previously. One, which is the least important of the three, is that the explanatory coherence theory seems to have no answer to the question of why sentences that satisfy H3, or BR3 or BR4, for appropriate evidence, are to be explained. The explanatory foundational theory answers this question by stating that these reports are acceptable for s at t independently of being explained, and thereby constitute the data that are to be explained. But if these reports are not acceptable if not explained, as this coherence theory requires, it is difficult to see why they, rather than some other sentences, should be explained. The second difference, which is the most damaging to the coherence theory, is that it, but not F3.22, withholds acceptability from the basic-reports, observation-reports, and basic memory-reports in foundational set F if no explanation of the members of F is the best for s at t. Yet it is often true that no one explanation will be singled out as the best. Indeed, a person might well have no explanation available. It is surely implausible in such a situation, and clearly contrary to what is commonly believed, that none of these reports is acceptable for this person at this time.

The third difference between the two theories that favors the minimal theory is that it provides a plausible restriction on when the members of F are to be explained. That is, in clause (3) of F3.221 it requires that their conjunction be acceptable. This enables this theory to avoid the lottery paradox. A similar restriction occurs in clause (5). The explanatory coherence theory, however, cannot rely on requiring the independent acceptability of this conjunction, and so must devise some other sort of requirement. But it is far from clear how this is to be done. Once again, a difference favors F3.22. Consequently, because these three differences favor F3.22, and there is no other difference that favors the explanatory coherence theory, which I have argued is the most plausible theory of type N2, we can conclude that the minimal explanatory foundational theory is more reasonable than any nonfoundational theory.

The Minimal Theory Versus Other Foundational Theories

By the end of Chapter 5, it had become quite clear that four of the most common kinds of foundational theories are inferior to the minimal explanatory foundational theory. Each theory of these four kinds takes basic-reports, with analytic sentences, as the foundation of justification. The crucial differences are the means each kind of theory allows for extending acceptability beyond this narrow base. The first kind, which is primarily Cartesian, allows only deductive inferences from the base; the second or Lewisean kind also allows enumerative and analogical induction; the third adds hypothetical induction; and the fourth increases all this by introducing Chisholmian epistemic rules. I argued in Chapter 4 that even if we were to grant that deduction and all analogical or enumerative inductive inferences are justified, none of them provides any extension of acceptability. Thus, all of them fail to provide bases for any decisions that require the acceptability of some nonbasic sentences. It is clear, then, that F3.22 is superior to theories of these two kinds, because it does extend acceptability well beyond the foundation, as so often is required for our decisions. Furthermore, even if a theory of one of these kinds were to be as reasonable as F3.22, except for the extent of agreement with commonly accepted beliefs, it is clear that F3.22 would agree with appreciably more of these, just because of its extension of acceptability beyond the base.

In Chapter 4, I also found the other two sorts of foundational theories to be deficient, but the reasons were quite different. I argued that hypothetical induction does not provide a way to infer the nonbasic from what is merely basic. In each case that form of inference requires a premise to the effect that a particular hypothesis is the best explanation of what is to be explained for a person, s, at a time, t, and this premise is not to be established by evidence taken solely from the foundation. Chisholm's epistemic rules, however, were originally designed to warrant inferences from the nonbasic to the basic, although it is far from clear that Chisholm's later amended versions still succeed in this. Nevertheless, even if they do, I found counterexamples to all the amended versions I could devise, and this, I argued, makes it reasonable that all Chisholmian epistemic rules fall before counterexamples. It was because of this problem that I designed and proposed BR3 and BR4. These principles construe 'p is probable relative to q' as a relative probability sentence – '$Pr(q/p) > 0.5$' – rather than as 'If q, then p is probable', which closely resembles Chisholm's rule. Because of this, I maintained, F3.22, which incorporates BR3 and BR4, avoids the counterexamples to Chisholm's theory, and the uselessness of hypothetical induction for inferences from the basic to the nonbasic. Once again, then, F3.22 proves to be superior.

With the four preceding sorts of foundational theories rejected for F3.22, the next question is whether there is likely to be some unexamined sort of foundational theory that is a stronger competitor for F3.22 than those four. I have been able to locate only five more types, the first four of which differ from the preceding four only by being more liberal about what is basic. A good example of such theories is one that takes whatever F3.22 allows in set F to be basic. Even though I argued against this extension in Chapter 5, I am willing to grant it here in order to see whether it helps appreciably. Each of these second four theories, then, allows basic-reports, observation-reports, and basic memory-reports at the foundation. They differ, as did the first four, according to the kinds of inferences they allow. It is clear, however, by arguments that parallel those I used in Chapter 4, that neither deduction nor that plus enumerative and analogical induction extend acceptability beyond this broader base. But, as Chapter 10 illustrates, F3.22 clearly extends acceptability well beyond set F. So F3.22 remains undaunted.

The new third sort relies on hypothetical induction to extend acceptability beyond F, and so it is very similar to F3.22. Nevertheless, unlike F, this new theory requires that inferences from the basic to the nonbasic be inferences to the best explanation, and that requires a premise to the effect that some explanation satisfy something like that complex set of conditions in clause (3) of F3.22. But it seems quite clear that this premise is neither a basic-sentence found in F, nor is justified by evidence that comes from F. Once again, F3.22 triumphs.

The last new type proposes Chisholmian epistemic rules to warrant inferences from sentences in F to nonbasic sentences, such as those about physical objects that are not now perceived. However, given Chisholm-like restrictions on the antecedents of these rules, I see no prospects of these succeeding when Chisholm's actual attempts have failed. The new sort of rule would be limited in its antecedent to eternalized versions of basic-reports, observation-reports, and basic memory-reports, plus, presumably, an epistemic conjunct like one in Chisholm's amendments of his rule B. The consequent, for unperceived physical objects, would be something like 'it is reasonable, for s at t, that there is an object that s is not perceiving at t'. The opportunities for counterexamples created by someone like our obstinate old friend seem quite extensive. I see no threat to F3.22 from this quarter.

There is one last foundational theory that we should examine. This is the theory of John Pollock that resembles Chisholm's theory in certain respects, but differs from it in two important ways. According to Pollock, previous theories of justification have failed to refute skepticism because they require that foundational or basic evidence provide what he calls 'conclusive' reasons for what is nonbasic, rather than merely *prima facie* reasons. Once these are understood to be *prima facie*, skepticism can be refuted and foundationalsim vindicated. The crucial difference between these two sorts of reasons is that if p is a conclusive reason for q, then p entails q, but if p is a *prima facie* reason for q, then some r is a 'defeater' of p as a reason for q. That is although p is a 'logical' reason for q, $(r \cdot q)$ is not.

Why is this change supposed to allow success where past theories have failed? After all, Chisholm's amended versions of B surely allow that basic evidence can be defeated, yet those rules fail. Indeed, unfortunately, that very same irrationally obstinate person with his conveniently poor memory who played havoc with Chisholm's rules, does the same with Pollock's theory. To see why this is so, let us consider Pollock's principle (3.5), which can be used to make inferences from something basic to what is nonbasic.[2] Let $P = $ 'Something looks yellow to me', and $Q = $ 'Something is yellow'. Pollock agrees that P is a *prima facie* reason for s to believe that Q. Given this, we can derive from (3.5) the following:

(3.51) If s justifiably believes-that-P, and believes-that-Q on the basis of his belief-that-P, and s does not believe any defeaters for P as a reason for him to believe-that-Q (that is, s does not believe any R, such that $(R \cdot Q)$ is not a logical reason for Q), then s is justified in believing-that-Q.

The preceding conditional differs from Chisholm's various versions of his rule B in two relevant ways. The first, helpful difference is that (3.51) and (3.5) are not attempts to provide a rule with an antecedent limited to basic-reports and analytic sentences. This is clear from Pollock's discussion of what it is for someone to base a belief that Q on a belief that P. This requires that his believing that P is causally responsible for his believing that Q. In this respect, Pollock's (3.5) is closer to F3.22 than to what Chisholm requires. The second difference, however, is of no help in avoiding the problem facing Chisholm. Where Chisholm amended the antecedent of his original B to require, in effect, that nothing with a particular epistemic status overrides or defeats the justification of Q by the relevant belief-sentence, Pollock requires that the person base his belief that Q on his belief that P, and that he believe nothing that defeats P's justification of Q. But it is just this lack of belief in defeaters that characterizes our obstinate friend who forgets so easily. So since he clearly is justified in believing that P, and we can easily elaborate the story to include his basing his belief that Q on his belief that P, principle (3.51), and so (3.5), yield the false conclusion that this person is justified in believing that something is yellow. Thus Pollock's theory fails because of flaws very much like those that defeat Chisholm's critical cognitivism. I conclude, then, that the minimal explanatory foundational theory is superior to Pollock's.

I have canvassed what, after careful investigation, I have found to be the major foundational and nonfoundational theories of empirical justification, and have concluded that the minimal foundational view is more reasonable than all the others. Consequently, unless I have overlooked some plausible kind of theory, we can further conclude that, as of today's date, it is more reasonable for us to adopt the minimal theory to provide bases for human decisions than to adopt any other theory of empirical justification for that purpose. That is, premise IX of the master argument is justified. It might be objected, however, that this conclusion is premature, because even granting that I have established the superiority of F3.22 over all foundational and nonfoundational theories, I have not examined any theories that fit neither category. One example of this is a 'mixed' theory that requires foundational justification for some empirical sentences, and a nonfoundational justification for others. Nevertheless, I see no reason to expect success for such a 'mixed' theory regarding the sentences that are to receive nonfoundational justification when, as I have argued, all 'pure' nonfoundational theories fail.

It might also be objected that I should examine another sort of theory that is neither foundational nor nonfoundational before I conclude the premise IX is justified. We might call these 'lottery' theories, because they instruct each person to choose which of a group of empirical sentences is acceptable by random choice. One such theory would require that for each difficult decision a person must make, he is to conceive of as many empirical sentences as he can that form different bases for the decision. Then he is to assign each of these sentences a number, pick one of the numbers randomly, assign the corresponding sentence acceptability, and decide what to do on the basis of that sentence. This 'lottery' theory has a clear advantage over F3.22 in providing results in every situation requiring a decision.

The preceding objection to my conclusion is wrong about one point. "Lottery" theories are clearly foundational, because, by definition D2, every acceptable empirical sentence is initially acceptable. Furthermore, it is interesting that those, like the previous example, imply nothing inconsistent with their being nonfoundational. This is because they imply nothing about how, if there were inferentially acceptable sentences, they would be justified. This seems to make these theories unique. Nevertheless, they are far from unique in begin quite implausible, as an example will show. Consider a juror who uses a lottery theory to determine how he ought to vote in a murder trial. Assume that the judge gives him but three alternatives: (1) innocent, (2) manslaughter, and (3) murder, and that he randomly chooses the number 3. This surely does not make it acceptable for the juror to say that the defendant committed murder and so does not justify his voting for that verdict. So 'lottery' theories should be rejected.

It would clearly be much more reasonable for the juror to try to arrive at the best explanation of the evidence presented to him during the trial. If no explanation that implies guilt clearly stands out as the best, then, by relying on the principle of reasonable doubt, he should vote that the defendant is innocent. Otherwise, he should decide between manslaughter and murder. It is this clearly preferable procedure that the explanatory foundational theory suggests. Of course, the minimal theory does not have the resources needed for this juror to use it to reach a conclusion about what is acceptable for him. He would need some way to assign acceptability now, when he is deliberating, to some of what he now believes are his past perceptions of exhibits and testimony during the preceding trial. I believe, however, that the addition of principle PP1 to F3.22 would go a long way toward providing what he requires to make acceptable for him now particular sentences about his past perceptions. It would then be his task to seek the best explanation of these sentences, and base his vote on what he discovers. The prospects of there being such plausible extensions and uses of F3.22, I would argue, clearly add to the reasonableness of the minimal theory.

With the demise of these last two types of theories of empirical justification – the 'mixed' theories and the 'lottery' theories – I find that there is no reason to object further to our concluding that premise IX is justified. Now, today, we have ample reason to prefer the minimal explanatory foundational theory for the purpose of providing bases for human decisions over any other theory, whether it be foundational, nonfoundational, unmixed. I have previously argued in this chapter that we are also justified in accepting the other three premises of the master argument that had not yet been justified – premises II, X, and XI. With all four of them now justified, and with the other none previously justified, we can at last conclude that the master argument, including its extension regarding skepticism about induction, justifies for us today, all its conclusions, whether intermediary or final. The three most important of these conclusions are XIII ('It is reasonable today for human beings to adopt the minimal explanatory foundational theory of empirical justification'); the final conclusion of the master argument, XVI ('It is unreasonable today for any human being to believe any form of moderate$_1$ skepticism about physical objects, the past, the future, and other minds'); and the conclusion of the extension of the argument, XIX ('Skepticism about induction is false').

We have finished the central task of this book which was to refute weak$_2$-moderate$_1$ skepticism. We have done this by showing that, contrary to that skeptical thesis, it is reasonable for us now to reject moderate$_1$ skepticism, that it is reasonable for us to reject the view that it is never reasonable for human beings to believe any claim entailing there are particular unperceived physical objects, past events, future events, or mental phenomena of others. The long, tortuous route to this conclusion forced us to justify a particular theory of empirical justification, and enabled us to refute skepticism about induction. These are three results whose importance, I believe, well outweighs the difficulty of completing the task. Yet, although we have finished this task and drawn the final conclusions of this book, none of the conclusions are final, because there are too many ways they may be overturned in the future. I propose, therefore, as I have always done, that we consider these conclusions to be tentative and provisional.

CONCLUDING REMARKS

I have insisted that the conclusions of this book are merely provisional. Let me finish by indicating some of my reasons for this.

NOTES

[1] J. S. Mill, *Utilitarianism*, New York: The Liberal Arts Press, 1953, pp. 24–26.
[2] John Pollock, *Knowledge and Justification*, Princeton, N.J.: Princeton University Press, 1974, p.44.

SKEPTICISM, JUSTIFICATION, AND EXPLANATION: A BIBLIOGRAPHIC ESSAY

This is a selective bibliography in which references are classified by topics. The topics are listed roughly in the order in which they are taken up in the text.

SKEPTICISM

Positions of Skepticism: A Historical Survey

Ontological Skepticism. Since the distinction between ontological and epistemological skepticism is generally conflated in the literature it is often difficult to isolate those authors who are genuine ontological skeptics. Probably the first serious ontological skeptic and nihilist was the sophist Gorgias who argued in his treatise 'On That Which Is Not, or On Nature', that nothing exists. There have been a number of ontological skeptics and nihilists regarding God's existence including Bertrand Russell in *Sceptical Essays* (New York: W.W. Norton, 1928) and *Why I Am Not a Christian* (New York: Simon and Schuster, 1957) and Albert Camus in *The Myth of Sisyphus* (New York: Random House, 1955). Although perhaps no one was ever a genuine ontological skeptic concerning the existence of other minds, a true solipsist, arguments for solipsism can be found in Johann Fichte, *The Vocation of Man* (Indianapolis: Bobbs-Merrill, 1956), chs. 5 and 6; and Russell, *Human Knowledge* (New York: Simon and Schuster, 1948), pt. 3, ch. 2. The most famous ontological skeptic regarding the existence of a nonmental external world is undoubtedly Bishop George Berkeley in *Three Dialogues Between Hylas and Philonous* and *A Treatise Concerning the Principles of Human Knowledge*. Other famous idealists include Hegel, *Phenomenology of Mind*; and F.H. Bradley, *Appearance and Reality* (London: Oxford University Press, 1930). Several versions of phenomenalism are discussed in detail in Cornman, *Perception, Common Sense, and Science* (New Haven, Conn.: Yale University Press, 1975), which contains numerous bibliographic references – see especially the appendix.

315

Epistemological Skepticism. Beginning with Socrates' assessment of his own wisdom as not thinking "that I know what I do not know", found in Plato, *Apologia* 21d, there have been a great many outright epistemological skeptics and philosophers who have advanced epistemological skeptical arguments. The most famous, and last, Pyrrhonian was Sextus Empiricus whose principle works were *Pyrrhoniarum Hypotyposes* and *Adversus Mathematicos.* Translations of these works are contained in *Sextus Empiricus* (Cambridge, Mass.: Harvard University Press, 1933). Erasmus appeared as a religious skeptic in a controversy with Luther in the sixteenth century. His views are expressed in *In Praise of Folly* and *De Libero Arbitrio.* Montaigne, in *Apologie de Raymond Sebond,* was another religious skeptic who argued that human powers alone were incapable of achieving true knowledge which could only be attained through faith. A major skeptic who greatly influenced Hume was Pierre Bayle, *Dictionnaire Historique et Critique.*

Secondary sources on skepticism in ancient philosophy include E.R. Bevan, *Stoics and Sceptics* (Oxford: Clarendon, 1913); Norman Maccoll, *The Greek Sceptics, from Pyrrho to Sextus* (London: Macmillan, 1869); and Eduard Zeller (Oswald J. Reichel, trans.), *The Stoics, Epicureans, and Sceptics* (New York: Russell and Russell, 1962).

David Hume as Skeptic. Hume's skeptical views are contained in David Hume (L.A. Selby-Bigge ed.), *A Treatise of Human Nature* (Oxford: Clarendon, 1888); *An Enquiry Concerning the Human Understanding . . .* (Oxford: Clarendon, 1894), and David Hume, *Dialogues Concerning Natural Religion* (Indianapolis: Bobbs-Merrill, 1947). Principal commentaries on these works include A.G.N. Flew, *Hume's Philosophy of Belief* (New York: Humanities Press, 1961); T.H. Green, *General Introduction to Hume's Treatise* (London: Oxford University Press, 1874); N. Kemp Smith, *The Philosophy of David Hume* (London: Macmillan, 1941); J.A. Passmore, *Hume's Intentions* (Cambridge: Cambridge University Press, 1950); and David C. Stove, *Probability and Hume's Inductive Scepticism* (Oxford: Clarendon, 1973).

Articles devoted to Hume's skepticism are legion but the following constitute some of more recent: W.L. Robison, 'Hume's Scepticism', *Dialogue* **12** (1973), 87–99; J.O. Nelson, 'Two Main Questions Concerning Hume's "Treatise" and "Enquiry" ', *Philosophical Review* **81** (1972), 333–360; J. Kekes, 'Beliefs and Scepticism', *Philosophical Forum* **1** (1969), 353–358; J.E. Adler, 'Stove on Hume's Inductive Scepticism', *Australasian Journal* *of Philosophy* **53** (1975), 167–170; and T.L. Beauchamp and T.A. Mappes, 'Is Hume Really a Sceptic About Induction', *American Philosophical Quarterly* **12** (1975), 119–129.

For an extensive treatment of skepticism in the modern period of the history of philosophy including Hume, see the following works by Richard H. Popkin: 'David Hume: His Pyrrhonism and His Critique of Pyrrhonism', *Philosophical Quarterly* **1** (1950–1951), 385–407; 'Berkeley and Pyrrhonism', *Review of Metaphysics* **5** (1951–1952), 223–246; 'David Hume and the Pyrrhonian Controversy', *Review of Metaphysics* **6** (1952–1953), 65–81; 'The Sceptical Crisis and the Rise of Modern Philosophy', *Review of Metaphysics* **7** (1953–1954), 132–151, 307–322, 499–510; 'The Skeptical Precursors of David Hume', *Philosophy and Phenomenological Research* **16** (1955), 61–71; *The History of Scepticism From Erasmus to Descartes* (New York: Humanities Press, 1964); and 'The High Road to Pyrrhonism', *American Philosophical Quarterly* **2** (1965), 1–15.

Contemporary Works on Skepticism

Skeptics. One of the growing list of philosophers who has seriously attempted to defend skepticism in the twentieth century is Peter Unger. His book *Ignorance: A Case for Scepticism* (Oxford: Clarendon, 1975) contains revised versions of the following papers; 'A Defense of Skepticism', *Philosophical Review* **80** (1971), 198–219; 'An Argument for Skepticism', *Philosophical Exchange* **1** (1974), 131–155; 'Propositional Verbs and Knowledge', *Journal of Philosophy* **69** (1972), 301–312; 'The Wages of Scepticism', *American Philosophical Quarterly* **10** (1973), 177–187; 'Two Types of Scepticism', *Philosophical Studies* **25** (1974), 77–98; and 'Truth', in M.K. Munitz and P. Unger (eds.), *Semantics and Philosophy* (New York: New York University Press, 1974). Various responses to Unger's position are listed in the next section.

Another serious argument for epistemological skepticism is in K. Lehrer, 'Why Not Skepticism', *The Philosophical Forum* **23** (1971), 283–298. See also, Lehrer, 'Skepticism and Conceptual Change' in R. Chisholm and R.J. Swartz (eds.), *Empirical Knowledge* (Englewood Cliffs, N.J.: Prentice-Hall, 1973). See also I.T. Oakley, 'An Argument for Scepticism Concerning Justified Beliefs', *American Philosophical Quarterly* **13** (1976), 221–228.

Critics of Skepticism. G.E. Moore vigorously attacked skepticism after the turn of the century. His antiskeptical papers are included in these collections of his essays: *Some Main Problems of Philosophy* (London: George Allen and Unwin, 1953), *Philosophical Studies* (London: Routledge and Kegan Paul, 1922), and *Philosophical Papers* (New York: Humanities Press, 1959). Moore's position was strongly criticized by Wittgenstein although he remained a staunch antiskeptic himself. Most of Wittgenstein's criticisms are collected in G.E.M. Anscombe and G.H. von Wright (eds.) (D. Paul and G.E.M. Anscombe, trans.), *On Certainty* (Oxford: Blackwell, 1969). The following are relatively recent articles which are generally critical towards skepticism: P. Olscamp, 'Wittgenstein's Refutation of Skepticism', *Philosophy and Phenomenological Research* **26** (1965–1966), 239–247; J. Wolfe, 'Dreaming and Skepticism', *Mind* **80** (1971), 605–606; J. Agassi, 'The Standard Misinterpretation of Skepticism', *Philosophical Studies* **22** (1971), 49–50; J. Kekes, 'Skepticism and External Questions', *Philosophy and Phenomenological Research* **31** (1971), 325–340; R.L. Purtill, 'Some Varieties of Epistemological Skepticism', *Philosophia* **1** (1971), 107–116; R.L. Purtill, 'Epistemological Skepticism Again', *Philosophical Forum* **3** (1972), 138–144; T. Clarke, 'The Legacy of Skepticism', *Journal of Philosophy* **69** (1972), 745–769; G.W. Barnes, 'Unger's Defense of Skepticism', *Philosophical Studies* **24** (1973), 119–124; K. Nielson, 'On Refusing to Play the Skeptic's Game', *Dialogue* **11** (1972), 348–359; C.E. Marks, 'Verificationism, Scepticism, and the Private Language Argument', *Philosophical Studies* **28** (1975), 151–171; R. Almeder, 'Defeasibility and Scepticism', *Australasian Journal of Philosophy* **51** (1973), 238–244; J. Door, 'Scepticism and Dogmatism', *Inquiry* **16** (1973), 214–220; and J. Margolis, 'Skepticism, Foundationalism, and Pragmatism', *American Philosophical Quarterly* **14** (1977), 119–128.

FOUNDATIONAL THEORIES OF JUSTIFICATION

Traditional Foundationalism

Descartes' Foundationalism. The classical English translation (1911) of Descartes' works is E.S. Haldane and G.R.T. Ross, *The Philosophical Works of Descartes* (New York: Dover, 1955). A more recent translation is G.E.M. Anscombe and P.T. Geach (eds. and trans.), *Descartes: Philosophical Writings* (London: Nelson, 1954). Descartes' principal writings concerning foundationalism are *Meditations on First Philosophy*, *Discourse on Method*, and *Principles of Philosophy*.

Contemporary sources on Descartes' foundational theory of knowledge include: H.G. Frankfurt, 'Descartes' Validation of Reason', *American*

Philosophical Quarterly **2** (1965), 149–160; A.K. Stout, 'The Basis of Knowledge in Descartes', *Mind* **38** (1929), 330–342, 458–472; and N. Malcolm, 'Dreaming and Skepticism', *Philosophical Review* **63** (1956), 14–37. Some of the above and other articles on Descartes' epistemology are collected in the following anthologies: A. Sesonske and N. Fleming (eds.), *Meta-meditations* (Belmont, Cal.: Wadsworth, 1966); and W. Doney (ed.), *Descartes: A Collection of Critical Essays* (New York: Doubleday, 1967).

Lewis's Foundationalism. C.I. Lewis's books, *Mind and the World Order* (New York: Scribner's, 1929), and *An Analysis of Knowledge and Valuation* (La Salle, Ill.: Open Court, 1946) contain the core of Lewis's foundational theory of knowledge. His important articles on epistemology include: 'Experience and Meaning', *Philosophical Review* **43** (1934), 125–146; 'Professor Chisholm and Empiricism', *Journal of Philosophy* **45** (1948), 517–524; and 'Replies to my Critics', in P.A. Schilpp (ed.), *The Philosophy of C.I. Lewis* (La Salle, Ill.: Open Court, 1968), pp. 653–676.

There is a great deal of literature on Lewis's epistemology. Two of the more important works are: H. Reichenbach, 'Are Phenomenal Reports Absolutely Certain?' *Philosophical Review* **61** (1952), 147–159; and N. Goodman, 'Sense and Certainty', *Philosophical Review* **61** (1952), 160–167. Lewis's 'The Given Element in Empirical Knowledge', *Philosophical Review* **61** (1952), 168–175, is a reply to these two papers and all three are collected in R.M. Chisholm and R.J. Swartz (eds.), *Empirical Knowledge* (Englewood Cliffs, N.J.: Prentice-Hall, 1973). Also included in *Empirical Knowledge*, pp. 203–223 and 459–470, are R. Firth, 'The Anatomy of Certainty', *Philosophical Review* **76** (1967), 3–27, and 'Coherence, Certainty, and Epistemic Priority', *Journal of Philosophy* **61** (1964), 545–557. Among other important critical works are R.M. Chisholm, 'The Problem of Empiricism', *Journal of Philosophy* **45** (1948), 512–517; R.M. Chisholm, 'Theory of Knowledge', in R. Chisholm *et al.* (eds.), *Philosophy* (Englewood Cliffs, N.J.: Prentice-Hall, 1964); R. Firth, R.B. Brandt, *et al.*, 'Commemorative Symposium on C.I. Lewis', *Journal of Philosophy* **61** (1964), 545–570; M.A. Slote, 'Empirical Certainty and the Theory of Important Criteria', *Inquiry* **10** (1967), 21–37; and M. Pastin, 'C.I. Lewis's Radical Foundationalism', *Noûs* **9** (1975), 407–420.

Chisholm's Foundationalism. Among Chisholm's many works the following are more directly concerned with his version of foundationalism: *Per-*

ceiving: A Philosophic Study (Ithaca, N.Y.: Cornell University Press, 1957);
Theory of Knowledge, 1st ed. (Englewood Cliffs, N.J.: Prentice-Hall, 1966);
2nd ed., 1977; 'The Foundation of Empirical Statements', in K. Ajdu-
kiewicz (ed.), *The Foundation of Statements and Decisions* (Warsaw: Polish
Scientific Publishers, 1965), pp. 111–120; 'Russell on the Foundations of
Empirical Knowledge', in P.A. Schilpp (ed.), *The Philosophy of Bertrand
Russell* (Chicago: Northwestern University Press, 1944); 'On the Nature
of Empirical Evidence', in *Empirical Knowledge, op. cit.*; 'On a Principle
of Epistemic Preferability', *Philosophy and Phenomenological Research* **30**
(1969), 294–301; " 'Appear', 'Take', and 'Evident' ", *Journal of Philosophy*
53 (1956), 722–731; 'The Logic of Knowing', *Journal of Philosophy* **60**
(1963), 773–795; 'Sentences About Believing', *Proceedings of the Aristotelian Society* **56** (1955–1956), 125–148; and *The Problem of the Criterion*
(Milwaukee: Marquette University Press, 1973).

There have been a great many articles and books which have addressed
Chisholm's epistemology. The following is a list of works that Chisholm
has cited in the second edition of *Theory of Knowledge*: F.L. Will, *Induc-
tion and Justification* (Ithaca, N.Y.: Cornell University Press, 1974); K.
Lehrer, *Knowledge* (London: Oxford University Press, 1974); N. Rescher,
The Coherence Theory of Truth (London: Oxford University Press, 1973);
W. Sellars, *Science, Perception and Reality* (London: Routledge and
Kegan Paul, 1963); W. Sellars, 'Empiricism and the Philosophy of Mind',
in *Empirical Knowledge, op. cit.*; W. Sellars, 'Givenness and Explanatory
Coherence', *Journal of Philosophy* **70** (1973), 612–624; P.L. Quinn, 'Some
Epistemic Implications of "Crucial Experiments" ', *Studies in the History
and Philosophy of Science* **5** (1975), 59–72; R. Keim, 'Epistemic Values and
Epistemic Viewpoints', T.J. Steel, 'Knowledge and the Self-Presenting',
and J.T. Stevenson, 'On Doxastic Responsibility', in K. Lehrer (ed.),
Analysis and Metaphysics (Dordrecht: Reidel, 1975) pp. 79–92, 145–150,
229–253 resp.; W.P. Alston, 'Two Types of Foundationalism', *Journal
of Philosophy* **73** (1976), 165–185; H. Kyburg, 'On a Certain Form of
Philosophical Argument', *American Philosophical Quarterly* **7** (1970),
229–237; J. Pollock, *Knowledge and Justification* (Princeton, N.J.: Princeton University Press, 1974); J. Pollock, 'Chisholm's Definition of
Knowledge', *Philosophical Studies* **19** (1968), 72–76; C.I. Lewis, 'Professor Chisholm and Empiricism', *op. cit.*; and especially H. Heidelberger,
'Chisholm's Epistemic Principles', *Noûs* **3** (1969), 73–82. *Analysis and
Metaphysics* is a *Festschrift* dedicated to Professor Chisholm which con-

tains many articles on Chisholm's epistemological views written by his former students. Articles concerning epistemology in this anthology not listed above include J.F. Ross, 'Testimonial Evidence'; K. Lehrer, 'Reason and Consistency'; M. Hanen, 'Confirmation, Explanation, and Acceptance'; and J. Canfield, ' "I Know That I am in Pain" Is Senseless'.

Other Recent Foundational Theories. Some other foundational theories of justification can be found in John A. Pollock, *Knowledge and Justification* (Princeton, N.J.: Princeton University Press, 1974); A. Quinton, *The Nature of Things* (London: Routledge and Kegan Paul, 1973); and D.M. Armstrong, *Belief, Truth, and Knowledge* (London: Cambridge University Press, 1973).

Skeptical Arguments Against Foundationalism

Arguments Against a Foundation of Certainty. Both Reichenbach's 'Are Phenomenal Reports Absolutely Certain?', *op. cit.*, and Goodman's 'Sense and Certainty', *op. cit.*, are critical of the possibility of an absolutely certain foundational base of knowledge. Cornman has responded to both in 'On the Certainty of Given Reports', *Noûs* **12** (1978), 93–118. Other significant papers which discuss the problems of establishing a certain foundation of knowledge and the different senses of certainty, incorrigibility, indefeasibility, and so on, include R. Firth, 'The Anatomy of Certainty', *op. cit.*, and 'Coherence, Certainty, and Epistemic Priority' *op. cit.*; W. Sellars, 'Givenness and Explanatory Coherence', *Journal of Philosophy* **70** (1973), 612–624; H. Heidelberger, 'Knowledge, Certainty, and Probability', *Inquiry* **6** (1963), 242–250; and D. Rynin, 'Knowledge, Sensation, and Certainty', in A. Stroll (ed.), *Epistemology* (New York: Harper and Row, 1967).

The attempt to secure a certain foundation for knowledge led to the debate among the logical positivists concerning the existence and status of protocol or basic statements. Two main protagonists on this debate were O. Neurath in 'Sociology and Physicalism' (M. Magnus and R. Raico, trans.), and 'Protocol Sentences', (F. Schick, trans.), both in A. J. Ayer (ed.), *Logical Positivism* (New York: Free Press, 1959) and *Foundation of the Social Sciences* (Chicago: University of Chicago Press, 1941); and M. Schlick in 'The Foundation of Knowledge', (D. Rynin, trans.), in *Logical Positivism* and in *Empirical Knowledge, op. cit.* Other positivists concerned with basic statements include R. Carnap (M. Black, trans.),

The Unity of Science (London: Kegan Paul, Trench, Trubner, 1934), and *The Logical Syntax of Language* (Atlantic Highlands: Humanities Press, 1964); C. Hempel, 'On the Logical Positivists' Theory of Truth', *Analysis* **2** (1934–1935), 49–59; and A.J. Ayer, *Language, Truth and Logic*, 2nd ed. (New York: Dover, 1946), *Foundations of Empirical Knowledge* (New York: St. Martin's, 1940), ch. 2, 'Basic Propositions', in M. Black (ed.), *Philosophical Analysis* (Ithaca, N.Y.: Cornell University Press, 1950), and *The Problem of Knowledge* (New York: St. Martin's, 1956). I. Scheffler, *Science and Subjectivity* (Indianapolis: Bobbs-Merrill, 1967) has an enlightening discussion of this controversy.

More recently some philosophers have attacked the certainty of observation reports on the grounds that all observations are necessarily 'theory-laden' and that there is no distinction to be drawn on the basis of some epistemic priority between an observational vocabulary and a theoretical vocabulary. Included in this group are N.R. Hanson, *Patterns of Discovery* (Cambridge: Cambridge University Press, 1958); T.S. Kuhn, *The Structure of Scientific Revolutions* (Chicago: University of Chicago Press, 1962); P.K. Feyerabend, 'Explanation, Reduction and Empiricism', in H. Feigl and G. Maxwell (eds.), *Scientific Explanation, Space, and Time* (Minneapolis: University of Minnesota Press, 1962); P. Achinstein, 'The Problem of Theoretical Terms', *American Philosophical Quarterly* **2** (1965), 193–203; 'Theoretical Terms and Partial Interpretations', *British Journal for the Philosophy of Science* **14** (1964), 89–105, and *Concepts of Science* (Baltimore: Johns Hopkins Press, 1968), chs. 5 and 6; M. Spector, 'Theory and Observation', *British Journal for the Philosophy of Science* **17** (1966), 1–20, 89–104; and M. Hesse, *The Structure of Scientific Inference* (Berkeley: University of California Press, 1974), ch. 1.

Defenders of the thesis that there is a class of observation sentences where truth or falsity can be determined independently of theoretical considerations, or at least that there are epistemic grounds for drawing an observational-theoretical distinction, include E. Nagel, *The Structure of Science* (New York: Harcourt, Brace, and World, 1961), ch. 5; G. Maxwell, 'The Ontological Status of Theoretical Entities', in H. Feigl and G. Maxwell (eds.), *op. cit.*, pp. 3–27; R. Carnap, 'Testability and Meaning', *Philosophy of Science* **3** (1936), 419–471; and E. Nagel, 'Theory and Observation', in M. Mandelbaum (ed.), *Observation and Theory in Science* (Baltimore: Johns Hopkins Press, 1971). Cornman, in chapter 4 of *Perception, Common Sense, and Science, op. cit.*, replies to critics who oppose any sort of observational-theoretical dichotomy.

Among those who have advanced skeptical arguments concerning the certainty of memory reports are Bertrand Russell, *The Analysis of Mind* (London: George Allen and Unwin; New York: Macmillan, 1921), chs. 4 and 9; *An Inquiry into Meaning and Truth* (New York: W.W. Norton and Co., Inc.; London: George Allen and Unwin, Ltd., 1940), ch. 11; C.D. Broad, *Mind and Its Place in Nature* (London: Kegan Paul, 1925), ch. 5; and H.H. Price, 'Memory Knowledge', *Proceedings of the Aristotelian Society*, (supplement) **15** (1936), 16–33. C.I. Lewis, *An Analysis of Knowledge and Valuation, op. cit.*, ch. 11, advances an "a priori justification" of memory; and N. Malcolm, 'Three Lectures on Memory', in *Knowledge and Certainty* (Englewood Cliffs, N.J.: Prentice-Hall, 1963), and G.E.M. Anscombe, 'The Reality of the Past', in M. Black (ed.), *Philosophical Analysis, op. cit.*, have criticized Russell's skepticism about memory reports.

On the Nonfoundational as Certain or Probable Relative to the Foundational: The Entailment of Nonbasic Sentences by Basic Sentences. Various phenomenalists have held that basic sense-data sentences entail non-basic physical object sentences. See, for instance G.E. Moore's papers in *Philosophical Studies, Some Main Problems of Philosophy*, and *Philosophical Papers*; Bertrand Russell in 'The Philosophy of Logical Atomism', in R.C. Marsh (ed.), *Essays in Logic and Knowledge* (London: George Allen and Unwin, 1956), pp. 175–282; and *An Inquiry into Meaning and Truth, op. cit.* R. Chisholm's famous objection to phenomenalism of this sort appears in *Perceiving, op. cit.*, pp. 189–197. Subjunctive analyses of physical object sentences in terms of sense-data sentences were offered by A.J. Ayer in *Language, Truth and Logic, op. cit.*, chs. 7 and 8; *Foundations of Empirical Knowledge, op. cit.*, ch. 5, and "Phenomenalism", in *Philosophical Essays* (New York: St. Martin's, 1954). Ayer rejects this theory in *The Problem of Knowledge, op. cit.*, ch. 3. C.I. Lewis offered a probabilistic analysis in *An Analysis of Knowledge and Valuation, op. cit.*, chs. 7 and 8, which was criticized by Cornman in chapter 3 of *Perception, Common Sense, and Science*. Chisholm criticized the theory in 'The Problem of Empiricism', and Lewis replied in 'Professor Chisholm and Empricism'. For more complete bibliographic references on phenomenalism and the analysis of physical object sentences, as well as detailed discussions of various sorts of phenomenalism, see Cornman's *Perception, Common Sence, and Science,* appendix and pt. 1, respectively.

Inductive Inference from Basic Sentences to Nonbasic Sentences: Enumera-

tive Induction. A.J. Ayer's argument in *The Problem of Knowledge* that the existence of other minds is justified can be viewed, as it is in Chapter 10 of this book, as an enumerative inductive inference. A. Plantinga discusses Ayer's argument and criticizes this approach in *God and Other Minds* (Ithaca, N.Y.: Cornell University Press, 1967), ch. 10.

Analogical Arguments. Analogical arguments for the existence of God have their primary source in Aquinas, *Summa Theologica*. The analogical argument for other minds was suggested by Descartes in *Discourse on Method*, pt. 5, and Locke in *Essay Concerning Human Understanding*, book 4, ch. 3, par. 27, and it was explicitly stated by Hume in *Treatise of Human Nature*, book I, pt. 3, section 16. More recent proponents include C.I. Lewis, *An Analysis of Knowledge and Valuation*, p. 143; C.D. Broad, *Mind and Its Place in Nature*; S. Hampshire, 'Analogy of Feeling', *Mind* **61** (1952), 1–12; H.H. Price, 'Our Evidence for Other Minds', *Philosophy* **13** (1938), 425–436; and B. Russell, *Human Knowledge* (Atlantic Highlands: Humanities Press, 1948), pp. 438–486. Plantinga criticizes these arguments in *God and Other Minds*, ch. 8.

Hypothetical Induction and Inference to the Best Explanation. G. Harman has argued that all reasonable inductive inferences are inferences to the best explanation in 'The Inference to the Best Explanation', *Philosophical Review* **74** (1965), 88–95; 'Knowledge, Inference, and Explanation', *American Philosophical Quarterly* **5** (1968), 164–173; and *Thought* (Princeton, N.J.: Princeton University Press, 1973). W. Gregory, 'Explanationism', unpublished; and R. Ennis, 'Enumerative Induction and Best Explanation', *Journal of Philosophy* **65** (1968), 523–529, are critical of Harman's position. Harman replies to Ennis in 'Enumerative Induction is Inference to the Best Explanation', *Journal of Philosophy* **65** (1968), 529–533. I. Niiniluoto and R. Toumela, *Theoretical Concepts and Hypothetico-Inductive Inference* (Dordrecht: Reidel, 1973) discusses hypothetical induction as it relates to scientific realism. R. Chisholm objects to hypothetical induction in *Theory of Knowledge*.

Nonfoundational Theories of Justification

The views of many nonfoundationalists can be found in the references cited in the section above entitled "Skeptical Arguments Against Foundationalism". We should at this point however list those philosophers who are understood to be the dominent contemporary nonfoundationalists.

Although Rescher's *Coherence Theory of Truth* is primarily a defense of a nonfoundational theory of truth it contains material relevant to a coherence theory of justification as well. Sellars and Quine are also commonly thought to be nonfoundationalists, although it is argued in this book that they need not be interpreted this way. Sellars's most important works on the topic appear in 'Givenness and Explanatory Coherence'; *Science, Perception, and Reality*, and 'The Structure of Knowledge', Machette Foundation Lectures given at the University of Texas in 1971. Quine's works on justification include *The Web of Belief*, with J. Ullian (New York: Random House); and 'Epistemology Naturalized' in *Ontological Relativity and Other Essays* (New York: Columbia University Press, 1969), pp. 69–90. Other nonfoundationalist views are expressed in L. Bonjour, 'Can Empirical Knowledge Have a Foundation', *American Philosophical Quarterly* **15** (1978), 1–14; 'The Coherence Theory of Empirical Knowledge', *Philosophical Studies* **30** (1976), 281–312; and D.B. Annis 'A Contextualist Theory of Epistemic Justification', *American Philosophical Quarterly* 15 (1978), 213–220.

Theories of Probability and Rational Belief

General Discussions of Probability. An outstanding introductory text on probability and inductive logic is B. Skyrms, *Choice and Chance*, 2nd ed. (Encinco, Cal.: Dickenson, 1975). Among other comprehensive surveys of the field are E. Nagel, *Principles of the Theory of Probability* (Chicago: University of Chicago Press, 1939); I.J. Good, *Probability and the Weighing of Evidence* (London: C. Griffin, 1950); R. Carnap, *Logical Foundations of Probability* (Chicago: University of Chicago Press, 1950); W. Kneale, *Probability and Induction* (Oxford: Clarendon, 1949); I. Hacking, *The Emergence of Probability* (Cambridge: Cambridge University Press, 1975); and W. Salmon, *The Foundation of Scientific Inference* (Pittsburgh: University of Pittsburgh Press, 1966). See R.L. Slaght, 'Induction, Acceptance and Rational Belief', in M. Swain (ed.), *Induction, Acceptance and Rational Belief* (Dordrecht: Reidel, 1970), for an extensive listing of references on probability as well as other related areas.

A.N. Kolmogorov, *Foundations of the Theory of Probability* (New York: Chelsea, 1950) is the classical work on the axiomatic mathematics of probability. Other mathematical treatments of probability include H. Cramer, *The Elements of the Probability Theory* (New York: Krieger, 1955); W. Feller, *An Introduction to Probability Theory and Its Applications* (New York: John Wiley and Sons, 1950); and R. Carnap and R.C.

Jeffrey (eds.), *Studies in Inductive Logic and Probability*, vol. 1 (Berkeley: University of California Press, 1971).

Interpretations of Probabilities: Frequency Theory. J. Venn, *The Logic of Chance* (New York: Chelsea, 1962) is one of the earliest frequency theorists. Another is R. von Mises, *Probability, Statistics, and Truth*, 2nd ed. (New York: Macmillan, 1939). Reichenbach's views are expressed in *The Theory of Probability* (Berkeley: University of California Press, 1949) and *Experience and Prediction* (Chicago: University of Chicago Press, 1938), section 5. W. Salmon has defended Reichenbach's theory in *The Foundation of Scientific Inference*; and 'Vindication of Induction', in H. Feigl and G. Maxwell (eds.), *Current Issues in the Philosophy of Science* (New York: Holt, Rinehart and Winston, 1961), pp. 245–256. I. Hacking discusses Salmon's views in 'One Problem about Induction', in I. Lakatos (ed.), *The Problem of Inductive Logic*, (Amsterdam: North-Holland Publishing, 1968), pp. 44–57, and 'Salmon's Vindication of Induction', *Journal of Philosophy* **62** (1965), 260–266. See also I. Levi, 'Hacking Salmon on Induction', *Journal of Philosophy* **62** (1965), 481–487.

Logical and Epistemic Interpretation. J.M. Keynes in *A Treatise on Probability* (London: Macmillan, 1921) is the classical statement of the logical interpretation of probabilities, with Carnp's *Logical Foundtions of Probability* being the most thorough statement of the view. J.G. Kemeny, 'Carnap's Theory of Probability and Induction', in P.A. Schilpp (ed.), *The Philosophy of Rudolf Carnap* (La Salle, Ill.: Open Court, 1963), pp. 719–738, is a clear account of Carnap's theory. H.E. Kyburg, *Probability and the Logic of Rational Belief* (Middletown, Conn.: Wesleyan University Press, 1961) is a more recent work written from the logical standpoint, and *Studies in Inductive Logic and Probability* contains Carnap's most recent elaboration of his epistemic and 'personalistic' view. W. Salmon's *The Foundation of Scientific Inference*; 'Carnap's Inductive Logic', *Journal of Philosophy* **64** (1967), 725–739; 'The Justification of Inductive Rules of Inference', in *The Problem of Inductive Logic*, pp. 24–43; and 'Vindication of Induction', contain substantial criticism of the logical interpretation of probabilities.

Propensity Interpretation. K. Popper gives his propensity interpretations in 'The Propensity Interpretation of Probability and the Quantum Theory', in S. Körner (ed.), *Observation and Interpretation: A Symposium of Philosophers and Physicists* (New York: Dover, 1957); and 'The Propensity Interpretation of Probability', *British Journal for the Philosophy of Science* **10** (1959–1960), 25–42. I. Levi, *Gambling with Truth* (New York: Alfred A. Knopf, 1967), ch. 14, gives a statement of the theory. L. Sklar criticizes the view in 'Is Probability a Dispositional Property?', *Journal of Philosophy* **67** (1970), 355–366; and 'Unfair to Frequencies', *Journal of Philosophy* **70** (1973), 41–52; and Levi responds in '. . . But Fair to Chance', *Journal of Philosophy* **70** (1973), 52–55. J.H. Fetzer defends the theory in 'A Single Case Propensity Theory of Explanation', *Synthese* 28 (1974), 171–198; and H.E. Kyburg criticizes it in 'Propensities and Probabilities', *British Journal for the Philosophy of Science* **25** (1974), 358–375. I. Hacking, *Logic of Statistical Inference* (Cambridge: Cambridge University Press, 1965) takes a modified Popperian propensity point of view.

Subjective Interpretation. A valuable anthology on the subjectivist's interpretation of probabilities is H.E. Kyburg and H.E. Smokler (eds.), *Studies in Subjective Probability* (New York: John Wiley and Sons, 1964). This collection contains de Finetti's classic 'Foresight: Its Logical Laws, Its Subjective Sources', pp. 93–158. Other proponents of the theory include F.P. Ramsey, *The Foundations of Mathematics and Other Logical Essays* (London: Routledge and Kegan Paul, 1931), pp. 74–82; L.J. Savage, *The Foundation of Statistics* (New York: Dover, 1954); and R.C. Jeffrey, *The Logic of Decision* (New York: McGraw-Hill, 1965). K. Lehrer has argued for a subjectivist interpretation in 'Evidence, Meaning, and Conceptual Change: A Subjective Approach', in G. Pearce and P. Maynard (eds.), *Conceptual Change* (Dordrecht: Reidel, 1973), pp. 94–122; *Knowledge*, pp. 136ff.; and 'Truth, Evidence, and Inference', *American Philosophical Quarterly* **11** (1974), 79–92. Critics of subjectivism include H.E. Kyburg, 'Bets and Beliefs', *American Philosophical Quarterly* **5** (1968), 54–63; W. Salmon, *The Foundations of Scientific Inference*, pp. 68, 79–82; and W. Gregory, 'Evidence, Subjectivism, and Lehrer', unpublished.

Strict Coherence, Conditionalization, and the Lottery Paradox. Concerning the topics of coherence, strict coherence, and Dutch Book bets, see A. Shimony, 'Coherence and the Axioms of Confirmation', *Journal of Symbolic Logic* **20** (1955), 1–28; R. Carnap and R.C. Jeffrey, *Studies in Inductive Logic and Probability*, pp. 12–15, 105–117; R.C. Jeffrey, *The Logic* *of Decision*; B. Skyrms, *Choice and Chance*, pp. 186–189; and W. L. Harper, 'Rational Belief Change, Popper Functions, and Counterfactuals', *Synthese* **30** (1975), 221–262.

Conditionalization is discussed in Carnap and Jeffrey, *Studies in Inductive Logic and Probability*, pp. 15–16; R. Hilpinin, *Rules of Acceptance and Inductive Logic* (Amsterdam: North-Holland Publishing, 1968), pp. 15–23; B. Skyrms, *Choice and Chance*, pp. 170–198; R.C. Jeffrey, *Logic of Decision*, pp. 153–161; 'Probable Knowledge' in I. Lakatos (ed.), *The Problem of Inductive Logic* (Amsterdam: North-Holland Publishing, 1968), pp. 166–180; 'Dracula Meets Wolfman: Acceptance *vs.* Partial Belief', in M. Swain (ed.), *Induction, Acceptance, and Rational Belief*, pp. 157–185; W. Harper and H.E. Kyburg, 'The Jones Case', *British Journal for the Philosophy of Science* **19** (1968), 247–251; I. Levi, 'If Jones Only Knew More!', *British Journal for the Philosphy of Science* **20** (1969), 153–159; 'Probability and Evidence', in *Induction, Acceptance, and Rational Belief*, pp. 134–156; 'Probability Kinematics', *British Journal for the Philosophy of Science* **18** (1967), 197–209; and P. Teller, 'Conditionalization and Observation', *Synthese* **26** (1973), 218–258.

H.E. Kyburg first discussed the lottery paradox in *Probability and the Logic of Rational Belief*. His other statements on the topic are in 'Probability and Randomness', *Theoria* **29** (1963), 27–55; 'Probability, Rationality, and a Rule of Detachment', in Y. Bar-Hillel (ed.), *Proceedings of the 1964 Congress for Logic, Methodology, and Philosophy of Science*, (Amsterdam: North-Holland Publishing, 1965), and 'Conjunctivitis', in M. Swain (ed.), *Induction, Acceptance, and Rational Belief*. Other writings on the topic include Hilpinin, *Rules of Acceptance and Inductive Logic*, chs. 2 and 4; G. Harman, *Thought*, chs. 2 and 10; K. Lehrer, *Knowledge*; 'Justification, Explanation, and Induction', in M. Swain (ed.), *Induction, Acceptance, and Rational Belief*; and I. Levi, 'Induction, Reason and Consistency', *British Journal for the Philosophy of Science* **21** (1970), 103–114.

INDEX OF NAMES

329

INDEX OF SUBJECTS

Bold face entries indicate primary or definitional uses of the term indexed.

332

PHILOSOPHICAL STUDIES SERIES
IN PHILOSOPHY

Editors:

WILFRID SELLARS, Univ. of Pittsburgh and KEITH LEHRER, Univ. of Arizona

Board of Consulting Editors:

Jonathan Bennett, Alan Gibbard, Robert Stalnaker, and Robert G. Turnbull

1. JAY F. ROSENBERG, *Linguistic Representation*, 1974.
2. WILFRID SELLARS, *Essays in Philosophy and Its History*, 1974.
3. DICKINSON S. MILLER, *Philosophical Analysis and Human Welfare*. Selected Essays and Chapters from Six Decades. Edited with an Introduction by Lloyd D. Easton, 1975.
4. KEITH LEHRER (ed.), *Analysis and Metaphysics*. Essays in Honor of R. M. Chisholm. 1975.
5. CARL GINET, *Knowledge, Perception, and Memory*, 1975.
6. PETER H. HARE and EDWARD H. MADDEN, *Causing, Perceiving and Believing*. An Examination of the Philosophy of C. J. Ducasse, 1975.
7. HECTOR-NERI CASTAÑEDA, *Thinking and Doing*. The Philosophical Foundations of Institutions, 1975.
8. JOHN L. POLLOCK, *Subjunctive Reasoning*, 1976.
9. BRUCE AUNE, *Reason and Action*, 1977.
10. GEORGE SCHLESINGER, *Religion and Scientific Method*, 1977.
11. YIRMIAHU YOVEL (ed.), *Philosophy of History and Action*. Papers presented at the first Jerusalem Philosophical Encounter, December 1974, 1978.
12. JOSEPH C. PITT, *The Philosophy of Wilfrid Sellars: Queries and Extensions*, 1978.
13. ALVIN I. GOLDMAN and JAEGWON KIM, *Values and Morals*. Essays in Honor of William Frankena, Charles Stevenson, and Richard Brandt, 1978.
14. MICHAEL J. LOUX, *Substance and Attribute*. A Study in Ontology, 1978.
15. ERNEST SOSA (ed.), *The Philosophy of Nicholas Rescher: Discussion and Replies*, 1979.
16. JEFFRIE G. MURPHY, *Retribution, Justice, and Therapy*. Essays in the Philosophy of Law, 1979.
17. GEORGE S. PAPPAS, *Justification and Knowledge: New Studies in Epistemology*, 1979.
18. JAMES W. CORNMAN, *Skepticism, Justification, and Explanation*, 1980.
19. PETER VAN INWAGEN, *Time and Cause*. Essays presented to Richard Taylor, 1980.
20. DONALD NUTE, *Topics in Conditional Logic*, 1980